CLARK
1980

CLASSIFIED STUDIES IN TWENTIETH-CENTURY DIPLOMATIC AND MILITARY HISTORY

Series Editor: Paul L. Kesaris

THE ROTE KAPELLE

THE
ROTE KAPELLE

The CIA's History of
Soviet Intelligence and Espionage Networks
in Western Europe, 1936-1945

UNIVERSITY PUBLICATIONS OF AMERICA, INC.

ISBN: 0-89093-203-4

Library of Congress Catalog Card Number: 79-51270

Manufactured in the United States of America

TABLE OF CONTENTS

PART ONE
Narrative History of the Rote Kapelle

SWITZERLAND

THE ROTE KAPELLE ELSEWHERE

PART TWO
Modus Operandi of the Rote Kapelle

PART THREE
Personalities

INTRODUCTION

The term "Rote Kapelle" ("Red Orchestra," "Red Band," "Red Choir," or "Red Chapel") was a cryptonym coined by the German central security office, the Reichssicherheitshauptamt (RSHA), to designate the Soviet networks of espionage and subversion discovered in Western Europe after the outbreak of the Russo-German war in 1941. The espionage reports were transmitted primarily by radio. The "music" on the air had its pianists (radio operators), a maestro in the field (the Grand Chef), and its conductor in Moscow (the Director). This analogy was not new to German counterintelligence. "Kapelle" was, in fact, an accepted Abwehr term for secret wireless transmitters and the counterespionage operations against them. The term "Rote Kapelle" was originally applied only to the secret operation started by Ast[1] Belgien (Abwehr III F.)[2] in August 1941 and conducted against a station of the Soviet intelligence service which had been detected in Brussels by the Funkabwehr (W/T intercept and cryptanalytic component of German military counterintelligence). The investigation, however, soon extended into Holland, Germany, France, Switzerland, and Italy; and the designation "Rote Kapelle" was adopted for these expanded operations also.

In July 1942 the investigation of the Rote Kapelle was taken over from Ast Belgien by Section IV. A.2. of the Sicherheitsdienst (SD, the security service of the RSHA). After the arrest of the two leading Russian agents, Leopold Trepper and Victor Sukolov, a small independent Gestapo[3] unit, "Sonderkommando[4] Rote Kapelle," was

---

[1] Ast: abbreviation of Abwehrstelle, a major field office of the Abwehr, the German military counterintelligence service.

[2] Abwehr III F.: Section III (counterintelligence) working against the intelligence services of the enemy.

[3] Gestapo: Geheime Staatspolizei, or Secret Federal Police.

[4] Sonderkommando: a special detail or task force.

formed in Paris in November 1942. There has been some misunderstanding about the term "Rote Kapelle" because it was also used to denote this special counterespionage group of the Gestapo, which was responsible for penetrating the Soviet apparatus and doubling its agents. As commonly used, therefore, the term "Rote Kapelle" could mean both the Soviet networks and the branch of the GIS responsible for combatting these agents. In the course of this study the term "Rote Kapelle" will be used exclusively to designate the Soviet networks. The term "Sonderkommando" will be used to designate a German counterespionage group.

Strictly speaking, therefore, the Rote Kapelle case was an internal security investigation by the Abwehr and the Gestapo of Soviet spies in Germany, Belgium, Holland, France, Switzerland, and Italy during World War II. But several of the Soviet agents in the wartime networks were recruited and became active years before World War II. Many of them had survived the great purges of Stalin and the difficult period of the non-aggression pact between Germany and the USSR. The Rote Kapelle was not, in fact, a wartime creation, but derived directly from the Soviet prewar networks in Europe. This study, therefore, includes the origins of the prewar networks; the period covered is approximately 1936-1945.

In addition, the activities of the Rote Kapelle agents were not limited to the countries mentioned above. Several connections with the Rote Kapelle were found in England, Scandinavia, Eastern Europe, the United States, and elsewhere. This study contains frequent references to the ties that existed between these areas and the major networks of the Rote Kapelle in Belgium, France, Germany, Holland, Switzerland, and Italy.

Most of the information about the Rote Kapelle was obtained from statements made by Soviet intelligence officers who belonged to the organization and who were seized in the course of the German counteraction in 1941-1943. Some information derives from observations made by German security agencies around 1941-1942. The leading Soviet Rote Kapelle officers independently gave corroborating testimony to the effect that Moscow began to set up the first Rote Kapelle nets in Europe as early as 1935 and 1936. For this purpose, specially trained and first-rate Red Army intelligence officers were employed. Some matriculated as students in European universities, whereas others applied for positions as technicians and as merchants in need of practice and experience abroad. Some former Comintern agents were also induced to participate in the nets being established by the Rote Kapelle organizers.

The Soviet intelligence networks in Europe before World War II had as their targets the United States and all the countries of Western Europe, particularly England. In the beginning they were primarily engaged in establishing and building up agent nets, installing radio and other communication facilities, and training the various units. Later, specific targets of Soviet intelligence were assigned: the development of aviation in the Western countries; the development of heavy weapons; and comprehensive information about the great fortification lines in the West. The broad objectives of the Rote Kapelle presupposed the existence in all the countries involved of a special apparatus of thoroughly trained and qualified intelligence officers, agents, and auxiliary workers, and an entirely original system of intelligence transmission services.

Early in 1940 the main target of the Rote Kapelle was changed to Germany, despite the non-aggression pact then in effect between the Third Reich and the Soviet Union. In the course of the war the Rote Kapelle expanded to such a degree and took on such proportions with respect to personnel, technical aspects, and increasingly comprehensive assignments that at the peak of its development in 1942-1943 it had become the principal component of the Soviet Military IS. The Rote Kapelle, considered as a whole, was a tremendous undertaking; it provides one of the best examples so far available of the intricate working methods of Soviet espionage as then conducted.

The chart on the next page depicts the basic organizational structure of the Rote Kapelle in Belgium, Holland, France, Germany, and Switzerland during the period 1938 to 1945. Only the main individuals and lines of communication are shown here; detailed charts for each country appear later in the study.

THE ROTE KAPELLE

DIAGRAM 1

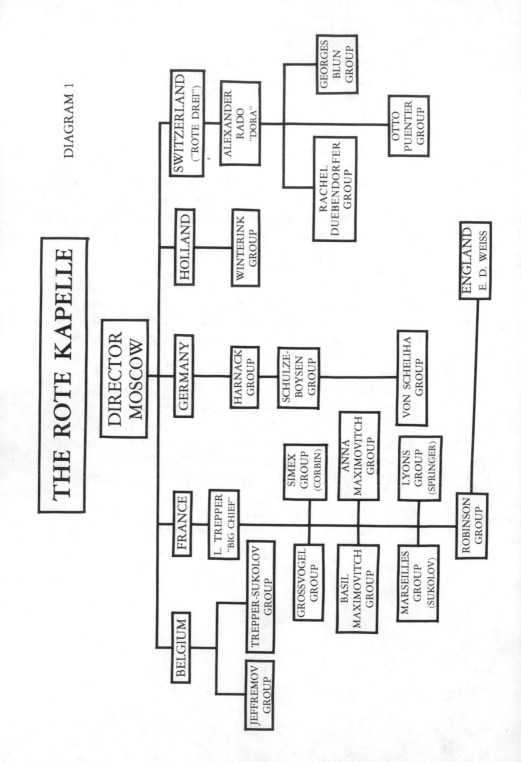

PART ONE

NARRATIVE HISTORY
OF THE ROTE KAPELLE

CHRONOLOGY OF THE ROTE KAPELLE IN BELGIUM

January 1936	Comintern agent Johannes Wenzel arrived in Belgium from Germany. He later provided technical assistance to the Trepper, Sukolov, and Jeffremov networks.
1936-1939	Soviet intelligence officer Konstantin Jeffremov was active somewhere in Western Europe, probably in the Low Countries.
1936	Franz and Germaine Schneider were recruited as Soviet agents in Brussels, possibly by Jeffremov.
1936	Leopold Trepper was made technical director of RU intelligence in Western Europe. In December 1936 he established a base for himself in Paris.
1936-1938	Trepper engaged in organizing missions for Soviet intelligence in Western Europe. He paid several visits to Scandinavia (1936-1938), met with Leon Grossvogel in Brussels (1937), and visited the British Isles (1937 and 1938).
1937-early 1939	Victor Sukolov, a Soviet intelligence officer, probably resided in France.
Autumn, 1938	Trepper made several visits to Brussels.
December 1938	Leon Grossvogel founded the Foreign Excellent Raincoat Company as a cover for intelligence operations.
early 1939	Mikhail Makarov, a Soviet intelligence officer, was sent from Moscow to Paris, via Stockholm and Copenhagen. In Paris Makarov was provided with new identity papers and $10,000.

6 March 1939	Trepper (alias Adam Mikler) officially arrived in Belgium with his wife and child. His cover was as a Canadian businessman associated with the new firm, Foreign Excellent Raincoat Company.
25 March 1939	Makarov (alias Carlos Alamo) arrived in Belgium to assist Trepper.
April 1939	Makarov became proprietor of the Ostende branch of the Excellent Raincoat Company, replacing Mrs. Grossvogel.
April 1939	Sukolov, presumably stationed in France, went to Germany to reactivate the Schulze-Boysen network and to establish a courier link.
1939	Anton Danilov was sent to Paris as a clerk in the Soviet Embassy. He later worked at Vichy with a Captain Karpov. Danilov would eventually be transferred to Belgium to assist the Sukolov network.
Spring, 1939	Grossvogel introduced Abraham Rajchmann, an expert forger, to Trepper. Grossvogel had been acquainted with Rajchmann since at least 1934.
Spring and Summer, 1939	Grossvogel visited Denmark, Sweden, Norway, and Finland on Foreign Excellent Raincoat Company business.
17 July 1939	Sukolov (alias Vincent Sierra) arrived in Belgium and met with Trepper at Ghent.
Summer, 1939	Sukolov visited Switzerland.
Fall, 1939-1941	Sukolov studied languages and commercial subjects at the University of Brussels. He also learned coding from Trepper and was ordered by Moscow to build a radio set and to establish communications.
6 September 1939	Jeffremov (alias Eric Jernstroem) arrived in Belgium. He was to work independently, and Trepper was not aware of his activities.
October 1939- c. January 1940	As "Clement," Sukolov probably utilized the Gouwlooze W/T link between Holland and Moscow.

March-April 1940	Sukolov made a three-week visit to Switzerland and saw Alexander Rado while there.
10 May 1940	The Germans invaded Belgium, Holland, and Luxemburg.
May 1940	Rajchmann fled from Belgium and went to France.
May 1940	Jules Jaspar fled to France. He salvaged 200,000 Belgian francs from the Foreign Excellent Raincoat Company. Escaping with him were Mrs. Jaspar, Mrs. Grossvogel, and Nazarin Drailly with his family.
May 1940	The Ostende branch of the Excellent Raincoat Company was destroyed by German bombing. Makarov moved to Brussels and established there a W/T link with Moscow.
mid-May 1940	Trepper made a tour of the combat zone in the company of Grossvogel and Durov, the Bulgarian consul in Brussels. He prepared a lengthy report based on his observations and sent it to Moscow.
28 May 1940	King Leopold III surrendered to the Germans.
from c. June 1940	Sukolov probably supplied Moscow with Schulze-Boysen's and Trepper's material by W/T.
early July 1940	Grossvogel and Trepper, in the automobile of the Bulgarian Petrov, left Belgium for France. Sukolov became the leader of the Belgian organization.
August 1940	The wife and child of Trepper went to France, and then to the USSR with Soviet assistance.
late September or early October 1940	Rajchmann returned to Belgium at Trepper's request and with the assistance of Malvina Gruber. He resumed his duties as the group's documentation expert.
Fall, 1940	Simexco was founded by Sukolov in Brussels as a cover for intelligence operations. The firm was not officially registered until March 1941.
c. December 1940	Johannes Wenzel was probably transmitting to Moscow for Jeffremov. These two may have

	worked together as early as 1936.
early 1941	Sukolov made a visit to Switzerland to inspect the network there.
early 1941	Jeffremov had a contact in Switzerland. His go-between was "Chimor," possibly Franz Schneider.
5 January 1941	Nazarin Drailly was persuaded by Trepper to return to Belgium to collaborate with Sukolov in the organization of Simexco.
27 March 1941	Simexco was officially registered in Brussels. Sukolov and Nazarin Drailly were listed as the principal stockholders.
28 June 1941	The Germans began to intercept Sukolov's W/T traffic to Moscow.
June or July 1941	Danilov (alias Desmets) arrived in Brussels to assist Makarov. He was escorted from France to Belgium by Malvina Gruber, the mistress of Rajchmann.
c. Summer 1941-Sept. 1942	The German penetration agent Mathieu (alias Carlos) was in close contact with Rajchmann. It was at a rendezvous with Mathieu in July 1942 that Jeffremov was arrested. Trepper's repeated orders to Rajchmann to break off contact with Mathieu were ignored.
October 1941	Sofie Posnanska was sent to Belgium to serve as an encipherer for Makarov. She was escorted from France to Belgium by Malvina Gruber.
Oct.-Nov. 1941	Sukolov travelled to Germany to aid the networks there. He probably also visited the Leipzig Fair during this trip. Sukolov then met with Maria Rauch at Raudnitz, Czechoslovakia, and with another contact in Prague.
12-13 Dec. 1941	Makarov, Danilov, Sofie Posnanska, and Rita Bloch were arrested at 101 Rue des Attrebattes, Brussels. Bloch immediately turned informant.
c. 15 December 1941	Sukolov and Isidore Springer fled from Brussels to France. The rest of the Belgian network went

into hiding. Nazarin Drailly took over as the manager of Simexco.

c. 15 May 1942   The Belgian network was turned over to Jeffremov at a meeting in Brussels, held in the Schneider home.

May 1942   Wenzel began transmitting for the new Jeffremov group.

June 1942   Trepper began to use Wenzel's W/T link after the arrest of the Sokols in Paris.

c. June 1942   Jeffremov introduced Maurice Peper to Rajchmann. Peper was to be liaison between Jeffremov and Rajchmann.

24 June 1942   John Wilhelm Kruyt, Sr., a Soviet agent, was parachuted into Belgium to assist the Jeffremov network. His accommodation was to be provided by Elizabeth Depelsenaire. Kruyt had two meetings with Irma Salno.

30 June 1942   Kruyt was arrested by the Gestapo. Information obtained from him led to the arrests of the Depelsenaire sub-group.

early July 1942   Martha Vandenhoeck was arrested and under duress helped the Germans stage other arrests.

early July 1942   Elizabeth Depelsenaire was arrested by the Gestapo in Brussels, betrayed by Vandenhoeck.

13 July 1942   Jean and Jeanne Otten were arrested by the Gestapo in Brussels.

22 July 1942   Jeffremov was arrested in Brussels at a meeting with the German-controlled agent Mathieu. This meeting had been set up by Rajchmann.

late July 1942   Wenzel and Jeffremov agreed to collaborate with the Germans. A large amount of back radio traffic was deciphered. Information in this traffic led to the first arrests in the German networks.

c. 25 July 1942   Isbutski and Peper were arrested in Brussels; they were betrayed by Jeffremov.

30 July 1942	By direction-finding techniques the Germans located Wenzel and arrested him in Brussels. Germaine Schneider, implicated by letters in Wenzel's possession, convinced the Germans of her innocence and was released. She immediately went to Paris to give warning to Trepper. Franz Schneider was also interrogated and then released.
early August 1942	Augustin Sesee was arrested in Brussels; he was betrayed by Peper.
6 August 1942	The radio playback of Wenzel ("Weide") began.
18 August 1942	Anton Winterink was arrested in Amsterdam; he was also betrayed by Peper.
mid-August 1942	The Germans had Jeffremov write a letter to Rajchmann, stating that all was well. Rajchmann received the letter and passed the information to Grossvogel. This was a deception tactic by the Germans designed to conceal Jeffremov's arrest from the rest of the network.
2 September 1942	Rajchmann was arrested by the Gestapo in Brussels and agreed to collaborate.
22 September 1942	The Winterink playback ("Tanne") was started in Brussels.
end of Sept. 1942	Sofie Posnanska committed suicide in a military prison at Brussels.
12 October 1942	Malvina Gruber was arrested in Brussels. At the urging of Rajchmann she agreed to collaborate. Rajchmann and Gruber were later used in Paris to break up Trepper's network there.
17 Oct. 1942	The Jeffremov playback ("Buche-Pascal") was started.
24 Oct. 1942	The Isbutsky playback ("Buche-Bob") was started.
November 1942	Germaine Schneider was arrested in Lyons, where she was working with the Springer group. Franz Schneider was arrested in Brussels.
November 1942	The Germans, after months of surveillance, raided Simexco and arrested the officers and employees.

17 Nov. 1942	Wenzel escaped from the Germans. He probably went to Holland, but his exact whereabouts after his escape are unknown.
11 Dec. 1942	Jeanne Ponsaint was arrested.
December 1942	Edward Vanderzypen was arrested. He had been one of Jeffremov's most important agents because of his employment with the Hentschel Works in Kassel.
January 1943	Jean Janssens and Josephine Verhimst were arrested by the Germans.
6 Jan. 1943	Nazarin Drailly was arrested.
7 Jan. 1943	Joseph and Renee Blumsack were arrested in Brussels. Yvonne Poelmans was also arrested.

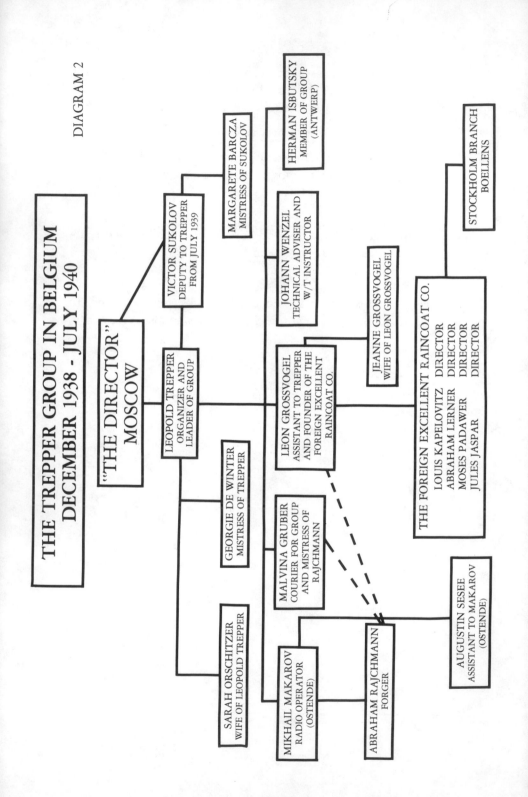

DIAGRAM 2

THE TREPPER GROUP IN BELGIUM
DECEMBER 1938 - JULY 1940

"THE DIRECTOR"
MOSCOW

LEOPOLD TREPPER
ORGANIZER AND
LEADER OF GROUP

VICTOR SUKOLOV
DEPUTY TO TREPPER
FROM JULY 1939

MARGARETE BARCZA
MISTRESS OF SUKOLOV

HERMAN ISBUTSKY
MEMBER OF GROUP
(ANTWERP)

JOHANN WENZEL
TECHNICAL ADVISER AND
W/T INSTRUCTOR

JEANNE GROSSVOGEL
WIFE OF LEON GROSSVOGEL

STOCKHOLM BRANCH
BOELLENS

LEON GROSSVOGEL
ASSISTANT TO TREPPER
AND FOUNDER OF THE
FOREIGN EXCELLENT
RAINCOAT CO.

THE FOREIGN EXCELLENT RAINCOAT CO.
LOUIS KAPELOVITZ   DIRECTOR
ABRAHAM LERNER   DIRECTOR
MOSES PADAWER   DIRECTOR
JULES JASPAR   DIRECTOR

GEORGIE DE WINTER
MISTRESS OF TREPPER

MALVINA GRUBER
COURIER FOR GROUP
AND MISTRESS OF
RAJCHMANN

SARAH ORSCHITZER
WIFE OF LEOPOLD TREPPER

MIKHAIL MAKAROV
RADIO OPERATOR
(OSTENDE)

ABRAHAM RAJCHMANN
FORGER

AUGUSTIN SESEE
ASSISTANT TO MAKAROV
(OSTENDE)

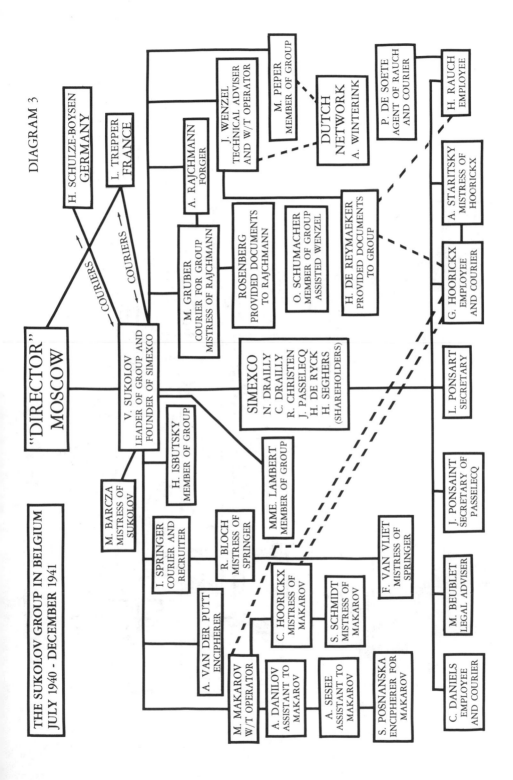

DIAGRAM 3

THE SUKOLOV GROUP IN BELGIUM
JULY 1940 - DECEMBER 1941

"DIRECTOR" MOSCOW

H. SCHULZE-BOYSEN GERMANY

L. TREPPER FRANCE

COURIERS

COURIERS

V. SUKOLOV LEADER OF GROUP AND FOUNDER OF SIMEXCO

M. BARCZA MISTRESS OF SUKOLOV

A. RAJCHMANN FORGER

J. WENZEL TECHNICAL ADVISER AND W/T OPERATOR

M. PEPER MEMBER OF GROUP

DUTCH NETWORK A. WINTERINK

P. DE SOETE AGENT OF RAUCH AND COURIER

H. RAUCH EMPLOYEE

A. STARITSKY MISTRESS OF HOORICKX

M. GRUBER COURIER FOR GROUP MISTRESS OF RAJCHMANN

ROSENBERG PROVIDED DOCUMENTS TO RAJCHMANN

O. SCHUMACHER MEMBER OF GROUP ASSISTED WENZEL

H. DE REYMAEKER PROVIDED DOCUMENTS TO GROUP

G. HOORICKX EMPLOYEE AND COURIER

SIMEXCO
N. DRAILLY
C. DRAILLY
R. CHRISTEN
J. PASSELECQ
H. DE RYCK
H. SEGHERS
(SHAREHOLDERS)

L. PONSART SECRETARY

H. ISBUTSKY MEMBER OF GROUP

MME. LAMBERT MEMBER OF GROUP

J. PONSAINT SECRETARY OF PASSELECQ

I. SPRINGER COURIER AND RECRUITER

R. BLOCH MISTRESS OF SPRINGER

F. VAN VLIET MISTRESS OF SPRINGER

M. BEUBLET LEGAL ADVISER

A. VAN DER PUTT ENCIPHERER

C. HOORICKX MISTRESS OF MAKAROV

S. SCHMIDT MISTRESS OF MAKAROV

M. MAKAROV W/T OPERATOR

A. DANILOV ASSISTANT TO MAKAROV

A. SESEE ASSISTANT TO MAKAROV

S. POSNANSKA ENCIPHERER FOR MAKAROV

C. DANIELS EMPLOYEE AND COURIER

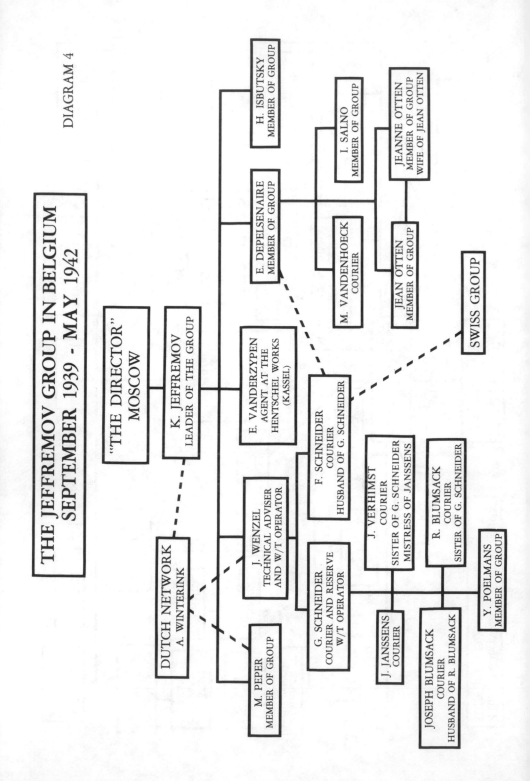

DIAGRAM 4

THE JEFFREMOV GROUP IN BELGIUM
SEPTEMBER 1939 - MAY 1942

"THE DIRECTOR"
MOSCOW

K. JEFFREMOV
LEADER OF THE GROUP

E. VANDERZYPEN
AGENT AT THE
HENTSCHEL WORKS
(KASSEL)

H. ISBUTSKY
MEMBER OF GROUP

E. DEPELSENAIRE
MEMBER OF GROUP

I. SALNO
MEMBER OF GROUP

JEANNE OTTEN
MEMBER OF GROUP
WIFE OF JEAN OTTEN

M. VANDENHOECK
COURIER

JEAN OTTEN
MEMBER OF GROUP

SWISS GROUP

F. SCHNEIDER
COURIER
HUSBAND OF G. SCHNEIDER

DUTCH NETWORK
A. WINTERINK

J. WENZEL
TECHNICAL ADVISER
AND W/T OPERATOR

G. SCHNEIDER
COURIER AND RESERVE
W/T OPERATOR

J. VERHIMST
COURIER
SISTER OF G. SCHNEIDER
MISTRESS OF JANSSENS

R. BLUMSACK
COURIER
SISTER OF G. SCHNEIDER

M. PEPER
MEMBER OF GROUP

J. JANSSENS
COURIER

JOSEPH BLUMSACK
COURIER
HUSBAND OF R. BLUMSACK

Y. POELMANS
MEMBER OF GROUP

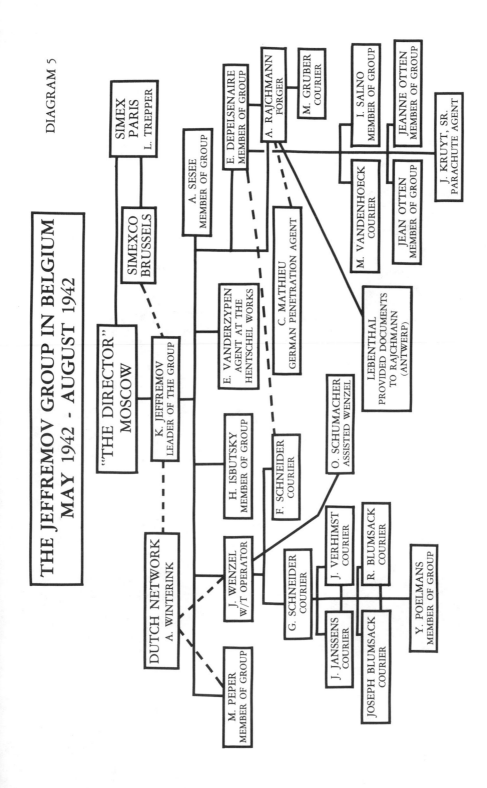

DIAGRAM 5

THE JEFFREMOV GROUP IN BELGIUM
MAY 1942 - AUGUST 1942

"THE DIRECTOR"
MOSCOW

SIMEX
PARIS
L. TREPPER

SIMEXCO
BRUSSELS

K. JEFFREMOV
LEADER OF THE GROUP

A. SESEE
MEMBER OF GROUP

E. DEPELSENAIRE
MEMBER OF GROUP

A. RAJCHMANN
FORGER

M. GRUBER
COURIER

I. SALNO
MEMBER OF GROUP

M. VANDENHOECK
COURIER

JEANNE OTTEN
MEMBER OF GROUP

JEAN OTTEN
MEMBER OF GROUP

J. KRUYT, SR.
PARACHUTE AGENT

E. VANDERZYPEN
AGENT AT THE
HENTSCHEL WORKS

C. MATHIEU
GERMAN PENETRATION AGENT

LEBENTHAL
PROVIDED DOCUMENTS
TO RAJCHMANN
(ANTWERP)

H. ISBUTSKY
MEMBER OF GROUP

F. SCHNEIDER
COURIER

O. SCHUMACHER
ASSISTED WENZEL

DUTCH NETWORK
A. WINTERINK

J. WENZEL
W/T OPERATOR

G. SCHNEIDER
COURIER

J. VERHIMST
COURIER

R. BLUMSACK
COURIER

Y. POELMANS
MEMBER OF GROUP

M. PEPER
MEMBER OF GROUP

J. JANSSENS
COURIER

JOSEPH BLUMSACK
COURIER

NARRATIVE OF THE ROTE KAPELLE IN BELGIUM

I. EARLY DEVELOPMENT

Belgium was a favorite base for Soviet intelligence operations before World War II. It was geographically ideal because of its proximity to all the other major countries of Western Europe. It provided good cover possibilities because commercial contacts between Belgium and the rest of Europe were widespread; Belgian businessmen could travel extensively on the Continent and in the British Isles without attracting notice. Even more important, however, was the fact that the Belgian government was indifferent to espionage carried on within its territory so long as it was directed against other powers. The Belgian Penal Code provided penalties only for espionage conducted against the Belgian government itself. For these reasons, Belgium was widely used in the 1930s by Red Army intelligence as a training ground and depot for agents trained and assigned to work in and against various countries.

A fairly simple procedure was followed to establish the first Soviet intelligence organizations in Belgium. Moscow headquarters sent out through the Soviet diplomatic representative in Belgium prepared lists of names of persons considered useful for the Belgian intelligence network. The lists contained all the necessary background information on these people. As a rule, strict care was observed not to include people who had appeared in public as Communists or Communist sympathizers. Every kind of investigation as to their suitability and dependability had already been undertaken by the Director in Moscow. They were to be "mobilized" by a kind of induction order and summoned to appear at a certain place and time, for which they had been given detailed instructions as to recognition signals, methods of procedure, and cover. The Soviet intelligence officers whom these people were to contact had received similar instructions. This system proved very practical and effective; it solved the problem of filling slots in the agent nets with almost clocklike precision. Persons of different backgrounds and varying motivations were joined together to form a vast and effective intelligence organization.

The Belgian networks of the Rote Kapelle were made up of:

(1) Agents who had been working for the Comintern for many years, such as:

> Johannes Wenzel,
> Franz and Germaine Schneider,
> Abraham Rajchmann,
> Malvina Gruber, nee Hofstadjerova, and
> Leon Grossvogel;

(2) Soviet officers, such as:

> Leopold Trepper (alias Mikler),
> Victor Sukolov (alias Sierra),
> Mikhail Makarov (alias Alamo),
> Anton Danilov (alias Desmets), and
> Konstantin Jeffremov (alias Jernstroem); and

(3) Agents recruited by Trepper, Sukolov, Makarov, and Jeffremov, such as:

> Rita Arnould, nee Block,
> Sofie Posnanska,
> Herman Isbutsky,
> Elizabeth Depelsenaire, nee Sneyers,
> Isidore Springer,
> Margarete Barcza, nee Singer,
> Augustin Sesee,
> Maurice Peper, and many others.

The first important Soviet agents to arrive in Belgium were technicians, and among them was Johannes Wenzel, who came to Belgium from Germany in January 1936. He had previously served with the clandestine military section of the German Communist Party. He was taken over by Red Army intelligence, and his principal use was to be as a wireless technician able to operate a radio and to train new operators.

Wenzel, a former Comintern agent, probably entered into relations with Franz and Germaine Schneider of Brussels in 1936. The Schneiders were new RU recruits in 1936, but they had previously been managers of a safe house and couriers for the Communists and the Comintern. Their first direct RU assignment was as couriers. Franz Schneider was employed by Unilever, an affiliate of Lever Brothers, and he occasionally went through Belgium to Switzerland, his county of origin. He was probably used as a courier in that direction.

II. LEOPOLD TREPPER

Leopold Trepper, who was later to take over the direction of the Belgian network of the Rote Kapelle, had already visited Belgium in 1931. In fact, there is a record of him at the Free University of Brussels, where he was allowed to follow a political science course during 1931.

Trepper was born 23 February 1904 at Neumark, Poland. He did not arrive in Belgium officially until 6 March 1939, but he seems to have made several visits there in 1937 and 1938. He may already have been using cover as a businessman.

Trepper was an old-time intelligence officer who had mastered his craft completely. His knowledge was not only theory learned at Soviet intelligence schools, but was also the product of many years of experience in Palestine and France. His actions were disciplined by careful deliberation, and he never said one word more than was absolutely necessary. Drawing him into conversation was almost impossible. He was completely at home in the West; there was little chance that he would betray his Soviet and Eastern European background.

Trepper lived well, but his private life was always concealed. Good conspiratorial working methods were observed, and there was no one who could give precise information on his private life. In public his manner was modest, and he blended almost invisibly into the background. He had complete control over his subordinates, and some of them actually worshipped him. They believed anything he told them and were so accustomed to obeying him that they betrayed their comrades unhesitatingly when he ordered them to do so.

Trepper's special talents and greatest strength were his organizational ability and ability to penetrate significant social groups. He was a very keen judge of people, even of people from backgrounds foreign to him. He had built up an unbelievably large reservoir of potential and working sources of intelligence in the West through his many years' association with the French CP. He had been well supported financially and had been allowed the freedom to develop his own work.

III. The Foreign Excellent Raincoat Company

Trepper began to build his cover some time before his operation was launched. He was of the belief that satisfactory work could be accomplished only with the use of commercial cover. Furthermore, such cover should be able to finance the espionage activities undertaken. He surveyed the situation on his trips to Western Europe, reported back to Moscow, and was told to organize a commercial enterprise that would suit his purpose. There is considerable evidence that cover firms—so-called "shadow enterprises"—had already been set up in several Western European countries many years before the beginning of World War II. In this procedure the Soviets followed a practice which had already been employed during World War I by the Central Powers and the Allies and which had proved successful then.

In order to establish his cover, Trepper turned to his old friend, Leon Grossvogel, whom he had known in Palestine. Grossvogel, a former Comintern agent, had been employed by the Brussels firm, Roi du Caoutchouc, since 1929 and in 1935 was manager of its foreign subsidiary, the Excellent Raincoat Company.

In 1937 Grossvogel, who had lived in Belgium since 1926, was transferred from the post of General Manager of the Excellent Raincoat Company to that of traveling inspector for the firm. It is significant that Trepper had met Grossvogel in Brussels the same year. The next year Grossvogel was to become an important figure in Trepper's long-term plans against the United Kingdom, then the primary target of Soviet intelligence operations in Western Europe.

Grossvogel had become unpopular with his employers, the owners of the Excellent Raincoat Company. Though they recognized his ability and though he was related to one of them, Louis Kapelowitz, by marriage, they knew that he had Communist sympathies; and they found him awkward during a strike which took place at their Brussels plant in 1938. Accordingly they accepted with relief Grossvogel's proposal that he set up an independent (or subsidiary) company in the same line of business. As a matter of fact, his employers subscribed half the funds (about eight or ten thousand dollars) toward the new firm and held, between them, half the shares issued. The other half was held by Grossvogel himself. The directors of the company were Louis Kapelowitz (Grossvogel's brother-in-law), Abraham Lerner, Moses Padawer, and Jules Jaspar.

Actually, Trepper had persuaded Grossvogel to form this company, which was created in December 1938 and was known as the Foreign Excellent Raincoat Company. It is certain that Grossvogel was supported in his endeavor by Trepper on behalf of the RU. Grossvogel became manager of the new concern, which was expressly designed to deal in the export of raincoats to Denmark, Finland, Norway, and Sweden (the territories in which Trepper planned to set up bases for his operations against the United Kingdom).

With the creation of the new firm, intentional rumors were circulated in business circles in Brussels to the effect that the financial backer was a wealthy Canadian, Adam Mikler, who provided ten thousand American dollars as capital. Thus, it was no surprise when Trepper (alias Mikler) became associated with the firm. The firm was established with the full sanction of the Belgian authorities. Belgian records show that a certain Mikler, with his wife and child, arrived in that country, from Quebec, 6 March 1939, and settled in Brussels.

The "Grand Chef"—as the name implied—was to function as supreme chief. He immediately assumed rigid control of the agent groups, reorganized them, and started the work of setting up installations for the radio network. His assignment was to inspect preparations already made by other intelligence officers, to expand the intelligence network still further, and to activate large-scale cover firms as bases for intelligence operations. With Trepper's arrival in Belgium the Rote Kapelle began to assume definite shape.

By 1940 Trepper was well-rooted. He gave Belgian authorities and business acquaintances the impression that he intended to stay in Belgium about two years only and that he had put only a portion of his capital into this export company. In the meantime he was actively engaged in recruiting agents for his intelligence network. (See diagram 2.)

At about the time Trepper came to Brussels, Grossvogel made a tour of the Scandinavian countries, with the object of establishing branch offices of the Foreign Excellent Raincoat Company. Local regulations made it difficult to create the type of branch company required. One office, however, was set up in Stockholm. It was put under the charge of a Belgian named Boellens, who was recommended by the Belgian Consulate in Sweden.

The business of the firm was handled overtly; local regulations were closely followed, and contact with local government officials was maintained. It was Trepper's intention that persons engaged in the purely commercial aspects of the business were to be kept in complete ignorance of its true purpose. Intelligence officers, sent from or recommended by Moscow, were only to be brought in after the commercial company was well established in its own right. Then, little by little, intelligence agents would be inserted as shareholders, business managers, or heads of departments. Trepper was setting about building a strong cover organization slowly but securely. Because of the imminence of war, however, his plans were disrupted by Moscow, and he was instructed to set to work collecting intelligence immediately.

IV. TREPPER'S DOCUMENTATION

As stated above, Trepper used the alias Adam Mikler when he arrived in Belgium. He carried Canadian passport #43761, issued in Ottawa 12 July 1937. Canada is one of the few countries which issues passports by mail and does not require a personal appearance before an official. Broadly speaking, all anyone needs to pose as a Canadian citizen, complete with passport, is the initiative to visit a travel agency, to have a reasonable cover story, to lie under oath, and to pay a $5 fee. Accordingly, Soviet "illegals" like Trepper are easily documented in Canada.

The records of the Belgian Police show that Adam Mikler, his wife, Anna, and their son, Edgard, entered Belgium on 6 March 1939, traveling ostensibly from Quebec, Canada. Their papers indicated that Adam Mikler was born 5 April 1903 at Rudki, Poland. His father was Andre Mikler, born in 1875 in Rudki; his mother was Maria Jagodrinski, born in 1870 in Tarnov, Poland; and his wife was Anna Orschitzer, born 25 May 1908 in Drohobucz, Poland. They were married 15 May 1928 in Rudki. Their son, Edgard Mikler, was born 4 December 1936 in Vancouver, Canada. It was indicated that Adam Mikler, his wife Anna, and son Edgard were Canadian nationals. Their address in Quebec was 131 rue St. Louis. The Mikler family established itself at 198 ave. Richard Neyberg, in Brussels. Trepper's wife had Canadian passport #45584, issued in Ottawa on 5 August 1937. Her son used her passport.

The records of the Canadian authorities tell a different story. According to the immigration authorities, no person by the name of Adam Mikler has ever entered, resided in, or left Canada. The address given in Quebec is fictitious. The Department of Vital Statistics has no record of the birth of Edgard Mikler.

Canadian passport #43761 was issued on 7 July 1939 to one Michael Dzumaga, born in Winnipeg on 2 August 1914. This man fought in the Spanish Civil War as a volunteer in the Mackenzie Papineau Brigade. In 1946 Dzumaga was not in possession of his passport, which he claimed was lost while he was in Spain. The Spanish Civil War produced a bonanza in passports for Soviet espionage. Members of the International Brigade invariably had their passports confiscated "for safekeeping" when they arrived in Spain, and usually these had been "lost" when they wanted to return home.

Canadian passport #45584 was issued on 5 August 1937 to Mrs. William Syme, nee Agnes Lockie, who is reported to have been involved with the Dutch Communist Party in Amsterdam and to have escaped arrest in the summer of 1942. During an investigation made by Canadian authorities about 1946 it was claimed that Agnes Syme still had her passport in her possession.

It appears that passports #43761 and #45584 were authentic Canadian passports, fraudulently altered by the Soviets and then used by Trepper, his wife, and son. Trepper's wife was Sarah Orschitzer, nee Broide, born at Radzivilov, Poland, in 1904. Their son with them in Belgium was born at Moscow in 1936. They also had another son, born at Paris in 1931. The older son had been left in the Soviet Union for schooling.

In the many years Trepper operated for the Soviet intelligence services he used a great number of passports, each one in a different name. The first to come to attention is an old Polish passport, in the name of Trepper, visas for which were procured in Belgium. He used this one in 1932 to travel to the USSR. In 1936 he was sent to France from the USSR on an intelligence mission. He then used an Austrian passport in the name of Sommer. This passport, which indicated that he had come from the USSR, was exchanged for him in Paris to conceal the fact that he had connections with the USSR, and he assumed the identity of Herbst, an Austrian. In 1937 he returned to Moscow, via Berlin, carrying a Luxemburg passport in the name of Majeris. After his cover firm had been established in Brussels, Trepper was ready to take his place in the organization and appeared in Belgium as Adam Mikler. Thus he traveled between the USSR and Western Europe many times, by different routes and using different identities. He had about twenty aliases and used Austrian, Polish, Luxemburg, French, and Canadian papers.

V. MIKHAIL MAKAROV

On 25 March 1939 Trepper was joined in Brussels by the Soviet intelligence officer Mikhail Makarov, who had been sent from Moscow via Stockholm and Copenhagen to Paris at the beginning of 1939. In Paris Makarov, who had been an aviator in the Spanish Civil War, was given $10,000 and a Uruguayan passport in the name of Carlos Alamo. The Uruguayan passport, issued in New York on 16 October 1936, indicated that Alamo had been born in Montevideo on 12 April 1913. Makarov went with the Alamo passport to Belgium, where he operated in that name.

His primary purpose was to assist Trepper with documentation. He was an expert in the preparation of false documents and in the use of secret inks. Soon after Trepper arrived in Brussels, however, Grossvogel managed to introduce Abraham Rajchmann to the group. An accomplished forger, Rajchmann had procured for Grossvogel in 1934 or 1935 two Syrian visas for a Polish passport, and in 1937 he was able to supply Grossvogel with two Polish passports. Rajchmann was henceforth used as the group's forger of documents, and Makarov was released for other duties. Rajchmann was able to procure false identity cards and papers for couriers and for other agents, as needed. Documents for traveling were particularly necessary when Trepper was developing his cover firm in Brussels and when Grossvogel was visiting outlying areas to establish branch companies.

Makarov started to work as a W/T operator, and his posting to Ostend by Trepper in April 1939 suggested that he was intended to serve in the front line of Trepper's communications with the British Isles. Makarov's cover in Ostend was fortified by the "sale" to him of a branch of the Excellent Raincoat Company, hitherto managed by Grossvogel's wife, Jeanne, nee Pesant. Makarov immediately set about establishing a wireless link and training operators. He recruited Augustin Sesee, who assisted him with transmissions. In May 1940 the Ostend branch of the Excellent Raincoat Company was destroyed by German bombing, and Makarov moved back to Brussels. From May 1940 to December 1941 Makarov's transmitter in Brussels was the only unofficial link Trepper had with Moscow.

VI. VICTOR SUKOLOV

Victor Sukolov, another Soviet intelligence officer, arrived in Brussels in July 1939, appearing as Vincente Sierra and traveling on a Uruguayan passport, which had been issued in New York 17 April 1936. It gave the holder's date and place of birth as 3 July 1911, Montevideo, and listed his parents as Spanish. His permanent address was noted as Calle Colon 9, Montevideo.

Sukolov had probably been active as a Soviet agent in France from 1937 to early 1939. There are records to indicate that in 1938, and during the first half of 1939, money was sent from Mexico to a bank in Marseilles for Sukolov. Who sent the money, how it was transmitted, and for what it was to be used are not known.

In April 1939 Sukolov visited Berlin on instructions from Moscow to revive Schulze-Boysen as a source and to arrange communications with him via courier. Sukolov was given Schulze-Boysen's telephone number and was told to phone him and arrange for a rendezvous. On no account was he to meet him at his home. When Sukolov made the telephone call, Mrs. Schulze-Boysen answered. Since Sukolov had been informed that she, as well as her husband, was to be involved in the work for the Soviet intelligence services, he arranged a rendezvous with her. Sukolov and Mrs. Schulze-Boysen met on the platform at the underground station, and Schulze-Boysen joined them there a little later. Then the three went to a cafe in the vicinity to discuss their business. Sukolov was probably posted to Brussels to establish a reception point for Schulze-Boysen's information and a means of relaying it from Belgium to Moscow.

The first meeting between Trepper and Sukolov took place at Ghent shortly after Sukolov's arrival, in accordance with instructions from Moscow. It was arranged that Trepper would instruct Sukolov in the export business until the fall of 1939. At the same time Sukolov was to take lessons in languages and business administration. It is also known that in 1939 Trepper gave coding instructions to Sukolov.

Sukolov's original cover was that of a student of languages traveling through Europe, with temporary residence in Belgium. Using the alias Vincente Sierra and carrying his Uruguayan passport, he posed as the son of a rich South American. Under this cover Sukolov was able to make a trip to Switzerland shortly after his arrival in Belgium. After this journey he enrolled as a part-time student at the Universite Libre in Brussels. His registration as a student made it possible for him to obtain a six months' resident's permit which he extended for further periods of six months.

According to German sources Sukolov had been originally destined for Copenhagen. The outbreak of war, however, caused the cancellation of the plan to send him to Denmark, and he stayed on in Belgium. It then became necessary to incorporate him gradually into the Belgian network. Orders to this effect were received from Moscow.

In March and April 1940 Sukolov made a three weeks' visit to Switzerland to see Alexander Rado. It is known that one purpose of this trip was for Sukolov to deliver $3,000 to Rado for the financing of the Swiss network.

During part of 1939 and 1940 Sukolov was associated with Trepper, but he handled his own traffic with Moscow. There is no doubt, however, that in all matters Sukolov was subordinate to Trepper.

VII. Konstantin Jeffremov

The foundations of another independent network in Belgium were laid by the arrival of Konstantin Jeffremov in Brussels from Zurich on 6 September 1939. He came under a Finnish alias, Eric Jernstroem, as a student of chemistry, ostensibly to study at the Ecole Polytechnique in Brussels. He carried a Finnish passport, issued in New York 22 June 1937, indicating that he had been born 3 November 1911 in Vasa, Finland, and had lived in the United States since 1932. It is not known where he obtained the passport; it is possible that it was issued to him in the USSR. It is also not known how Jeffremov lived his cover for the next year and a half, but he appeared to have plenty of American currency and a U.S. passport. No information suggesting that he had ever been in the United States is available.

Jeffremov had been employed before the war in the collection of technical information about chemicals, and chemistry may have been the immediate interest of his mission. The target and outcome of the mission are unknown. Jeffremov's arrival in Belgium a few days after the outbreak of war was too opportune to be wasted on a short-term mission, however, and he was instructed to build up a network. For this purpose he was put in touch with Wenzel, whom he may have known before, and he also made use of his friends, the Schneiders, who had been recruited for the RU in 1936. The Schneiders were possibly recruited by Jeffremov, who from 1936 to 1939 had lived somewhere in Western Europe, probably in the Low Countries. From September 1939 to May 1942 Jeffremov ran his own RU service from Brussels. (See diagram 4.) Wenzel in Belgium and Anton Winterink in Holland had established W/T links with Moscow by December 1940, and Jeffremov used them to pass his traffic.

Jeffremov's team seems to have maintained its independence in the Low Countries until 1942. There were, however, connections between Jeffremov's group and the Trepper-Sukolov group. Johannes Wenzel, for example, worked as a radio operator for Jeffremov but also provided technical assistance and instruction to members of the Trepper-Sukolov network. Herman Isbutsky performed services for Trepper as early as 1939, and in 1941 he worked for Jeffremov as well. Maurice Peper was simultaneously a member of the Jeffremov and Sukolov networks, although his primary responsibilities were to Jeffremov. It is known, also, that Jeffremov was aware of Sukolov's operation, at least by 1941. Likewise, it must be presumed that Trepper and Sukolov eventually knew of Jeffremov's presence, even though his arrival in September 1939 had not been announced to them. There is even evidence that Mikhail Makarov and Jeffremov had been classmates together at a Soviet intelligence school in Moscow and had met completely by chance one day on a street in Brussels.

Only infrequently did Jeffremov provide Moscow with intelligence of good quality, and he was frequently reprimanded for his lack of activity and poor production. On the other hand, his top agent, Germaine Schneider, was a competent courier and organizer. Another of his agents, Elizabeth Depelsenaire, headed a sub-group which was primarily responsible for the accommodation of Soviet agents parachuted into Belgium. One of these, John Kruyt, parachuted into Belgium 24 June 1942 and was captured by the Germans six days later. Information obtained from him led to the arrests of members of the Depelsenaire sub-group.

VIII. COMMUNICATIONS

Soviet diplomatic offices in the Low Countries were available to the Rote Kapelle, and there is evidence that Trepper did on occasion refer to the Soviet Embassy in Brussels. However, regular use of the diplomatic links could have endangered his cover, and he must have been anxious to establish his private line of communication. It is not known whether Trepper during 1939-40 had any quantity of intelligence to pass, because his operations against the British were still in the early stages. Because the Schulze-Boysen line was his, Sukolov must have been under some pressure, and it is likely that it was he who sought out a link with the Dutch Communist Party. Once this link was working, Trepper may have used it too. The networks in Belgium also maintained a communications link with Moscow through the Soviet Trade Delegation in Brussels.

By the time World War II broke out in Western Europe, the Rote Kapelle had an efficient radio organization at its disposal. In Northern Europe—England and Scandinavia—this intelligence apparatus was supplemented by an auxiliary agent and radio network which at the time (mid-1940) was still comparatively small-scale but which functioned well. Detached from the political intelligence service of the Comintern, it served the "Grand Chef" for a long time as an alternate routing system for messages, via London and Stockholm.

IX. THE GERMAN INVASION

When the Germans invaded Belgium in May 1940, several persons connected with the Rote Kapelle in Belgium escaped to France. One of these was Jules Jaspar. Arrangements were made to supply Jaspar with about two hundred thousand francs, money salvaged from the Belgian firm, so as to enable him to establish a new and secure base in unoccupied France by creating a fresh commercial company as soon as the opportunity arose. Abraham Rajchman also fled from Belgium to France in May 1940.

Through his contacts with Bulgarian diplomatic circles Trepper was able to tour the war-torn areas of Belgium in mid-May 1940, on the assumption that he was checking the damages to his business resources. He then wrote a lengthy report on his observations and the discussions he had had with people enroute, and forwarded it to Moscow.

The Foreign Excellent Raincoat Company and its parent firm were taken over by the Germans not long after the occupation of Brussels. In July 1940 Trepper and Grossvogel fled to France in the automobile of the Bulgarian Petrov.

Before leaving, Trepper made arrangements for his wife and son to go to France also. In August 1940 Sarah Orschitzer and her son were able to reach Marseilles, and from there they returned to the Soviet Union, supposedly with the assistance of Soviet officials in France. Later, in March 1941, Trepper had his American-born mistress, Georgie de Winter, come from Brussels to join him in Paris. Trepper had met Georgie in Brussels in 1938 or 1939. It is probable that he is the father of her son, Patrick de Winter, born 29 September 1939 at Brussels.

After the invasion of the Low Countries, Sukolov anticipated no difficulties from the German authorities, since he was passing as a Uruguayan. When Trepper and Grossvogel had to flee to France, Trepper made Sukolov the head of the Belgian network and turned over to him the agents who were active in this network, including a W/T operator (Makarov), several couriers, and a number of subagents. As soon as things quieted down, Sukolov began to reorganize the network. (See diagram 3.) He thereafter referred to Trepper only on fundamental points of policy.

X. SIMEXCO

A new cover firm was urgently needed by the network to replace the "Foreign Excellent Raincoat Company," which had been seized by the Germans. This company, called Simexco, was founded by Sukolov in the fall of 1940.

The firm was established as a genuine business and was even granted telephone and telegraph facilities by the German authorities. Like its sister firm, Simex, in Paris, Simexco was designed for general dealings and contracting in support of the German occupation, and it provided regular and privileged means of communication between Trepper and Sukolov. It is likely that Sukolov passed over his wireless transmitter a good deal of Trepper's intelligence and business messages to Moscow, even before the Soviet embassies were withdrawn from France in June and July 1941. After that date Sukolov's transmitter was probably the sole means of communication for both Trepper and his new partner, Henri Robinson. There is no evidence of an alternative line through Rado's service in Switzerland during this period, although in June 1941 Robinson expressed the hope of a regular contact with Rachel Duebendorfer.

Early in 1941 Sukolov, as head of Simexco, made a business trip to Switzerland on Moscow's instructions, probably to inspect Alexander Rado.

The official Soviet establishments in Belgium having been

closed down, one of the most important problems became wireless communications. Sukolov was supplying Moscow with Schulze-Boysen's intelligence through his W/T station in Brussels. He may also have contributed intelligence collected in the Low Countries, some from his own agents in Belgium, such as Isidore Springer, and some from agents bequeathed to him by Trepper in July 1940. Makarov, transmitting for Sukolov in Brussels, had more traffic than he could handle.

In the summer of 1941 Moscow, seeking to alleviate these difficulties, sent Makarov an assistant, Anton Danilov, formerly a clerk in the Soviet Embassy at Paris and then Vichy. He went to Brussels to receive W/T training from Makarov and to assist with transmission work for Sukolov's network. Even this aid, however, was not enough, and in October 1941 Sofie Posnanska was transferred to Brussels from Paris to do enciphering work for Makarov. Both Danilov and Posnanska worked diligently for Makarov until their arrest in December 1941.

In late October 1941 Sukolov went to Germany on orders from Moscow. Among other assignments, he was to check the transmitter sets of Schulze-Boysen and Harnack to see why their communications were not getting through to Moscow and, if possible, to repair the sets. He was not able to make the repairs.

On this trip Sukolov was also supposed to deliver a cipher key to Ilse Stoebe, but she had moved to Dresden, and he was unable to locate her. He delivered the key instead to Kurt Schulze, who was directed to establish a W/T link with Moscow. The trip to Germany was made through the assistance of Sukolov's German contacts, who arranged for him to visit the Leipzig Fair. Sukolov had been instructed to hide 1,000 marks at 2 Eichen, Leipzig. For whom this money was intended and whether it was recovered or not has not been determined. Sukolov apparently surveyed the situation of the German networks during this trip and sent a report on the topic to Moscow. He was also able to report to Moscow on the political situation in Germany. Sukolov had one final mission to accomplish while he was in Germany. He was to arrange for the dispatch of an agent to the Soviet Trade Delegation in Istanbul and of another to the Soviet Consulate in Stockholm. It is not known whether Sukolov successfully completed this last assignment.

Sukolov then proceeded to Czechoslovakia, where in early November 1941 he met Maria Rauch, the wife of Simexco employee

Henri Rauch, at Raudnitz. He had also been instructed by RU headquarters to visit Wojatschek and Frantischek, picture dealers in Prague, in order to be put in touch with one "Rudi." This individual had probably been working for Moscow through the Soviet Military Attache in Prague, but he had not been heard from since June. Sukolov failed to contact Frantischek or Wojatschek because they had been captured by the Gestapo shortly before his visit.

XI. THE FIRST ARRESTS

In the course of 1941 a direction-finding service working in Berlin reported the existence of a secret radio transmitter operating in contact with Moscow. Around October or November 1941 Henry Piepe of the Abwehr was ordered to take charge of the investigation of this station, believed to be located somewhere in Belgium. As a result of Piepe's D/F activities, the Abwehr narrowed the search down to the Etterbeck section of Brussels.

Sukolov's W/T operator, Danilov, was arrested early in the morning of 13 December 1941 while transmitting from a safehouse at 101, rue des Attrebates, Etterbeck. The two women who ran the house, Rita Arnould and Sofie Posnanska, were arrested at the same time. The day after Danilov's arrest Makarov went to the safehouse and was taken into custody by the Germans.

Trepper, too, happened to be in Belgium at the time of the arrests and went unsuspectingly to the house on 13 December. His cover (a businessman from France) and his documentation were so authentic that he was released immediately. He was thus in a position to forewarn others in the network of the impending dangers.

Sukolov was among those warned by Trepper. His first concern was for the safety of his mistress, Margarete Barcza, and he asked Abraham Rajchmann to arrange for her to go to France. Rajchmann was eventually able to do so; and with the help of Malvina Gruber, Barcza and her son, Rene, reached France in late December 1941. Sukolov hid in the house of Nazarin Drailly for a few days while he made arrangements for the closing of his affairs at Simexco. He also visited Robert Christen and left with him a radio set. Approximately 15 December 1941 Sukolov fled to France. His agent Isidore Springer went with him. The minor characters in the organization were instructed to lie low for several months. They were all in great danger, particularly since Rita Arnould had turned informant shortly after her arrest.

At the time Sukolov pulled out, Simexco was not only providing him with good contacts but was a well-established, thriving, and profitable enterprise. According to the records the profits for the year 1941 amounted to a million ninety thousand francs. Sukolov was able to withdraw most of the assets from Simexco. Later, in July 1942, he completed the sale of the firm's holdings to a person who was probably entirely outside the espionage organization, Louis Thevenet.

XII. REORGANIZATION

In May 1942 Trepper met Jeffremov in the Schneiders' house in Brussels at a rendezvous arranged by the RU. Trepper handed over to Jeffremov the surviving parts of the network that Sukolov had had in the Low Countries—a network which embodied parts of the organization established by Trepper between 1938 and 1940.

Probably the most important and urgent part of Jeffremov's new commission was to continue the transmission of Schulze-Boysen's material, received by courier from Germany. According to the Dutch agent Goulooze, Jeffremov had been in wireless communication with Moscow through Wenzel and his assistants since December 1940. It is not impossible that Jeffremov's traffic, including the Schulze-Boysen material, was routed through Trepper himself from February to April 1942, for Trepper during this period was in touch with Moscow through a French CP transmitter, and he is known to have been visited during this period by Germaine Schneider as a courier from Jeffremov. Johann Wenzel was working only infrequently for Jeffremov at this time, but he agreed in May 1942 to resume full-time work as the W/T operator for the new group.

XIII. THE SECOND ARRESTS

While he was in the act of transmitting, Wenzel was arrested by the Germans in Brussels on 30 July 1942. Letters found at his residence incriminated Germaine Schneider, the courier and safehouse keeper for the network. She, too, was arrested; but with the aid of her husband, Franz Schneider, she masqueraded as Wenzel's mistress and was released as of no intelligence interest. She quickly fled to Paris, where she reported the news to Trepper.

Under interrogation Wenzel was broken to a point where he was regarded as "turned" to German purposes. At no time does

Wenzel appear to have resisted too much, and by August 1942 he was being played back by the Germans.

With Wenzel's information on codes and enciphering techniques the Germans were able to make use of previously intercepted wireless traffic. They had been intercepting Sukolov's W/T traffic since 28 June 1941. After Wenzel's collaboration they were able to decipher almost all of it. Samples of the decrypted messages, taken from captured German documents, reveal how damaging these messages were to the entire Rote Kapelle organization, particularly to the German networks. A message intercepted on 28 August 1941 by the German short wave station at Prague, for example, instructed the Soviet agent "Kent" (Sukolov) in Brussels to seek out "a certain Ilse Stoebe, alias Alte, at Wielandstr. 37, Berlin-Charlottenburg." She was described as an important agent. As a result of this message and the subsequent German investigation Stoebe was arrested in Berlin on 12 September 1942. Other messages led to even earlier arrests, such as that of Harro Schulze-Boysen on 30 August 1942. The networks in Germany owed their demise to Johann Wenzel.

It may be that Wenzel had made with Moscow previous arrangements whereby it was agreed that, if he was arrested, he could divulge certain information to the Germans. If so, these arrangements may have included an escape plan, for on 17 November 1942 Wenzel escaped from his captors and was never heard from again. No further information is available on Wenzel's escape, except for one unconfirmed report that he was in Holland in 1943. It may be that his escape, like Trepper's several months later, was part of a triple-cross plan. On the other hand, if he betrayed all he knew to the Germans, without previous approval from Moscow, it is possible that he fled in fear of both sides and retired from the field of intelligence.

After the arrest of Wenzel the rest of the Belgian network soon fell. Trepper, who had received word of the disaster from Germaine Schneider, sent word to Jeffremov to establish for himself a new identity as soon as possible. For this purpose Jeffremov naturally addressed himself to the group's documentation expert, Abraham Rajchmann, who agreed to provide Jeffremov with new identity documents.

Rajchmann, however, had been under close observation by the Gestapo for several months. The German penetration agent Charles Mathieu was even supplying Rajchmann with false documents for members of the organization. Rajchmann arranged a meeting between Mathieu and Jeffremov on 22 July 1942, at which time Jeffremov was to receive his new documentation. Jeffremov was arrested a short distance away from the rendezvous spot.

Jeffremov was almost immediately regarded as "turned" by the Germans. From prison he was induced to write to Rajchmann a letter stating that he had been hiding recently but that all was well and that Rajchmann should not be concerned about his absence. This information, as the Germans had hoped, was passed from Rajchmann to Grossvogel and then to Trepper. The Germans were planning radio playbacks and were attempting to conceal Jeffremov's arrest from the rest of the network.

Apparently the Germans tried to operate both the Wenzel and Jeffremov transmitters, but Moscow had certainly been warned about Wenzel's arrest. The W/T deception through Wenzel and Jeffremov may therefore have been played back by the RU, with or without the prisoners' connivance. It is, nevertheless, a fact that Wenzel and Jeffremov not only betrayed a number of their fellow agents but also revealed what was far more damaging to the RU, their W/T cipher.

After Jeffremov was arrested by the Germans, he gave them details of his various rendezvous with subagents, so that a few days later two of them, Isbutsky and Peper, were arrested. Peper revealed that he was the liaison officer with a network in Holland and that he had scheduled a rendezvous with the leader of the Dutch network, Anton Winterink, for a few days later. The meeting was to take place in the afternoon at a point in a busy street in Amsterdam. Winterink attended the meeting and was arrested by the Germans. The arrest took place in Holland, and possibly because of Wenzel's evidence, the Germans were under the impression that Winterink's station had been operated under Wenzel's indirect control.

XIV. THE GERMAN VERSION

The German version of the capture of the Soviet agents in Brussels, taken from the final report on the Rote Kapelle that was submitted by Abwehr III F. Ast Belgien and dated 24 March 1943, follows:

"Chemnitz' [Makarov's] radio activity in Brussels led to it that on 12 and 13 December 1941, the transmitting system was seized during work by the police radio detachment. The report by the Belgian Office of 31 December 1941, Br. B. No. 1290/41 g. Kdos III F, should be pointed out in this respect. The arrests made had endangered the position of the Belgian group. The Grand Chef, who arrived at the place of action the day after the seizure and was arrested, could prove with the aid of the credentials at his disposal that he was harmless and he was released. In this manner he had been able to get a picture of the situation and was in the position to warn all participants who had not yet been arrested. One of these was Kent [Sukolov]. As the outbreak of war with the United States was imminent, it did not attract any special attention at Simexco when he disassociated himself from the firm under the pretext that he wanted to avoid internment as South American. And so it did not astonish anyone when he withdrew a part of his allegedly invested fortune from the firm and fled with his mistress, Mrs. Barcza, to France. The Simexco firm was well-established and has been able to do good business with the aid of its commercial representatives, especially with the German authorities. In this connection, Kent also tried to make personal contacts with the various group leaders of the German Government departments. He succeeded only in part, however. He made the personal acquaintance only of staff paymaster Kranzbuehler and of his secretary, Miss Amann. He has been able to use them only to a very small extent for intelligence purposes. It is interesting in this connection to repeat the statements of the Grand Chef verbatim:

> I have never tried, indirectly or directly, to get information from a German officer. On the one hand I have to admit that German officers generally are not a good subject in this respect, for they are very uncommunicative. On the other hand one can state the opposite for the officials of officer rank and other followers of the Wehrmacht. The officer is mostly taciturn, but administrative officials and other personnel are gossips in my opinion.

"Romeo [Springer] who had been recognized as an intelligence courier, was able to escape with Kent. All other lesser members of the organization stayed at first in hiding and were told to keep quiet for a few months. The Grand Chef intended to set up immediately a reserve group that Moscow had placed at his disposal. The fact, recognized by counter-espionage, that there must be still other groups and very small groups in Belgium led to a III-F type of game that was executed by four contact people. With the aid of a contact-man it was possible to get near the 'Fabrikant' [Rajchmann]. After the dispersion, the latter had received from Grossvogel of the Kent group a spare wireless communication set which then was kept hidden in the house of our contact man. Other contact-men had informed the AST that a section of the group had gone to Marseille and Nice. Another contact person found out where they received their mail. III F Ast Belgium thus was very well informed. In this respect we also want to refer to the report of Ast Belgium III F of 12 October 1942 Br. 8 No. 4/42 g. Kdos. The Grand Chef found out by couriers about the further development of the inquiries and decided, in spite of the danger involved, to continue the existence of 'Simexco' in Brussels, for with the exception of Drailly all other associates were true dummies, and the departure of Kent had been connected with the fact of the imminent war between Germany and the United States. The legal status of the Simexco firm also was absolutely solid, for it was recognized as a conservative firm with the aid of German service departments, and on the recommendation of the administrative staff at the military command it had through III N Ast Belgium even been granted long distance and telegram communications. Drailly, who gradually had recognized the true nature of the business, reproached the Grand Chef and threatened to betray him. The Grand Chef said that, despite this threat, he did not eliminate and liquidate him, for he still needed him as a commercial expert.

"Radio direction findings in June 1942 showed the renewed presence of a red transmitter in Brussels. Contact-man Charles [Mathieu] had brought the news earlier that the group had been re-established and was working again. The greatest activity of the above-mentioned contact-men could merely establish that Germans or German-speaking people were participating in the new group. Police action related to the new transmitter took place on 30 June 1942 and led to the arrest of the wireless operator 'Hermann' [Wenzel]. The first short interrogations established the surprising result that he was a Communist leader who had been sought by the Reich since 1929 and whose dangerousness was an established fact. As the contact-man had reported that serious resistance could be expected, troops had been activated, besides the GFP, under the direction of

III F officers of Ast Belgium, and a short shooting engagement took place. The fact that the new group had been eliminated was soon reported to the Grand Chef in Paris. Hermann's papers showed that he had contacts with a Mrs. Germaine Schneider, with whom he maintained intimate relations. She was arrested by the GFP but was able to deceive the arresting officials and was released. Mrs. Schneider really was the 'Schmetterling' mentioned in the first situation plan, who later went under the name of 'Odette.' As it turned out later, she was not only Hermann's assistant, but was the courier of Harry [Robinson]; was arrested in Paris; and made trips on behalf of the French and Belgian organization to the Reich and to Switzerland and England. Immediately after her release she fled to Paris and informed the Grand Chef of the situation. (Report of Ast Belgium of 12 October 1942 Br. B. No. 4/42 Kdo. g. 13 Rote Kapelle). The Grand Chef realized the dangerousness of the situation and instructed the successor of Kent, 'Paul' or 'Pascal' [Jeffremov], to prepare new forged papers with the aid of the Fabrikant. By the able contact work of a III F contact-man it was possible to induce Fabrikant to let the necessary papers be manufactured by our contact-man. Photographs etc. were handed over to our contact-man and thus also reached the III F Ast Belgium. Fabrikant had received a very detailed description of one man. It was possible to arrange a meeting between our contact-man Carlos and this person. After the delivery of the papers produced by Ast Belgium, this person was inconspicuously arrested 500 meters from that spot in a side street. He was soon recognized as the above-mentioned 'Paul'—'Pascal.' Pascal had been sent to Belgium by Moscow, without the knowledge of the Grand Chef, as a relief troop leader. As the Grand Chef was without direct communication to Moscow after 13 December 1941, further information from Moscow reached him via a technical auxiliary line in Paris. This is a radio circuit of the French Communist Party, with which the military Russian intelligence generally must never be connected. (We shall report about this auxiliary line within the framework of the groups ascertained in France.) Moscow had instructed the Grand Chef to arrange for a meeting with Pascal in Belgium. The meeting took place at the residence of Mrs. Schneider. It was agreed that Pascal now should take over the remainder of the group dispersed on 13 December 1941, and he did. For this purpose Pascal received 100,000 Belgian francs from the Grand Chef. Pascal was known by a Finnish name and had Finnish identification papers. He allegedly was in Brussels for study purposes and was enrolled at the Brussels University. His main subject was chemistry (Report Ast Belgium Br. B. No. 4/42 g. Kdo. 3 December 1942). The Grand Chef informed Pascal about the existence of the 'Simexco' firm, but forbade him to establish contacts with this firm for conspiratorial reasons, for it was possible that the 'Simexco' Director, Drailly, would also betray him if Pascal ever went there. Pascal, who had concealed himself completely since his arrival in Belgium, now established—in accordance with the orders received—the contact with the remaining part of the group. Hermann, who already in the full group had acted as a technical adviser and was known under the cover name of 'Professor,' was connected with Pascal by the Grand Chef on orders from Moscow. Another meeting took place with Bob [Isbutsky], who for his part contacted Fabrikant again with Pascal. Romeo, who in the meantime had learned that the police were looking for him, dropped out of the residual group. It was now possible to establish a new group. Hermann was in the possession of a transmitter and was also able to make some auxiliary devices himself, as he did in his spare time, and he also instructed Bob and Sesee, who has been mentioned with the first Kapelle, in the activities of a wireless operator. It was intended to form again, next to the existing working group, a relief group for cases of emergency. Pascal received the assignment to establish wireless communication with Moscow as quickly as possible. This occurred approximately in May 1942. Pascal generally worked independently, but under the supervision of the Grand Chef. A standard meeting was arranged every month with the Grand Chef and Pascal, which Pascal was to keep in any case, while the Grand Chef would put in an appearance only whenever he believed it necessary. During the next weeks Grossvogel was brought together with Pascal and Hermann, so that the total communication of the Belgian group with France now seemed to be sufficiently assured. At the beginning of June 1942 Pascal, who until then had occupied himself mainly with organizational questions and the technical reconstruction of his group, received the assignment from the Grand Chef to send intelligence via the wireless transmitter of Hermann to Moscow. This had become necessary, for the Sokol transmitter in Paris had been seized. We shall discuss Sokol to a greater extent later in connection with the French group. During the night from 29 to 30 June 1942 the transmitter of Hermann was seized. (Report Ast Belgium of 12 October 1942 Br. B.

No. 4/42 g. Kdo.). In the meantime, four contact-men of III F Ast Belgium worked together with Fabrikant and other small figures of the group. The contact-men had the full confidence of Fabrikant in particular. However, the Grand Chef already had expressed doubts about our contact-man Carlos, who concealed the above-mentioned apparatus at his residence. Fabrikant dispelled this suspicion, and the contact continued to exist with the approval of the Grand Chef, for Fabrikant urgently needed our contact-man Carlos for his forging activities. Further shadowings and surveillances of meetings by contact-men of III F established the letter-reception places and the standard meetings of individual members of the group. Fabrikant, who in the meantime had been recognized as an important man, was constantly shadowed, so that a clear picture had evolved about his individual meetings.

"The first brief questionings of Paul-Pascal after his arrest showed that the young man was unable to stand up under severe interrogation and that he broke down. He soon revealed his cover name, 'Bordo,' used in wireless communications, and also his transmission code. He also revealed standard meetings with his deputy agents, and on the third day after his arrest Bob and Wassermann [Peper] were arrested on the street during the holding of such a meeting. Bob remained silent, but it was possible to get something out of Wassermann. The brief statements revealed that Wassermann was the contact agent to a group in Holland. He also revealed that he would have a meeting with the Dutch group leader in a few days. The operating III-F officer and some officials transported Wassermann in a police car to Amsterdam for the holding of the meeting. The meeting was to take place on an afternoon at a predetermined place on a busy Amsterdam street. Under the observance of great precaution and security measures, Wassermann was released and sent to the meeting. However, the group leader did not appear. Wassermann returned. Other questionings of Wassermann in Amsterdam showed that he was able to name the residence of the Netherlands group leader with a Dutch family. It was therefore decided to send Wassermann to the family in question and to arrange a meeting for the same evening. Again under strict security measures, Wassermann was sent to the house and returned with the news that the meeting was to take place in the evening between 8 and 8:30 in the IS-Dutch regular restaurant in Amsterdam. Wassermann was again alone in the restaurant during the meeting, while security personnel were sitting nearby in the same restaurant. At about 9 o'clock a person appeared, went toward Wassermann, and took a seat on his table. At an agreed upon sign they were seized and arrested. On the way to the police car that was standing by, the arrested person put up considerable resistance, and a brief scuffle took place. During the arrest the person had called out a name into the crowd that had assembled, so that it had to be assumed that he had arranged to be shadowed during the meeting and was warning those who shadowed him by calling out a name. The identification papers found on his person did not give any information about his address. It was therefore necessary to take action at the above described cover place and to arrest the occupants of the dwelling. It was a couple by the name of Hillbolling. The cover name of the person was learned through the couple. It was 'Tino' [Winterink], a Communist official already known to the Executive. With the aid of the Hillbolling couple it was possible to find the clandestine residence of Tino, which was searched the following night. The search of the residence showed that Tino was not only the group leader of the Holland group but also its wireless operator. His mistress, who had lived with him, apparently had fled, warned by the arrest. A complete wireless apparatus, including all technical data, was seized at the residence. (See also the report of Ast Belgium of 12 October 1942, Br. B. No. 4/42 g. Kdo. Rote Kapelle.) Tino was taken to Brussels and at first remained silent. The action with Pascal was continued. Pascal was induced to write to Fabrikant from the prison. The deception succeeded. Fabrikant informed the Grand Chef that Pascal had not come to several meetings but that he was at large and was remaining in hiding for the time being. After it had become known that Mrs. Schneider was not only Hermann's mistress but a very important collaborator and courier, Pascal was induced to arrange a meeting with her husband at a streetcar stop. That also was successful. Schneider did not give any information about the whereabouts of his wife, and only later was it learned that Schneider was playing a double role and that he had sent word to the Grand Chef that Pascal probably was the informer. Fabrikant, who very adroitly had questioned the guards at the prison, was able to find out that Pascal really had been arrested and that Bob and Wassermann were also imprisoned.

"Fabrikant had given our contact-man Carlos at the same time another assignment for the manufacture of forged papers for a woman. The papers were produced with the assistance and approval of III F, and police action was to take place again during the transfer of the forged papers. Only Fabrikant appeared at this meeting and not Grossvogel, who, as was learned later, had been requested to procure the papers for Mrs. Schneider and deliver them to her. Fabrikant was arrested on this occasion. He was a very weak Jew and soon admitted his relationship with his mistress, Malvina [Gruber]. From prison he persuaded her to work from now on with us. Bob confessed during further interrogations that Grossvogel was the Andre we knew from the wireless messages. Everything now depended on breaking up the group in France, for Malvina had learned in the meantime that a far-spread group existed in Paris under the leadership of the Grand Chef. The known cover firm of Simexco in Brussels was at first permitted to continue, but mail and telephone surveillances were introduced and soon produced incriminating material. It could be discerned that the coproprietors and associates of the firm had become concerned and were warning each other. Through Malvina it was learned that Mrs. Grossvogel had been delivered of a child at a Brussels clinic. Malvina and another contact-woman of III F were continued on the case, and it became clear that other women were informed about the organization. There was no further police action for the time being. All reports from contact-men showed that the Russian intelligence organizations which had existed for a long time had been destroyed and, above all, that further radio communications, even with the aid of the radio interception group, could no longer be perceived." [Report of Abwehr III F Ast Belgien, 24 March 1943.]

XV. The Playbacks

From August to October 1942 the Germans instituted a series of W/T playbacks. Wenzel was made to operate a "Funkspiel" called "Weide" in his own character in August, and in September a substitute for Winterink was set up with another transmitter. This station was called "Tanne." In October there were two more instituted: one operated by Jeffremov, called "Buche-Pascal," and the other by a substitute for Herman Isbutsky, called "Buche-Bob." Not one of these playbacks is likely to have achieved any success with Moscow. Apart from the early warning of Wenzel's arrest, delivered to Trepper by Germaine Schneider, there is evidence that Moscow was given news of the disaster from Bulgaria. Wenzel, too, may have sent a warning to Moscow after his escape in November 1942. According to one report, Wenzel joined a Dutch resistance group and was able to inform the Soviet Embassy in London, via a British communication line, that Jeffremov had been doubled and that the radio playbacks were being conducted to confuse Moscow.

TRANSLATION OF A STATEMENT MADE BY ABRAHAM RAJCHMANN TO THE BELGIAN AUTHORITIES

INTRODUCTORY NOTE

Abraham Rajchmann worked successively for the Trepper, Sukolov, and Jeffremov networks of the Rote Kapelle in Belgium. He was arrested by the Belgian authorities 23 July 1946 and tried for espionage and collaboration. The following is a statement made by him shortly after his arrest. The material in brackets has been inserted by the translator. Rajchmann's statement corresponds well with the known facts and is an important source of information on the operations and working methods of the Rote Kapelle.

STATEMENT BY ABRAHAM RAJCHMANN

[I. CONTACTS WITH GROSSVOGEL (1934-1939)]

I wish to express myself in French.

About 1934 or 1935, while I was having a meal in a little Jewish restaurant on the Rue des Tanneurs in Brussels, run by a certain Reinstein, two gentlemen came to ask for me. I do not know who had sent them to me. All that I can say is that they knew my nickname, "Adash," the Polish diminutive of Adam, a first name corresponding in French to Abraham. They asked me if I could get them visas for Syria to attach to two Polish passports. I procured these visas for them for a few hundred francs.

A few months later, if my memory is correct, they asked me to get them a visa for a country in South America. I got them this visa.

I did not know the identity or the place of residence of these gentlemen.

About 1937 one of them came to see me again and this time asked me if, on the basis of official documents, I could get Polish

passports for some people without their being obliged to go to the
Polish Consulate. He also asked me to accompany some people, who
he said were Jewish refugees, to act as interpreter so they could obtain passports more easily. These people were in possession of official documents, such as birth certificates and certificates of nationality. I accepted this proposition. After this conversation he arranged
another meeting with me. I was supposed to see him again at the
Cafe Metropole in Brussels. On the set date I went to the rendezvous and met him. I knew him at this time by the name of "Leopold." During our conversation at the Cafe Metropole my friend,
Lejzor Bugajer, walked by and said hello to "Leopold." The latter,
noting that we had a common friend, then admitted to me that he
was related to the directors of the Excellent Raincoat Company [Le
Roi du Caoutchouc]. Later my friend Bugajer told me that "Leopold" was really named Leon Grossvogel. He told me also that this
man was involved in politics and that I should be careful.

A short time later I had another rendezvous with Grossvogel.
Because of what I had learned, I hesitated to help him this time. To
conquer my fears Grossvogel appealed to my feelings and reminded
me that I myself had been in difficult situations. He told me that
the people he wanted me to help were in the same condition as I
was because of their racial backgrounds. I was convinced by his arguments and got for him what he wanted. There was then a long interruption in our relationship.

In 1938 I associated myself in Brussels with my friend, Lejzor
Bugajer, and a certain Max Unikowski for the purpose of running
jointly a business dealing in simulated leather. Our offices were in
the City, Rue Neuve, Brussels. This enterprise was liquidated late in
1938 or early in 1939 because of disagreement among the associates.

[II. SERVICES FOR THE TREPPER NETWORK (1939-1940)]

In the spring of 1939 I again met Grossvogel at a rendezvous
arranged by Bugajer. In the course of the conversation he very cleverly let me understand that I was in his hands and that I would have
to provide him with services. Then he said that he wanted to introduce me to someone whose identity he did not reveal to me, for
whom I would have to render the same services I had already rendered to him. I accepted, and he gave me a rendezvous for about
two weeks later. I went to this rendezvous, and Grossvogel introduced to me a man whom he called "Uncle," a heavy-set man, very

calm, with a very serious look [Trepper]. "Uncle" told me that my business would not be to procure visas. My role would be that of an expert who would be consulted on the validity of documents submitted to him. It was agreed that liaison between "Uncle" and me would be through a certain "Charles" [Makarov], whom I met in a cafe at another meeting. "Charles" gave me a telephone number where I could reach him if needed. I no longer remember this telephone number.

On 16 September 1939 I went to the Commissariat of Police to register as required by the local laws in effect for foreigners residing in Belgium. I was immediately arrested and interned at St. Gilles Prison as a foreigner under suspicion. I learned later, through my family, that "Charles" had gone to my house shortly after my imprisonment and, hearing of my arrest, declared that he would come back to receive news about me. Moreover, he told a member of my family that after my liberation I should call the telephone number he had given me.

About the end of October or the beginning of November [1939] I was released from prison. I called "Charles" to tell him of my liberation. He arranged a rendezvous for a few days later in a cafe downtown. I remember neither the name nor the location of this cafe. I went to the rendezvous and met "Charles." Right away he reprimanded me for having gone to the Commissariat to register and said that I should have been more careful. He also said I should prepare a new identity for myself. I replied that this was not possible because I was too well known in Brussels. It was then agreed between us that I would hide in a quiet house with a garden where they would come to consult with me, as had been arranged with "Uncle." After this conversation I found a place to stay in Brussels, Rue du Progres, with a Jewish family named Rybski or Rybsky. I do not remember whether it was "Charles" or I who found this place. "Uncle" and "Charles" came to see me from time to time for advice. It was thus that one day "Uncle," having found a person supposedly able to obtain visas in a certain manner, which he explained to me in detail, asked me if this procedure conformed to the regulations then being followed in the various consulates. Another time "Uncle" came to explain to me that a person in possession of a Polish passport had obtained a visa to go to Mexico. It was, however, necessary for this person to get a visa of transit from the American authorities. An individual whose name I do not know was given the job of procuring this visa, but claimed that the passport had been kept by the American Consulate. He undertook to get it back for the sum of $800. "Uncle" asked my opinion. I replied that he had been "tricked"; then "Uncle" gave "Charles" the order to have the passport destroyed.

A little before the declaration of war against Belgium "Uncle" proposed that I should leave for Brazil. I did not want to go to that country because I really suspected that if I accepted his proposition I would be required to perform services I did not wish to perform. I know, however, that for the purpose of this departure "Uncle" and "Charles" undertook to get for me a regular passport from the Polish Consulate. It is true, as you point out to me, that the Consulate at my request then approached the *Surete Publique* to obtain authorization for me to go to Brazil or to any other foreign country. I learned later from "Uncle" and from "Charles" that their project to get me a Polish passport had failed because of some trouble with a certain Malvina Hofstadjerova, the wife of Adolf Gruber. In order to be complete, I should say that I had introduced this woman to "Uncle," and especially to "Charles," before I went to hide with the Rybskys. "Uncle" had in fact asked me to introduce to him someone who could perform certain services for him, notably going to the different consulates to find out what formalities were necessary to obtain visas.

When "Uncle" told me about Malvina's trouble, which resulted in my getting the passport, he said that in a short time Belgium and France would be attacked by Germany, but that in any event I should stay in Belgium and not become frightened. On that occasion he advised me to prepare for myself a new identity. During this conversation he made known to me in an official manner that he was part of a secret Soviet organization. Because I wanted to know more details, in view of the fact that the Soviets had signed a nonaggression pact with Germany, "Uncle" explained to me that the Russians and the Germans would never get along together, and that the activity of his organization was directed against Germany. I told "Uncle" that if his work was against the Germans, I was completely ready to help him if I could. At the time of the invasion of Poland by the Germans my whole family had been killed, and for that reason I decided to do everything possible to hurt the Germans if the occasion ever arose. "Uncle" told me that one day perhaps I would have the chance to do just that.

[III. Flight to France]

On 10 May 1940 [the day of the German invasion of Belgium] I was still in hiding with the Rybskys. The area had been bombed; so I went to find my wife at her parents' house—32, avenue Jean Volders in St. Gilles—and advised her to flee. It was decided that the wife and child of Lejzor Bugajer would leave with my wife for France. Bugajer took from me the sum of five thousand francs with the promise to procure for us an automobile, in which we could escape together. I never again saw Bugajer. I recently heard that during the occupation he had been deported to Germany and was never seen again. In any event, not seeing Bugajer with the automobile he had talked about and for which I had given him the five thousand francs, I left by train for France with my father-in-law and brother-in-law. My brother-in-law left us at Tournai. My father-in-law and I after several days of travel arrived at Mont-Rejeau in the South of France. In accordance with the Mandel Law I was interned at the Camp de St. Cyprien. My father-in-law, whose papers were in order, was not interned. I was liberated at the time of the French armistice, after succeeding in getting in with a group of Italians and in that manner receiving a hearing from the Commission.

Once free, that is, in July or August 1940, I went to Revel, near Toulouse, where my father-in-law was staying. I had received his address through the intermediary of the family of my brother-in-law, Henri Borman, living in Paris at 58, rue Vieille du Temple.

In about August 1940 I received in Revel a letter from "Uncle," mailed from Vichy, in which he asked me to let him know how I was. I wrote back to him, as previously agreed, by a letter addressed in the name of Peiper, I believe, in care of General Delivery, Vichy.

A week later he wrote me a second letter, asking me to phone him at the Poste Centrale on a particular day and time. I was supposed to ask that they call a Monsieur Peiper to the phone. I am not at all certain about this name or its spelling. I called, as he asked, and in the course of the conversation he gave me orders to leave for Paris as soon as possible. I was supposed to meet him there two weeks later at a place he indicated and which I no longer remember. At that time I had been planning to flee to Portugal in order to escape the Germans. I did not do anything about this, however, and I decided to leave for Paris as I had promised.

Two or three days later I learned at Revel that a woman was trying to find me. She wanted to take me back to Belgium. At least that is what she said when I met her at Toulouse. This woman was Malvina Hofstadjerova, whom I have already mentioned. She assured me that she had in her possession repatriation permits for several persons to return to Belgium. Since I knew that these permits cost a lot of money, I pointed out to Malvina that my father-in-law and I had no money at all. Malvina told me that that did not make any difference.

A few days later we left by train with her and other refugees toward the first demarcation line, where we were turned back. We then headed for Bordeaux by another route and succeeded in crossing the demarcation line, thanks to Malvina, who convinced the Germans at the control point to let us pass. I then left for Paris, where I joined my wife at the Caron Hotel, Place Caron, in the third arrondissement. At this hotel, Bob [Isbutsky], whom I had never met before, came to say that "Uncle" wanted to see me. I was supposed to meet him in a restaurant located opposite the Hotel de Ville, on the first floor. I went to this rendezvous and saw "Uncle," who asked me to change a thousand dollars for him, which I agreed to do. I was to give him the equivalent in French francs at a metro station a few days later.

I took care of this matter and met "Uncle" as we had planned. During this meeting he told me that I would have to find some way of returning to Belgium. Since I knew that Malvina handled the transporting of refugees into Belgium, I went to my home at 32, avenue Jean Volders, St. Gilles. I wish to point out that these events took place at the end of September or the beginning of October 1940.

[IV. Services for the Sukolov Network (1940-1942)]

After my return to Brussels, Charles came to see me at my home and again insisted that I take a new identity. I refused.

In January 1941 I obtained a temporary identity card in my own name.

In February 1941 I received on several occasions from a person named Rosenberg in Antwerp, for Charles, blank identity cards with seals attached, certificates of good conduct, etc.

On 19 February 1941 I was arrested by the Belgian Police for violation of the expulsion order and was sentenced to two months in prison.

On 20 April 1941, after my release from prison, Charles contacted me and said that henceforth I would have to participate actively in the fight against the Germans.

I expressed to Charles my desire to get my family into safety, but he replied that this was not necessary.

The first thing he asked me to do was to get together some identity documents for members of the organization. Then he gave me the job of finding out which German unit was stationed in Ghent at the time.

I accepted and successfully completed these assignments.

Later Charles asked me to learn Morse code, but a few days afterwards he said not to do so.

He then asked me to get for him a list of persons sought by the Germans. It was at this time that I thought of Chief Inspector Mathieu of the P.J.P., and I asked him to get these lists for me. Before doing so, however, I tested his loyalty by having him try to get several identity cards for me, which he did to my complete satisfaction. Mathieu promised to try to get the lists I needed. He was successful and continued to furnish them to me at irregular intervals. Our purpose was to warn the persons being sought and to protect them from the risk of being taken by the Germans. I also obtained from Mathieu information on units stationed in the rural areas. I knew Mathieu's name and he knew mine. We also knew each other's addresses. In my group Chief Inspector Mathieu was known by the alias "Cousin." My superiors knew that he was an inspector in the P.J.P. At about this same time Mathieu gave me photos of German atrocities in Russia, such as collective hangings. I remind you that the events described above took place in 1941.

One day Charles gave me the job of bringing from France to Belgium, with maximum security, an individual [Anton Danilov] for whom he would hold me responsible. I proposed Malvina for this job, nevertheless making reservations to Charles about her discretion. My proposition, however, was accepted and here, if my memory is correct, is how the operation was carried out. Charles gave me the address of a cafe in Paris where Malvina was supposed to be contacted by a member of the group. I no longer remember the address of the cafe, and the identity of the person was never revealed to me. This person would indicate to Malvina the address of a dentist in Paris, where the unknown person to be conducted to Belgium was staying. My assignment was to contact this person at the home of Malvina upon his arrival in Brussels and to give him a telephone number by which he could get in contact with Charles. Everything went as planned. This took place in the summer of 1941. I cannot tell you from memory the name or the alias of the unknown person brought into Belgium by Malvina. I know, however, that he was a "musician," that is, a radio operator. I also know that he was arrested in December 1941, at the same time as Charles. It was "Uncle" who reported this to me much later.

Next I was given the job of bringing from France a foreign woman [Sofie Posnanska]. She was also a "musician." This woman was also arrested in December 1941, at the same time as Charles.

After the entry of the United States into the war I had a meeting with Charles. We agreed to meet again a few days later. But the same day [probably 13 December 1941], while I was at Malvina's house on the Rue du Marche du Parc, "Uncle" came to announce that some members of our organization, including Charles, had been arrested. Contrary to his habit, "Uncle" had gone without warning to their address and had been taken by the Gestapo. He had declared to the Germans that he had gone to the wrong house and that the house he was looking for was that of a firm dealing in automobile parts. As if by chance, there was a garage nearby. Because "Uncle's" papers were in order and he could prove the truth of his statement, he was released by the Germans.

In view of the circumstances I advised "Uncle" to return to Paris by an indirect route.

After the arrest of Charles I had no further direct contact with the group. This situation did not last very long, though, because at the beginning of 1942, I think, I had a new superior, replacing Charles, in the person of Bob [Isbutsky], whom I had already met in Paris.

One day Bob came to get me at six o'clock in the morning to take me to Place Venderkindere, Uccle, to meet a so-called Argentine, who by his accent was certainly a Russian [Sukolov]. After complaining about "Uncle," who had left just when everything was in a "mess," the Argentine asked me to do whatever was necessary to take his wife and child to France [Margarete Barcza and her son, Rene]. He also gave me twenty thousand francs, forbidding me to use it without his instructions. He told me he was a director or shareholder in a company called Simexco.

I gave to Malvina the job of taking the Argentine's wife, as well as her little boy, across the French border. Malvina took them to Paris and put them into the hands of a second person belonging to our group, who would see that they were transferred to the non-occupied zone. The passport of this woman was Czechoslovak and stated that she was "Aryan" or "Catholic." I personally assured myself that Malvina actually left with the wife and little boy of the Argentine.

During my first meeting with the Argentine, he asked me to find a place where it would be possible to hide a radio transmitter. After looking around, I found no secure place except at the home of Chief Inspector Mathieu. I talked to him about it, and he agreed to hide the transmitter. Bob was supposed to bring me the set about a hundred meters from the Barriere of St. Gilles. I went there, and he handed over to me the suitcase containing the transmitter. This was a large traveling suitcase, measuring approximately 90 x 50 x 20 cm., dark brown in color, and fairly well-used. This suitcase belonged to Bob, whom I did not tell where I intended to hide the transmitter that was inside. I then carried the suitcase to the Barriere of St. Gilles and gave it personally to Chief Inspector Mathieu, who took it to his home. I saw him get on streetcar number nine with the suitcase.

Two days later I met Chief Inspector Mathieu, who told me that the place in which he had planned to hide the suitcase was not large enough to hold it. I therefore bought for him three smaller suitcases, and it was decided that the transfer of the transmitter from the large suitcase to the three small ones would take place in my presence one day when Mathieu's wife was not home.

In January or February 1942 I was invited by Mathieu to make the transfer with him. I went for this purpose to his home, 65 Avenue des Tilleuls. The transfer was carried out in a front room. I believe that the large suitcase was locked up in a closet, which I think was a clothes closet. When the transfer was completed, I carried away the large suitcase and gave it back to Bob.

During subsequent meetings with Bob he asked me to get word to "Uncle" that he was out of money. I had a chance to send this message by the intermediary of a woman who came on behalf of "Uncle" to find out from Malvina whether Vera had arrived safely. Let me explain myself. Malvina previously had brought from France a woman named Vera and had failed to send news of her arrival in Brussels. If I remember correctly, this Vera told me that she was staying with a friend [masculine]. [Vera is probably Annemarie van der Putt, who worked for Trepper in France in 1941 and 1942.]

The woman sent by "Uncle" informed me that he wanted to

see me in Paris in a week or ten days at the Cafe Boule d'Or or Boule d'Argent, not far from the St. Michel metro station. She told me also that I could dispose of the twenty thousand francs given to me by the Argentine [Sukolov] in the following manner: two thousand francs for Bob; four thousand francs for Vera; four thousand francs for me; and ten thousand francs to give to Bob for the use of "Prof" [Johannes Wenzel]. This latter, according to what I learned later, was an expert in codes who had disappeared after the first arrests in December 1941. I point out in passing that it was possible for me to contact Vera by going every three or four days to the cafe "Le Grillon," rue de l'Ecuyer, Brussels.

As "Uncle" had asked me, I went to Paris and met him at the agreed place. We talked at first about unimportant things; then we left the cafe to take a short walk. While walking, "Uncle" announced to me that he would see me the next day. Then he turned me over to a person who took me to an apartment, the location of which I could not determine because of the darkness. The next day "Uncle" came to see me at the apartment. We stayed inside all day, discussing several matters relating to our clandestine work. In the evening "Uncle" suggested that I return to Brussels, promising that he would come to see me shortly.

[V. SERVICES FOR THE JEFFREMOV NETWORK (1942)]

When I saw "Uncle" in Brussels he told me that, from then on, my direct superior would no longer be Bob but Bordo [Jeffremov]. I think I made contact with Bordo as follows: Bob came to get me, and together we met "Uncle," who was waiting for us in the Parc du Cinquantenaire, Brussels. Two or three hours later "Uncle" introduced me to Bordo, not far from there, if my memory is correct. In the course of our conversation "Uncle" asked me about the person to whom I had given the transmitter given to me by Bob. I replied that I had given it to "Cousin." He also asked me to find out what had happened to a certain Gilbert, who had lived at Molenbeck. For this I went to Mathieu and learned through him that the man in question had left his home without leaving a new address. It seems to me that "Uncle's" desire was "to double" this Gilbert, because while talking he asked me if I had not procured for him an identity in this name. After I gave the result of Mathieu's inquiries to "Uncle" he asked me to establish an identity for him in the name Gilbert. He insisted that the paper and seals be authentic.

For this I went to Antwerp, to a shop on Rue du Pelican run by a certain Lebenthal, whom Malvina had recommended to me, I think. This store was a candy shop or a pastry shop. Lebenthal promised to furnish me with authentic documents, as well as certificates of good conduct and morals. He kept his word, and I had Malvina take the documents to "Uncle," who was at that time in Paris. Returning from Paris, Malvina was accompanied by a woman whom I knew by the name of Jeanne [probably Jeanne Grossvogel]. This woman was about forty years old, of average size, and slightly greying hair, spoke with a Flemish accent, and had quite an ordinary look about her. She stayed one or two days in Brussels, then returned to Paris with Malvina, who on this occasion carried secret information hidden in a button of her blouse, as well as false identity papers for "Uncle."

After that I regularly saw Bordo, who insisted upon being informed about train and troop movements in Belgium. One day he asked me if I could find a way to get a job for one of his men in the Usines Gevaert at Antwerp. I could not help him in this last matter. Another time he told me he was happy to have found again "Prof" [Wenzel], who was a code specialist. A short time later Bordo told me that "Prof" had been arrested with another person whose name I do not know [probably a reference to Germaine Schneider]. The entire area had been surrounded; and "Prof," who had tried to escape by the roof of the building from where he was transmitting, was captured. Bordo had found out about this by asking a few questions around the neighborhood where this had occurred. He did not know, however, whether the Germans were able to seize the code. The code was frequently changed, especially in 1942. Bordo, I think, was able to recover a reserve transmitter that had been hidden in Prof's house.

During the summer of 1942 Bordo introduced me to a Dutchman called Peper who was supposed to serve as liaison between him and me because Bordo, for reasons of security, did not want to see me except in cases of emergency. In those cases I was supposed to go to the corner of Rue Berckmans and Chaussee de Charleroi about noon; and if Bordo saw me, we would meet an hour later in a street according to a procedure determined in advance. One day Bordo asked me for a new identity for himself. For this I went to see Mathieu, who got it for me. I know that he proceeded as follows to get identity papers of this kind: He sent a written request to the local administration of a place that had been destroyed in order to find out whether a certain person at a certain address was known. They answered that the records had been destroyed and it was not possible to furnish the desired information, except to say that the address had existed. On this basis the identity card was delivered a few days later. It was thus that Bordo went to get his identity card at the Maison Communale of St. Josse Ton Noode. I had followed him without his knowledge to make sure that everything went all right. I did, in fact, see him come out holding in his hands different papers which looked exactly like food stamps. He left in the direction of the Gare du Nord. I followed him for a few more minutes but then stopped because I had not noticed anything suspicious. I did not see him reach the Rue Royale. I was supposed to see Bordo the same afternoon to confirm that there had been no difficulty. He did not come to the meeting. This took place about July 1942. Since I was very worried about not having seen him again, I spent several days in the neighborhoods where I knew I could run across him. I never saw him again. On the other hand, I met Peper, who was also looking for him. This was the first time I had seen Peper since Bordo had introduced us. Two or three weeks later I saw Grossvogel completely by chance. He told me he had no money for me because the organization was going through a bad period. He also asked me if I had any news from Bordo. Now, I had just found in my mailbox a few days before a letter from Bordo worded approximately as follows: "Dear friend, I had to leave for Lieges to take care of a very urgent matter. I have been delayed and will return to Brussels in a few days. Signed, 'Bordo.' " I was very concerned because it was not Bordo's habit to act that way. I told Grossvogel about this, but he did not think that it was in any way unusual. [The Germans had induced Jeffremov to write this letter to Rajchmann in an attempt to conceal his arrest from the rest of the network.] Grossvogel asked me to get him some identity cards. They were, he said, for some very important agents [one of whom was Germaine Schneider]. He told me that the photos would be given to me the next day by Bob, about noon, and he left after giving me a small sum of money for my personal use. The next day I went to the rendezvous arranged for the delivery of the photos, but Bob did not come. I was supposed to see Grossvogel a few days later, so in order not to waste any time I went to find Mathieu and asked him to prepare two false identity cards for which I would furnish the photos later. A few days later I met Grossvogel and told him that I had not seen Bob as planned. Grossvogel promised to get me two other photos that afternoon. He gave me these photos hidden in a pack of cigarette papers. I delivered this pack to Mathieu a little later somewhere downtown. When I gave him the photos, I told him not to take them out of the pack until he was ready to put them on the cards. A few days later I saw Grossvogel again, and he wanted the identity cards for the next day. I promised to give him an answer that afternoon and agreed on a rendezvous for that purpose. I then telephoned Mathieu, who told me he would be able to have the cards for the next day. I informed Grossvogel of this at our meeting. Grossvogel at that time gave me a calendar in which I was supposed to hide the identity cards.

[VI. ARREST AND COLLABORATION (1942-1944)]

On 2 September 1942 I had a rendezvous with Mathieu at the Cafe Isy, Avenue de la Porte de Hal, Brussels. He came and handed over to me the two identity cards he had promised. I hid them in Grossvogel's calendar. Then, for security reasons, I decided to have Malvina take the identity cards to the meeting I had arranged with Grossvogel. This meeting was supposed to be on the Avenue Albert, near the Police Station of Forest. After dining at my place, I went on foot by way of the Chaussee de Waterloo to make sure I was not being followed. At the Barriere de St. Gilles I got on streetcar number fourteen to go to Avenue de Fleron, number one, where Malvina lived, with the intention of giving her the identity cards and her new assignment. After changing streetcars at Place Wielemans Couppons, I got off at Place St. Denis in Forest. I then went on foot toward Malvina's house, but en route a car of the Gestapo stopped beside me, and I was told to get in. This car contained German policemen in civilian clothing. They took me to Avenue Louise, where they searched me. They found on me the calendar as well as the identity cards which were hidden in it. I was immediately asked where and to whom I was to deliver the identity cards. I answered that I was to deliver them at the Coin de la Chaussee de Waterloo in the place called "Ma Campagne" at six o'clock in the evening, to a Jew whom I had met in the Cafe Metropole and who offered me a large sum of money if I would get him these identity cards. I was kept at Avenue Louise until six o'clock, and then Colonel Wolf came to say that I had been lying. I was taken the same evening to Breendonck. As soon as I arrived, I was taken to the torture chamber. I was there interrogated and tortured. My interrogators were

Colonels Wolf, Berg, and an individual they called "Doctor." They were all in civilian clothing. They tried to get me to tell the real place of the rendezvous and the name of the person to whom I was to deliver the identity cards. I was interrogated three days without interruption. To make me confess, they gave me whippings on the back and blows on the testicles; they hung me up by the arms and tried to separate my gums from my teeth; and finally, they blinded me for several minutes with an extremely strong light which moved back and forth. When I could take no more and fainted, they threw buckets of cold water in my face or let drops of cold water fall into my ears. After three days I told them the place of the rendezvous was Avenue Albert in Brussels. There was at that time no chance for the Germans to meet Grossvogel, with whom I had agreed that in case of non-appearance at the first meeting there would be a second the next day at the same time and place. Moreover, I always maintained that it was a woman, and not a man, whom I was supposed to meet. Nevertheless, the Germans kept the place under surveillance, but obviously they had no results. They were furious, and then informed me that it was not a woman, but a man named "Leopold," whom I was to meet. I admitted this but declared I did not know the real identity of this "Leopold." They answered that I was lying and that I knew very well that his name was Grossvogel and that he was one of the directors of the firm, "le Roi du Caoutchouc." Two days later I was taken to Brussels, Avenue Louise, at the headquarters of the Gestapo. From there they took me by car to the Porte de Hai in St. Gilles, where we stopped. The car was parked in such a manner that we could see the persons entering and leaving the Cafe Isy. The Germans told me to point out to them immediately any person whom I knew and who was entering or leaving the cafe. A little later I saw Inspector Mathieu arrive at the cafe and go in. Since I pretended not to recognize him, the Germans gave me a slap and said, "You do not recognize the Inspector?" I answered that I was near-sighted and that I could not distinguish clearly from the distance we were. A few minutes later Malvina also entered the cafe. The same scene was repeated because the Germans knew her also. After an hour and a half Mathieu came out. At that moment a German came to the car and told the driver to follow the woman who would be coming out, and that he would take care of the Inspector. When Malvina came out, the car followed her all the way to her house. When she was going into her house, the Germans said to me, "It is there that she lives." I did not answer. I was then taken back to Avenue Louise, where Berg was waiting for me. He interrogated me on the role played by Malvina, and I said that we were only social acquaintances. He said, "That is what we will find out at Breendonck." I was taken there and again interrogated. I then learned that the Germans knew about Malvina's role in helping me cross the demarcation line and then the Franco-Belgian border in 1941, as well as all she had done after that. I refused to admit her role and was again tortured for about three hours. The next day I was confronted with Malvina, and they asked me what I had hidden at the Inspector's house. The Germans told me to tell Malvina what I knew about Grossvogel. I stated that I knew nothing more than what I had already told them. They showed me some photos, among which were different members of the organization, but I did not point out to them the photo of Grossvogel. The next day I was subjected to another interrogation. This time the Germans told me that it was a transmitter that I had left with Inspector Mathieu. They even knew that the set had been transported in Bob's suitcase and that I had transferred the contents of this suitcase into three smaller ones at the home of Inspector Mathieu. Despite this, I swore that I knew nothing about a radio set. A few days later I was again confronted with Malvina. On this occasion the Germans showed me a letter supposedly coming from my group. According to them, this letter, which requested news of me, had been received at Malvina's. The Germans forced me to write the following reply: "For the moment it is impossible for me to show myself because there is danger. If someone wishes to see me, he should go to the Boulevard Botanique (Porte de Schaerbeck) on such a date and such a time. He will there see Malvina, whom he must not accost, but instead follow. She will lead him to me."

On the day set by the above letter I was taken to a cafe, Place Communale de Laeken, at the corner of the Rue Marie Christine. I no longer remember the date or the name of the cafe. All that I can say is that it was in October 1942. I was taken under heavy guard to the Maison Communale of Laeken. Then I was instructed to go alone to the cafe mentioned above to have a drink and to wait for three quarters of an hour. They gave me money to pay for my drink. Inside the cafe there were three couples, obviously agents of the Gestapo. I waited for three quarters of an hour, but nothing happened, and I returned to the car. I still do not know why they took me to that place.

I was next taken back to Breendonck, where a few days later I was confronted with Bob. He admitted knowing me.

About 28 October 1942 I was taken to Brussels, where I was put in the presence of a certain Giering [Karl Giering of the Gestapo]. He announced to me that I was going to be allowed to move about freely, but that I would still be considered as a prisoner. Then I had to write at his dictation a statement by which I agreed to divulge nothing of what I had seen or learned, under penalty of reprisals which would be taken against my wife and three children, who would be held as hostages. I was taken back to my home and instructed that I should stay there and telephone twice a day to Giering to let him know how things were going. I could communicate with Malvina. I could not see the Inspector. If anyone came to get in touch with me in any way at all on behalf of my organization, I was to let Giering know immediately.

A few days later, while I was at Malvina's house, a German came on behalf of Giering to tell her that she had to leave for Paris. Malvina followed these instructions; and when she came back a few days later, she told me that in Paris she was placed in prison, in a cell with other prisoners. Her mission was to tell these prisoners that she had been arrested for a trifle, was going to be freed, and could eventually deliver a message to the outside. According to Malvina, she behaved in a manner to arouse mistrust, and because of that she reported no message. About January or February of 1943 Malvina came to tell me that I was supposed to accompany her to Paris. We made the trip by train under the surveillance of a German. At Paris this German took us to a German police station. I do not know the address of this station. I was then shown the identity card I had prepared for "Uncle" in the name "Gilbert." I admitted having made this identity card. They also showed me some photos of persons who had been brought to Brussels by Malvina. They told me that I had been involved with these people. I did not answer, but Malvina admitted having brought them to me. I was then taken to a place which I would not be able to locate again. They gave me a note written by "Uncle," and I was told to send this note to an Italian who lived in one of the nearby buildings.

After completing this task, I was driven to the outskirts of Paris to a villa where I saw a person named Andre [probably Hillel Katz], whom I had previously met in 1942 at the time of my conversation with "Uncle" in Paris. I was able to talk with this Andre, who told me that he had been tortured and confronted with "Uncle," who was arrested and advised him to talk. He confided to me that in his opinion it was the Soviet Military Attache in Paris in 1941 who had been the traitor. After the conversation the Germans did not interrogate me and took me back to Brussels at the same time as Malvina.

Later I was again taken to Paris, this time to a villa where "Uncle" was. When I wanted to speak to him, the Germans stopped me and Berg said: "Microphones are installed. Someone is supposed to come here to talk with 'Uncle.' When 'Uncle' leaves with this person, you will go with him."

We waited for three hours, but no one came. Berg then stated: "I'm sure someone will come to see you because Moscow is interested in you."

This arrangement lasted for a week. After this time Berg declared that if no one came that evening, I would return to Brussels. No one came that day, just like the other days.

The next day Berg came to see me very excited: "Uncle" had just escaped [16 September 1943]. I saw that he had the intention to torture me because he was convinced that I had helped "Uncle" to escape. Nevertheless, he sent me back to Brussels in the hope that "Uncle" would go to look for me there. I have had no news about "Uncle" from that date until the present.

A short time later in Brussels I was called to an office on Avenue Louise, where a German interrogated me on the subject of "Uncle." He especially wanted to know where "Uncle" was hiding. I remember that he showed me an identity card in the name of a certain de Winter. The photo attached to the card was of a young woman of twenty or twenty-two, with black hair, a long face, big eyes, and a well-shaped mouth. The German asked me if it was I who had prepared this card. I denied this, even though I remember having made it. In fact, if my memory is correct, it was an identity card in the name of a certain Georgette de Winter, to which I was to attach the photo and to complete the seal by hand. It was probably an authentic identity card to which I was supposed to attach the photo of another person. I continued to see Malvina, who was earning a lot of money in the currency traffic. I went out with her often and several times saw her do business in cafes.

After the Allied landing, on 11 July 1944, the Germans again arrested me and imprisoned me at St. Gilles. I was interrogated there several times, but not tortured. These interrogations mostly concerned the places where "Uncle" could be hiding, and they stopped five or six days before the total evacuation of the prison.

On 2 September 1944 I was put on the last convoy, which never arrived in Germany.

I was freed 3 September 1944 at the Gare de la Petite Ile, Brussels.

After reading, I verify and sign . . . witnessed . . . .

CHRONOLOGY OF THE ROTE KAPELLE IN HOLLAND

1935-1937	August Johannes van Proosdy, a Dutch communist, received training in Moscow as a W/T technician and operator.
January 1936	Johannes Wenzel was sent from Moscow to Belgium as a W/T technician, instructor, and adviser for the RU in the Low Countries.
1936-1937	Daniel Gouwlooze, a publisher and a leading Dutch communist, helped form an undercover "information" service in Holland. Gouwlooze served as the link between this service and the Dutch Communist Party (CPN).
1937	Gouwlooze visited Moscow to receive intelligence training. Upon his return to Amsterdam he established a W/T service between Amsterdam and Moscow.
September 1937	Van Proosdy was appointed by Gouwlooze as the W/T operator for the Dutch network. The transmitter was hidden in van Proosdy's house at Orteliusstraat, Amsterdam. This set also handled CPN traffic.
5 October 1937	Wenzel was denied permission to remain in Belgium. He went to Holland, where he discussed with Gouwlooze the plans for the construction of an intelligence network in the Low Countries.
1938	Jan de Laar, a member of the CPN, received six months of intelligence training in Moscow. He returned to Moscow and became van Proosdy's assistant.

early 1938	Wenzel returned to Belgium, illegally and with an assumed identity. He was sheltered by Germaine and Franz Schneider in Brussels.
late 1938	Van Proosdy constructed a second transmitter for Gouwlooze's service.
December 1938	Wenzel visited Gouwlooze in Amsterdam. Gouwlooze introduced to Wenzel an official of the CPN, Anton Winterink. Winterink returned to Brussels with Wenzel to train as a W/T operator.
1939	Gouwlooze went to Moscow for final discussions regarding the operation of the Dutch net. He was given a reserve W/T code.
June 1939	Adam Nagel was recruited by Gouwlooze from the ranks of the CPN to work with Wenzel in Belgium.
1939	Jacobus Dankaart became Gouwlooze's deputy in the information service of the Dutch CP. Dankaart was in charge of finances for the service.
September 1939	Konstantin Jeffremov, a Soviet intelligence officer, arrived in Brussels under cover as a Finnish student. His instructions were to build up a network in Belgium and Holland for the collection of military, political, and economic intelligence. Anton Winterink was assigned to Jeffremov as a W/T operator.
October 1939	Victor Sukolov, another Soviet intelligence officer operating in Belgium, sought out Gouwlooze as a contact with the CPN. Sukolov asked that a temporary W/T link with Moscow be arranged for his use. This line was used by Sukolov until about January 1940.
October 1939	Gouwlooze arranged, at a meeting in Belgium with Clement (probably identical with Sukolov), to relay the latter's reports to Moscow over the CPN link in Amsterdam. The material was taken by Clement or his couriers to Gouwlooze for transmission.

Spring 1940	Gouwlooze travelled to Brussels on "publishing business" and visited Wenzel.
May 1940	The establishment of Clement's own radio operator in Brussels (probably Makarov) terminated Gouwlooze's responsibilities for relaying Clement's reports to Moscow.
mid-1940	Alfred Knochel, the leader of a group of German refugee communists in Holland, began to organize a CP intelligence service inside Germany. Knochel remained in Holland but developed a network of informants in Germany.
July 1940	Sukolov again approached the CPN for a communications link with Moscow. Gouwlooze provided Sukolov with the reserve code he had been given in Moscow in 1939.
Summer 1940	Gouwlooze sent the W/T technician van Proosdy on temporary loan to Clement in Brussels. Van Proosdy's assignment was to train an operator for Clement's service and to repair a transmitter (probably Makarov's).
late 1940	The Dutch group was given the code name "Hilda" and placed under the direction of Winterink. Winterink returned to Amsterdam, where he succeeded almost immediately in establishing radio communications with Moscow. From this time until May 1942 Jeffremov, in Brussels, was probably dependent on Winterink for W/T communications. Adam Nagel also returned to Amsterdam to assist Winterink.
late 1940–August 1942	Maurice Peper (alias Wasserman) acted as a courier between Jeffremov and Winterink.
early 1941	Van Proosdy gave a transmitter to a Frau fnu Eller-Meyer, a member of the CPN.
1941	Material obtained by Knochel from sources inside Germany was transmitted to Moscow over the W/T links of Gouwlooze and Winterink.
early 1942	Gouwlooze sent van Proosdy to Germany to help

	Knochel's net set up its own W/T link.
early 1942	Winterink and Adam Nagel disagreed on operating procedures and separated. Moscow attempted to bring about a reconciliation but was only partially successful. Winterink recruited Johannes Luteraan to serve as his deputy. Winterink and Luteraan had previously worked together for the Rote Hilfe, a communist aid organization.
Spring 1942	Knochel himself went to Germany, leaving his fiancee, "Elly," as his deputy in Amsterdam.
mid-1942	Lambertus Portegies-Zwart, a Dutch communist, was recruited by Dankaart as an agent for Gouwlooze's information service.
22 June 1942	Jan Kruyt, Jr., was parachuted into Holland at Hulshortsche with a W/T set and false Dutch identity papers. Kruyt made contact with Gouwlooze, but apparently intended to conduct an independent operation, probably for the MGB.
30 June 1942	By technical means the Germans located a clandestine transmitter in Brussels and arrested the operator, Johannes Wenzel.
July 1942	Adam Nagel warned Gouwlooze of the arrest of Wenzel.
Summer 1942	Van Proosdy trained Portegies-Zwart as a W/T operator and provided him with a transmitter. Portegies-Zwart installed the transmitter at the home of a fnu Gnirrep. Portegies-Zwart trained Gnirrep in W/T, and the latter became a reserve operator for the group.
Summer 1942	Gouwlooze's service was operating at least five transmitters in Amsterdam.
18 August 1942	Anton Winterink, betrayed by Maurice Peper, was arrested by the Gestapo in Amsterdam.
late August 1942	Jakob and Hendrika Hilbolling, safehouse keepers and couriers for Winterink, were arrested in Amsterdam.

22 Sept. 1942	The Germans began a playback of Winterink's radio set. This station, called "Beam Tanne," was continued until March or April 1944. Moscow, warned by Nagel or Gouwlooze of Winterink's arrest, was not deceived.
Autumn 1942	Unable to recruit his own radio operator, Jan Kruyt was supplied by Gouwlooze with Jan de Laar. Gouwlooze also gave Kruyt a new transmitter.
November 1942	Gouwlooze provided assistance to the Soviet parachute agent Peter Kousnetzov (alias Franz Cuhn), who was intended for Knochel's service in Germany. Gouwlooze was out of touch with Knochel and suspected a German penetration of Knochel's service, so he sent Kousnetzov to Jan Kruyt instead. Kousnetzov replaced Jan de Laar, who had proved to be an unsatisfactory operator. De Laar returned to Gouwlooze's group.
17 November 1942	Wenzel escaped from his German captors and went into hiding, probably in Holland.
December 1942	Kruyt contacted an Anna Voute (unidentified).
December 1942	Van Proosdy was sent to Germany as a radio operator for Knochel's service. His cover was as an electrician for the Quastenberg firm in Berlin.
early 1943	Van Proosdy was probably arrested by the Germans and may have operated under control for a short time.
Spring 1943	Kruyt trained agents for planned operations inside Germany.
Spring 1943	It became evident to Gouwlooze that van Proosdy had been captured by the Germans. In fact, the whole group in Germany under Knochel had probably been liquidated. The interrogation of van Proosdy, Knochel, and others led to the penetration of Gouwlooze's group in Holland.
mid-1943	De Laar was arrested.
28 July 1943	Kruyt and Kousnetzov were arrested. Kousnetzov

	may have committed suicide while in the hands of the Germans.
July 1943	Portegies-Zwart succeeded in evading arrest at the time of the German round-up in Holland.
c. August 1943	Jacobus Dankaart was arrested by the Germans.
Autumn 1943	With the assistance of Gouwlooze, Dankaart escaped from a hospital in The Hague.
15 Nov. 1943	Gouwlooze was arrested by the Gestapo in Utrecht and deported to Germany.

DIAGRAM 6

THE WINTERINK GROUP IN HOLLAND
(GROUP "HILDA")

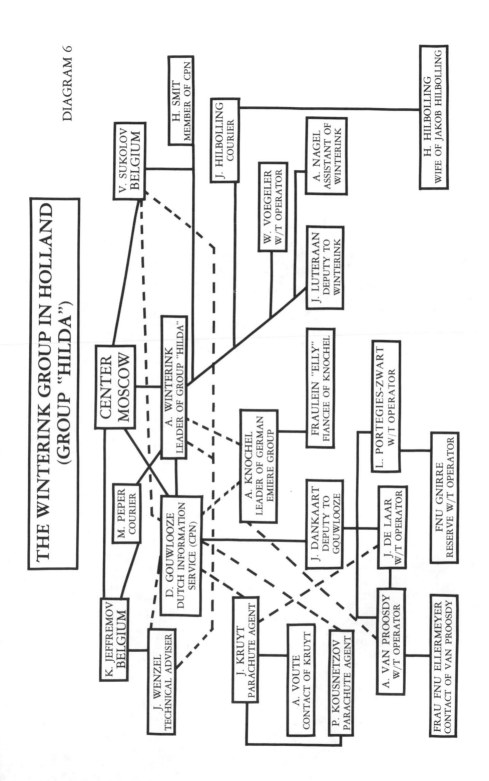

NARRATIVE OF THE ROTE KAPELLE
IN HOLLAND

I. BACKGROUND

Johannes Wenzel, a German communist refugee, entered Belgium on 29 January 1936. According to Belgian police records, Wenzel, who was born 9 March 1902 at Niedau near Danzig, carried a tourist visa valid for one month. This visa was extended by the Belgian Ministry of Foreign Affairs until 8 October 1937, but Wenzel was informed in September 1937 that he would receive no further extensions. His request for a six-month extension for the purpose of enrolling in a mechanics course in Brussels was refused. Wenzel left Belgium on 5 October 1937.

Wenzel's visit to Belgium was in accordance with instructions he had received from the RU in Moscow. For about ten years he had worked for the AM-Apparat (Military Section) of the Comintern in Germany, but in 1935 he was recruited for the RU. After thorough training he was sent to Belgium as the W/T technician, instructor, and adviser for the RU network to be organized in the Low Countries.

A report from the French police dated 15 November 1939 described Wenzel as a member of a group of saboteurs operating in Belgium and Holland for the Soviet-inspired Internationale der Seeleute und Hafenarbeiter. This organization was founded in Hamburg in 1930 under the influence of the Comintern; it later established branches in France, Belgium, Holland, and Scandinavia. Its original purpose was to spread communist propaganda among seamen and associated workers, but after 1937 it was used as a vehicle for sabotage directed against the merchant shipping of the Axis powers.

These reports show clearly what Wenzel's career must have been. He was a communist political agitator of long standing who was later transferred to espionage duties. The Germans probably exaggerated the importance of his position in the Soviet intelligence service, but it is known that Wenzel was in touch at one time or another with the networks of Soviet military intelligence in France, Belgium, and Holland. He was probably not the "Technical Chief for Western Europe," as the Germans claimed. He was certainly, however, the most capable and experienced W/T technician for the RU in Europe, and he provided assistance at various times to the Jeffremov, Sukolov, Trepper, Robinson, and Winterink groups.

In October 1937, when Wenzel moved from Belgium, he went to Holland and called on Daniel Gouwlooze, a leading Dutch communist. He told Gouwlooze that he wanted to settle in Holland and to work for the Dutch Communist Party. Gouwlooze agreed to help, but shortly thereafter Wenzel was instructed to report to Moscow for additional training and a new assignment. Early in 1938 Wenzel returned illegally to Belgium. He lived with Franz and Germaine Schneider in Brussels and probably used the alias Hegenbarth.

II. Anton Winterink

Towards the end of 1938 Johannes Wenzel revisited Gouwlooze and told him of his resettlement in Belgium. He asked for a man from the Dutch Communist Party to help on some unspecified task; Gouwlooze provided him with a young communist official, Anton Winterink. It was not until later that Gouwlooze learned of Winterink's training by Wenzel as a wireless operator.

Anton Winterink (alias Tino) was born 5 November 1914 at Arnhem, Holland. He was a leading functionary of the Rote Hilfe organization in Holland, but in 1938 he gave up that job to devote full-time attention to his intelligence duties. Winterink was taken by Wenzel into Belgium for his W/T training. Winterink proved to be an apt student, and in September 1939 he was assigned as a W/T operator for the network then being organized in Belgium by the Soviet intelligence officer Konstantin Jeffremov. Jeffremov, who posed as a Finnish student, was trying to build up a network in Belgium and Holland for the collection of military, political, and economic intelligence.

In June 1939 Wenzel asked Gouwlooze for another recruit from the Dutch Communist Party, and Adam Nagel, a photographer, was sent to him in Belgium. Wenzel trained Nagel in W/T procedures, just as he had trained Winterink. Nagel (alias Velo) and Winterink worked for Jeffremov in Brussels throughout most of

1940, but it is likely that they continued to make frequent trips back to Holland to recruit agents and to organize a network there. Late in 1940 Winterink was ordered to return to Amsterdam to take charge of the Dutch group. This step was probably taken upon the recommendation of Jeffremov, who had quickly recognized Winterink's potential for leadership. Nagel also returned to Amsterdam in a role subordinate to Winterink's. In Amsterdam Winterink succeeded almost immediately in establishing radio contact with Moscow.

The Dutch group, which operated under the code name "Hilda," continued to receive orders from Jeffremov, even after it had its own communications channels with Moscow. Maurice Peper (alias Wasserman) acted as the courier between Jeffremov in Brussels and Winterink in Amsterdam. Johannes Wenzel went to Holland regularly to provide technical assistance to the "Hilda" group. In addition to Nagel, Winterink's network included Wilhelm Voegeler, a W/T operator, Jakob Hilbolling, a courier and a safehouse keeper, Hendrika Smith, a member of the Dutch Communist Party. The Winterink group provided information on German troop movements in Holland and also sent by W/T to Moscow reports of political and economic interest.

Early in 1942 Winterink and Nagel disagreed on operating procedures and on the role Nagel should play in the organization. Nagel insisted that he and Winterink were equals and should run the network together. Winterink, on the other hand, was not willing to share his authority and ordered Nagel to comply with his orders. This disagreement developed into a bitter quarrel, and Moscow was extremely concerned that the intelligence collection efforts of the group would suffer as a result. Winterink and Nagel separated, despite the remonstrations from Moscow that a reconciliation should take place. Johannes Wenzel was instructed to contact Nagel, and by mid-1942 he was successful in persuading him to return to work. Nagel and Winterink, however, were irreconcilable and Moscow finally agreed that they should work independently. Winterink was ordered to continue to provide communications services for Nagel, which he grudgingly agreed to do. Winterink, without Moscow's knowledge or approval, recruited as his deputy to replace Nagel Johannes Luteraan, whom he had known in the Rote Hilfe.

On 30 June 1942 the Germans in Brussels, using radio direction-finding equipment, located the transmitter operated by Wenzel and arrested him. On 22 July 1942 Konstantin Jeffremov was also arrested in Brussels. Wenzel and Jeffremov both broke under the German interrogation. Jeffremov revealed the names of his sub-agents. On about 25 July 1942 Maurice Peper was arrested by the Gestapo in Brussels. Peper agreed to collaborate.

The following is an excerpt from a report by Section III F (Counterintelligence Service) of the Abwehr in Brussels, dated 24 March 1943:

"Wasserman [Peper] talked. His statements revealed that he was the courier to a group in Holland. He also revealed that he would have a meeting with the leader of the Dutch group [Anton Winterink] in a few days. The III-F officer in charge [Henry Peipe] and some other officials transported Wasserman in a police car to Amsterdam on the day of the meeting. The meeting was to take place during the afternoon at a predetermined place on a busy Amsterdam street. Under the strictest conditions of security Wasserman was released and sent to the meeting. The group leader, however, did not appear. Wasserman returned. Further questioning of Wasserman revealed that he knew the name of a Dutch family with whom the group leader was in contact. It was therefore decided to send Wasserman to the family in question and to arrange a meeting for the same evening. Again under strict security measures Wasserman was sent to the house and returned with the news that the meeting was to take place that evening between eight and eight-thirty at a restaurant in Amsterdam. Wasserman sat alone at a table in the restaurant, with security personnel sitting nearby in the same restaurant. At about nine o'clock a person appeared, went toward Wasserman, and took a seat at his table. At an agreed-upon signal, this man was seized and arrested. On the way to the police car that was standing by he put up considerable resistance and a brief scuffle took place. While being arrested, this man had called out a name to the crowd that had assembled, so that it had to be assumed that he had arranged to be watched at the meeting and was warning his comrades who were there. The identification papers found on this person did not give his address. It was therefore necessary to arrest the Dutch family mentioned above. They were a couple by the name of Hilbolling. The alias of the arrested person was learned through the couple. It was "Tino," a communist official already known to the Gestapo. With the aid of the Hilbolling couple it was possible to find the clandestine residence of "Tino," which was searched the following night. The search of the residence showed that "Tino" was not only the group leader of the Holland group but also its wireless operator. His mistress, who had lived with him, had fled, apparently warned by the arrest. A complete W/T set, including all technical data, was seized at the residence."

Winterink was taken to Brussels, where he resisted interrogation for about two weeks before he agreed to cooperate with the Germans. Beginning on 22 September 1942 the Germans played Winterink's radio back against the Soviets. This station was called by the Germans "Beam Tanne." Moscow, however, was not deceived by the playback, because both Nagel and Daniel Gouwlooze had escaped arrest, and one or both of them had warned Moscow of Winterink's arrest. In an attempt to counter this situation the Germans instructed Winterink to report to Moscow that he himself had barely escaped the Gestapo and that it must be assumed that some members of his group, specifically Nagel and Gouwlooze, had been arrested.

In the summer of 1943 "Beam Tanne" asked Moscow for funds to continue its work. After several evasive replies Moscow finally asked for an address where the money could be deposited. The Gestapo in Amsterdam furnished the address of a former member of the Communist Party, and this address was relayed to Moscow. A few days later Moscow reproached "Tanne" for having sent the address of a man who, according to their knowledge, was suspected of having relations with the Gestapo. This incident reportedly infuriated the Gestapo chief, Heinrich Mueller, who strongly reprimanded the senior Gestapo officer in Amsterdam.

In March or April 1944 Moscow ordered Winterink to discontinue his transmissions and to join an active resistance group. Winterink's ultimate fate is not known, but it is presumed that he was executed.

The Winterink group was closely associated from 1940 to 1942 with two other pro-Soviet groups operating in Holland. One of these groups was the Dutch Information Service run by Daniel Gouwlooze; the other was a group of German emigres led by Alfred Knochel.

III. DANIEL GOUWLOOZE AND THE DUTCH INFORMATION SERVICE

Daniel Gouwlooze was born 28 April 1901 in Amsterdam. He was a Dutch Jew and had originally been employed as a carpenter. In 1930 he became the manager of the publishing company Pegasus, which specialized in communist literature. Gouwlooze had been an active communist since 1925, and in 1932 he became a member of the Executive Committee of the Dutch Communist Party. In 1934 he was arrested in connection with a plot to assassinate Queen Wilhelmina.

In 1935 and 1936 Gouwlooze helped to form the Dutch Information Service, a group organized for the purpose of providing information to Moscow. Gouwlooze served as the link between this service and the Dutch Communist Party. Gouwlooze went to Moscow in 1937 and received intelligence training. On his return to Amsterdam he established a regular W/T service between Amsterdam and Moscow. Gouwlooze utilized as W/T operators two members of the Dutch Communist Party, August Johannes van Proosdy and Jan de Laar, both of whom had received technical training in Moscow. The transmitter of the Dutch Information Service also handled traffic for the Dutch Communist Party.

Gouwlooze had contacts with KPD (German Communist Party) members in Berlin and with Comintern members in Belgium, France, and Great Britain. He rendered considerable assistance to Johann Wenzel's communications service in the Low Countries, providing recruits from within the Dutch Communist Party and W/T links with Moscow when Wenzel's own lines failed.

Gouwlooze went to Moscow in 1939 for final discussions before the outbreak of war on the role his Dutch Information Service should play and the support he should provide to the intelligence networks in Western Europe. Gouwlooze was given a W/T code to hold in reserve.

On at least two occasions Victor Sukolov, a Soviet intelligence officer operating in Belgium, visited Gouwlooze in Amsterdam to request assistance. In October 1939 Sukolov requested that a temporary W/T link with Moscow be arranged for his use. Gouwlooze provided Sukolov with this service until about January 1940. In July 1940 Sukolov again visited Gouwlooze and received from him the reserve code which Gouwlooze had been given in Moscow the year before.

Gouwlooze was used by the RIS as a receptionist for two parachute agents dropped into Holland in 1942. Jan Wilhelm Kruyt, Jr., was parachuted into Holland on 22 June 1942 with a W/T set and false papers. According to one report, Kruyt was dropped for the Soviets by the British SOE (Special Operations Executive). He made contact with Gouwlooze almost immediately after his arrival in Holland. Kruyt, however, had received MGB training in Moscow and probably intended to conduct an independent MGB operation in Holland. In the autumn of 1942 Kruyt, who was unable to recruit his own radio operator, was supplied by Gouwlooze with Jan de Laar. Kruyt also received a new transmitter from Gouwlooze.

On 30 November 1942 a Soviet agent named Peter Kousnetzov (alias Franz Cuhn) was parachuted into Holland. Kousnetzov was intended to reinforce the network of Alfred Knochel in Germany, and he approached Gouwlooze for contact instructions. Gouwlooze told Kousnetzov that he was out of touch with Knochel and that he suspected that there had been a German penetration of the Knochel group. Gouwlooze requested permission from Moscow to send Kousnetzov to work with Jan Kruyt as a replacement for Jan de Laar. De Laar, an extremely high-strung individual, had proved to be unsuitable for clandestine W/T work. Moscow agreed to Gouwlooze's proposal, and Kousnetzov joined Kruyt in about March 1943. Together they trained agents in Holland for planned operations inside Germany. Kruyt and Kousnetzov were arrested by the Germans on 28 July 1943. Kousnetzov may have committed suicide after his arrest in order not to betray his comrades.

IV. The Emigre Group of Alfred Knochel

Gouwlooze provided assistance to Alfred Knochel, the leader of a group of German refugee communists in Holland. About mid-1940 Knochel organized the group, trained the members, and then sent them back to Germany to collect intelligence. The material collected by the agents in Germany was delivered by courier to Knochel in Amsterdam. It was then forwarded by W/T to Moscow via the transmitters of Gouwlooze's Dutch Information Service. On several occasions Knochel handed the material collected by his sources in Germany to Anton Winterink, who sent it to Moscow over his own W/T link.

Early in 1942 Knochel decided that he would try to establish in Germany a separate W/T link for the group. The risks and delays involved in sending couriers with compromising information back and forth between Holland and Germany were becoming too great. Knochel asked Gouwlooze for help in establishing this link. Gouwlooze sent his W/T expert, van Proosdy, to Germany to help the Knochel group. Van Proosdy returned to Holland after a few months, and it appears that his trip to Germany was not completely successful. Knochel himself went to Germany in the spring of 1942 and reported back to Gouwlooze that there were still serious communications difficulties. By the summer of 1942 Gouwlooze had lost all contact with Knochel and suspected that the group had been liquidated. Moscow sent the parachute agent, Kousnetzov, to Holland in November 1942 with the mission of going to Germany as a W/T operator for Knochel. As described earlier, however, Gouwlooze convinced Moscow that the risks were too great, and Kousnetzov stayed in Holland. It is interesting, therefore, that in December 1942 Gouwlooze agreed to send van Proosdy back to Germany. Van Proosdy had a cover position arranged with the Quastenberg firm in Berlin, but both Gouwlooze and van Proosdy must have known that the chances of coming back were very dim. Van Proosdy was, in fact, arrested by the Germans shortly after his arrival in Berlin.

V. THE LIQUIDATION OF THE GOUWLOOZE GROUP

By the spring of 1943 Gouwlooze knew that van Proosdy and most of the members of the Knochel group had been arrested. He warned the members of his group and went into hiding.

The Germans broke van Proosdy by interrogation, doubled him, and in July 1943 began a round-up of his communist contacts in Holland. Jan de Laar was the first to be arrested. In August 1943 Gouwlooze's deputy, Jacobus Dankaart, was arrested. A W/T operator recruited by Dankaart, Lambertus Portegies-Zwart, escaped arrest, as did Gouwlooze.

In the autumn of 1943 Gouwlooze learned that Dankaart was interned in a hospital at The Hague. At great personal risk he assisted Dankaart in escaping from the hospital. On 15 November 1943 in Utrecht Gouwlooze was arrested, probably because of the risks he had taken in rescuing Dankaart. He was sent, along with other prisoners, to Oranienburg. He later stated that he had avoided rough treatment in Oranienburg by using an alias at the camp. After the liberation Gouwlooze returned to Holland, where he again became active in communist politics, often in opposition to the leadership of the Dutch Communist Party. Gouwlooze died in September 1965.

CHRONOLOGY OF THE ROTE KAPELLE IN FRANCE

1928	Leopold Trepper was expelled from Palestine and went to Paris where he lived until 1932.
c. 1930	Comintern agent Henri Robinson arrived in Paris and began intelligence operations against France, Germany, Switzerland, Belgium, and the United Kingdom.
1935	Harry II (unidentified), a Red Army agent in Paris, took over the direction of Ernest Weiss in the U.K. Harry II communicated with Moscow via the military attache in the Soviet Embassy.
December 1936	Trepper completed his intelligence training in Moscow and returned to France as technical director for RU intelligence in Western Europe.
1936-1938	Based in Paris, Trepper traveled to Belgium, England, and Scandinavia, as well as inside France, organizing Soviet military espionage.
1937-early 1939	Victor Sukolov, a Soviet intelligence officer, probably resided in France.
1937	Harry II turned over his net, targetted against the U.K., to Henri Robinson. Harry II returned to Moscow; Robinson stayed in Paris.
early 1939	Mikhail Makarov was sent from Moscow to Paris, where he was provided with new identity papers and 10,000 dollars.
March 1939	Makarov moved to Brussels, where he worked as a W/T operator for the Belgian branch of the Rote Kapelle.

Spring 1939- Summer 1940	Trepper was in Brussels where, under cover as a Canadian businessman, he organized an RU network.
April 1939	Victor Sukolov, presumably stationed in France, went to Germany to activate networks there and to establish a courier link.
July 1939	Sukolov moved to Brussels to work with Trepper.
1939	Anton Danilov went to Paris as a clerk in the Soviet Embassy. He later worked at Vichy with Captain Karpov.
1939	Jean, living in London, was Robinson's chief agent in England.
May 1940	The Germans invaded Belgium. Abraham Rajchmann, Jules Jaspar, Nazarin Drailly, and others fled from Belgium to France.
June 1940	The fall of France.
June 1940- February 1941	After the German occupation of France, Robinson's communications with Jean failed. By February 1941 Moscow was still unable to establish communications with Jean.
early July 1940	Trepper and Leon Grossvogel, in the automobile of the Bulgarian, Petrov, left Belgium for France. Trepper established contact with the Soviet military attache in Vichy, who was his immediate superior.
August 1940	As a security precaution Trepper arranged for his wife and son to leave Belgium for France. With Soviet assistance they then returned to the USSR via Marseilles.
Autumn 1940	Leon Grossvogel, a key assistant to Trepper, was instrumental in founding the Simex firm in Paris. While Grossvogel concentrated upon the legitimate business of Simex, Trepper developed its potential as cover. In Belgium the sister company, Simexco, was established. Trepper used the name Jean Gilbert and posed as a Frenchman in his role as director of Simex.

late 1940 or early 1941	Robinson sent a courier to Rachel Duebendorfer (Sissy) in Switzerland. The courier brought her 2,000 dollars.
March 1941	Trepper's mistress, Georgie de Winter, and their son, Patrick, joined Trepper in Paris.
22 June 1941	The Germans invaded the USSR. Trepper had been communicating with Moscow via the Soviet Military Mission in France, but now he established direct W/T contact.
Summer 1941	Anton Danilov was transferred from France to Belgium to assist Sukolov.
August 1941	Moscow directed Trepper to establish contact with Robinson, who had a very active network.
early September 1941	Trepper met Robinson. Thereafter Robinson received his incoming W/T via the Makarov set as a result of a Trepper-Robinson agreement to share this communications link.
end of 1941	The courier link by which funds had been received from Switzerland was broken. Moscow made arrangements by W/T for each subsequent transmission of money.
13-14 Dec. 1941	The Germans arrested Makarov, Danilov, Sofie Posnanska, and Rita Arnould. Trepper and Robinson were left without radio contact in France. The Brussels network was broken up. Victor Sukolov and Isidore Springer fled to France.
January 1942	Trepper ordered Sukolov to go to Marseilles to set up a new network under the cover of a Simex branch office.
February 1942	Trepper re-established W/T contact with Moscow through a transmitter of the French Communist Party located at Le Raincy.
April 1942	Hersog and Mariam Sokol, having been trained by Grossvogel, tried to reach Moscow by radio but failed. They made contact, however, with London, whence their messages were relayed to the USSR.

June 1942   The Sokols were arrested. Traffic from Trepper's
                     network was then relayed by Wenzel, the W/T
                     operator for the Jeffremov Group.

30 July 1942   Wenzel was arrested while transmitting for the
                     Jeffremov network in Brussels. Thereafter Trep-
                     per was forced to revert to the radio link of the
                     French Communist Party, which he had wished to
                     avoid for security reasons.

12 Nov. 1942   Sukolov and his mistress, Margarete Barcza, were
                     arrested in Marseilles. It was the interrogation of
                     Sukolov that produced for the Germans their first
                     operational, non-intercept leads into the Rote
                     Drei in Switzerland. Abraham Rajchmann and
                     others were also arrested and turned.

November 1942   The premises of Simex in Paris were occupied and
                     searched. The known proprietors and associates
                     of the firm were arrested. Among them was the
                     firm's director, Alfred Corbin. The Germans be-
                     gan an intensive manhunt for Trepper (alias Jean
                     Gilbert).

5 December   German intelligence trapped Trepper through a
1942   dental appointment. Trepper promptly offered to
                     collaborate. The Germans required proof of good
                     faith, and Trepper began to betray his associates,
                     beginning with the "kleiner Andre," Hillel Katz.
                     The betrayal of Robinson, Grossvogel, and others
                     soon followed.

25 December   The Germans began to play Trepper back against
1942   the Soviets by means of a controlled W/T opera-
                     tion dubbed "Eiffel." It appears likely, however,
                     that Trepper had managed to warn the Russians
                     and that they were aware of the attempted decep-
                     tion from the outset.

June 1943   Through leads given them by Henri Robinson, the
                     Germans discovered at Le Raincy the W/T station
                     of the French Communist Party.

July 1943   Acting under German control, Sukolov reactivated
                     Waldemar Ozols (alias Solja).

16 Sept. 1943	Trepper escaped from German custody.
late Sept. 1943	Georgie de Winter brought Jean Claude Spaak in contact with Trepper, who recruited Spaak for support functions.
December 1943	Ozols got in touch with Paul Legendre, chief of a French resistance organization called the "Mithridate" network.
January 1944	Ozols brought Sukolov and Legendre together. The latter gave Sukolov the identities of all of his people in Marseilles. The Gestapo was able to penetrate the Mithridate network.
August 1944	The Germans retreated from Paris.
16 August 1944	Sukolov and Heinz Pannwitz of the SD Sonderkommando left Paris. They continued the radio playback from various locations until May 1945.
7 November 1944	The DST arrested Ozols in Paris, but he was released through the intercession of a Colonel Novikov, who was a member of the Soviet Military Mission. Legendre was similarly arrested and released.
January 1945	Trepper accompanied Alexander Rado and Alexander Foote of the Rote Drei on their trip by air from Paris to Moscow.
3 May 1945	Sukolov and Pannwitz were captured by a French military force in a mountain hut near Bludenz, Vorarlberg, Austria.
7 June 1945	Sukolov and Pannwitz were flown from Paris to Moscow.

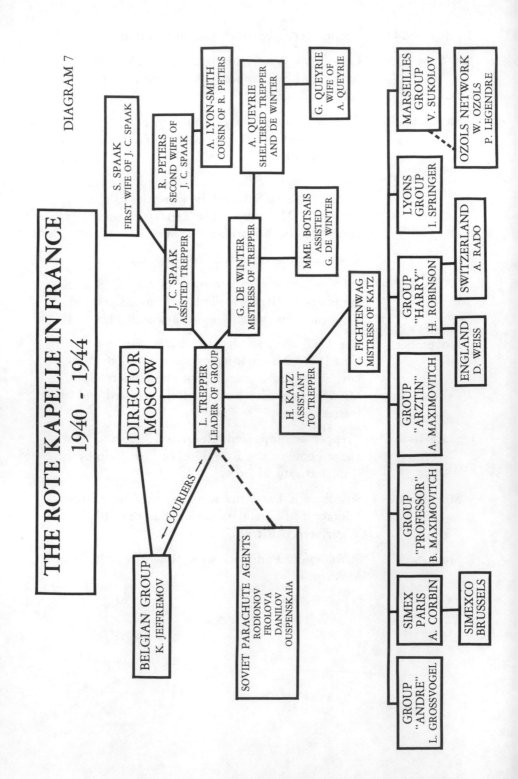

THE ROTE KAPELLE IN FRANCE
1940 - 1944

DIAGRAM 7

DIAGRAM 8

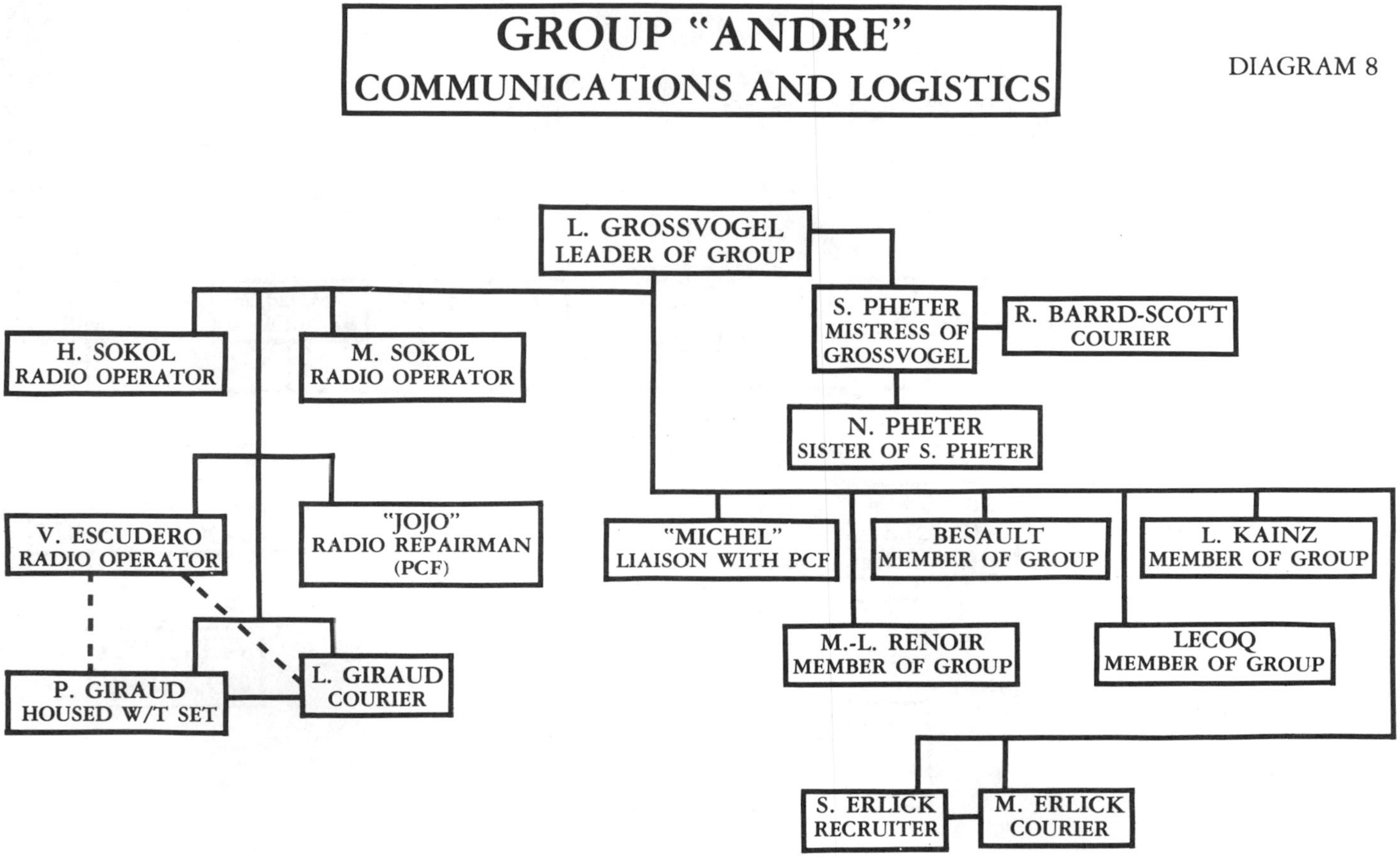

GROUP "ANDRE"
COMMUNICATIONS AND LOGISTICS

L. GROSSVOGEL
LEADER OF GROUP

S. PHETER
MISTRESS OF GROSSVOGEL

R. BARRD-SCOTT
COURIER

N. PHETER
SISTER OF S. PHETER

"MICHEL"
LIAISON WITH PCF

BESAULT
MEMBER OF GROUP

M.-L. RENOIR
MEMBER OF GROUP

L. KAINZ
MEMBER OF GROUP

LECOQ
MEMBER OF GROUP

S. ERLICK
RECRUITER

M. ERLICK
COURIER

M. SOKOL
RADIO OPERATOR

H. SOKOL
RADIO OPERATOR

"JOJO"
RADIO REPAIRMAN
(PCF)

V. ESCUDERO
RADIO OPERATOR

L. GIRAUD
COURIER

P. GIRAUD
HOUSED W/T SET

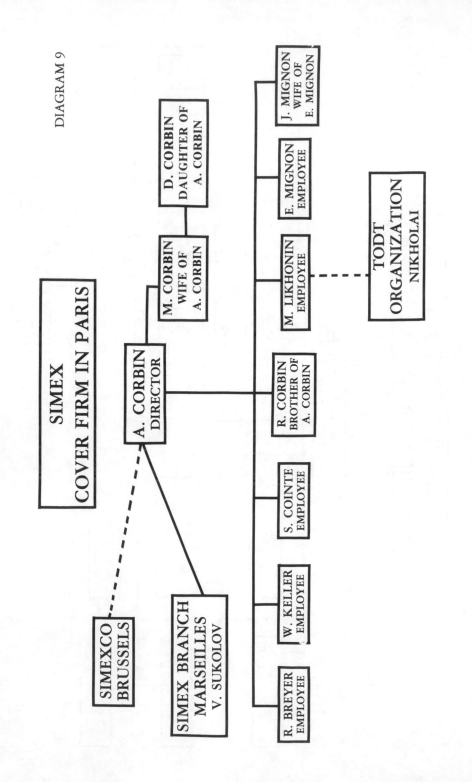

DIAGRAM 9

SIMEX
COVER FIRM IN PARIS

A. CORBIN
DIRECTOR

M. CORBIN
WIFE OF
A. CORBIN

D. CORBIN
DAUGHTER OF
A. CORBIN

SIMEXCO
BRUSSELS

SIMEX BRANCH
MARSEILLES
V. SUKOLOV

R. BREYER
EMPLOYEE

W. KELLER
EMPLOYEE

S. COINTE
EMPLOYEE

R. CORBIN
BROTHER OF
A. CORBIN

M. LIKHONIN
EMPLOYEE

E. MIGNON
EMPLOYEE

J. MIGNON
WIFE OF
E. MIGNON

TODT
ORGANIZATION
NIKHOLAI

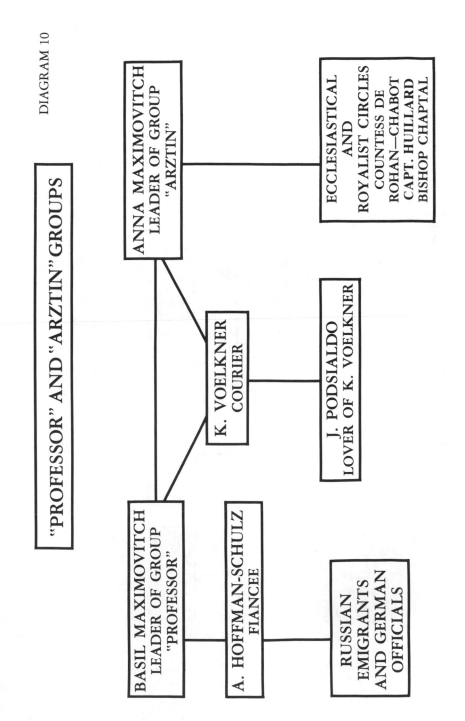

DIAGRAM 10

"PROFESSOR" AND "ARZTIN" GROUPS

ANNA MAXIMOVITCH
LEADER OF GROUP
"ARZTIN"

ECCLESIASTICAL
AND
ROYALIST CIRCLES
COUNTESS DE
ROHAN—CHABOT
CAPT. HUILLARD
BISHOP CHAPTAL

K. VOELKNER
COURIER

J. PODSIALDO
LOVER OF K. VOELKNER

BASIL MAXIMOVITCH
LEADER OF GROUP
"PROFESSOR"

A. HOFFMAN-SCHULZ
FIANCEE

RUSSIAN
EMIGRANTS
AND GERMAN
OFFICIALS

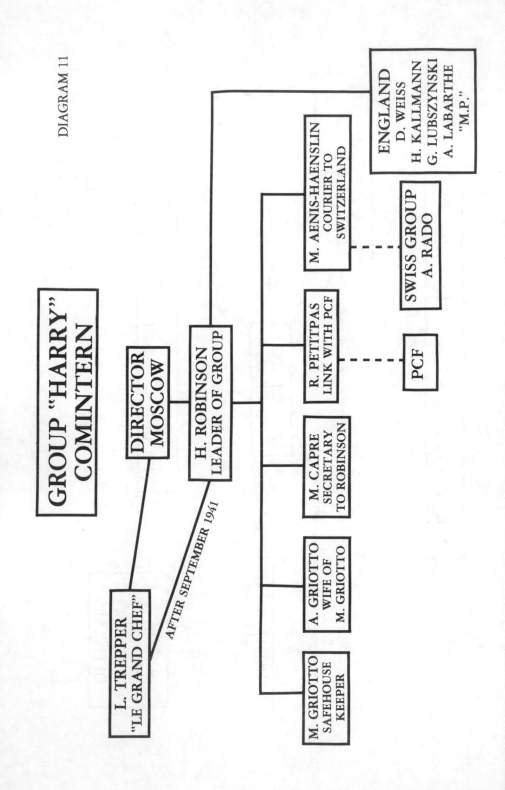

DIAGRAM 11

GROUP "HARRY" COMINTERN

DIRECTOR MOSCOW

H. ROBINSON LEADER OF GROUP

L. TREPPER "LE GRAND CHEF"

AFTER SEPTEMBER 1941

M. GRIOTTO SAFEHOUSE KEEPER

A. GRIOTTO WIFE OF M. GRIOTTO

M. CAPRE SECRETARY TO ROBINSON

R. PETITPAS LINK WITH PCF

M. AENIS-HAENSLIN COURIER TO SWITZERLAND

ENGLAND
D. WEISS
H. KALLMANN
G. LUBSZYNSKI
A. LABARTHE
"M.P."

SWISS GROUP A. RADO

PCF

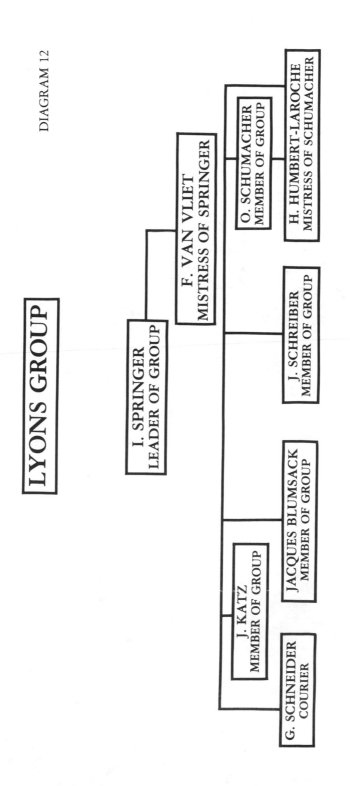

DIAGRAM 12

LYONS GROUP

I. SPRINGER
LEADER OF GROUP

F. VAN VLIET
MISTRESS OF SPRINGER

O. SCHUMACHER
MEMBER OF GROUP

H. HUMBERT-LAROCHE
MISTRESS OF SCHUMACHER

J. SCHREIBER
MEMBER OF GROUP

J. KATZ
MEMBER OF GROUP

JACQUES BLUMSACK
MEMBER OF GROUP

G. SCHNEIDER
COURIER

MARSEILLES GROUP

DIAGRAM 13

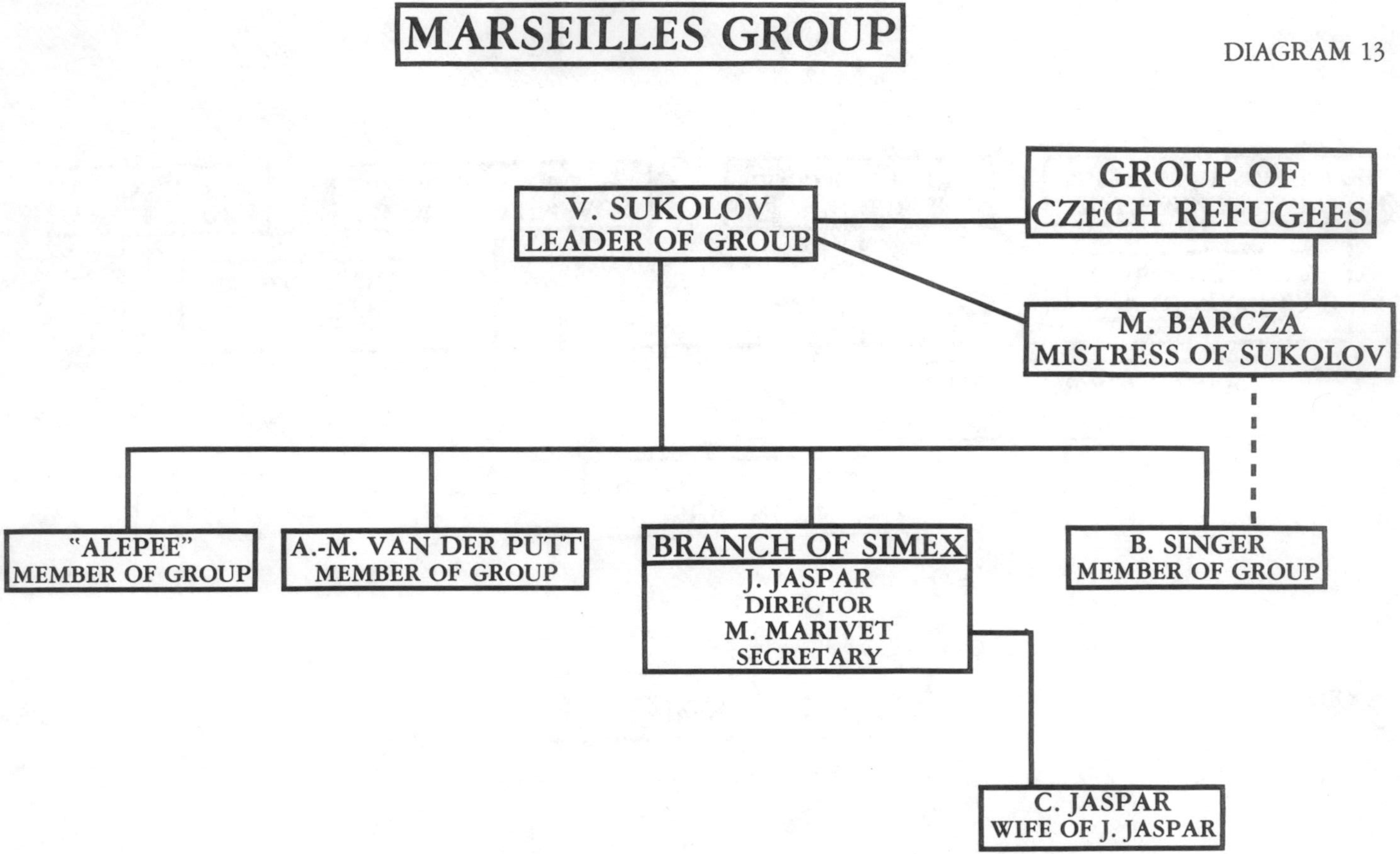

GROUP OF
CZECH REFUGEES

M. BARCZA
MISTRESS OF SUKOLOV

B. SINGER
MEMBER OF GROUP

C. JASPAR
WIFE OF J. JASPAR

V. SUKOLOV
LEADER OF GROUP

BRANCH OF SIMEX
J. JASPAR
DIRECTOR
M. MARIVET
SECRETARY

A.-M. VAN DER PUTT
MEMBER OF GROUP

"ALEPEE"
MEMBER OF GROUP

DIAGRAM 14

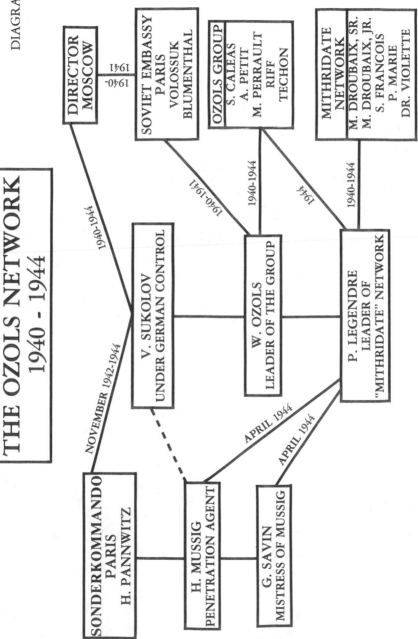

THE OZOLS NETWORK
1940 - 1944

NARRATIVE OF THE ROTE KAPELLE IN FRANCE

I. LEOPOLD TREPPER

When Leopold Trepper fled from Belgium to France in July 1940 after the German invasion of the Low Countries, he had already accumulated a great deal of experience in France. In 1928, after he was expelled from Palestine, he had gone to Paris and lived there in poverty until 1932. Upon completion of his intelligence training at Moscow in 1936, Trepper returned to France as the technical director for RU intelligence in Western Europe. His primary mission seems to have been as a general technical adviser in Western Europe, rather than as a collector of intelligence in any particular country.

Paris was Trepper's base from 1936 to 1938 while he engaged in planning and reorganization missions in France, Belgium, England, and Scandinavia. In the spring of 1939 he moved to Brussels, where under cover as a Canadian businessman he organized a Soviet intelligence network.

Soon after Trepper reached France in the summer of 1940, he renewed his direct contact with Moscow by getting in touch with the Russian Military Attache in Vichy. We have proof that upon Trepper's return to Paris, he came under the supervision and control of the Soviet Military Attache and was charged with building an organization with military intelligence targets.

Trepper arranged for his wife and son to return to the Soviet Union in August 1940 as a security measure. His mistress, Georgie de Winter, stayed in Belgium with their son, Patrick, but in March 1941 she moved to Paris to be with Trepper.

In Paris Trepper's assistants were Leon Grossvogel and Hillel Katz, both of whom he had known from his days in Palestine. Although he was not the leader of any group, Hillel Katz (alias Andre Dubois, alias Petit Andre), who was Trepper's secretary, played a leading role in the Rote Kapelle operations. Grossvogel, of course, had founded the Foreign Excellent Raincoat Company and had worked closely with Trepper in Brussels.

With the help of Grossvogel and Katz, Trepper began to develop acquaintances with persons favorable to the Soviet Government or sympathetic to the Communist cause, and recruited them as his agents. Trepper also continued to exercise some control over the Belgian network of the Rote Kapelle under Sukolov, and he made many trips to Brussels, posing as a French businessman.

II. SIMEX

In the fall of 1940 a new firm, Simex, was established in Paris through Grossvogel's efforts. (The name was derived from *S* for *Societe*, *IM* for *import*, and *EX* for *export*.) It was set up on a grand scale and, in addition to the funds salvaged from Belgium by Jules Jaspar, it was heavily subsidized by Soviet funds.

In the new firm Trepper appeared as a Frenchman, named Jean Gilbert. Actually it was Grossvogel's task to build the firm as a sound and respectable business in France, while Trepper concentrated on the development of the clandestine activities that were to use this firm for cover. This firm eventually spread far afield, and at the time of its collapse in 1942 it was said to have representatives in Germany, Scandinavia, and the Balkans.

The new French firm and its sister firm in Belgium, Simexco, were general dealers and contractors expressly set up to handle contracts arising from the German occupation. They dealt extensively with the Todt organization. The firm thus provided direct contact with the Germans and obtained in the course of its business valuable privileges, such as freedom of movement in occupied territory.

Through the firms of Simex and Simexco Trepper was brought into contact with a number of industrialists and businessmen. He was always careful to remain in the background. Before a business deal he would prime the representative of Simex or Simexco with suitable questions to put to the other side. In this way he heard much while saying very little. He was careful to ensure that negotiations were always conducted with persons in important or responsible positions. Here, Grossvogel was of great assistance to him.

From 1940 to 1942 Director "Gilbert" appeared to be a solid businessman and the manager of a large export firm. He was a welcomed and much respected personage in the Paris and Brussels business world. The "Grand Chef," moreover, played this role with great skill and delicacy for years, without anyone's imagining that he was dealing with a highly accomplished Soviet intelligence officer. The "Grand Chef's" instructions were always sent out as business communications, or similarly disguised, so that there was no evidence of their intelligence nature. He familiarized his business partners with "progressive ideas" and soon succeeded so well that they would inform him of all kinds of innovations to please him. Maintaining that "a businessman who wants to be superior must be informed about everything and must continually keep abreast," and "without a sound inquiry service no business transaction can be carried out successfully," he acquired cheap, dependable sources of information in Belgian and French business circles, which were already equipped with excellent natural camouflage.

III. THE SEVEN NETWORKS

Trepper commanded seven separate groups or networks of Soviet intelligence in France, each active in its own field and under its own chief. Trepper's seven groups were constructed centrally, with parallel but completely independent networks in which only the group leader had direct contacts with the "Grand Chef." The contacts consisted of regular meetings and a system whereby the Grand Chef could reach the group leaders at predetermined contact places. This latter type of communication was not possible in the other direction. Stringent measures of security and compartmentation were built in everywhere.

The seven groups had the following tasks and leaders:

(1) "Andre" (Andre Grossvogel): Information concerning economy and industry; the wireless communication of the organization.

(2) "Harry" (Henri Robinson): Information from French military and political circles, from Vichy intelligence (Deuxieme Bureau), from the Central Committee of the illegal Communist Party, and from U.K. and Gaullist circles. (In contact with Trepper only after September 1941.)

(3) "Professor" (Basil Maximovitch): Information from White Russian emigrant circles; special contacts with various sections of the German Wehrmacht.

(4) "Arztin" (Anna Maximovitch): Information from French clerical and royalist circles; special contact with Bishop Chaptal.

(5) "Simex" (Alfred Corbin): Information from German administrative departments and firms; financing of the organization.

(6) "Romeo" (Isidor Springer): Leader of the Lyons group; contacts with U.S. and Belgian diplomats.

(7) "Sierra" (Victor Sukolov): Leader of the Marseilles group; information from circles around Darlan and Giraud; contacts with French authorities and administrative departments.

Grossvogel, who was actually running the business end of the Simex firm, feared that his status as a Jew might interfere with the German contacts that the firm maintained. He therefore withdrew from the firm and directed his efforts to the clandestine communications of the network. In his place a man named Alfred Corbin, a Communist sympathizer, took over the directorship. At first Corbin was not aware of the espionage activities of the firm; in time he began to suspect them. Ultimately he served as a courier with the networks in Lyons and Marseilles, using as cover his business journeys to the unoccupied zone. He was on good terms with the German authorities and in his capacity as director of Simex further maintained this favorable relationship.

As part of his assignment in supervising communications for Trepper's network, Grossvogel was responsible for finding houses and lodgings which could be used as rendezvous sites, letter drops, and so forth. Sometimes he would turn this task over to his agents. For example, the Girauds were asked to find safe addresses to be used by couriers and for housing wireless equipment.

IV. FINANCES

Trepper's network was financed by the profits returned from the cover firms, as well as by additional funds provided by Moscow. It is believed that from eight to ten thousand dollars monthly were put at his disposal. Trepper told the Germans that no definite sums of money were provided for financing the espionage organizations. The amounts required were requested by wireless as each assignment was undertaken.

Until the outbreak of the Russo-German war Trepper made his requests through the Soviet Military Mission, and the funds were received through the Soviet Military Attache in Paris. After the outbreak of war and the withdrawal of the Soviet Mission Trepper made his requests directly to Moscow by wireless, and the funds are reported to have been sent via Switzerland by courier in dollar currency. For a while a Swiss businessman handled these transactions. At the end of 1941 this link broke, and thereafter Moscow indicated to Trepper in W/T messages that the required cash had been assigned, and told him where, when, and under what circumstances the money was to be collected. A description of the person who was to hand over the money, the password, and any other necessary data that would ensure the safe transfer of the funds was also outlined in the wireless messages.

The cash was used for the purpose of maintaining Trepper and his agents, as well as for the expenses of carrying out special assignments. Included were the maintenance of a social life in business circles from which information and material were forthcoming, the buying of special equipment, and the payment of rents for various flats and safehouses. Trepper was responsible for the receipt and expenditure of money received from Moscow.

Before the war Trepper received a salary of about three hundred and fifty dollars a month, which was reduced to two hundred and seventy-five dollars when his family returned to the USSR. Grossvogel received about one hundred and seventy-five dollars a month, which sum was later increased to two hundred and twenty-five dollars. These salaries were supposed to cover normal expenses; additional sums were available for exceptional circumstances and travelling expenses.

After June 1941 considerable economies had to be made, and salaries were radically cut, to about one hundred dollars a month. At this time, however, both Simex and Simexco were doing well, were drawing substantial profits, and it is reasonable to assume that the difference in salaries was made up from these profits.

The agents who were recruited locally, as opposed to those sent out from Moscow, did not receive a regular salary. Instead, they received occasional payments in proportion to the value of their work. As a rule Trepper paid his women agents at the rate of about one thousand French francs a month. This was more than his men agents received because, he said, the women required more for their clothes. Trepper also expended a total of between four thousand and ten thousand French or Belgian francs on miscellaneous cutouts and sub-agents.

Trepper made all of his calculations in U.S. currency or converted all of them to dollars, because during the war years U.S. currency was stable, whereas Belgian and French francs were continually depreciating.

At the time of his arrest Trepper showed the Germans a balance sheet reflecting his receipts and expenditures, amounting to over twenty thousand dollars each year for 1941 and 1942. The original notes on which this balance sheet was based were hidden by Trepper in a clock in one of his houses, but were recovered by the Germans with Trepper's assistance. The original receipts and financial statements were destroyed for security reasons, according to Trepper, but he kept his notes as the basis of a future report to Moscow.

A reserve fund was built up for emergencies. As a matter of fact, Trepper had two emergency funds, and possibly more. One consisted of gold sovereigns, to the value of about one thousand dollars, which were packed in cork in jam jars. These were in the custody of one of Trepper's agents. (With Trepper's assistance these caches were recovered by the Germans.) The other fund, of an unknown amount, was certainly not brought to the attention of the Germans. It had been left with Jean Claude Spaak, who kept the money and some indentification papers for Trepper hidden in a steel box for eighteen months. Trepper picked these up after he made his escape from the Germans.

V. HENRI ROBINSON

In August 1941 Moscow instructed Trepper to make contact with the Soviet agent Henri Robinson, who was in charge of a very active intelligence network of his own. The first meeting between Trepper and Robinson took place early in September 1941 at the home of Anna Griotto. Henri Robinson had been working as a Soviet agent in Western Europe since about 1930, when he was put in charge of the intelligence apparatus of the French Communist Party. During the 1930s Robinson acted as head of the OMS, the Comintern's Liaison Section, in Western Europe. He was well known during the 1930s to Red Army intelligence and was probably equally useful to the NKVD.

During the 1930s one of Robinson's agents in England had a sub-agent who worked for the Royal Aircraft Establishment. The sub-agent "borrowed" official documents and took them to his home, where he photographed them before returning them to his office.

Harry II, an unidentified Red Army intelligence agent, seems to have been based in Paris, at least from the spring of 1934, when he took over the management of Ernest Weiss as a secondary agent in the British Isles. By March 1936 Harry II had his headquarters in Paris. Harry II's link to Moscow seems to have been through the military attache at the Soviet Embassy in Paris.

In the first half of 1937 Harry II handed over his net against the U.K. to Robinson. Possibly Harry II's return to Moscow was connected with the general upheaval in Red Army intelligence at that time. Paris appears to have remained Robinson's base, but he engaged in widespread planning discussions. In Paris he discussed the Scandinavian network; and on a visit to Switzerland he supposedly took part in talks about Czechoslovakia, the Balkans, Greece, and Italy. He seems to have continued his technical functions and to have visited the British Isles for a similar purpose.

Robinson's agent in England was in contact with him through a postal link, possibly combined with a courier service. A book code was used to conceal the most secret parts of their correspondence. Names used at the beginning and end of letters had no relation to any of the agents in the network. It was customary, in letters of this kind, to invent both an addressee and a signatory for each occasion. The following instructions for the book code used by Robinson and his agent in England (Jean) were found in Robinson's apartment after his arrest:

"Each letter *or* each word is indicated by 6 figures:

> E.G.　59　04　22
> 59- 　page 59
> 04- 　4 lines from the top
> 22- 　22 letters in the line

590422-Wings: The 22nd letter is the first letter of a word; the whole word is therefore meant. If only one letter is meant, then the first letter of a word must be avoided, e.g., 590423—i.

"In order to save time whole words are to be adopted as far as possible. Figures are to be written out and enciphered, e.g., 9-nine. In order to avoid mistakes, lines which contain figures (in the book) ought not to be used. The same applies to pages of the book which contain a chapter heading.

"The enciphered text must be in English; the uncoded, *en clair* part of the message can be in French or German for deception purposes.

"For greater security the page number is concealed as follows: Before the beginning of the enciphered text three figures are placed, e.g., 017. That means that page 17 of the book is indicated in cipher by 01, and so on. In order to encipher the word "wings," therefore, you do not write 590422, but 430422 (if page 17 is represented by 01 and the 16 preceeding pages are to be ignored, which means that they are subtracted from 59).

"In order to observe the system chosen, the figures can be broken into arbitrary groups. If the text is partly *en clair* every enciphered portion must have an individual three-figure key number. EXAMPLE: Meeting permitted determined by letter for Saturday.

1. To encipher:
   M—1770409
   E—1541208
   E—1272215
   T—1650138
   I—1230405
   N—1622711
   G—1901822
   permitted—1591811
   determined—1913202
   by—1820505
   letter—1631507
   for—1922617
   Saturday—1470808

2. To conceal the page number:
   Key number, e.g.
   121, i.e., 120 to
   be subtracted.

570409	341208
072215	450138
030405	422711
701822	391811
713202	620505
431507	722617
270808	

3. The key number is placed on top and all figures are arbitrarily grouped.
   E.g., 121
   57040   934   120-
   8072   221   5450
   x13   803040   54
   2271   170182   239
   1811713   20262   050
   543150772   2617270
   808"

On several occasions Robinson had Max Habjanic in Basle obtain passports for him through Anna Mueller. These passports were probably intended for his agents. It is possible, however, that Robinson wanted them, or some of them, for his own use, because when he was arrested by the Germans and an investigation was made, it was found that in addition to identification in the name of Henri Robinson he also had the following documents: a Swiss passport in the name of Otto Wehrli, issued in Basle in February 1935, renewed in Basle in April 1938, and valid until April 1941; a Swiss passport in the name of Albert Gottlieb Bucher, issued in Basle in May 1938 and valid until September 1940; a Swiss passport in the name of Alfred Merian, issued in Basle in May 1938, valid until May 1939, renewed in July 1939, and valid until July 1942. In addition, he had an identity card in the name of Alfred Doyen, issued in Herseaux, Belgium, in October 1921. He may have had additional identification documents which did not come to light in the course of the investigation.

There is evidence to indicate that Robinson had available a source of funds which he kept as a reserve and that he disposed of large sums of money, mostly as payment for agent work. For many years prior to the war he continued to pay one of his agents in England at the average rate of eight to ten pounds a week, including expenses.

At the end of 1940 or early in 1941 Robinson sent a courier to contact Rachel Duebendorfer in Switzerland. On the basis of material she had collected from her agents, for which she had no funds to pay, Robinson sent her two thousand dollars from his reserves without waiting for approval from Moscow.

Before September 1941 it appears that Robinson handed his reports to a cutout who passed them on to the Soviet Embassy in Paris for transmission to Moscow, possibly by diplomatic pouch. He probably met his cutout at fixed rendezvous points. It seems, however, that no arrangements for emergencies or for the handling of especially urgent messages were made; and during a period when Robinson was ill, toward the end of 1940, they were unable to keep up the liaison.

After September 1941 Robinson's incoming messages came over Makarov's set, in accordance with an agreement that had been made between Robinson and Trepper when they met for the first time. At that time they were forced to amalgamate and to share their communication links until Robinson could put his set into operating condition. Robinson's group had made no adequate preparations for long-range W/T traffic to Moscow. He had the equipment and codes but no operator. He never did succeed in getting his set to operate.

The office of the Soviet Military Attache in Paris was used to transmit the material received from Robinson and possibly from several other agents. In addition to his contact with the Paris Military Attache, Robinson handed some of his reports to an intermediary who passed them to the Military Attache in Vichy for transmission to Moscow.

VI. THE ROBINSON PAPERS

Betrayed by Trepper, Robinson was arrested by the Germans in December 1942. He revealed a hotel address used by him. This room was searched thoroughly by the Germans, and among the papers were some containing intelligence information which had been concealed in a briefcase under the floorboards. The papers also included his identity documents, reports, coding data, and messages to and from him. The originals of these seized papers were never obtained by the Americans. Probably they went to RSHA headquarters and fell eventually into Soviet hands among the "Gestapo files" seized by the Soviets and known to have been held after World War II in Potsdam, East Germany.

Abwehr III F. (CE) in France had sent photostats of these "Robinson papers" to Ast Belgien, the Abwehr station in Belgium. These photostats in Belgium came into the custody of the British, presumably in the course of the liberation of Belgium. They were reportedly mislabeled or misfiled in processing by the CI War Room (Joint British-OSS CE Center in London during and immediately after World War II) and "lost" until 1947, when they were rediscovered by the British, who translated some of them.

The British commented in 1966 that:

> the Robinson papers, apart from Weiss, did not give any positive lead to spies *in situ* in the U.K. They do, however, indicate that Robinson played an important part in the running of Russian operations in the U.K. in the 1930s, and it seems . . . that even at this late stage there are a number of points arising out of the Robinson papers worthy of further study on both sides of the Atlantic.

In transmitting the "Robinson papers" to Ast Belgien, the Abwehr in Paris, in a report dated 19 January 1943, commented that the Soviet agent known as "Harry" was being sent to Berlin at the request of the RSHA because he has been searched for in the Reich since 1930 and his contacts in party-political circles reach into the Reich.

As regards party politics, he was an exceptionally important person and was at the time of the occupation of the Ruhr already fully active. At the outbreak of the Soviet-German war, he also occupied himself with military intelligence, according to his own admission. He appears to be intelligent and versatile, which is confirmed by Trepper, and was on the best terms with the highest circles of the de Gaullist movement. When he returns to Paris, Harry should be closely questioned about this.

Among the several hundred documents in the Robinson papers are the coded names of a number of persons, many of whom have never been positively identified. But some of the identities have been established. For example, "Sissy" has been positively identified as Rachel Duebendorfer, a Soviet agent operating in Switzerland against Germany during World War II.

Notes in Robinson's possession indicated that he had an agent who used the cover name of "Jenny." She is probably identical with Rose Reudi Luschinsky, nee Hepner, sister of Rachel Deubendorfer.

Rose Luschinsky and Dr. Heinz L. Luschinsky entered the United States in 1941. On 4 January 1951 Rose Luschinsky and her husband, Heinz, of 5555 Netherlands Avenue, New York City, were interviewed by the FBI. Rose Luschinsky denied knowing Henri Robinson and denied any involvement in Soviet espionage operations. She admitted that her sister, Rachel, was a Communist and said that she had read of Rachel's work as a Soviet agent in Switzerland. She stated, however, that she had not seen her sister since the late 1930s. Rose denied being "Jenny." Investigation disclosed, however, that her address book contained the notation, "Dr. Z. Angeluscheff, 120 East 86th Street, New York City."

He is probably identical with Dr. Schivko Angeluscheff, a medical doctor who resides and maintains an office at 131 E. 93rd Street, New York City. A report from an unidentified French intelligence source which is described as an alphabetical listing of Soviet agents in France prior to World War II reads in part:

Angeluscheff, Schivko, alias Angueloucher, born 15 January 1897 in Meglish, Bulgaria. Parents: Dimitri and Beslat Islka. Bulgarian nationality, German citizenship by naturalization. Married Helene Georgieff on 16 June 1926 in Berlin. She was born 18 March 1902 in Philippoli, Bulgaria, and is also naturalized German. Because of his anti-French activity he was expelled from France on 16 October 1938 and disappeared from his home, 35 rue de Danzig, Paris, where his wife remained.

Rose Luschinsky was also accompanied to the U.S. by Helene Matouskova and Frantisek Studnicka. She said that she met Matouskova and Studnicka immediately before her embarkation for the U.S. and welcomed their friendship. She admitted knowing that Matouskova was employed at the United Nations. She did not know Studnicka very well other than that he was a "boyfriend" of Matouskova. She added that she knew that Matouskova was married to one Frantisek Matousek, a painter who came to the U.S. shortly after the war for an exhibition of his paintings in New York City.

A comparison of the information in the Robinson papers about Jenny and facts developed through the investigation of Rose Luschinsky reflect that she is probably "Jenny," and that she lied when interviewed.

Several other code names mentioned in the Robinson messages and related to "Jenny" have never been satisfactorily identified. Among these are "Dubois" (male and female), "Sanger," and "The Painter." It appears from the messages that Jenny knew Sanger and The Painter and that she was at Mont Dore with the woman Dubois, the man Dubois being in England at the time. On the basis of available information it seems that "The Painter" could be identical with Frantisek Matousek, and that "Sanger" and "Dubois" could be Helene Sommerova Matouskova and Frantisek Studnicka. Rose Luschinsky admitted being at Mont Dore during the pertinent period.

The identification of Sissy and Jenny is important in the study of the Robinson papers, because revolving around Sissy and Jenny are "Jean," the "Professor," "M. P.," "Jerome," and others who have not been positively identified to date.

Robinson's agent in England, who was named Jean, controlled a subgroup, one member of which was the "Professor," whose field of specialization was television.

On 6 April 1939 Jean wrote to Harry (Robinson):

> Prof—Herewith some dozen weekly reports and a variety of other material—his old friend Kallmann migrated altogether to the U.S.A. in February and it was possible beforehand to take a look into his most important plans/drawings. . . .

It appears from Robinson's 24 July 1940 message that "Jean" had lacked contact with a superior since the beginning of the war. In a 15 November 1940 message regarding his suggestions to the management that the agent "M. P." should be sent to England, Robinson remarked anxiously:

> I don't know whether you have contact with Jean, for he should have first-hand information. His financial situation must be extremely bad.

The following are excerpts from Robinson's papers concerning M. P.:

> I should tell you that the friend of M. P. whom we tried to have here is actually down there and holds one of the highest and most important offices from our point of view. My plan consists of trying to find M. P., who should be a prisoner . . . making him come here and then you would have to find the means of moving him down there. . . . [Robinson to Center, 24-7-40]
>
> I have just found M. P. again and I have begun to interest him in the work. . . . [Robinson to Center, 10-9-40]
>
> I have just . . . let you know that he was working with me and I had informed you of my idea whether an attempt should not be made to send him to England. . . . He should also have a chance of getting a place which could be of great interest for us, next to one of the directors of de Gaulle. . . . Thorez knows that M. P. is working with us . . . what payment should I make to M. P. [Robinson to Center, 15-11-40]
>
> We have established a direct link with the friend of M. P. We have agreed with you to call M. P. Jerome, who is to be found at present with de

> Gaulle . . . consequently it is useless to send Jerome to join him, all the more since his friend is at loggerheads with his management . . . [the de Gaulle management] . . . and he can no longer produce much profit. We consider it a better idea to use Jerome in your show [chez vous] . . . to acquire more clients in your country. We authorize you to give him 2,000 francs a month. We will arrange things with his party manager [direction du parti]. [Center to Robinson, 20-12-40]

In the light of information received from the DST in 1968—information indicating that Robinson was once Kim Philby's case officer—it is obviously important from a counterintelligence standpoint to identify "Jean," "M. P.," and "Jerome." The Robinson traffic clearly shows that Jean was living in England and that there was enciphered communication between Jean and Harry.

According to British sources, Jean, who lived in London, was Robinson's chief agent in the U.K. in 1939. Further, Robinson's traffic with Jean before their lines of communication were broken may have been reproduced by Robinson for the management at a later date. For example, in the message of 24 July 1940 Robinson said that he sent various materials on his liaison with the U.K. to the management "in his [i.e., Jean's] time."

On the basis of the above it would appear reasonable to assume that Jean was in London during the 1939-40 period. But Philby was not in England during the 1939-40 period, a fact which rules out the possibility that Philby was Jean. Philby had been out of the country almost continuously since early 1937. Between leaving the Spanish civil war in July 1939 and setting off with the BEF as the *Times* No. 1 war correspondent, Philby had only a little time to arrange the details of his divorce. By October 1939 he was at British headquarters in Arras, and he stayed in Europe until the fall of France in June 1940.

An earlier Rote Kapelle study states that Ernst David Weiss (alias Walter Lock), who worked for both Harry II and Henri Robinson, could have been Jean. A message in March 1941 from Robinson to Moscow, apparently in response to questions, contained a reference to Ernst Weiss (with telephone number PAD 7501, which was that of Weiss' London address since 1933) in conjunction with the "Professor" and the Professor's wife, "Sheilla." Robinson's communications with Moscow suggest that Robinson's agent, Jean, and his network in England were in financial difficulties and that by February 1941 Moscow had not been able to establish a link with Jean in replacement of Robinson's own line of communication, which failed after the German occupation of France. Despite Weiss' denials, it is possible that he had connections with Jean in England or even that he is identical with Jean.

During the past five years investigation has disclosed that "Jerome" is probably Andre Labarthe; "M. P." is probably Marcel Prenant or Marcel Perrault (who belonged to the Ozols network); the friend of M. P. is probably Jacques Soustelle; Hans Gerhardt Lubszynski is probably the "Professor"; Dr. Heinz Erwin Kallmann is the colleague of the Professor. Biographical summaries of Labarthe, Prenant, Perrault, Soustelle, Lubszynski, and Kallmann are included in the personalities section of this study.

VII. COMMUNICATIONS

Throughout the latter part of 1940 and most of 1941 Trepper attempted to build up a wireless station in France. He had received a transmitter, call-signs, and codes, and it only remained to find a suitable operator. He had selected one of the operators working with the Belgian network; but before the operator could be transferred to France, he was arrested by the Germans when they closed in on the Makarov transmitter. At the same time Trepper and Grossvogel were training several W/T operators in France.

Trepper was in Brussels on a business trip on 13 December 1941, the day that one of Makarov's operators was arrested by the Germans. Makarov was apprehended the following day. As a matter of fact, Trepper went to the safehouse the day after the arrest and was taken into custody along with the others on the premises at the time. With the assistance of his false papers and with a good cover story he was able to secure his release. He thus had a full picture of the situation and was in a position to warn those members of the group, particularly Sukolov, who had not yet been arrested. Sukolov fled to France almost immediately thereafter. After the arrests of December 1941 Trepper forbade the communications staff in France to have any personal contact with him or with other agents.

Makarov's arrest in December 1941 caused a breakdown in communications and left Trepper in an embarrassing position. He had no wireless communications in France, although he, like Robinson, had the equipment and codes ready and was in the process of establishing a line. The loss of the link through Makarov meant that the traffic from both Trepper's and Robinson's organizations was blocked. The Soviet missions had been evacuated, and the French Communist Party had gone underground.

Trepper fell back on an emergency rendezvous in Paris that he had pre-arranged with Moscow. The arrangements had indicated that for the safety signal certain newspapers were to be carried to the rendezvous spot, newspapers not normally sold on the streets.

Trepper did not succeed in making contact until February 1942. He recognized the agent who had been sent by the newspaper he carried; the password was exchanged and contact was established. Trepper learned that his contact was connected with the French Communist Party and that he came prepared to make arrangements for Trepper to use the Party channel wireless transmitter. Normally there would have been no formalized association between the Soviet intelligence services and the local Communist Party, but in an emergency like this the Soviet intelligence services were forced to fall back upon the services of the Party.

The Communist Party link is believed to have run through an automatic transmitter in the press wireless station of the Comintern. The normal function of the Party transmitter was to carry press messages, presumably for *Tass*, and it is unlikely that it ever was intended to be an undercover or illicit station.

Robinson, too, was eventually compelled to make use of the French CP transmitter. When he had his first meeting with Trepper in September 1941 it was agreed that he should set up a direct wireless link with Moscow immediately; he had been given his own transmitter, code, and call signs. In the meantime, until he could do so, his incoming messages were to be routed via Brussels. Robinson's attempts to establish a wireless link were not successful, partly for lack of materials and partly because he could not find reliable operators. Accordingly, when the Brussels network was broken up in December 1941, Robinson turned to the Party link and continued to use it until Trepper's operators started to transmit from Paris. Then Robinson transferred his signals to their set for transmission.

It is said that special arrangements for the transmission of Trepper's and Robinson's material over the Party channel were made through the wireless expert of the Party. He and his assistant took over the construction and development of transmitter and receiver sets. On the outskirts of Paris they had a workshop fitted with all modern machinery and are reported to have had a stock of about twenty completed or partly completed sets.

The military attache in Vichy had assisted Trepper in recruiting personnel for the network he was organizing in France. For example, the military attache's office had drawn up a list of Soviet citizens desiring repatriation. This list was shown to Trepper, who selected the name of a radio dealer as a possible agent recruit. Through the Communist Party in France inquiries were made in Belgium, where this man previously resided. It was discovered that this man and his wife, Hersog and Marian Sokol, had been active Communists and had been expelled from Belgium for their activities. They had taken no part in political work since their arrival in France. They were eventually selected, recruited, and trained to be W/T operators for Trepper's Paris network.

Grossvogel had been given the task of establishing a reliable wireless line and supervising the agents concerned in communications work. Three W/T sets had been made available to the organization, although only one was ever used. One set belonged to Robinson, and it was never usable. The other was an American set which was operated by the Sokols. The third was a set which had been given to the Girauds by the French Communist headquarters and which was never used.

One of Grossvogel's functions was to train W/T operators. Sokol was one of his trainees; Mrs. Sokol had studied coding previously. By April 1942 the Sokols were ready to begin transmitting and were given a W/T set. Their set apparently was not able to contact Moscow directly, and their messages went to London, whence they were relayed to Moscow. Trepper's information was delivered to the operators through his personal courier.

The Sokols were originally recruited through the French CP; and although information on their W/T service is limited, they may have had connections with the Party's W/T service and system. Some resemblance to the Party W/T links appears in Spaak's statement that the Sokols were able to transmit messages to Moscow via London. It is not known how much incriminating evidence was obtained by their arrest in June 1942, but it is possible that Trepper succeeded to a large extent in sealing off the incident, just as he had done in the Low Countries in December 1941.

After the arrest of the Sokols the traffic of Trepper's network was transferred to the transmitter of the Jeffremov network in Brussels, operated by Wenzel; the woman agent who was encoding for

Trepper fled, but the Girauds continued their courier services. Possibly the Sokols, if they had talked, could have compromised the Party communications system, and this threat might account for Trepper's diverting his traffic for the USSR not to the French CP but back to Jeffremov's station in Brussels. The new line lasted hardly a month, because Wenzel was arrested while transmitting for Jeffremov on 30 July 1942.

After Wenzel's arrest Trepper was forced to revert to the Communist Party link. He was allowed to send only two to three hundred groups over this link in any one week. He used the Girauds as cutouts between himself and the Communist Party. For this purpose the Girauds were in touch with Grossvogel. They collected reports from him and passed them on. In the fall of 1942 they took a house at Le Pecq. A transmitter was installed, and an operator was dispatched to operate it. The set did not work, however, and was later found by the Germans, concealed in the garden.

It is strongly suspected that Trepper had contact with the Soviet military attache in London. There are several substantiating indications. It will be recalled that Trepper's organization originally was designed to obtain information from and about England and, logically, would have come under the control of the military attache's office in London. On the other hand, arrangements for contact between Trepper and London may have been made through the military attache in Vichy in 1941.

One contact with London may have been made when Trepper was transmitting by W/T from Paris. There is some evidence that his traffic was picked up in London by the wireless station at the Soviet Embassy and was then relayed to Moscow. If so, the practice may have come about for some purely technical reason; for example, the transmitter in Paris may have had insufficient power to maintain satisfactory communications directly with Moscow.

VIII. VICTOR SUKOLOV

When Victor Sukolov fled Belgium in December 1941, he came to Paris. In January 1942 Trepper sent him to Marseilles with instructions to organize a new network there. In Marseilles Sukolov lived with his mistress, Margarete Barcza, under the cover of a branch office of Simex. Together they organized a network of Czech agents, but they apparently were in constant fear of discovery and limited their intelligence activities as much as possible. For a while

Sukolov and Barcza even considered discontinuing their work and fleeing to Switzerland.

It was only after the arrest of Sukolov in Marseilles in November 1942 that the Germans managed to do something about the Rote Drei in Switzerland. Sukolov's interrogation produced the fact that in the summer of 1940 he had brought code books to Geneva and that these books had been left in the rue de Lausanne. The address, Alexander Rado's, housed the headquarters of the Soviet net in Switzerland.

IX. TREPPER'S ARREST

The Germans in Paris suspected that there was espionage going on in Simex, and they attempted deception with the help of a member of the Todt organization, which had dealings with Simex. After they had arrested Abraham Rajchmann and some of the people in Jeffremov's network, the Germans decided to seize both Simex and Simexco.

The premises of Simex in Paris were occupied and searched in November 1942, and the known associates and proprietors of the firm were arrested. No espionage material, however, was found. Immediate interrogations of the subjects failed to determine the whereabouts of "Monsieur Gilbert," who had not been found and who could not be discovered. It was revealed later that none of the arrested had ever known Gilbert's real address.

For conspiratorial reasons Trepper had ordered that no member of the firm should ever know his whereabouts, and especially not his address or cover addresses. Through a piece of good luck it was learned from the arrested Director of Simex in Paris, Alfred Corbin, that Gilbert had asked Corbin about the address of a dentist who was supposed to live on the rue Rivoli. The dentist in question was found, and his appointment book was inspected unobtrusively by the Sonderkommando. One of the names found was that of a certain Gilbert, and it was learned that Gilbert had an appointment at 2 p.m. on 5 December 1942, at which time the "Grand Chef" was arrested in the dentist's chair.

Following his arrest Trepper was very communicative. He said that he had never felt secure since the Germans first arrested the Sukolov group in Brussels in December 1941. He made an offer of collaboration with the Germans. Although they refused it, they told him that the proposal would be reconsidered if he first gave concrete proof of his intent to collaborate fully. Trepper then gave them the name of "Kleiner Andre" as his chief assistant, and as further proof of his good faith telephoned Hillel Katz in the presence of German officials.

Trepper explained to the Germans that his motive for collaboration was that he wished to save the lives of his relatives and family in the USSR. He stated that he knew his entire family would be liquidated if the fact of his arrest became known to the Soviets.

It was finally agreed upon that Trepper should collaborate in rounding up the organization which he directed in return for a guarantee that his arrest should be concealed from the Soviets. Trepper thereupon betrayed Robinson, Grossvogel, and other members of his network.

During the next few weeks Trepper amply fortified the confidence of the Germans. Directly or indirectly he had put his finger on an impressive collection of agents, including Robinson and Grossvogel in Paris and members of the Springer group in Lyons. By Christmas Day Trepper seems to have lulled all the suspicions of the Germans, and a playback to Moscow was started on a wireless transmitter which Trepper was supposed to have set up in Paris.

X. The Playback

Trepper's W/T playback, or Funkspiel, known as "Eiffel," began transmissions on 25 December 1942. The interval between the time of Trepper's arrest and the transmissions, the Germans thought, could be explained by the fact that Trepper at the time of his arrest did not have an effective transmitter. The Sokol set which Trepper had used had been off the air since June 1942, and Trepper is believed to have used the French CP transmitter between June 1942 and his arrest.

Although this playback began soon after Trepper's arrest—he was arrested on 5 December 1942 and the playback started twenty days later—it is presumed that Moscow was aware of the deception from the start. There are various reasons for supposing that the manner in which Trepper handled his arrest and the situation during the few weeks after his arrest were part of a preconceived plan. Trepper's offer of collaboration was probably by pre-arrangement with Moscow. Trepper had apparently kept Moscow informed of the situation and the arrests up to the time of his apprehension; therefore, it is plausible that some agreement was made between Moscow and Trepper for him to follow a triple-cross plan. To preserve his pose, Trepper was bound to divulge much information that was true. Presumably he also fed the Germans deception material, concealing some facts and distorting others. He was evidently untruthful about his Communist Party connections, and he protected from German discovery at least one agent, the person who was responsible for passing on the reports he smuggled out under the eyes of his German guards.

Of all types of counterespionage operations, a W/T playback is one of the most difficult to handle, although ordinarily it has exceptional capabilities for profitable development. Operations of this sort have long displayed a tendency toward disaster; in many instances the attempted playback has been blown or suspected almost from the time of its inception. The German playback of Trepper provides an excellent example.

As a result of the arrests in the Low Countries Trepper undoubtedly had seen the handwriting on the wall and had realized the probability of his own capture. He had ample time before his arrest to discuss this likelihood with Moscow, and it is probable that he and his superiors drew up a "triple-cross plan" against such an eventuality. His activities while working for the Germans show some evidence of such a pre-arrangement. According to German accounts, Trepper appeared neither surprised nor dismayed by his arrest. Instead he congratulated his captors on their skill and offered them his wholehearted collaboration.

According to an RSHA member, Wilhelm Berg, Trepper made the following suggestions without any prompting at his first interrogation after his arrest:

1. He stated that he was prepared to name all his assistants, agents, and sources of information. He advised that after these persons were checked, a decision should be made as to who should not be arrested. (Later he did provide the names.)

2. He was insistent that wireless contact with the "Direktor" (Direktor was the W/T code name for the Chief of Section I of the Office of Operations of the RU) in Moscow should not be broken off, but rather developed by setting up new transmitting stations. This proposal is interesting in view of the fact that Trepper at the time of his arrest had no W/T station of his own and was using the French CP W/T transmitter. The information which was to be sent over the W/T station was to be obtained from the sources already known by Moscow to be in the network.

Trepper's suggestions were discussed and approved by the RSHA, which hoped to achieve the following objectives: the arrest of remaining members of the organization or any other RU organizations operating in Western Europe; the discovery of the French CP transmitter and the penetration of Communist and Soviet intelligence organizations in Switzerland; and the passing to Moscow of misleading political and military reports about Germany and the occupied territories in the West, in the hope of disguising actual German intentions, especially as to operational plans on both the Eastern and Western Fronts.

The arrests of the agents were made, and those arrested were housed in a villa in Paris on the Boulevard Victor Hugo. According to Berg, Trepper secured the personnel who had been arrested (largely through his information) as his assistants, and each of these went to work without any difficulty.

After his escape in September 1943 Trepper told Claude Spaak, who helped him get away undetected, that two or three weeks after his capture he had been able to smuggle a message to the "Center" in Moscow. Trepper told Spaak that on the pretext of learning German he was able to obtain complete privacy for one evening shortly after his capture. During this evening he wrote out (presumably in code) a full account of his arrest, his situation, and his plans. His understanding with the Germans was by this time so excellent that he was able to forward this report undetected, under the pretense of collaboration.

The Germans regarded the arrest of Trepper as one of their most important operational achievements. In the beginning he showed such deliberation in offering his services that his sincerity was questioned. Shortly thereafter, however, Trepper gave his captors proof of his desire to collaborate by phoning, in the presence of German officers, his aide and technical secretary, Hillel Katz. This deed was accepted as a sign of good faith, and in the weeks that followed Trepper aided the Germans in rounding up agents of his own network and other RU agents in France.

Thus the confidence of the Germans in Trepper was rapidly established, and their findings were colored deeply by his interpretations. To preserve the appearance of collaboration, Trepper had to divulge a great deal of true information. In fact, as will be seen from the traffic, the Germans took Trepper's opinions very seriously. But if, as the evidence suggests, Trepper was carrying out a preconceived triple-cross plan, the Germans were undoubtedly duped by him occasionally from the time of his arrest in December 1942 until his escape in September 1943, and it is very likely that he distorted some facts and concealed others.

One of the things that Trepper told the Germans in the beginning of the playback was that Moscow must remain unaware of his arrest so that there would be no reprisals against his family. To assure headquarters that he was allright, it would be necessary that he appear from time to time in various parts of Paris for recognition meetings. The Germans agreed to this proposal and were content to watch such meetings from a distance. By visiting the Bailly Pharmacy, Gare St. Lazare, which was one of the rendezvous for these meetings, Trepper was able to pass his report, without being seen by the Germans, to a woman agent whom he had not betrayed to the Germans. We have no knowledge of the length of time it took the report to reach Moscow, but it is certain that any pre-arranged "triple-cross plan" between Moscow and Trepper could not have come into effective operation until "The Center" knew the circumstances and results of Trepper's arrest.

XI. TREPPER'S ESCAPE

Trepper continued to work for the Germans until 16 September 1943, when he escaped. During this period he appears to have had outside lines of communication with the RU, possibly through the French CP transmitter which he had used prior to his arrest. Just after his escape Trepper told Spaak that the reason he had fled was that he had learned during his captivity that the Germans had acquired a "secret Russian code" and feared that as a result of that code the Germans might uncover from previously intercepted traffic the report which he had smuggled to Moscow.

In June 1943, through the leads given them by Henri Robinson, the Germans discovered the French CP W/T station at Le Raincy. It is possible that the Germans showed Trepper the cipher from this station and that Trepper, recognizing it as a code used by the French CP, decided to escape.

After Trepper's escape the deception operation, of necessity, was discontinued. In an effort to cover up Trepper's escape the Germans sent a message in Sukolov's code over the W/T playback set, Mars, to the effect that Trepper was missing and had probably been captured by the Germans. Any possible success of this message, even assuming that the real situation was not already known in Moscow, must have been shortlived; for in October 1943, when the Germans still had not captured Trepper, they circulated wanted-person notices (including a photograph and description of him) throughout France. Because there were separate unblown RU networks operating in France at the time, it seems likely that at least one of these networks would have noticed the wanted circular and relayed the information to Moscow. It is interesting to note that according to Sukolov's mistress, Margarete Barcza, Sukolov appeared to be the only person who was not upset or surprised at Trepper's escape, a still further indication that Sukolov may have been a part of Trepper's "triple-cross plan," if such a plan existed.

The generally accepted view that Trepper was engaged in a triple-cross, though plausible, is not supported by Heinz Pannwitz, who replaced Reiser after Trepper's arrest, or by some western authorities on the Rote Kapelle. In his history of the Sonderkommando Rote Kapelle, Pannwitz states that Trepper told "much more than we [the Germans] ever hoped and much more than was necessary under the circumstances." No physical means of persuasion were used on Trepper; yet, according to Pannwitz, Trepper betrayed Hillel Katz, the Robinson group, which was unknown to the Germans, the Maximoviches' groups, Voelkner, Podsiadlo, and others. Pannwitz also claims that the result of Trepper's revelations and his willing cooperation in the Funkspiel against Moscow was that the Rote Kapelle was "completely exposed, totally paralyzed." Pannwitz claims that he discovered no indication that Trepper's cooperation with the Germans was pre-arranged with Moscow during his interrogation by Soviet authorities after the war.

The alacrity with which Trepper agreed to cooperate with the Germans might seem to support the triple-cross theory. However, by the time of Trepper's arrest, Soviet nets in Belgium and Germany had, for the most part, been silenced. This left only the Rote Drei, which was plagued with difficulties, to provide Moscow with intelligence from Western Europe.

Consequently, the state of Soviet intelligence operations at the time of Trepper's arrest raises two important—but still unanswered—questions. What motive could Moscow have had for directing Trepper to expose his net? If Trepper was acting on orders from Moscow, why was he imprisoned by the Soviets after the war and why are the Soviets still refusing (in 1973) to allow Trepper to leave Poland? Until satisfactory answers to these and other questions are forthcoming, it would seem that those who reject the triple-cross theory have a strong case.

XII. AN EVALUATION OF THE PLAYBACK

After their decision to operate the playback the Germans built two stations in the outskirts of Paris. These were wireless units of the German Schutzpolizei and employed their apparatus and equipment. Even if the Soviets had not been notified by Trepper of his arrest and future plans, it must be assumed that their suspicions would have been aroused immediately by the sudden ease with which communications were now established after the difficulties which Trepper had encountered in the past. The Germans failed to take this change into consideration and during the playback did not even attempt to invent communications difficulties. Set out below are the various W/T stations used by Trepper from the fall of 1941 until his arrest. One cannot fail to note the contrast between the difficulty he encountered in this period and the ease of his means of communications after 25 December 1942.

1941, Fall

Until the roundup of the Sukolov network in Brussels in December 1941 Trepper passed his information to Moscow via Sukolov's W/T set. The information was sent by courier from Paris to Brussels, and vice versa.

1942, Early

After the arrest of the Sukolov group, Trepper used a W/T station of the French CP, to which he had access through Henri Robinson. He used this link from February 1942 to April 1942.

1942, April

In April 1942 the Sokols got their W/T set in working condition, and from April 1942 to sometime in June 1942 Trepper passed his information over this station, which was located in a Paris suburb.

1942, June

In June 1942 the Germans arrested the Sokols, and Trepper again initiated a courier service to Brussels and passed his information over the W/T link in Brussels which had replaced Sukolov's. The chief of this network was Jeffremov, and its radio technician was Johann Wenzel. In the summer of 1942 the Germans arrested Wenzel while he was transmitting.

1942, Summer

After the breaking up of the Jeffremov group and up to the

time of his arrest Trepper used the W/T station of the French Communist Party.

The Germans who were involved in drawing up the messages and having them sent appear to have employed them carelessly, and in several instances sent out the same material on different days. For instance, parts one and two of a two-part message were sent to Moscow on 22 March 1943. Part one was again sent out as a separate message on 5 April 1943. Parts one and two went out as a two-part message on 16 April 1943, and part two went out as a separate message on 27 April 1943. On 27 February 1943 information purportedly coming from Fabrikant (Abraham Rajchmann) was sent to Moscow. The same message, giving no source of information, was repeated on 16 March 1943 and again on 23 March 1943.

In another instance, the Germans on 30 July 1943 sent out through another playback a message which read word for word the same as the message Trepper sent out on the same day, even though one RU agent was supposed to be in Paris and the other in Marseilles. The other agent, Sukolov, who was operated by the Germans as playback Mars, had been brought by them to Paris in the summer of 1943 and had been housed with Trepper. Even had Moscow been unaware that Sukolov was also working under German control (he may even have been included in Trepper's triple-cross operation), this duplicate message would have been enough to make the headquarters suspicious of both agents.

One of the vital achievements in any playback operation is the successful passing of false information. Of necessity the information must have enough validity to fool the recipient and yet, and especially where military information is concerned, it must be so sanitized that it will not jeopardize any military operations or disclose any important military secrets, such as numbers of military units, their locations, strength, and arms. Against the Soviets this deception is especially difficult, because, as we know, the general practice of the Soviets is to assign the same task to several completely different networks, thereby cross-checking the validity of the information received.

The Germans did not suceed in overcoming this problem. Through the RU apparat in Switzerland, the Soviets were getting at the time very high-level information from the OKW, OKH, etc., in Berlin almost as soon as the various German high commands were receiving the material. Moscow thus had an adequate cross-check against German attempts to pass misinformation on military movements and locations.

Throughout the Trepper W/T playback the Germans passed to Moscow only general information, claiming for one reason or another that more detailed information was impossible to ascertain. This evasion was completely out of character for Trepper, who for years had been passing the Soviets high-level information and whose work had not been characterized by poor performance or excuses.

The false information which the Germans were passing to Moscow could only be dispatched as general statements with no actual disclosure of military OB. Moscow, on the other hand, presumably knowing that the line was under German control, repeatedly asked for detailed and precise information.

Moscow's demands for precise, concrete, and detailed information became more and more insistent. The German intelligence officers of the Special Command who were handling the playback were dependent upon the Chief of Command, West, for the release of espionage material which could be passed to Moscow. The more demanding Moscow became, the more grudging was the release of information from the Chief of Command, West. On the fifth of June 1943 the Chief of Command, West, advised by letter that he was opposed to the release of espionage material for the continuation of the SD's W/T playback, "Eiffel," beamed to Moscow. His position was that the Moscow station had for some time been putting questions of a military type in such a precise form that a continuation of the playback was possible only if the precise questions were also answered in a precise form, "since otherwise the Moscow station will see through the Spiel." He thereupon advised that for military reasons he could no longer be responsible for answering, in the form of espionage material, the questions sent by Moscow. He also took the stand that there was no interest, considering the military situation of the Germans in the West at that time, in a policy of confusing Moscow.

The opinion of the RSHA Special Command which was running the playback was, of course, that there was a continuing German interest in clarifying the RU organization of Trepper within certain limits, and that the playback must, therefore, be continued and confusion material prepared and passed. The SD and SIPO specialists on playbacks were informed of the conflicting views. The results are not known, but on 17 June 1943 the Chief of Command, West, released additional material for the playback; and although Operation Eiffel had to be discontinued after Trepper's escape in

September 1943, the German playback of Sukolov (Operation Mars) continued to the end of the war.

A review of the messages available for the Trepper playback reflects that the Germans on a number of occasions relayed to Moscow information which had allegedly been collected by Fabrikant. This sourcing in itself would have suggested to Moscow that Trepper was operating under German control, for Fabrikant was a relatively unimportant cog in the RU apparat in Brussels. His primary function in the network had been the procurement of false documentation for members of the group; his motivation was primarily financial. He had not often been assigned duties in direct procurement of intelligence information. In addition, Moscow—at least by the time the playback was instituted—was probably aware of the fact that both Rajchmann and his mistress, Malvina Gruber, had been arrested and turned by the Germans in 1942.

A further alleged intelligence source was one Rene, although it seems unlikely that an RU agent with the cover name of Rene ever was a member of Trepper's group in either Belgium or France. Of this fact the Germans should have been aware as a result of the interrogations of the Rote Kapelle personnel arrested in both Belgium and France.

Therefore, when the Germans suddenly activated a Rene who appeared to be a fairly important member of Trepper's network, the Center, had they not been aware of the fact that Trepper was being played back, probably would have raised numerous questions as to the identity of this new source.

Although a few of the Special Command who were concerned in the Eiffel playback eventually became suspicious that Moscow might have seen through the operation, most of the German Intelligence Officers connected with this operation regarded it as highly successful. A review of the traffic, however, reflects that Moscow profited much more than did Berlin.

On one occasion, at least, Moscow received valuable intelligence from Trepper. In 1943 Trepper succeeded in obtaining from German Intelligence an up-to-date report on the German knowledge of British forces in the Mediterranean area. This information, released by the Germans in order to bolster the confidence of Moscow in the playback, was urgently needed at the time by the Soviets in estimating the possibility of securing a second front.

A successful attempt at deceiving the Germans occurred in August 1943. Moscow advised Trepper that headquarters was sending an agent to Paris to contact him and wanted to know Trepper's operational address and name so that a rendezvous could be effected. The Germans were greatly intrigued by this prospect. Whatever plan "the Center" had in mind was never disclosed, however, for Trepper escaped from the Germans before the plan could be carried out.

There is also evidence that Moscow, at least in one instance, may have launched a psychological warfare attack on the Germans through the playback. On 29 May 1943 Moscow sent to Trepper a message urgently requesting that Fabrikant determine whether or not the German occupation army was preparing to use poison gas, and submitted various other questions relating to poison gas. As soon as this information was received, it was forwarded to the Chief of the SIPO and SD. On 2 June the Chief of the SIPO and SD forwarded the message, by letter, to the Chief of the Army Amt. Ausland Abwehr, Abwehrabteilungen III and IIID. The letter also contained the following statement:

> The urgency about the question of German gases and preparation for gas war indicated the possibility that the Soviets have ideas along this line and maybe even the British and the Americans. The Grand Chef (Leopold Trepper), who was asked about it, says that because it is so urgent, he thinks the Axis opponents could very possibly soon begin to use poison gas and similar material. I inform you of this and ask you for playback material for answering this message from Moscow.

In his papers Pannwitz includes an apologia for running complicated double-agent and radio playback operations as opposed to arresting and imprisoning spies. Nevertheless, Pannwitz was probably wrong in his assumption that his Sonderkommando had almost complete control of all Soviet and Communist espionage underground nets in France and the Low Countries. The British advance a fairly firm theory that the two Soviet principal agents, Trepper and Kent, played back against the GRU headquarters in Moscow by the Germans, were able to notify Moscow through French CP communications channels, unknown to the Germans, of German control of the Soviet espionage networks.

Trepper made very elaborate plans for his getaway. Two things are clear: first, that he had not told the Germans everything; and second, that he had made provisions for escaping and living underground. By letting the Germans in on some things, he was able to throw them off the track on others.

Trepper had set aside two emergency funds. One consisted of gold sovereigns to the value of about one thousand dollars, which were packed in cork and kept in jam jars. At the time of Trepper's arrest these jars were in the custody of Trepper's right-hand man. With Trepper's assistance this sum of money was recovered by the Germans.

The other emergency fund he had left in Spaak's safekeeping. He made no reference to this fund, and the Germans had no reason to know of its existence or to anticipate that Trepper could fall back on such a fund in making his escape.

According to Pannwitz, only a fraction of Trepper's contacts in France were uncovered:

> because we simply did not have the opportunity or means to carry out such an enormous investigation. Only those were arrested who were absolutely essential for the Funkspiel operation. Those who were not vital to the operation were not alerted or allowed to become suspicious, in order to protect our operation. He had friends, but they were also his agents and subordinates, such as Grossvogel, (Hillel) Katz, etc. He did not allow any other type of friendship. We could learn nothing about his family and relatives in the West. He himself would tell us nothing about his family.

The W/T deception proceeded smoothly (or so the Germans thought) until September 1943, at which time Trepper escaped and was not recaptured.

After Trepper's escape from the Germans the playback was continued with the assistance of Sukolov's transmitter, which was known as the "Mars" playback. Until March 1943 Sukolov's set had been operated from Marseilles. In the spring of 1943 Sukolov was brought to Paris, and "Eiffel" and "Mars" were joined. In the summer of 1943 Trepper and Sukolov were housed together and had an adequate chance to discuss their future plans.

XIII. THE OZOLS AND THE MITHRIDATE NETWORKS

There is little doubt that Moscow knew in early 1943 that Sukolov had been arrested and that he had been doubled by the Germans. It is, therefore, interesting to note that on 14 March 1943 Sukolov received a message from Moscow giving information concerning one Waldemar Ozols (alias Solja). The information included the last known address of Ozols in Paris. The Germans finally located Ozols in Paris; and in July 1943 Sukolov, using a pre-arranged word furnished by Moscow, contacted Ozols and reactivated him. He had been out of contact with Moscow since July 1941. Sukolov did not inform Ozols of his arrest by the Germans; and Ozols, believing Sukolov to be a bona fide Soviet agent, immediately furnished Sukolov with information concerning his activities from July 1941 to July 1943. The Sukolov playback continued well into 1944 and possibly up to August 1944, when the Germans retreated from Paris and took Sukolov with them.

Waldemar Ozols (alias Solja, alias Sokol, alias Marianne, alias "The General") was born 17 October 1898 in Riga. Other reports indicate that Waldemar Ozols-Priede was born 17 October 1884 in Riga. He was a general in the International Brigades during the Spanish Civil War, and according to one account he had been working for the GRU in France since 1926. He is said to have visited the U.K. on occasion from 1934 to 1939; but he appears to have been independent of Robinson and Trepper, although his direction, like theirs, came through the Soviet military attache in Paris. During the German invasion Ozols may have lost contact with the Soviet MA after the withdrawal of Embassy officials to unoccupied France.

In the message of 14 March 1943 Moscow requested Kent (Sukolov) to contact Solja, a former Latvian general who had fought for the Loyalists in Spain during the Civil War. The Center advised that Ozols could furnish information about German troop movements and had a W/T set, but the Center had not heard from Ozols after the German occupation of France. Kent was told to be very careful in contacting Ozols because the "Greens" (Nazis) were probably still looking for him.

In this message, received four months after Trepper's capture, Karl Gierling, who was then directing the Sonderkommando and reading the Soviet radio traffic, saw the possibility of getting his hands on another Soviet network. With the facilities of the Gestapo Ozols was located. Sukolov informed the Center. Pursuant to the

Director's instructions a meeting was arranged, and Ozols met Sukolov on 1 April 1943. Apparently Ozols had no reason to be suspicious of Sukolov. Ozols noted that Sukolov spoke a modern Russian and concluded that the latter was a young Soviet officer rather than the son of an emigre working for Germany.

Ozols told Sukolov that he had sought refuge in France after the Spanish Civil War. In 1940 he had been requested by the Air Attache of the Soviet Embassy in Paris to organize an intelligence network. Ozols had recruited about a dozen agents; and when the Soviet diplomats left Paris, he was given a W/T set. But Ozols had not been able to find an experienced radio operator, and his attempts to contact Moscow had failed.

After the Germans arrived in France, Ozols had gone underground in Normandy. Ozols did not mention to Sukolov that he had been in contact with Trepper in 1940. This fact appeared to him unimportant. He did not know that the Center had recommended to Trepper that he be most prudent in his contacts with Ozols; the latter was suspected of working for the Deuxieme Bureau, the Gestapo, or both.

Sukolov ordered Ozols to reassemble the remnants of his network and to bolster it by recruiting French technicians and officials capable of furnishing intelligence of a political, economic, and military nature.

Four months later, in December 1943, Ozols was placed in contact by a common friend with Paul Legendre, a reserve captain, age 65. For three years Legendre had been chief of the Mithridate network for the Marseilles region. Mithridate was one of the most important organizations of the French Resistance. Ozols recruited Legendre, but the latter assumed that Ozols was working for the Soviets and that they were both working against the Germans. In January 1944 Ozols organized a meeting between Legendre and Sukolov. During this meeting Legendre mentioned that his wife had been arrested and deported. Sukolov promised to get her released, and he did; so Legendre concluded that the Soviet intelligence services were indeed powerful.

Legendre was completely captivated by Sukolov and turned over to him the complete list of his agents in Marseilles. This roster permitted the Gestapo to penetrate the Mithridate network, to exploit it, and even to set up another clandestine organization under the Kommando's control. Upon the advice of Sukolov, France was divided into eight military regions, and Legendre was placed in charge of the Marseilles and Paris regions. Legendre recruited numerous agents, among them Maurice Violette, former Minister in the Third Republic and Mayor of Dreux.

At first the Mithridate network, penetrated by the Germans, was utilized in order to manipulate the French Resistance, but in the spring of 1944 Pannwitz decided he would use the Mithridate network to gather and relay information to the Gestapo from behind Allied lines. Accordingly, Sukolov instructed Legendre to advise his contacts that:

> Washington and London are not advising Moscow of their military planning, and this is too bad because it is impossible to formulate a common Allied strategy. We don't even know if the next disembarkation is going to be a raid like that at Dieppe or a Second Front. In advising us of the number and nature of the landing forces, you will permit the Soviet high command to have a more precise idea of what is going on and to harmonize its strategy accordingly and thus advance the defeat of Germany.

Some of Legendre's agents were skeptical about this request, but others saw Sukolov's logic and followed his instructions.

Ozols was arrested in Paris on 7 November 1944 by the DST. He was indicted for espionage and imprisoned at Fort de Charenton. A short time after his arrest he was liberated through the personal intercession of Colonel fnu Novikov of the Soviet Military Mission. Novikov was a working colleague of General Pierre Koenig during this period. Arrested with Ozols and likewise charged with espionage was Legendre, who was also freed upon the intercession of Novikov. After his release Ozols remained in Paris and worked for the Soviet Commercial Attache's office.

An American named Moses Gatewood became involved with the Mithridate network in the summer of 1944. The following excerpt is from a 1945 OSS report:

"A naive young American airman named Moses Gatewood was shot down over the village of Flexanville. He was given shelter by a group of persons whom we can identify as members of Sokol's organization. These included a Mme. Bernoit; an old man named Violette, who is said to have been Governor of Algiers; a French general described as having previously belonged to the Deuxieme Bureau;

and a Belgian army officer. This curiously assorted group arranged for Gatewood to be taken to Paris, where he was lodged in a flat near Les Invalides in the charge of a young textile engineer from Lyons, named George. In Paris, Gatewood also met a man described as Arthur, or Le Chef. A series of discussions followed in which it was proposed that Gatewood should be smuggled out to Spain and should take with him certain documents for transmission to the American authorities. These included a codebook to be used in communications between the Americans and the resistance group who, it was implied, were already in contact with each other. Gatewood was also to carry a private letter from the Belgian officer to his brother-in-law in England. It was impressed upon him that these papers were to be handed to the American authorities only and not to the British, for whom all the members of the group expressed great dislike and distrust.

"Gatewood accepted these proposals. Shortly thereafter he set out by car from Paris, accompanied by an individual named Jean, the latter's girlfriend, Pat, and a third person who went under the name of George. We are able to identify these three persons. Jean was a disreputable Frenchman, Jean Varon (alias Hans Mussig), who was at that time employed by the Germans as a penetration agent; Pat was his mistress; and George was a minor Gestapo official from Sonderkommando Pannwitz named Rolf Werner Richter. Thus accompanied, Gatewood was conveyed to the Spanish frontier in circumstances which would have suggested to a more perspicacious man that he was not in the hands of a simple resistance group. From the village of Port Rameau on the French side of the frontier he established contact with the U.S. Consul in Barcelona and was conveyed across into Spain.

"We must assume from Gatewood's story that by June 1944 the Sokol group had been very fully penetrated. Whether its members were aware of this, and how many of those whom Gatewood saw were acting in good faith, must remain more doubtful. Gatewood's escape was clearly known to, and facilitated by, the Germans, presumably with the object of securing contact with other Allied-run resistance groups and thus widening their sphere of penetration. Why, in this case, Gatewood should have been warned against the British authorities is less clear, unless it was merely an oblique form of flattery. The incident of the letter is also curious. It does not appear ever to have been delivered, and we do not know the contents. The addressee has, however, been identified as M. J.

Fitzgerald, the present assistant secretary of the Chelsea Royal Hospital. He has confirmed that his brother-in-law, who could claim either French or Belgian nationality, was the principal figure in a small resistance group which was later rounded up by the Germans. His brother-in-law was arrested and finally shot in Buchenwald in July 1944. Mr. Fitzgerald was able to provide the address of his nephew, Marcel Droubaix, who was also active in the group, but who survived and is now resident in Paris.

"The Gatewood story represents almost our last information about Sonderkommando Pannwitz. The unit continued to operate until almost the end of the war; but its activities became increasingly nominal. Almost certainly the Russians had realized by the end of 1943, if not before, what was the real state of affairs, and it is probable that the Germans were aware of this. It is said that in the latter stages Pannwitz kept Kent's transmitter going—although he knew that it was already a critical stage in the war—as a channel of communication between Russia and the Nazi authorities. He is said to have been a convinced believer, as were many other RSHA officials, in the necessity for a compromise agreement with Russia. In August 1944 the Sonderkommando withdrew from Paris. It retired by stages, first to Tannenkirch in Alsace, then to Hornberg in the Black Forest, and finally to Bregenz am Bodensee, where it was reported at the end of April 1945. . . ."

In the above report it appears that "Sokol's organization" should read "Ozols' organization." The "French general" is undoubtedly Paul Legendre. Mussig's mistress, "Pat," is Georgette Savin, nee Dubois.

The codebook mentioned in the OSS report was handed to the U.S. Consul in Barcelona for onward transmission to OSS. In August 1944 the codebook was passed by OSS to the British-led SOE (Special Operations Executive), which returned it as of no interest.

David Dallin mentions the Mithridate organization in his book, *Soviet Espionage*. He states:

> It is not certain just when Ozols and Legendre were enlightened about the real meaning of their performance, but in 1943-44 Ozols was working directly for the Kommando, and Legendre was collaborating with "Hotel Lutetia" [the headquarters of the Abwehr in Paris]. Their connections with the resistance were the

main assets of this group. The German police who were receiving information from the group did not arrest all the underground militants; instead they recruited its agents for their own work and even controlled a number of radios of the resistance group. It is paradoxical that when Allied troops invaded the Continent some French resistance radio stations working from behind the Allied lines communicated with German headquarters.

The Ozols-Legendre network, wrote Colonel Wedel of German counterintelligence, was "controlled by the RSHA (headquarters of the Himmler police) and served to keep Moscow confident. In this way we succeeded in penetrating further into the organizations of the French Communist Party and learning more about the kind of messages in which Moscow was most interested.

XIV. Jean Claude Spaak

After Trepper escaped from the Germans, he asked Jean Claude Spaak to try to get a message through to the Soviet Military Attache in London. Sending this message to London implies that someone in England had the means of producing a safe and resourceful contact in France, despite the extensive German penetration of the Trepper and Robinson organizations. It is conceivable that such a contact might have been arranged or pre-arranged under French resistance cover, since there are indications, as far back as 1941, that Robinson had access to French resistance communications with England. The same facilities may have existed in the opposite direction.

The following extract concerning the preparations made by Trepper for his escape and his activities thereafter is based on a statement made by Claude Spaak to the Belgians during an interrogation in 1946:

"The Sokols were neighbors of Claude Spaak. At the end of 1941, or the beginning of 1942, in the course of a conversation with Spaak, they indicated that they were involved in some clandestine activities and asked Spaak to hold a sum of a hundred and fifty thousand French francs and some identity papers for them. They told Spaak that, in case they would not be able to retrieve the money and papers themselves, he was to give them to a person who would give his name as 'Henri.'

"About a month after the visit from the Sokols, Spaak, who had had no further news about the Sokols, was visited by a man who called himself 'Henri.' This man was Trepper. He told Spaak that the Sokols had been arrested by the Germans while in the act of transmitting, and he asked Spaak to continue holding the money they had left with him.

"In September 1943 Spaak, who had not heard from Trepper since his visit in 1942, was approached by Georgie de Winter, who asked Spaak for money on 'Henri's' behalf. Spaak told her to have 'Henri' come for the money himself. When she explained that it would be impossible for 'Henri' to travel, though he was in the vicinity of Paris, Spaak accompanied de Winter to see Trepper.

"According to Spaak, Trepper admitted to him that he was one of two chiefs of Soviet intelligence in Western Europe. He said he directed the networks in France, while the other operated in London, and they had both assumed their functions before the war.

"Trepper told Spaak he had been in business in Belgium, but that the business had served merely as a cover for his clandestine activities. He explained that he had to leave Brussels when the area became too hot, and he fled to Paris, where he resumed his espionage activities. The Sokols were his agents, and acted as liaison by W/T with London.

"During 1942 one of his agents had been captured by the Germans and had talked. As a result, Trepper was arrested while in his dentist's office in Paris, and forced to work under their control.

"Immediately after his escape, he went to the home of his mistress. Trepper left almost at once to take refuge in Suresnes, which is where de Winter escorted Spaak.

"After telling all this to Spaak, Trepper asked him for his cooperation on several matters. First, he wanted some of the money and identification papers that had been left in his safekeeping. Then, he wanted Spaak to place him in contact with the Communist Party in France, so that he could send a message to Moscow via this channel. Finally, he wanted Spaak to see that the following message reached the Soviet Military Attache in London: 'I will be at the church every Sunday morning between 10 and 11 a.m. Signed "Martik."'

"Spaak gave Trepper some money and one of the identity

cards, properly falsified. During the next few weeks he tried to handle the last two requests made by Trepper. Spaak contacted the French Communist Party, but they were skeptical about Spaak's request.

"By the end of September, 1943, Trepper sensed danger in Suresnes, and went to Spaak's home with de Winter. Spaak hid them for one night. The following day, Trepper and de Winter left for Bourg La Reine, where Spaak knew a woman who arranged to hide Jewish children. This woman was in contact with the owners of a boarding house, where she placed Trepper and de Winter. Trepper, being a very active person, wanted to resume his clandestine work, while his mistress, on the other hand, wanted him to stop this dangerous activity. In order not to be hindered in his work by his mistress, Trepper asked Spaak to get her through to the formerly nonoccupied zone.

"Spaak recalled that a woman of his acquaintance had a link with a certain doctor who lived at St. Pierre de Chartreuse and who knew of a safe address. He got this woman to write a letter of instruction to the doctor. The note was sent with de Winter. Enroute, she was arrested by the Germans, who found this letter on her.

"During this time Trepper used a woman, named Botsais, as intermediary between himself and Spaak. Trepper went regularly, every Sunday, to the Church d'Auteuil, where he hoped to meet the contact sent by the Military Attache in London. He did not know yet that the printer, who had been carrying his message to the Military Attache, had been arrested by the Germans. When he decided that he could no longer risk going to the rendezvous himself, Trepper sent Botsais in his place.

"On Sunday, 17 October 1943, when Botsais failed to return from the rendezvous, Trepper went to Spaak's house, from where he telephoned the boarding house where he was staying. He learned that the Gestapo had been there and was on his traces.

"From this time on, Spaak was also in danger. Trepper advised him to flee immediately but to leave word with the woman at Bourg La Reine as to where he would be. Spaak did that.

"On Tuesday, 19 October 1943, Spaak sent his wife and their two children to Belgium, to stay with his parents. He remained in Paris. That day he met with some delegates from the French Communist Party, at 1030 hours, at the Church de la Trinite, in Paris. The meeting itself took place on the outskirts of Paris.

"Spaak saw Trepper for the last time before the liberation on

Thursday, 21 October 1943, and told him the result of his meeting with the delegates of the French Communist Party.

"On Saturday, 23 October 1943, Spaak telephoned to his home and spoke to his housekeeper. He had arranged with her that, in case the Germans should be in his apartment, she was to answer the phone with, 'Bonjour, Monsieur,' and, if they were not there, she was to say, 'Bonjour, Monsieur Spaak,' at the beginning of the conversation. It so happened that, at the moment he called, the Germans were in the apartment. The housekeeper spoke the agreed phrase and, during the conversation, gave Spaak to understand that the Germans were there, physically, in his apartment, and had been for the past week. That day, the Germans arrested Spaak's brother and sister-in-law.

"On Monday, 25 October 1943, Spaak sent a message to his wife in Belgium to inform her of his whereabouts. Then he returned to Paris, where he hid out at the home of some friends, until the end of the war.

"In November, 1944, Spaak saw Trepper again. At this meeting, Trepper told Spaak he had just come back to Moscow, where he had gone immediately after the liberation. Trepper saw Spaak several times during November and December, 1944, and, for the last time, in December. As he bid him farewell, Trepper admonished Spaak to keep silent about the affair in which he had become mixed up, and to take care of de Winter's requests for money until the money left with Spaak by the Sokols was all used.

"Since the end of December, 1944, Spaak had not seen or spoken to Trepper. Spaak presumed Trepper had gone to Moscow."

There are three Spaak brothers: Charles Spaak is the well-known cinema personality who has lived most of his life in France; Paul Henri Spaak is the former Prime Minister of Belgium and Secretary General of NATO; Jean Claude Spaak, the writer, is the one who played an important part in the Rote Kapelle. Suzanne Spaak, the first wife of Jean Claude, was executed by the Gestapo.

On 23 October 1943 Jean Claude's brother, Charles, was arrested. Jean Claude Spaak and Ruth Peters escaped and hid independently. Jean Claude's wife, Suzanne, was arrested in the Ardennes and interned in Fresnes Prison until her execution on 12 July 1944. Trepper had given Jean Claude Spaak one hundred and fifty thousand francs for Georgie de Winter's use, and he handed this out to Georgie, who drew on it after her release from prison until it was exhausted in 1946.

Jean Claude Spaak's last known home address was 11 rue de Beaujolais, Paris.

The British study of the Rote Kapelle places emphasis on Claude Spaak as Trepper's assistant:

> The confidence which Trepper reposed in Spaak
> suggests that he was a well-known and well-
> tried friend of the USSR, if not of the GRU.

Ruth Peters, who lived with Spaak and assisted him in his work for Trepper, became Spaak's second wife early in 1946.

Concerning Suzanne Spaak, Pannwitz has commented as follows:

"In spite of her involvement with Trepper, Mme. Spaak was a very likeable woman who made an unforgettable impression. She was a serious, calm woman who looked at everyone with her large, protruding eyes in a composed fashion. Obviously she had followed her parlor-pink sympathies. She regarded all of her actions as an intellectual game and could never bring herself to sacrifice her comfortable living to become an effective and active worker for any cause. She was above all an artist with very modern taste in painting, which the pictures, painted by her and hung in her apartment, indicated. Although we felt a great pity for her, she was too deeply involved for us to help her. She and Mme. May were brought to court with the others and sentenced to death. Mme. May actually received two death sentences, one for aiding the enemy and the other for concealing weapons. An order existed at that time that Hitler must review every death sentence passed by the courts against foreign women. He changed Mme. May's into ten years in prison, but let the death sentence remain for Mme. Spaak. It was evident to us that his action resulted from the fact that Paul Henri Spaak was leader of the Belgian Government in exile in London. I personally petitioned Berlin to have the sentence commuted on the grounds that Mme. Spaak was needed in the search for her husband, the brother of the Minister President. My petition was immediately approved. I proposed to Berlin that Mme. Spaak be asked to assist in the search for her husband with the promise that the death sentence would never be carried out if her husband was found and both of them remained in prison for the remainder of the war. Berlin agreed clearly and unequivocally to this proposal. Mme. Spaak was in the military prison of Paris, Fresnes, in which the security police kept all their prisoners, but which was administered by the military authorities. The only exception to the rule were the 'noble prisoners,' security police prisoners who were housed in Boemelburg's villa and those prisoners, Kent, Barcza, and Lyon-Smith, housed in my villa. I proposed to Mme. Spaak that she send her husband a letter through her children in which she outline the German offer. She had asked the prison officials prior to writing the letter whether we would and could keep our word. The officials arranged for her to talk with me once more. I once more wrote Berlin, asking for reassurance and emphasizing that in this case I had to keep my word. I received a firm, positive answer that the promise would be kept. After the second assurance, Mme. Spaak wrote the letter as instructed and enclosed two small dolls which she had made out of her own hair for her children. The children, who were living with their grandmother in Brussels, received the letter. The father must have learned of the contents of the letter but he had not appeared as of the time we withdrew from Paris. At the time of the German withdrawal from Paris the transportation of the Paris-Fresnes prisoners was handled by the military prison administration. I knew positively that the commutation of the death sentence into a prison sentence in Mme. Spaak's case was never revoked. I had always believed that she was taken to a prison in Germany. This belief was supported by the fact that toward the end of the war, in April 1945, I received a radio message from Kriminaldirektor (Horst) Kopkow of the RSHA, while I was in Heiligenberg on Lake Constance, asking my opinion of an exchange of Mme. Spaak for German prisoners. Inasmuch as I had no particular opinions, I did not express myself one way or the other, but from this letter I had always assumed that Mme. Spaak had been exchanged before the end of the war. I was confronted in Moscow with the accusation that Mme. Spaak had been executed while still in Paris-Fresnes. I simply did not believe this. Since I returned from the Soviet Union, however, I have heard that she was reportedly executed. If that is a fact, a horrible mistake occurred somewhere, because as far as my Kommando and the Security Police were concerned, the change of death sentence to prison sentence had never been reversed. The responsibility can only lie with the administrative offices of the prison where the commuted death sentence may have been overlooked in the files. It was neither possible for, nor the responsibility of, my Kommando to supervise the prison transport from Paris during the final hectic days of the withdrawal.

It is most regrettable that all of our efforts to save this woman's life were in vain because of a stupid and horrible administrative mistake.''

When Pannwitz was interrogated in Moscow, the KGB was very interested in the case of Suzanne Spaak. Pannwitz states:

"In order to discredit me as a serious witness against him, Trepper had told them that shortly before the German retreat from Paris I had appeared in uniform in the company of several other people at the cemetery near Fresnes Prison. He alleged that I had introduced myself to the cemetery caretaker by true name, ordered him to dig a grave, shot Mrs. Spaak in the caretaker's presence, and then ordered him to close the grave. The Soviet interrogator tried unsuccessfully for nine months to get me to sign a statement confessing my responsibility for Mrs. Spaak's death. During these interrogations I learned that Mrs. Spaak had been carried in the Soviet agent card files under the cover name of 'Intelligentka,' and had once been a valuable and long-time agent. This came out repeatedly, and I am convinced it is true.''

The case of Suzanne Spaak was extremely poignant. While awaiting execution Suzanne knitted a necktie for her son, using two toothpicks as knitting needles. The Germans suspected she had somehow hidden a coded message in the necktie and refused to deliver it.

XV. The Return to Moscow

In January 1945 Trepper, Alexander Rado, and Alexander Foote, travelling under aliases, left Paris for Moscow by plane. All the passengers were supposedly Russian PW's who were being repatriated to the USSR, and all held Russian repatriation certificates which had been furnished by the recently established Soviet Repatriation Mission.

Sukolov left Paris with Heinz Pannwitz of the Sonderkommando on 16 August 1944. They continued the playback from various locations until May 1945. They were captured by a French military force in a mountain hut near Bludenz, Vorarlberg, Austria, on 3 May 1945. Sukolov declared that he was an RIS officer in the Red Army and that Pannwitz was in the German underground. As proof he showed to the French cables from the Center in Moscow.

Pannwitz and Sukolov were taken to Paris for interrogation. On

7 June 1945 they were flown to Moscow. Arrangements for the flight were made by Colonel fnu Novikov of the Soviet Military Mission.

CHRONOLOGY OF THE ROTE KAPELLE IN GERMANY

1930	Arvid Harnack, a lecturer in economics at Giessen University, began to organize groups of Communists and left-wing sympathizers. He was assisted by his American-born wife, Mildred, nee Fish, also a convinced Communist.
April 1933	Harro Schulze-Boysen, a young journalist, was arrested and tortured by the SS for his political views and activities and for his association with the leftist publication *Der Gegner*.
1934	Schulze-Boysen, through family connections, was appointed to the News Department of the Air Ministry.
c. 1935	Alexander Erdberg, under the cover of the Soviet Trade Delegation in Berlin, began laying the groundwork for an intelligence network in Germany.
1936	Schulze-Boysen married Libertas Haas-Heye, who came from a prominent German-Swedish family. He organized and led a Communist group in Berlin with the assistance of Libertas, who was deeply implicated in his illegal work.
	Schulze-Boysen, employed at the Air Ministry, passed a report on plans for military operations against Republican Spain to the Soviet Embassy in Berlin. Gisela von Poellnitz, a well-known Communist, acted as the intermediary.
1936 or 1937	Rudolf von Scheliha, a career diplomat in the German Foreign Office, was recruited for Soviet intel-

ligence in Warsaw by the journalist Rudolf Herrnstadt. Von Scheliha used the stenographer Ilse Stoebe as his cut-out to Herrnstadt.

April 1939 — Victor Sukolov, the leader of the Belgian network, traveled to Germany and probably made contact with Alexander Erdberg.

August 1939 — Rudolf Herrnstadt left Poland for Lithuania on the eve of the German invasion, leaving with Ilse Stoebe the responsibility for handling von Scheliha's reports.

September 1939 — Von Scheliha left Warsaw for reassignment at the Foreign Office in Berlin. In Berlin he secured employment for Ilse Stoebe at the Press Office.

late 1940 — Erdberg recruited Arvid Harnack for Soviet intelligence. Erdberg had already been exploiting Harnack as a source of information for several years, possibly since 1935. Harnack was instructed to recruit sub-agents and to develop communications channels.

early 1941 — Harnack introduced Harro Schulze-Boysen to Erdberg. Erdberg recruited Schulze-Boysen. Schulze-Boysen set out to recruit several of his left-wing friends for intelligence duties.

Harnack accepted a position in the German Ministry of Economics as an advisor on foreign exchange, probably at the urging of Alexander Erdberg.

January 1941 — Schulze-Boysen was appointed to the liaison staff of the Luftwaffe Chiefs of Staff.

Spring 1941 — Erdberg gave Hans Coppi a small battery transmitter. A few days later he gave him a more powerful transmitter concealed in a suitcase. Coppi was instructed to establish radio contact with Moscow. The set, however, did not function properly, and satisfactory communications with Moscow were not achieved.

22 June 1941 — The Germans invaded the USSR. The Soviet Em-

bassy and the Trade Delegation were withdrawn. There were no effective communications between Moscow and the Berlin groups.

November 1941 Victor Sukolov made a trip to Germany with instructions to contact Schulze-Boysen, Harnack, and Ilse Stoebe. The purpose of the trip was to restore a communications link between the German groups and Moscow.

Kurt Schulze gave Hans Coppi a new radio set (provided by Sukolov) and trained him as an operator. A courier channel established by Sukolov between Berlin and Brussels began to operate.

May 1942 Two Soviet parachute agents, Erna Eifler and Wilhelm Fellendorf, were dropped in East Prussia with instructions to contact Ilse Stoebe. They could not locate Stoebe and took shelter with Bernhard Baestlein in Hamburg.

5 August 1942 Two more parachute agents, Albert Hoessler and Robert Barth, were dropped near Gemel. Their mission was to go to Berlin and to provide assistance to the Schulze-Boysen group. Hoessler had several meetings with Schulze-Boysen in Berlin.

August 1942 Schulze-Boysen attempted to establish a courier link with Switzerland through Marcel Melliand, a businessman with excellent connections there.

Johann Wenzel, the arrested radio operator of the Belgian network, revealed his codes to the Germans. As a result, they were able to decipher messages they had intercepted earlier. One of these messages contained the name and address of Ilse Stoebe. Another contained the names of Harnack and Schulze-Boysen.

30 August 1942 Schulze-Boysen was arrested in Berlin. A warning from Horst Heilmann, who worked in the Cipher Section of the OKH (Army Chiefs of Staff), had failed to reach him in time. The arrests of the other members of Schulze-Boysen's group and of

Harnack's group followed shortly.

12 September 1942	Ilse Stoebe was arrested by the Gestapo in Berlin. After seven weeks of interrogation, she admitted that she was a Soviet agent.
27 September 1942	Robert Barth established wireless communications with Moscow and passed three messages announcing his arrival and his difficulty in finding quarters.
early October 1942	Albert Hoessler was arrested by the Germans. His radio was used in a playback operation until February 1943.
9 October 1942	Robert Barth was arrested.
20 October 1942	Wilhelm Guddorf, an important member of the Harnack and Schulze-Boysen groups, was arrested. His interrogation led to the arrest of Bernhard Baestlein and of several other Communists in Hamburg.
23 October 1942	Heinrich Koenen (alias Koester), a Soviet agent, was parachuted into Germany from the USSR. After the failure of Erna Eifler to contact Ilse Stoebe and to transmit von Scheliha's report, Koenen was dispatched for this purpose. He was equipped with a W/T set and the verbal recognition signal, "greetings from Rudi" (Rudolf Herrnstadt). He also carried a copy of a receipt for 6,500 dollars signed by von Scheliha in 1938. This was to be used, if necessary, to blackmail von Scheliha. Von Scheliha, fearing for his safety, had become a recalcitrant source.
26 October 1942	At a stakeout of Ilse Stoebe's residence in Berlin, the Germans observed Koenen as he tried to make contact with Stoebe. (A female employee of the Gestapo impersonated Stoebe.) The Germans followed Koenen and arrested him that evening in a cafe.
29 October 1942	Von Scheliha was arrested by the Gestapo at the frontier control point near Konstanz.

late October 1942	Erna Eifler and Wilhelm Fellendorf, probably betrayed by Wilhelm Guddorf, were arrested in Hamburg.
December 1942	At a secret trial in Berlin, Rudolf von Scheliha and Ilse Stoebe were convicted of treason and sentenced to death.
19 December 1942	Thirteen members of the German network of the Rote Kapelle were convicted of treason at a court martial in Berlin. Eleven of them received death sentences. Mildred Harnack was sentenced to six years in prison, and Erika von Brockdorf, to ten years. Hitler confirmed the death sentences but ordered new trials for Mildred Harnack and Erika von Brockdorf.
22 December 1942	Harro and Libertas Schulze-Boysen, Arvid Harnack, Hans Coppi, Kurt Schumacher, Elizabeth Schumacher, Horst Heilmann, Kurt Schulze, Johann Graudenz, Ilse Stoebe, and Rudolf von Scheliha were executed at Ploetzensee Prison in Berlin. In accordance with German law, the eight men were hanged and the three women were beheaded. (*All* future executions were by beheading.)
13 May 1943	Walter Husemann, Karl Behrens, Wilhelm Guddorf, Walter Kuckenmeister, Philippe Schaeffer, Hans-Helmuth Himpel, Erika von Brockdorf, and six other members of the Berlin group were executed.
5 August 1943	Marie Terwiel, Hilde Coppi, Adam Kuckhoff, Oda Schottmueller, Eva Buch, Anna Kraus, Rose Schloesinger, and eight others were executed in Berlin.

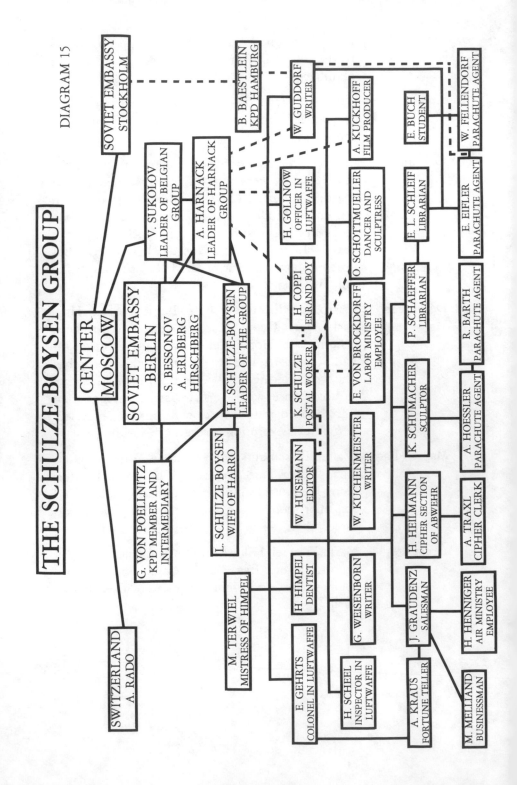

DIAGRAM 15

THE SCHULZE-BOYSEN GROUP

THE HARNACK GROUP

DIAGRAM 16

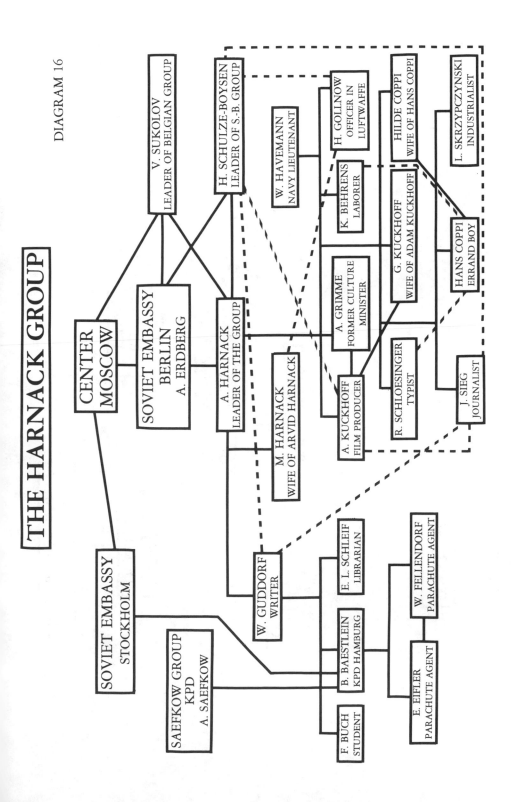

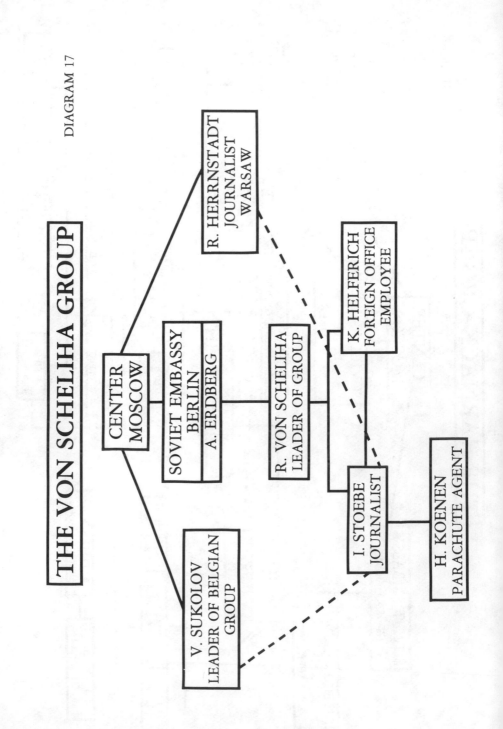

DIAGRAM 17

THE VON SCHELIHA GROUP

CENTER
MOSCOW

R. HERRNSTADT
JOURNALIST
WARSAW

SOVIET EMBASSY
BERLIN
A. ERDBERG

R. VON SCHELIHA
LEADER OF GROUP

K. HELFERICH
FOREIGN OFFICE
EMPLOYEE

V. SUKOLOV
LEADER OF BELGIAN
GROUP

I. STOEBE
JOURNALIST

H. KOENEN
PARACHUTE AGENT

NARRATIVE OF THE ROTE KAPELLE IN GERMANY

I. BACKGROUND

A far-reaching Soviet espionage network was discovered in Germany during World War II. This network was comprised of groups led by Harro Schulze-Boysen, Arvid Harnack, and Rudolf von Scheliha. The separate groups were linked together in Germany and also had occasional contacts with Rote Kapelle agents in other countries, particularly in Belgium and in France. According to Guenther Weisenborn, an author-dramatist who was a member of the Schulze-Boysen group, the Berlin branch of the Rote Kapelle had two hundred eighty-three members. This figure cannot be verified. It may be within reason for the total network, but more of the members of the three nets were engaged in covert anti-Nazi propaganda, not in espionage.

The first two active agents were Rudolf von Scheliha and his accomplice, Ilse Stoebe. They were both recruited in Warsaw by the journalist Rudolf Herrnstadt, the former in 1937 and the latter perhaps a little earlier. The next in succession was Arvid Harnack, recruited in Berlin by Alexander Erdberg of the Soviet Trade Delegation either at the end of 1940 or the beginning of 1941. (Erdberg was an alias. His true identity has not been ascertained.) The last of the major figures to be recruited was Harro Schulze-Boysen. He was introduced by Harnack to Erdberg and formally recruited by the latter early in 1941.

The organization as a whole was thus in three parts: Harnack's group, Schulze-Boysen's group, and the Stoebe-Scheliha group. Of these, the first two were so closely intermingled as to form in effect a single network. The third group, that of von Scheliha, functioned independently of the other two. (It is probable, however, as is confirmed by various interrogation reports, that some contact among all three groups did exist and especially between Stoebe and Schulze-Boysen.)

Stoebe and von Scheliha were active as agents over a period of more than five years. Schulze-Boysen and Harnack had much shorter careers. Their lives as agents did not last much more than a year, from a little before June 1941 until the end of August 1942. Although Schulze-Boysen and Harnack were both ardent Communists before 1941, they were not at that time *recruited* Soviet agents and had no effective link with Moscow. Their political activities against the Third Reich from 1933 to 1941 were therefore not carried out as part of the Rote Kapelle organization. Like numerous groups in other parts of the world, however, the undercover political factions led by Harnack and Schulze-Boysen later developed into espionage networks.

II. THE SCHULZE-BOYSEN GROUP

Harro Schulze-Boysen was known to the Gestapo as early as 1933. While he was still a student, he founded a resistance group, the Gegner Organization, with the object of bringing together discontented elements from all parties. His next step was to leave the Jungdeutschen Order for the Schwarze Front and to approach Thomas Mann, Ludwig Renn, Paul Loebe, the former president of the Reichstag, and other emigres. In 1933 Schulze-Boysen spent three months in prison because of his political agitation.

After his release from prison, Schulze-Boysen resumed his active opposition to the Nazi state. In Berlin he became the leader of a Communist group composed of artists and workers. He collected Communist propaganda pamphlets and leaflets, which he distributed to sympathizers and later to doctors, professors, and police officials in Berlin. These activities reached their peak at the time of the outbreak of the Russo-German war. Schulze-Boysen's pamphlets were then being sent to members of the Wehrmacht serving at the front.

At the time of the exhibition "Das Soviet Paradies," organized in the Lustgarten in Berlin in 1942, Schulze-Boysen ran a rival poster campaign throughout greater Berlin under the slogan:

> Exhibition: The Nazi Paradise
> War—Hunger—Lies—Gestapo
> How much longer?

The Schulze-Boysen network consisted of people belonging to all classes of German society. His organization grouped together in-

dividuals who for one reason or another were in opposition to the
National Socialist Party. With the help of his wife, Libertas, who
was a friend of Hermann Goering, Schulze-Boysen eventually suc-
ceeded in influencing intellectual circles along Communist lines.
The following persons were the most important members of the
Schulze-Boysen group:

> Erwin Gehrts, a colonel in the Luftwaffe;
> Johannes Graudenz, a salesman;
> Helmuth Himpel, a dentist;
> Gunther Weisenborn, a writer and drama
>   critic for the Berlin Schiller Theater;
> Philip Schaeffer, a librarian;
> Walter Husemann, an editor;
> Walter Kuchenmeister, a writer;
> Kurt Schumacher, a sculptor;
> Hans Coppi, an errand boy;
> Herbert Gollnow, a Luftwaffe officer;
> Horst Heilmann, an employee in the cipher
>   section of the Abwehr;
> Kurt Schulze, a postal worker;
> Adam Kuckhoff, a film producer;
> Wilhelm Guddorf, a writer;
> Erika von Brockdorf, an employee in the
>   Ministry of Labor in Berlin.

These persons were all regular recipients of Schulze-Boysen's pamphlets and read them with great interest. An example of Schulze-
Boysen's skill as a pamphleteer was the political essay he wrote on
Napoleon Bonaparte, which was circulated to a large number of intellectuals, Army officers, and other officials. Schulze-Boysen cited
historical authority to show that the policy on which Napoleon's
campaign in Russia was based and which led to his downfall was exactly parallel to the policy of Hitler and the Nazi Party.

Schulze-Boysen and his wife, Libertas, held at their house frequent evening discussions during which they sought to influence
their guests. Listening to enemy broadcasts was a matter of course.
Libertas was an impulsive woman of great personal ambition. She
was one of her husband's most active agents and exercised considerable influence over his opinions. She was fully aware of his activities
and took part in them as a courier, a writer of seditious pamphlets,
and a recruiter for the group. Whenever her husband was temporarily absent, she acted as his deputy in the organization. After

Schulze-Boysen's arrest, Libertas attempted to conceal or to destroy material evidence. She was also responsible for the warning given to other members of the group in September 1942 when the roundup began. Her warning, however, came too late.

Schulze-Boysen's intelligence-gathering activities began in the year 1936. Then employed at the Air Ministry, he was able to obtain information about the secret plans for military operations to be directed against the Republican government in Spain. With the help of his wife Schulze-Boysen passed a report on this matter to the Russian Embassy in Berlin through Gisela von Poellnitz, who was well known for her Communist activities. As a result of this information, the Republican authorities in Spain shortly afterwards took measures in the neighborhood of Barcelona to counter a projected undertaking by Franco forces.

In 1940, through Heinrich Scheel, an inspector in the Luftwaffe's Meteorological Service, Schulze-Boysen was brought into contact with a Communist discussion group composed of former students of the Scharfenberg-Augbau School in Berlin-Tegel. Hans Coppi was a member of this group. Early in 1941 he was recruited by Schulze-Boysen and became the latter's wireless operator. In the spring of 1941 Alexander Erdberg gave Coppi, with Schulze-Boysen's knowledge, a battery transmitter. This was intended to act as a mobile wireless station through which contact could be maintained with various small boats owned by members of the group. The power and frequency range of the set were limited. The transmitter was finally discovered in the house of a university professor, Dr. Gustav Roloff, where it had been hidden by his son, Helmuth Roloff, the well-known Berlin pianist.

A few days after the first transmitter was handed over, Erdberg, again with Schulze-Boysen's knowledge, gave Coppi a second set. This set was a modern transmitter and receiver concealed in a suitcase. While Coppi was testing this set, however, he plugged it into direct current and blew the transformer and the tubes. Coppi and other technicians tried to put the set into working order, but they were not entirely successful.

After these failures Coppi was put into touch with a certain Kurt Schulze (alias Berg), a Communist official who was then a driver in the postal service. Schulze had previously been a naval wireless operator. Schulze-Boysen arranged this meeting, which took place in November 1941, through Walter Husemann, the former editor of a Communist paper in Mannheim who had spent many years in prison because of his political activities. Schulze trained Coppi as an operator and at the end of 1941 gave him a transmitter and receiver of the most modern type.

In 1927 Kurt Schulze had been officially withdrawn from the Communist Party and transferred to illegal work. In 1928 he visited the radio school in Moscow and was afterwards employed in Berlin as an emergency wireless operator. During the next ten years three wireless sets delivered by the Russian Embassy in Berlin passed through his hands. All the Soviet officials with whom he was in contact were members of either the Embassy or the Trade Delegation. He was paid a few thousand marks, and some part of this sum was found when his lodgings were searched.

Using the set supplied to him by Schulze, Coppi made several attempts to establish wireless communications with Moscow. He worked first from his own house, then from that of Oda Schottmueller, and finally from that of Erika von Brockdorf. This last location was used by him at the end of 1941 and the beginning of 1942. Both Schottmueller and von Brockdorf were on intimate terms with Kurt Schulze and willingly placed their houses at Coppi's disposal.

Johannes Graudenz, a salesman, was one of Schulze-Boysen's most valuable informants. In addition, he produced a large number of propaganda leaflets, which he printed on two machines. Early in 1942 Graudenz informed Schulze-Boysen that he knew Marcel Melliand, a businessman who sympathized with their left-wing opinions and who had very good contacts in Switzerland. Schulze-Boysen then asked Graudenz to establish a link with Switzerland through Melliand, and the latter agreed. This link was tried for the first time in August 1942. Schulze-Boysen instructed Graudenz to ask Melliand to make a trip to Switzerland for the purpose of forwarding a report from there to England. This report contained the information that the German Army was in possession of an English radio code, knew that a convoy was assembling in Ireland, and also knew that it would be sailing early in August for the north Russian ports. This information did not in fact ever reach England because Melliand was unable to obtain a permit for the trip.

Graudenz subsequently produced a number of other political, military, and economic reports. He was, among other things, an agent for the firm Blumhardt of Wuppertal, which built aircraft undercarriages, and obtained his information through business and personal contacts with members of the Air Ministry. His most important coup was to obtain the production figures of the Luftwaffe for June and August 1942. He had managed to elicit these in a conversation with Hans Gerhard Henniger, an inspector in the Air Ministry.

Schulze-Boysen consistently tried to find new sources of information among persons holding military or official positions. He was successful in obtaining information from Horst Heilmann, a wireless operator and cadet, and from Herbert Gollnow, a lieutenant in the Luftwaffe. An active member of the Hitler Jugend and later of the Party, Heilmann was employed until the time of his arrest as a decipherer of English, French, and Russian conversations in the Cipher Section of the OKH (Army Chiefs of Staff). He came to know Schulze-Boysen, by whom he was much influenced, while the latter was conducting a class at the Institute of Foreign Affairs in Berlin. Schulze-Boysen took great pains with Heilmann and believed him to be an efficient worker. They collaborated in preparing a document which set out the general political problems of the First World War and made several comparisons to the current war. This document had a strong anti-Nazi bias. Heilmann was fully aware of Schulze-Boysen's illegal activities and offered to supply him with all of the important information which he learned in the course of his work. On the day of Schulze-Boysen's arrest, Heilmann passed to Libertas Schulze-Boysen a wireless message concerning the discovery of the group. His office had deciphered a message which constituted a warning to all the persons involved. Heilmann also managed to recruit a certain Alfred Trexl, employed in the Western Section of the Cipher Office.

Herbert Gollnow also came into touch with Schulze-Boysen through the Institute of Foreign Affairs in Berlin, where he was studying. Under the guise of assisting Gollnow in his work, Schulze-Boysen was able to exercise a political influence over him and to convert him to Communism, although he had previously been a Nazi. Gollnow was also in close contact with the Harnacks and had intimate relations with Mildred Harnack. Through his gross carelessness Gollnow gave away to the Harnacks a good part of the secrets of the Abwehr, which found their way into the Schulze-Boysen wireless messages sent to Moscow via Brussels. Later Gollnow became a witting source.

Schulze-Boysen was also a close friend of Colonel Erwin Gehrts of the Air Ministry. They had both taken part over a period of years in Communist discussion groups which had the goal of preparing the ground politically for a new Germany. Schulze-Boysen gave

Gehrts pamphlets which he had prepared and kept him informed of interesting events in the department of the Air Ministry where he worked. In return he received from Gehrts all the information which the latter received officially in his capacity as a staff officer. Schulze-Boysen used part of this information in his own reports and passed a part to Harnack. Gehrts, a member of the Confessional Movement, leaned toward metaphysics and the occult. So superstitious was he that he even resorted to Anna Kraus, a fortune teller, for advice on official matters and allowed himself to be influenced by her. Anna Kraus was later arrested. She also cast horoscopes for many of the other persons in the group, including Johannes Graudenz, whom she told that he would have a political role to play in the future. In trance-like states Anna Kraus described the political structure of the Reich after the collapse of the Nazi regime. She was fully informed about the activities of Schulze-Boysen and his group and frequently received pamphlets from them. She exercised a hypnotic influence on many of the officials involved in the Berlin group and greatly strengthened their attitude of opposition to the State.

The Schulze-Boysen group was having extreme difficulty in establishing a direct wireless link between Berlin and Moscow. Moscow therefore decided in August 1942 to send to Germany parachute agents who had received special training at schools in Moscow and the Urals. Their mission was to intensify the work which was being done and to establish a direct wireless link. On 5 August 1942 two persons were dropped from a Soviet long-distance bomber in the vicinity of Gemel: Albert Hoessler and Robert Barth, who both wore the uniforms of non-commissioned officers in the German artillery. The former was a Communist official who used the aliases Franz, Helmuth Wiegner, and Walter Stein. Barth, who had previously worked on the Communist newspaper *Rote Fahne* in Berlin, used the aliases Beck and Walter Kersten. After their landing these two travelled to Berlin, where they were to take up their work. Both Hoessler and Barth had been recruited by Alexander Erdberg.

Hoessler emigrated from Germany to Czechoslovakia in 1933. He later worked as a Communist official in Belgium and Holland; and in 1937 he fought in Spain on the Republican side. After the war he went to the Soviet Union. There, after thorough training in politics, intelligence, radio, parachute jumping, and sabotage, he was selected for work in the Rote Kapelle organization in Berlin. A few days after his arrival in Berlin, Hoessler made contact with one of Schulze-Boysen's closest associates, the sculptor Kurt Schumacher, and his wife. Schumacher gave Hoessler every assistance, sheltered him in his house at Tempelhof, and put him in touch with Schulze-Boysen. Recognizing Hoessler's importance, Schulze-Boysen had a number of meetings with him, including one in a Berlin army barracks, and introduced him to the W/T operator Coppi. From that time until their arrest Hoessler and Coppi attempted to establish a wireless link with Moscow. They operated from the houses of various Communists in Berlin and especially from the studio of Erika von Brockdorf. Satisfactory communications with Moscow, however, were never established.

The second agent, Robert Barth, was arrested in Berlin on 9 October 1942. During the war he had served as a soldier at the front and had been wounded and decorated. Later he was taken prisoner while fighting on the Eastern Front. He declared himself as an ex-employee of the *Rote Fahne* and was eventually, after long training, dispatched to Germany as a parachute agent. His mission was to recruit further agents in Berlin and to report on the economic and political situation in Germany. He was to remain in close touch with Hoessler. By 27 September 1942 Barth had already established wireless communication with Moscow and had passed three messages announcing his arrival and his difficulty in finding quarters. Hoessler and Barth had several meetings in Berlin, at which they exchanged experiences in the matter of finding quarters and living under cover.

III. The Harnack Group

Dr. Arvid Harnack was the son of Otto Harnack, a professor at Darmstadt who committed suicide in 1941 while of unsound mind. Arvid Harnack had been interested in socialism for many years and finally drifted to the Communist Party. His progress in this direction was accelerated by his friendship with various members of the Soviet Embassy in Berlin and the Soviet Trade Delegation. Harnack's contacts with the Soviet Embassy were systematically exploited for intelligence purposes. His principal Soviet friends during this period were Sergei Bessonov, a counselor at the Embassy, fnu Hirschberg, one of the secretaries, and two other members of the Embassy staff. In addition, the undercover member of the Soviet Trade Delegation who used the name Alexander Erdberg exercised great influence on Harnack until the outbreak of the Russo-German war and was able to persuade him to act for the Soviets as an intelligence agent.

Alexander Erdberg had been in Germany for several years prior to the outbreak of the Russo-German war, possibly since 1935. At some point he was directed to take charge of the German agent networks, probably as a replacement for Bessonov, who became a victim of the Stalinist purges. Bessonov disappeared from Berlin in February 1937 under unusual circumstances and was sentenced in 1938 to fifteen years in prison. It is likely that when Sukolov went to Germany in April 1939, he made contact with Erdberg. In October 1941 Moscow instructed Sukolov to make another trip to Germany and to get in touch with Erdberg. Erdberg recruited agents, gave them the necessary equipment and funds, and arranged for their W/T training. He also sent several agents to Moscow from Germany for training. Among these were the agents who were ultimately returned to Germany by parachute and directed to contact the Schulze-Boysen, Harnack, and von Scheliha groups. Erdberg may have been responsible for arranging monthly payments of one hundred fifty to two hundred fifty marks to owners of safehouses for harboring illegal visitors. These arrangements were made just prior to the withdrawal of the Soviet Embassy from Germany in June 1941.

Through Harnack, Erdberg was able to recruit without difficulty Dr. Adam Kuckhoff, a man of Communist sympathies who had been a friend of Harnack since 1930. In reply to a question about his political intentions, Kuckhoff stated:

> Harnack and I worked for a Communist Germany with a national planned economy. Our view was that such Communist states should be organized everywhere. In order to achieve this objective, Harnack and I set for ourselves the task of converting our friends to Communism.

Shortly before the outbreak of the Russo-German war in June 1941, Erdberg gave Kuckhoff, with Harnack's agreement, a complete wireless transmitter. This set was returned to Erdberg a week later because it could not be put in working order. The handing over and subsequent return of the transmitter took place, like most of the meetings of this group, in an underground railway station under conditions of strict secrecy.

Erdberg gave Dr. Harnack twelve thousand reichsmarks and Dr. Kuckhoff five hundred reichsmarks for the expenses of the group. Harnack distributed the money he received among his agents and acquaintances. Adolf Grimme received two thousand marks; Karl Behrens, five thousand; Leo Skrzipczynski, three thousand; and Rose Schloesinger, one thousand. The balance of the money was used by Harnack himself.

Adolf Grimme had been brought into the group in 1937. He had previously made the acquaintance of Kuckhoff during his period of office as Minister of Culture (1930-1933). Grimme, however, was a strongly religious socialist, and it required a considerable effort to convince him to go over to the side of Communism. Harnack and Kuckhoff finally succeeded, as the latter said, "in uniting Grimme firmly with Communism."

Prior to 1933 Adam Kuckhoff had been an editor of *Tat*. At that time he had been acquainted with Johann Sieg, a member of the Communist Party and formerly a member of the *Rote Fahne* staff. Sieg was brought into the organization in 1940.

Much hard work was done by the group in discussing and disseminating Communist theories. Previously these discussions had been based on material supplied by the individual members from their own resources—for example, from the secret material available to Harnack as a result of his employment in the Ministry of Economics. Johann Sieg now took the initiative and created an illegal newspaper, *Die Innere Front*, the first number of which had a large sale in Berlin. The group also discussed the latest pamphlets distributed by Schulze-Boysen and his fellow workers, as well as various economic essays produced by Harnack. It was the ultimate intention of the group to prepare for the break-up of Nazi Germany, which was expected to occur in 1943, and to organize the immediate creation of a Communist government which could then form an alliance with the Soviet Union.

In the summer of 1942 Sieg recruited another member of the troup, Wilhelm Guddorf, a Communist writer. He was born in 1902, the son of a German professor at the University of Ghent. He had been a member of the Communist Party since 1922 and had worked as the editor of the Communist newspaper, *Rote Fahne*. In 1930 he made a long visit to the Soviet Union. Sentenced in 1934 to three years in prison for treasonable activities, he was sent to a concentration camp where he remained until 1939. As soon as he was released, he resumed his illegal work, despite serious warnings. He later wrote:

The outbreak of war in the autumn of 1939

was the starting point for my renewed political
activity. I had the impression that the agreement with the Soviet Union formed the basis
for fresh Communist work. I began at the same
time to collect material about Russia from the
German press and also from Russian and other
foreign newspapers supplied to me by Schulze-
Boysen. Through Schulze-Boysen I also obtained military information to which he had access
as a Luftwaffe officer . . . We intended to create a Communist government in Germany . . .
We intended to destroy the Third Reich and to
create a Communist government which could
enter into negotiations with the enemy. We
hoped to hasten the end of the war by propaganda. Our view of the general situation was
that the German Front would collapse at the
end of 1943 and that this would be our opportunity.

After Guddorf's arrest on 20 October 1942, he revealed his illegal Communist contacts in Hamburg. As a result of this information, approximately eighty-five arrests were made, mainly in North
Sea dockyards. Through Bernhard Baestlein, a Communist official
in Hamburg, Guddorf had been in contact with two Soviet parachutists who had been dropped into East Prussia in May 1942 and
had taken refuge with sympathizers in Hamburg. Guddorf suggested to Harnack the possibility of establishing a direct wireless link
with Moscow through these agents. Harnack agreed and handed
over to Guddorf a report on German plans for operations in the
Caucasus, which was to be passed to Moscow through the Hamburg
link. (This report never reached its destination because the Gestapo
captured the transmitter before the necessary arrangements could be
made.) It was intended to move the parachute agents from Hamburg to Berlin. Guddorf had already found quarters in Berlin and,
through Harnack and Sieg, had obtained travel permits and ration
cards. This plan failed. Erna Eifler, a former member of the German
Communist Party, and Wilhelm Heinrich Fellendorf, the two agents
involved, were arrested in October 1942.

Harnack's attempt to establish a wireless link with Moscow
through the two parachute agents was in accordance with his agreement with Alexander Erdberg in 1941. Shortly before the outbreak
of the Russo-German war, he had put Erdberg, at the latter's re-

quest, into contact with his friend Schulze-Boysen. Erdberg attached great importance to Schulze-Boysen's work and saw in it the possibility of establishing a permanent wireless link with Moscow. Schulze-Boysen himself was delighted at this idea because it gave him the opportunity at last of doing really active anti-Nazi work.

Until his arrest, Dr. Harnack acted as an intermediary and also enciphered the messages sent to Moscow by wireless. The reports were brought to him by Schulze-Boysen or his wife; and Harnack passed them on to Hans Coppi, the wireless operator of the group. For this purpose he used as an intermediary Karl Behrens. When Behrens was called up by the Army, the typist Rose Schloesinger, whose husband was on the Eastern Front, took his place.

When Harnack's contact with the Soviet Embassy in Germany was disrupted and when he failed to establish a direct W/T link with Moscow, he arranged for his communications to be transmitted through the German Communist Party in Hamburg (Bernhard Baestlein) to the Soviet Embassy in Stockholm. From there they were sent on to Moscow. The subjects of reports sent by this means included the following, among many others:

(1) The existence of an important truck repair works at Iverlo in Finland.

(2) The operational and reserve strength of the Luftwaffe on the Eastern Front.

(3) Luftwaffe dispositions on the Eastern Front.

(4) The plans for troop movements down the Dnieper.

Harnack was consistently urged by Moscow to extend his espionage network. With this goal in mind he tried over a period of many months to bring influence to bear on his nephew, Wolfgang Havemann, an assessor at the Potsdam High Court who later entered the Navy. Havemann was aware of his uncle's activities. After his arrest, he said: "It is now clear to me that I was denounced because of conversations I had with my uncle and leaflets I received from him." There is no doubt that Harnack intended to recruit Havemann as an agent. In a radio message dated 30 August 1941, Harnack gave Havemann's name to the RIS under the code-name of "Italiener."

IV. The von Scheliha Group

On 28 August 1941 a coded wireless message was intercepted by a German shortwave station in Prague. In August of 1942 Johann

Wenzel, the arrested radio operator of the Belgian network, revealed his codes, and the Germans were able to decipher the message they had intercepted the year before. The message instructed the Soviet agent Sukolov in Brussels to seek out a certain Ilse Stoebe (alias Alte) at Wileandstr. 37, Berlin-Charlottenburg, and to ask her to get in touch with the group in Brussels. She was described as an important agent.

Ilse Stoebe was arrested in Berlin on 12 September 1942. After seven weeks of interrogation she admitted that she was a Soviet agent and had regularly given information for money to her friend Rudolf Herrnstadt, a former member of the *Berliner Tageblatt*. Stoebe was Herrnstadt's mistress. (She contracted a venereal disease from him and eventually became a chronic invalid.)

From the beginning of 1940 until August of the same year, and again from early 1942 until July 1942, Ilse Stoebe made contact with the German career diplomat Rudolf von Scheliha. She received from him information of all kinds which she passed to an attache in the Soviet Embassy. She also passed back to von Scheliha instructions given to her by Herrnstadt and made to him a payment of three thousand reichsmarks for work he had done.

Von Scheliha was arrested on 29 October 1942. He admitted that he had been employed as a Soviet agent since 1937 and had been recruited by Herrnstadt in Warsaw. He had then been attached to the German Embassy in Warsaw, where he served from 1930 until 1939. Von Scheliha also admitted that he had consistently sold to Herrnstadt political information obtained from the German Embassy in Warsaw. The extent of the damage done to the Germans by von Scheliha is difficult to assess, but it was undoubtedly grave. He was instructed by Moscow to report on such matters as the German-Polish situation, the outcome of the conversations between the Polish Foreign Minister and the German Ambassador in Warsaw, the adherence of various European states to the Three Power Pact, and the attitude of the Foreign Office towards the threat of an English invasion.

Von Scheliha was exploited as a source in Poland from 1937 until September 1939, when he returned to the Foreign Office in Berlin after the outbreak of war between Germany and Poland. He became chief of the Information Department in the Ministry of Foreign Affairs and attended the daily meetings of the chiefs of departments, where he had access to much important information.

Von Scheliha succeeded in placing Ilse Stoebe with the Press

Section of the Foreign Office, where she had official relations with the *Tass* representative in Berlin. Until June 1941 von Scheliha's intelligence passed through Ilse Stoebe to *Tass* and then to the Soviet Commercial Attache at the Berlin Embassy.

Moscow seems to have thought it unsafe to bring von Scheliha into the Schulze-Boysen or Harnack organizations. Apart from possible danger to the security of von Scheliha's delicate position, it may have been thought that as a purely venal source he would not blend well into the ideological background of the two main German groups.

Von Scheliha visited Switzerland in February, September, and October 1942 to bank part of his espionage income. He is supposed to have been of such great value to the Soviet intelligence services that the Germans calculated he was paid about fifty thousand dollars for his services. The Germans believed that most of this money was consumed by his domestic expenses, but at least some of it found its way into his account in the Swiss bank. Von Scheliha and his family lived far beyond their means in Berlin.

There are records of two payments made for von Scheliha's espionage work. In February 1938 he received six thousand five hundred dollars, which was paid into his account at Julius Baer and Company in Zurich by a check drawn on the Chase National Bank in New York and cleared through the Credit-Institut in Lyons. One other payment is known to have been made to von Scheliha, in February 1941, when Stoebe gave him the three thousand reichsmarks for work he had performed for the Soviet intelligence services.

The extent of Moscow's interest in von Scheliha's work is shown by the employment of a special parachute agent, who was dropped from a Soviet long-distance bomber over Osterode in East Prussia on 23 October 1942. He made his way to Berlin and there attempted to get in touch with Stoebe (previously arrested), and through her with von Scheliha. His instructions were to use his wireless transmitter for the purpose of sending von Scheliha's information to Moscow. This agent was arrested on 26 October 1942. His name was Heinrich Koenen (alias Heinrich Koester), the son of Wilhelm Koenen, a Communist member of the Reichstag and the Landstag. Heinrich Koenen left Germany in 1933 and travelled through Denmark and Sweden to Moscow, where he received training as an agent. His principal mission was to pass on from Berlin all the material collected by von Scheliha and Stoebe, but he also had scheduled meetings on various days of the month with another Soviet agent in Berlin.

These meetings did not take place because the agent concerned was Erna Eifler, the Communist official who had been dropped into Germany by parachute and who had already been arrested by the Gestapo in Hamburg. Shortly after her arrest another parachutist, Wilhelm Fellendorf, was taken into custody. As the result of these two arrests a number of safehouses in Berlin were searched in October 1942, and an organization for preparing false papers was discovered. The owners of the houses were all former Communist officials, some of whom had been giving shelter to illegal workers since 1928. For this work they received through the Soviet Embassy in Berlin payments of from one hundred fifty to two hundred fifty reichsmarks a month. The safehouse keepers were probably recruited and paid by Alexander Erdberg prior to his departure from Berlin.

V. THE ROLE OF VICTOR SUKOLOV

On 28 August 1941 Victor Sukolov in Brussels received information by radio from Moscow to contact Ilse Stoebe at an address in Berlin-Charlottenberg. Sukolov was prevented from making the trip immediately, however, because of the pressures of running his own espionage network in Belgium.

On 18 October 1941 Sukolov received another message concerning the proposed trip to Germany. His particular task was to reestablish between Germany and Moscow the link which had been severed by the outbreak of war. For this purpose he was given detailed instructions and the names and addresses of persons whom he was to contact in Germany. A summary of the actual wireless message follows:

Moscow to Kent (Victor Sukolov) 18.10.41

Instructions for Kent's trip to Germany:

1. To search out in Berlin Adam Kuckhoff or his wife Greta with the help of Alexander Erdberg.

2. To make contact with Arvid (Harnack) and Choro (Schulze-Boysen) through Kuckhoff.

3. To arrange meetings with the ''friends'' of the Arvid group, namely Italiener (Wolfgang Havemann), Strahlmann (Hans Coppi), Leo (Leo Skrzipczynski), and Karl (Karl Behrens).

4. To request the dispatch of a man to the Soviet Trade Delegation in Istanbul and of another to the Soviet Consulate in Stockholm.

5. To make preparations in Berlin for the reception of parachute agents.

6. To take steps to see that the transmitting sets available to the Choro group were repaired and put into use again.

In November 1941 Sukolov made the trip to Germany and later reported to Moscow that his tasks had been successfully completed. Through Adam Kuckhoff he made contact with both Harnack and Schulze-Boysen, to whom he handed over a new transmitter for the use of Hans Coppi. He was also in touch with Kurt Schumacher and his wife and arranged with them for the transmission of reports by post to Brussels. This link enabled Sukolov to receive reports from the German groups and to relay them by wireless to Moscow. At the same time Sukolov handed to Kurt Schulze a cipher to be used for Stoebe's traffic. This circumstance indicates that Stoebe was at least linked closely enough with the Harnack and Schulze-Boysen groups to be sharing their wireless transmitter.

Among the reports produced by the German groups and passed to Moscow by means of Sukolov's transmitter in Brussels were the following:

a. Information about the strength of the Luftwaffe at the outbreak of the Russo-German war.

b. The monthly production figures of the German aircraft industry for June and July 1941.

c. Advance information about the German attack on the Maikop oilfields.

d. Figures on the losses of German parachutists in Crete.

The communications of the German groups and their links with the network in Belgium require a brief summary. During the period before June 1941 all three groups—Schulze-Boysen's, Harnack's, and von Scheliha's—had a channel of communication through the Soviet Embassy or through the Soviet Trade Delegation. Thereafter they had to depend on wireless or courier channels of their own. The first transmitter that was available to Harnack or to Schulze-Boysen and was capable of communicating with Moscow was the set given to Coppi in June 1941. It was damaged shortly afterwards, though, and was never satisfactorily repaired. Some traffic was passed via this transmitter, including Harnack's message of 30 August 1941 relating to Italiener. Until November 1941 this set was the only one directly available to any of the three groups. After November 1941 all three groups used the courier channels to Brussels set up by Victor Sukolov, possibly supplemented to some small degree by the transmitters delivered later by the various parachute agents.

In all, five parachute agents were involved. The first two, Erna Eifler and Wilhelm Fellendorf, arrived in May 1942. They were originally intended to provide communications for the von Scheliha group; but Harnack, having learned of their arrival through his contacts in Hamburg, attempted unsuccessfully to make use of them. The next pair, Albert Hoessler and Robert Barth, arrived in August 1942. Hoessler was intended to reinforce the Schulze-Boysen group and did, in fact, join forces with Hans Coppi, the radio operator. Barth remained in touch with Hoessler but was not otherwise connected with the organization. Finally, in October 1942, Heinrich Koenen arrived with instructions to make contact with Stoebe and von Scheliha. He was arrested within a few days.

Hoessler's radio set was run by the Germans as a playback from 9 October 1942 until 25 February 1943. The sets of Erna Eifler and Heinrich Koenen were also activated and were still operative on 1 November 1943. Although Moscow had been warned that Wenzel's cipher was compromised and must have known the danger in which these German groups stood, it is possible that these playbacks had some initial success.

VI. THE COMMUNIST UNDERGROUND GROUP OF ANTON SAEFKOW

In his book *Germany's Underground* Allen Dulles wrote that, in June 1944, when it became clear that the American and British troops had secured a permanent foothold in France, Klaus Philip Schenk, Count von Stauffenberg, a leader of the twentieth of July group, looked for support from the Communists:

"He proposed that the Communists be taken into the coalition. When he was advised against it for security reasons, he induced his Socialist friends to establish contact with the Communist underground without the consent of the other key conspirators.

"On 22 June, (Julius) Leber and (Adolf) Reichwein, representing the conspiracy, and Anton Saefkow, Franz Jacob, and a third man whose name is not known, representing the Central Committee of the Communist underground, met clandestinely. The Communist ZK, or Central Committee, had only recently been reorganized. Saefkow, a one-time metal worker, had been particularly active in the Ruhr region and was a friend of Ernst Thaelmann, the head of the Communist Party before Hitler came to power. When Saefkow was caught by the Gestapo in Hamburg in 1933, the infamous Terboven, then Gauleiter of the Ruhr region and later of Norway, had him brought to his native Essen, where he was so tortured that there was grave doubt of his recovery. It is a miracle that he survived the ten years of concentration camp life which followed. Some time in 1943 he and Jacob succeeded in escaping and in getting to Berlin. Shortly before that time the Brandenburg leader of the Communist underground had been executed. Saefkow and Jacob immediately assumed leadership.

"At the 22 June meeting the proposal was made that the Beck-Goerdler post-Nazi government would include Communists. Saefkow and Jacob and their unnamed comrade were given the names of some of the leading conspirators. They asked for time to decide, and another meeting was arranged for 4 July at which Stauffenberg was to be present.

"The conference never took place. On 4 July the Gestapo arrested Reichwein, and, the next day, Leber, as well as hundreds of leftists who had relations with the Free Germany Committee. It was clear that the Gestapo had penetrated the Communist underground. Saefkow and Jacob were later executed."

A West German source stated in 1951 that the Saefkow group, "an anti-Hitler resistance organization" in Germany before and during World War II, had *no* connection with Moscow. The Saefkow group, however, was an important Communist underground organization with direct ties to the Rote Kapelle through Bernhard Baestlein, Wilhelm Guddorf, and Henri Robinson. In its ranks were mainly military Communists organized, controlled, and directed by the Third International.

The Saefkow group had many important contacts and maintained cells in at least thirty organizations in Hamburg and other German cities, Sweden, and Switzerland. It was in liaison with Henri Robinson and his group in France and coordinated and supported a vast network of espionage with interlocking connections both inside and outside Germany.

The most important personality in the Saefkow group besides Anton Saefkow ("Kurt"), Bernard Baestlein, and Franz Jacob was Wilhelm Guddorf (alias Paul Braun), who had connections with Baestlein in Hamburg and was a close associate of Arvid Harnack. Guddorf, who was born in Germany in 1902, joined the KPD at the age of twenty. His father was a professor at Ghent University in Belgium. In 1927 and 1928 Wilhelm was an editor and writer for the *Rote Fahne*. In 1930 he left Germany for the USSR, where he remained until 1933. He was arrested in Germany in 1934 and was imprisoned until 1939. During his imprisonment he became acquainted with Bernhard Baestlein and Johann Sieg. After his release he became editor of the weekly *Welt und Abend*. He resumed his illegal Communist activities. Through associations with fellow Communists, especially Baestlein, he became a member of the espionage network. In May 1942 Baestlein informed Guddorf of the arrival of two new agents, Erna Eifler and Wilhelm Fellendorf, who had parachuted into the Hamburg area. The Gestapo arrested Guddorf in the early fall of 1942, but he escaped with the help of Heinz Verleih, whom Guddorf had also met in prison. He was soon reapprehended, however, and his interrogation led to the arrest of Baestlein and, through the latter, Eifler and Fellendorf. Guddorf was executed in 1943. Baestlein's principal function had been to provide a courier service between the Harnack group in Berlin and the Soviet Embassy in Stockholm. Baestlein was executed in 1944.

Wilhelm Heinrich Hermann Fellendorf was born on 8 February 1903 in Hamburg. There he became a truck driver and a functionary of the Red Front Movement. He was engaged in sabotage, the staging of ambushes, and the procurement of arms. He used the aliases Welmuth, Willi Machmarov, and Eduard Heinrich Schramm. His illegal activity forced him to flee to Sweden in 1933. From there he went to Denmark, where he made contact with the Soviet Embassy. He arrived in the USSR in 1938. Later that same year he arrived in Spain, where he became a lieutenant in an armored tank corps. He returned to the USSR after the Civil War ended. The Soviets trained him in sabotage and related subjects. After the Gestapo arrested Fellendorf, he became a double agent for the Germans.

Erna Eifler (alias Kaethe Glanz, Gerda Sommer, "Rosita," and "Biene") was born in Berlin on 31 August 1908. By 1926 she was already an experienced Comintern agent and courier. In 1928 she was working for the Soviet Trade Delegation in Hamburg as a secretary. Sometime after 1928 she went to the USSR. By 1936 she was living in Vienna, and the following year she went to Harbin, China, on an intelligence mission. For this purpose she used the alias of Kaethe Glanz. About 1942 she and Fellendorf were members of the same group of persons trained near Moscow in sabotage, W/T, and parachute jumping. After her arrival in Germany she tried to reach the Harnack or von Scheliha group but was arrested by the Gestapo before she could do so. Like Fellendorf, she became a double agent under German control. She operated a transmitter in a W/T playback operation until March 1945. Her subsequent fate is not known.

The Saefkow group was so well organized and had so many important contacts inside and outside Germany that the members had little trouble in obtaining secret data for transmittal to Moscow. The activities of this group were concentrated largely in two fields:

(1) The establishment of cadres in all businesses of military importance in Berlin.

(2) The dissemination of propaganda to soldiers, both at home and on the front.

Despite the obstacle of strict security measures in the Wehrmacht, the Saefkow group succeeded in establishing sources on both fronts and even in the OKW. These men supplied valuable information and collected addresses of dissident soldiers, who then received letters containing political indoctrination from the group. Propaganda for the defection of entire units to the Free Germany Committee played an important role on the Eastern Front.

Considerable time was devoted to making contact with other organized anti-Fascist circles, including Social Democrats and labor groups. Liaison was arranged in 1943 with the Ulrich group, but it proved valueless when that group was arrested a short time later. In 1943 small groups of scientists and artists were being used as sources of information. In the spring of 1944 contact was established with the group of Dr. Leber and Professor Reichwein. The Saefkow group also had excellent connections in the Ministry of Armament and War Production, youth groups, the Luftwaffe Clothing Office, and the post office.

After the main Rote Kapelle apparatus was destroyed by the arrests of the Schulze-Boysen and Harnack groups, the Saefkow group continued its operations. Furthermore, not all the members of the group were liquidated when Saefkow, Baestlein, Jacob, and approximately one hundred others were arrested in 1944. It is probable that the Saefkow group continued to furnish information to Moscow even after its organization and leadership had been decimated.

In a speech by Berlin City Councilman Ottomar Geschke on 22 September 1946 commemorating the deceased members of the various resistance groups, the name of Anton Saefkow led all the rest.

VII. THE ARRESTS AND TRIAL

The Schulze-Boysen group was discovered as a result of German CI action in Belgium. After the Abwehr's D/F equipment located the clandestine W/T transmitter in Brussels and Johann Wenzel was arrested, the Germans were able to read Moscow's messages of 18 October 1941 instructing Sukolov to proceed to Berlin; in the message was the address of Harro Schulze-Boysen. During the search of Wenzel's apartment the Germans also found a message which had not yet been coded. It gave precise information about two thousand five hundred planes of the Luftwaffe at Stalingrad. Reportedly only three people in Berlin knew that the Germans lacked aviation gasoline for these planes, and one of these was Schulze-Boysen.

Investigation disclosed that the Soviet agents had high level contacts in governmental offices in Berlin, Hamburg, Dresden, and elsewhere. The case was considered so important that Goering and Himmler took personal charge of it, and a special group was organized to identify, arrest, and liquidate the Soviet spies in Germany.

The Gestapo's roundup of the organization began in the latter part of August 1942. Schulze-Boysen himself was arrested on 30 August 1942, and the arrests of the other members of his group and of Harnack's group took place in September. Ilse Stoebe was arrested on 12 September, but von Scheliha, the last or almost the last to be taken, was at liberty until 29 October 1942.

There were one hundred eighteen prisoners in the Rote Kapelle case in Berlin. The first to go on trial were Harro and Libertas Schulze-Boysen, Arvid and Mildred Harnack, Hans Coppi, Kurt and Elizabeth Schumacher, Horst Heilmann, Herbert Gollnow, Kurt Schulze, Johann Graudenz, Erwin Gehrts, Erika von Brockdorf.

Libertas Schulze-Boysen behaved badly at the trial. She had reportedly cooperated with the Gestapo and thought she would be acquitted. There was a Gestapo rumor that Libertas seduced a young SS guard the night before she was executed.

All were convicted except Mildred Harnack and Erika von Brockdorf, who got new trials. Hitler refused to commute the sentences. On 22 December 1942, three days after the trial, the first executions took place. The executions of Herbert Gollnow and Colonel Gehrts were postponed so that they could testify at the new trial of Mildred Harnack and Erika von Brockdorf. Ilse Stoebe and Rudolf von Scheliha, who had been convicted at a separate trial, took their place. Official records reflect that the deaths in the Berlin group of the Rote Kapelle consisted of two suicides, eight hangings, forty-one beheadings.

Dr. Manfred Roeder, the presiding officer at the trials, reported that of those condemned in the Schulze-Boysen and Harnack networks of the Rote Kapelle 29 percent were academicians and students; 20 percent were professional soldiers and government officials; 21 percent were artists, writers, and journalists; 17 percent were members of the armed forces; 13 percent were workers or laborers. According to Roeder, German counterintelligence estimated the number of additional losses caused by the Rote Kapelle agents in Germany at two hundred thousand men. Admiral Canaris' estimate was about the same.

Dr. Adolf Grimme, the former Prussian Minister of Culture, wrote an indictment on 15 September 1945 to the British military government in Hanover, accusing Dr. Manfred Roeder of crimes against humanity for ordering the executions of the Rote Kapelle members in Berlin. In addition to Grimme's indictment to the British military government, Guenther Weisenborn and Greta Kuckhoff composed an indictment, dated 1 February 1947, containing similar accusations which they submitted directly to the American military tribunal in Nurnberg. In this indictment Greta Kuckhoff stated:

> I am convinced that a very thorough investigation should be done of Dr. Roeder. Through his ruthless treatment of Dr. Harnack and Schulze-Boysen, one of the most pronounced resistance groups was destroyed. This group had tested the possibility of destroying the Nazi regime with internal measures and had come to the conclusion that only collaboration with democratic and socialistic peoples could successfully destroy the regime. This group was the only resistance group which had an American member (Mildred Harnack), a woman who had the honor of being the president of the American Women's Clubs in Berlin prior to the outbreak of war. Dr. Roeder feared that this group was endangering Nazism, not Germany . . .

The brochure "Widerstand im Dritten Reich" (Resistance in the Third Reich), published by the VVN (Verband der Verfolgten des Nazi Regimes—Association of Persecutees of the Nazi Regime), made the following remarks on the role of the Rote Kapelle in Germany:

> The group increasingly adopted the practice
> of assigning special tasks to certain members.
> Dr. John Rittmeister was to listen to foreign
> broadcasts. Information gleaned by him was
> used in indoctrination courses, leaflets, and in
> the journal *Die Innere Front* (The Internal
> Front). Warfare in the ether played a significant
> role during the last conflict. The Schulze-Boy-
> sen/Harnack resistance group also broadcast to
> the German people in an effort to convince the
> latter of the hopelessness and criminal nature of
> this war. It wanted to prove to the democratical-
> ly-minded people of other nations that the
> voice of freedom, of human dignity, had not
> been silenced among the Germans despite Hit-
> lerian terror and persecution. In this manner
> they fought heroically in the interest of Ger-
> many.

Roeder has commented that there could be no worse distortion of the facts than the above statement.

"Should one suppose that the radio messages were *coded* in an effort to gain the ear of the German people? Was it so heroic and was it so very much in the interest of Germany to relay coded information on tactical and strategic measures to Moscow?"

Ulrich von Hassel, who was executed after the failure of the 20 July 1944 plot to kill Hitler, wrote that the Schulze-Boysen group was "a vast Communist conspiracy":

> In appearance, the fanatics (because of their
> hate of the regime) pretend that their desire
> was to create a substitute organization in the
> eventuality of a Bolshevik victory . . . In the
> salons, in the antechambers of ministers, in the
> corridors of the headquarters, there was talk of
> this abcess, the smell of which was polluting the
> air of the Third Reich. Each professed to know
> it all; what one did not know, one invented.
> The affair became a myth and the suspicions
> knew no bounds.
> The price of secrecy is when it is no longer abso-

lute. Berlin trembled with horror because over there, on the banks of the Volga, at Stalingrad . . . How is it possible not to establish a link of cause and effect between the poison at Berlin and the deadly paralysis that seized the Wehrmacht?

Greta Kuckhoff, one of the Rote Kapelle agents who survived Hitler's executioner, wrote in an article in the *New Times*, November 19, 1966, that when one of the youngest members of their organization, Fraulein Cato Bontjes von Beek, learned that the death sentence had been pronounced against her, she said, "I regret only that I did not do more." Kuckhoff added that the words of von Beek have stayed with her:

They are a command to those of us who have remained alive. Today the German Democratic Republic is the heir of the cause for which the warriors of the common anti-Fascist front fought in the war. We must spare no effort that the entire German nation may grasp history's lesson. Our struggle continues.

In June 1948 the Nurnberg *Telegraf* printed the following item:

In the persecution of the members of the Schulze-Boysen/Harnack resistance group, the then-Judge Advocate, Colonel Manfred Roeder, presently in the Neustadt internment camp, played a particularly evil role. Roeder is to be charged with crimes against humanity. All members of the resistance movement are hereby urged to submit reports on Roeder's actions. Photostats of documents which may support the case against Roeder are also solicited. All material is to be addressed to Attorney Dr. Heinke, Nurnberg, Palace of Justice, Room 355.

In connection with the above, Dr. Roeder later wrote:

I informed Attorney Heinke that I considered this appeal of his as something irregular; he disclaimed any connection with it and explained to me that this appeal had been made by the parents of Horst Heilmann, who were now living in the East Zone.

This shows that there are still others, besides Grimme and Mrs. Kuckhoff, who are today working hard to make themselves appear as martyrs.

In conclusion it should be pointed out that the failure of the Harnack, Schulze-Boysen, and von Scheliha groups was primarily due to inexperience and lack of training on the part of the groups' leaders, to the inefficient and amateurish wireless communications, and to the constant readjustments which were made necessary thereby. The same thing was true of the Belgian network. It was the detection, first of Makarov's transmissions, and then of Wenzel's, which provided the Germans with the essential starting point in their investigations. Wireless communications were without a doubt the most vulnerable point in the Russian organization. Had it not been for this weakness the Rote Kapelle organization might have survived the war successfully.

VIII. POSTSCRIPT

In 1967 the East German Government issued commemorative postage stamps glorifying the heroism of the Rote Kapelle agents who were executed as "traitors" by the Nazis during World War II. The Communist "spies" honored as "heroes" for their anti-Fascist work were Harro Schulze-Boysen (1909-1942), Arvid Harnack (1901-1942), Mildred Harnack (1902-1943), Adam Kuckhoff (1887-1943), Anton Saefkow (1903-1944), Bernard Baestlein (1894-1944), Franz Jacob (1906-1944).

Several close relatives of Harro Schulze-Boysen and his wife are still alive and of intelligence interest. Among them are Hartmut Wolfgang Schulze-Boysen, Ruth Schulze-Boysen, and Johannes Haas-Heye.

Hartmut Wolfgang Schulze-Boysen is the brother of Harro. He was born 21 February 1922. In 1955 he was a counselor at the German Embassy in Washington, D.C. He resided at 6609 Radnor Road, Kensington. In 1961 Hartmut was chief German representative of the Political Commission of the NATO Permanent Council in Paris and assistant to the West German Ambassador to NATO.

The following comment was made about Hartmut Schulze-Boysen by an unidentified American source in 1955:

As far as young (Hartmut) Schulze-Boysen is

> concerned, he was here (Washington) as Second
> Secretary in the Embassy, charged with report-
> ing extreme rightist American political develop-
> ments. Young Schulze-Boysen is the younger
> brother of the famous Schulze-Boysen of the
> Rote Kapelle. He is an extremely bright man
> and a very pleasant person and no doubt is
> slated for a successful career in the German For-
> eign Service. I believe young Schulze-Boysen is
> as politically conscious as his brother was . . .

In 1963 Schulze-Boysen returned to Washington as the press attache. In 1967 he was a counselor and the fourth ranking member at the German Embassy. He returned to Germany in 1970.

Ruth Schulze-Boysen, nee Rudolf, is the wife of Hartmut Schulze-Boysen. She was born 10 September 1923 in Pforzheim. She was in contact with Hanna Liere, nee Schlegel, who was associated with Theodor Fink, a KPD member and a prominent Communist in southern Germany. Hanna Liere was a link to Theodor Fink and Dr. Otto John, whose brother was executed after the 20 July 1944 plot against Hitler.

Johannes Haas-Heye was born 16 March 1912 in Paris. He is the brother of Libertas Schulze-Boysen. In June 1953 he was an editor in the Frankfurt office of the United Press Agency and had been employed there since 1946.

CHRONOLOGY OF THE ROTE DREI
IN SWITZERLAND

1936-37	Maria Josefovna Poliakova headed Soviet military intelligence network in Switzerland.
May 1936	Alexander Rado moved to Geneva from Paris with his wife and family to begin activities in behalf of Soviet intelligence.
August 1936	Rado opened Geopress, a cartographic firm he used as a cover for his intelligence activities.
October 1938	Alexander Foote arrived in Switzerland and began work under Ursula Hamburger's direction.
March 1940	Victor Sukolov, an important figure in the Belgian net, journeyed to Switzerland for a meeting with Rado.
Summer 1940	Hamburger turned over her Swiss net to Rado.
August 1940	Edmond and Olga Hamel were recruited as W/T operators.
October 1940	Rado journeyed to Belgrade for a meeting with a courier sent by Moscow.
20 Dec. 1940	Hamburger left Switzerland for England.
February 1941	Hamburger arrived in England.
March 1941	Edmond Hamel began to transmit to Moscow for the Rote Drei.
May 1941	Rado established contact with Rachel Duebendorfer on instructions from Moscow.
October 1941	Georges Blun was recruited as a member of the Rote Drei.

October 1941	Ernst Lemmer was recruited as a source by Blun; Lemmer was first noted in communications on 22 October 1941.
October 1941	Margaret Bolli was recruited as a W/T operator.
April 1942	Otto Puenter became a source of the Rote Drei according to a message from Dora in July 1942.
April 1942	The Germans sent agents into Switzerland to track down the Rote Drei transmitters.
Summer 1942	Duebendorfer recruited Christian Schneider.
Summer 1942	Rudolf Roessler begins reporting to Duebendorfer via Schneider.
July 1942	Leon Beurton arrived in England to join Hamburger.
September 1942	Bolli moved to Geneva and began to transmit for Rado.
8 October 1942	This first reference to Schneider in a message sent by Rado to the Director describes him as a new source, although he is actually a cut-out.
mid-1943	Bolli began an affair with Hans Peters, a Gestapo agent; it compromised her and other members of the Rote Drei.
July-August 1943	Duebendorfer resists all attempts by the Center to identify Roessler or turn him over to Rado.
8 October 1943	Edmond and Olga Hamel were arrested by the Swiss police.
13 Oct. 1943	Bolli was arrested by the Swiss police.
mid-October 1943	Rado and his wife went "underground" to avoid arrest by the Swiss police.
late October 1943	Through Foote, Rado sent a message to the Director suggesting that he and Jim seek refuge from arrest at the British Embassy; in early November the Director refused.
5 November 1943	Rado received word that he had been awarded the Order of Lenin for his intelligence activities.

5 November 1943	The Director expressed concern about the possibility of Rado's being arrested.
20 November 1943	Foote was arrested and imprisoned by the Swiss police.
May-June 1944	Rudolf Roessler, Schneider, Duebendorfer, and Paul Boettcher were arrested by Swiss police.
July 1944	The Swiss released Edmond and Olga Hamel and also Bolli.
September 1944	The Swiss released Duebendorfer and Schneider.
6 Sept. 1944	Roessler was released by Swiss police.
8 Sept. 1944	Foote was released on bail by the Swiss.
19 Sept. 1944	Rado and his wife arrived in Paris after fleeing Switzerland to avoid arrest.
7 or 9 Nov. 1944	Foote arrived in Paris.
6 January 1945	Foote and Rado left Paris for Moscow via Cairo. Rado disappeared enroute. He sought refuge with the British in Egypt.
14 Jan. 1945	Foote arrived in Moscow.
July 1945	Rado arrived in Moscow.
23 July 1945	Duebendorfer and Boettcher, who escaped from his internment camp, escaped to France to avoid trial by the Swiss; they were sentenced *in absentia*.
1946-1955	Rado was imprisoned by the Soviets.
March 1947	Foote, prepared for a new mission by the Soviets, turns himself in to British authorities in Berlin and declares that he wishes to abandon his career as a Soviet agent.
Summer 1947	Roessler agreed to resume intelligence work, this time for the Czech Intelligence Service.
5 Nov. 1953	Roessler sentenced by a Swiss court to a year and nine months for espionage.
1955	Rado returned to Hungary.
1956	Death of Foote.

1958   Death of Roessler.

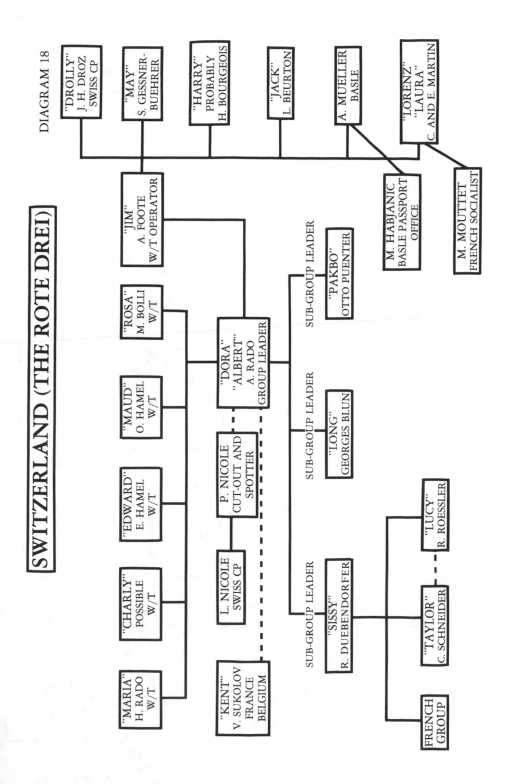

DIAGRAM 18

SWITZERLAND (THE ROTE DREI)

"DROLLY"
J. H. DROZ
SWISS CP

"MAY"
S. GESSNER-
BUEHRER

"HARRY"
PROBABLY
H. BOURGEOIS

"JACK"
L. BEURTON

A. MUELLER
BASLE

"LORENZ"
"LAURA"
C. AND E. MARTIN

"JIM"
A. FOOTE
W/T OPERATOR

M. HABJANIC
BASLE PASSPORT
OFFICE

M. MOUTTET
FRENCH SOCIALIST

"MARIA"
H. RADO
W/T

"CHARLY"
POSSIBLE
W/T

"EDWARD"
E. HAMEL
W/T

"MAUD"
O. HAMEL
W/T

"ROSA"
M. BOLLI
W/T

"DORA"
"ALBERT"
A. RADO
GROUP LEADER

P. NICOLE
CUT-OUT AND
SPOTTER

L. NICOLE
SWISS CP

"KENT"
V. SUKOLOV
FRANCE
BELGIUM

SUB-GROUP LEADER

"PAKBO"
OTTO PUENTER

SUB-GROUP LEADER

"LONG"
GEORGES BLUN

SUB-GROUP LEADER

"SISSY"
R. DUEBENDORFER

"LUCY"
R. ROESSLER

"TAYLOR"
C. SCHNEIDER

FRENCH
GROUP

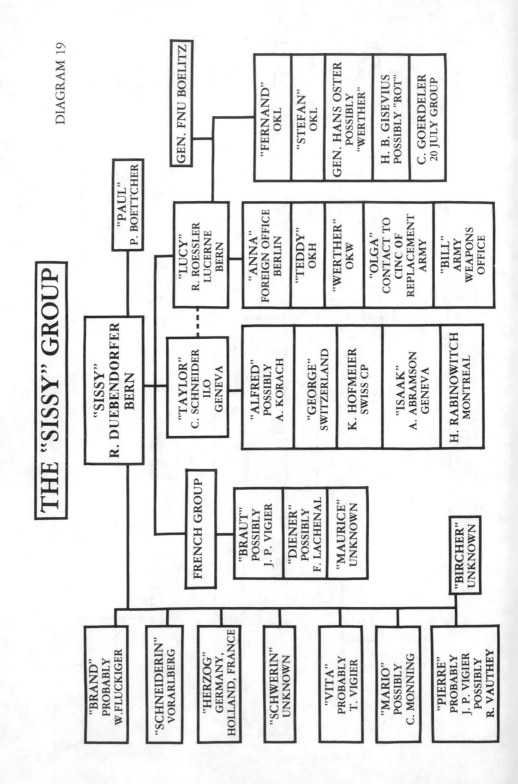

DIAGRAM 19

THE "SISSY" GROUP

DIAGRAM 20

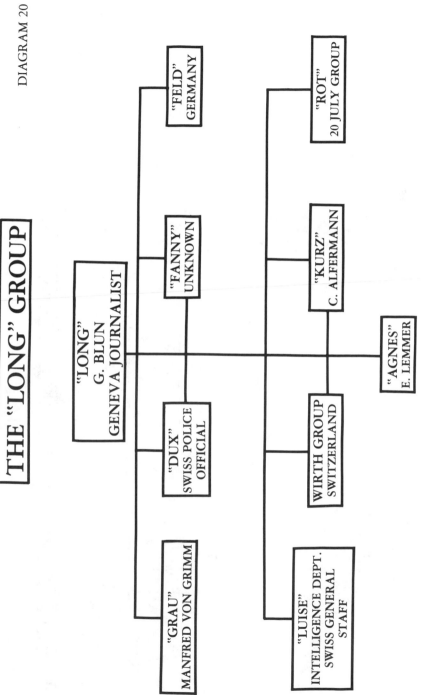

THE "LONG" GROUP

"LONG"
G. BLUN
GENEVA JOURNALIST

"FELD"
GERMANY

"FANNY"
UNKNOWN

"DUX"
SWISS POLICE
OFFICIAL

"GRAU"
MANFRED VON GRIMM

"ROT"
20 JULY GROUP

"KURZ"
C. ALFERMANN

"AGNES"
E. LEMMER

WIRTH GROUP
SWITZERLAND

"LUISE"
INTELLIGENCE DEPT.
SWISS GENERAL
STAFF

DIAGRAM 21

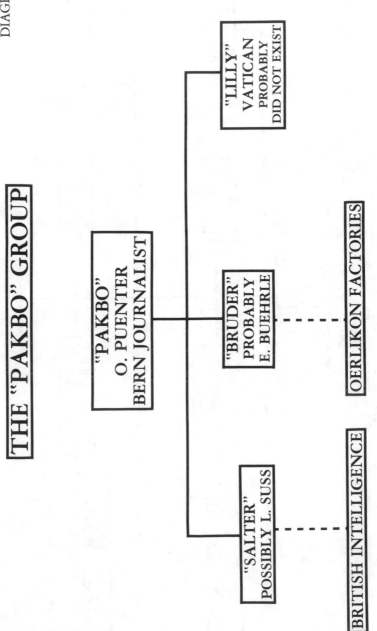

THE "PAKBO" GROUP

"PAKBO"
O. PUENTER
BERN JOURNALIST

"LILLY"
VATICAN
PROBABLY
DID NOT EXIST

"BRUDER"
PROBABLY
E. BUEHRLE

OERLIKON FACTORIES

"SALTER"
POSSIBLY L. SUSS

BRITISH INTELLIGENCE

NARRATIVE OF THE ROTE DREI
IN SWITZERLAND

I. THE RADIO MESSAGES EXAMINED

Any useful, accurate account of the Rote Drei must start with the radio traffic exchanged between the Center in Moscow and the network in Switzerland. The first question is quantitative: How many messages did the traffic contain? Wilhelm F. Flicke, a German cryptanalyst who worked on the traffic during the war, estimated the total at some five thousand five hundred, about five a day for three years. This estimate is not unreasonable. When Edmond and Olga Hamel, two of the Rote Drei radio operators, were arrested by the Swiss police on 9 October 1943, a total of one hundred twenty-nine messages were found in their flat. A comparison of these with those in other holdings has shown that forty appear elsewhere and eighty-nine are unique. The forty matching messages were all transmitted between 3 September and 5 October 1943. If it is assumed that the remaining eighty-nine were also sent to Moscow during the same period, as seems possible, then it can also be surmised that one hundred twenty-nine is the average number of transmissions per month. There have been a number of claims that the Rote Drei network was functioning before the war and that Lucy, as Rudolf Roessler was called, gave Moscow advance warning of Hitler's attack. The traffic proves, however, that Sissy (Rachel Duebendorfer) did not establish a clandestine association with Taylor (Christian Schneider) and Lucy until the late summer of 1942. More reliable information on total volume and time-span of the traffic will be forthcoming.

From various sources we have pulled together four hundred thirty-seven messages that appear authentic. This collection, unfortunately, contains only 8 percent of the presumed total. For this reason we are obliged to be circumspect when drawing from the traffic any quantitative conclusions. What is more important, the riddles resolved by the 8 percent are cause to believe that the remaining mysteries, or most of them, could be solved with the aid of the missing 92 percent.

This account of the Rote Drei is drawn chiefly from the radio messages. Supplementary research in classified files has yielded additional information. Although there are still gaps in our knowledge, we can at least present the first account of the Rote Drei that is not based chiefly on speculation, fantasy, and falsification.

Our collection of messages contains references to fifty-five sources. Most of them, of course, are listed only by a cover name. Of these fifty-five we can identify fifteen with certainty and make educated guesses about sixteen more. The remaining twenty-four appear rarely and inconspicuously. We also know the identities of some persons associated with the Rote Drei who do not appear in the traffic.

Digging out the facts and telling the story would have been decidedly easier if so much misinformation about the subject had not been published in the past. Even the name Rote Drei, a German appellation based on the number of transmitters or operators serving the network, is misleading, because at times there were four and even five.

II. Vera and the Beginnings of the Rote Drei

The story of the Rote Drei begins with Maria Josefovna Poliakova, a highly intelligent Russian Jewess and a dedicated Communist, born about 1910. When she was twenty-one, she was a very active member of the central committee of the Komsomol. She was recruited at that time by the IVth Department of the Soviet General Staff. Her aliases were Mildred, Gisela, and Vera. She was fluent in German, French, and English. Her brother, father, and husband were all executed in Communist purges; yet her devotion to the cause was unshaken.

In 1936-1937 she headed the Soviet military intelligence network in Switzerland. She made a quick trip back in 1941, when she ordered certain changes in the command structure of the Rote Drei. But mostly she spent the war years in Moscow, where she specialized on the Rote Drei operation. (She was not the "Director," however. All of the cables from Moscow to Switzerland were signed "Director," an indicator showing that they came from the Center. It is probable that Poliakova was the originator of many of these; her informal, fervent, Marxian style is distinctive. But this tone is often replaced by that of superiors who are much more authoritative and brusque.) At the end of 1944, when the Swiss operation had ended, Poliakova, then a major, became chief of the GRU's Spanish section. Alexander Foote suggests that she was purged less than two years later.

> The Director and Vera were removed from their posts and replaced in about May 1946. I never saw them again, nor were they ever mentioned. The Center has only one penalty for failure.

III. SONIA

In *Handbook For Spies* (second edition, 1964, Trinity Press, Worcester and London), Alexander Foote recounts that in Switzerland he was first directed by a lady whom he calls Sonia. Her true name was Ursula Maria Hamburger, nee Kuczynski. She was born on 15 May 1907 in Berlin, one of four sisters. She also had a brother, Professor Juergin Kuczynski, who introduced Klaus Fuchs to Soviet intelligence officers. Ursula and Rudolf Hamburger were Red Army espionage agents in Shanghai in 1930-1935. She went to Switzerland in the latter 1930s, travelling alone because her husband had been ordered to stay in China. In 1939 her position was jeopardized by the arrest of Franz Obermanns, a German Communist with false Finnish documents and a transmitter. On 23 February 1940 she married Leon Charles Beurton, an Englishman whom Foote called "Bill Philips." Beurton, a veteran of the Spanish Civil War, was recruited for Soviet espionage by Brigette Lewis, who turned him over to her sister Ursula on 13 February 1939. Ursula Hamburger trained both Beurton and Foote in W/T. The marriage to Beurton gave Ursula British citizenship, and she left Switzerland for England in December 1940. Her husband remained in Switzerland, where he trained Edmond Hamel in operating a W/T set. In July 1942, provided with a British passport in the name of Miller and the blessings of the Red Army staff, Beurton went via Portugal to England and his Ursula. In 1947 the Beurtons left England hurriedly for East Berlin.

IV. SISSY AND PAUL

A third person of importance in the swaddling days of the Rote Drei (or four or five) was also a woman. Rachel Duebendorfer was born on 18 July 1901 in Danzig. She became an active Soviet agent in 1920. Soon thereafter she married one Curt Caspari, and on 8 July 1922 she gave birth to a daughter, Tamara, who eventually married a Frenchman and who helped her mother with the housework, as did her husband, by serving as a Rote Drei courier. In the late 1930s Rachel contracted a marriage of convenience with a Swiss citizen named Duebendorfer. She took up residence in Bern, where she lived as the common-law wife of a German Communist named Paul Boettcher (alias Paul, alias Hans Saalbach). Boettcher was born on 2 May 1891 in Leipzig. Before fleeing Germany he had been a member of the Central Committee of the Communist Party, Minister of Finance in Leipzig, and editor-in-chief of the *Arbeiterzeitung* in Leipzig. Escaping to Switzerland from Germany after the Nazis came to power, he was twice expelled from Swiss territory, in 1941 and 1944, but managed to survive. Sissy not only took him into her flat but also gave him the papers of her Swiss husband whose identity Boettcher assumed. Boettcher, Duebendorfer, Tamara Vigier (nee Caspari), Roessler, and Christian Schneider were all arrested in May 1944. Neither Sissy nor Paul was present in the courtroom on October 22-23, 1945, when a Swiss military court sentenced each to two years. Both had escaped to France in July of that year. Boettcher went back to Saxony and in 1947 became editor of the *Leipziger Volkszeitung*. For a time he was a professor of Russian in Halle. By 1958 he was again an editor in Leipzig. Sissy's fate is not known.

In our collection of W/T messages, Sissy appears twenty-eight times between 8 October 1942 and 28 November 1943. These are the highlights:

8 October 1942
    Director to Dora (Alexander Rado) for Sissy:

> You must learn a code and receive additional instruction . . . Your new people Marius and Taylor are not bad workers, but one must always control them and keep them busy.

Two characteristics of this message are interesting. The first is that Sissy is the only one of Rado's sources to whom the Center directed messages by name and through Rado. Later, as is noted below, Moscow even eliminated Rado, the resident director, from the communications channel for certain messages, which were sent to Sissy in her own code. The second important element in this message is its reference to Taylor (Christian Schneider) as a new source. As we shall see, Taylor was first recruited by Sissy in the summer of 1942. Because Lucy reported only through Taylor, this fact means that Moscow received no messages from Lucy and his subsources until that time. (Foote claimed that Lucy's material began going to the Center in early 1941 and that he warned the Russians of Hitler's impending attack some two weeks in advance. Others, including Accoce and Quet in *A Man Called Lucy*, have copied the claim. But the traffic proves it false.)

20 November 1942

The Director instructed Dora to have Sissy determine and report the identities of the sources in the Lucy-Taylor group.

12 January 1943

Before this date Sissy had sent her first message in her own code, because the Center answered,

> We greet your first telegram. Try to work attentively and to be careful when working. Destroy immediately all notes and working papers.

The ordinary traffic continued to be channeled through Rado. But on 23 April 1943 Moscow sent its second message in Sissy's code, this one addressed to her and Paul. (Moscow did not usually use the true first name of an agent as his radio cover name, but evidence in the traffic itself makes it plain that Paul was Sissy's common-law husband, Paul Boettcher.) The message read as follows:

> 1. Dear friends, since the summer of 1942 you have worked with the Taylor-Lucy group, which has provided us with a great deal of varied material, some of it valuable. But despite the long cooperation this group remains wholly unclarified for us . . .
>
> 2. Determine and inform us by radio exact reports on Taylor, Lucy, Werther, Anna, Olga. Especially important is a personality sketch of Lucy. Who is he, what is his name, what were his circumstances earlier and what are they now, for what motives does he work for others and for us?
>
> 3. Answer this telegram in your own code. You do not need to inform Albert of our telegram or of your answer. He has received direc-

tions, as well as telegrams coming directly from
Sissy, without sending queries back (i.e., to
Moscow) . . .

4. To Sissy only: We send you the title of a
new book for your code; but, we shall give you
instructions about how to work according to the
book. Albert is not to know about the new
book. It is called *Tempete sur la Maison* . . .

5. How are you? What is Mara doing? Greetings to her and both of you from Gisela.

Although Sissy and Paul had their own code, it appears that
they did not have their own radio operator at this time and had to
go through Rado; hence Moscow's assurances that Rado was not being curious or testy but rather was accepting this traffic in a code
that he could not read without demur. Gisela was one of three code
names for Maria Josefovna Poliakova, the other two being Vera and
Mildred. Mara was Sissy's daughter, Tamara Vigier.

(Tamara had her own code name, Vita, and one may wonder at
Poliakova's indiscretion in not using it; but such lapses were not
rare. On 6 December 1943 a message from Dora informed Moscow
that Foote had been arrested. He was named openly as Foote instead
of being designated as Jim.)

18 May 1943
Dora to Director:

Sissy has just reported that Maurice has been
arrested by German authorities. She fears that
the Gestapo will thus come across her trail.
Maurice knows Sissy's true name. I have initiated discreet inquiries and shall report further.

24 May 1943
Director to Dora:

Sissy is to let us know immediately: How did
she learn of Maurice's arrest and to what extent
can his arrest be dangerous for her?

4 July 1943
Director to Dora:

We have been able to determine, just in the
past few days, that the courier from France, who
was supposed to pick up the money from Jim,

was arrested; and in his place a Gestapo agent came to Jim and, it appears, followed him to his apartment and in this way was able to learn his name. At the same time, but independently of this even, Maurice was arrested in France . . . For the time being, you must break off your connection with Sissy completely . . . She can be persuaded that it is in Taylor's interest to have a connection with someone else for a while . . . Try to convince Sissy. Tell her that it will be for only three months . . . Sissy could say it is because of Paul, who is under observation . . . She should keep her apartment absolutely clean and, above all else, not say a word too much . . . It is best that Paul not sleep in the apartment.

It has been suggested that Maurice was Maurice Emile Aenis-Haenslin, born 20 September 1893 in St. Denis, France. Aenis-Haenslin, a Swiss citizen and an engineer, was a member of the Central Committee of the Swiss Communist Party and later joined the French CP. He was involved in courier and funding activity on behalf of Soviet intelligence during World War II. There are conflicting reports about the date of Maurice's arrest by the Germans, one account dating it 1943; another, 1942. The latter is both more detailed and less derivative. It is therefore concluded that the Maurice who knew Sissy and whom the Germans arrested in France may have been someone else other than Aenis-Haenslin, who was released from a German concentration camp in Brandenburg in response to a Swiss demand.

At any rate, the traffic continued to mention Maurice and to reveal conflicting views about his arrest. On 8 July 1943 Poliakova repeated to Sissy, in the latter's code, some of the instructions radioed to Dora four days earlier. (In so doing Poliakova referred not to Maurice but to Marius, so that there is a possibility that the two were identical. It has also been suggested, however, that Marius was Marius Mouttet, a Frenchman and former Socialist minister.) She directed Sissy to leave Bern and go to Tessin (Ticino) or a spa for two or three months. Taylor and Lucy were to be turned over to someone else.

V. Sissy's Fight with Moscow

Sissy's reaction was unambiguous. On 8 July 1943 Dora sent the Director the following:

> Sissy and her men do not believe the story has anything to do with Maurice and the Gestapo. They believe that the man who asked about them came from the Center and just handled himself clumsily. They assume that the Center wants in this way to take away the Taylor group, and in such a manner that I too shall know nothing about it.

Presumably there were further exchanges, with Moscow insisting that Sissy identify Lucy and his sources and that she turn them over to Dora or someone else, and with Sissy adamantly refusing. But these are not in our collections. On 16 August 1943, however, the Center sent Sissy, via Dora, a stern message which substituted the formal second person for the intimate, and which appears to have been drawn up not by Poliakova but by her superiors:

> Dear Sissy,
> We, the Center, which has its people everywhere and can determine what is happening in other countries and around you, have told you clearly and explicitly that we have hard evidence that the Gestapo knows that you work for us and will try to uncover your connections into Germany. You, however, deny this possibility and interpret it as an attempt to take the Taylor group away from you. You must understand, inasmuch as you assume this position, that you know nothing of the danger which threatens you and Taylor's people, especially those in Germany. Your behavior is frivolous and irresponsible. We demand that you recognize the seriousness of the situation and place full confidence in our statements. We repeat: The Gestapo knows that you have or had a connection with us and will attempt all possible provocations . . .

But Sissy stayed tough. On 22 September 1943 Dora radioed to the Director:

In answer to your No. 157 and No. 158. Many thanks for your advice. I am myself convinced that much more could be gotten out of the Lucy group. However, I have no direct contact with this group, as you know, and every time I try to intensify the group's activity I encounter in Sissy and her man (this literal interpretation of "man" has been used because Sissy at this time was still married to Duebendorfer, a Swiss citizen) a resistance that I do not understand. I remind you that when I noted the possibilities of this group a year ago, I had to hold with Sissy discussions that continued for months before she was prepared to take it over and use it. . . . Sissy and her man . . . say that they cannot transmit criticisms to Taylor and Lucy because both would consider it an insult and would stop working. In accordance with your advice, I wrote Lucy a very friendly letter, but Sissy declared that Taylor could not pass it on because Lucy, beyond doubt, is already doing everything he can. Apparently Sissy and her man view the letter as an attempt by the Center or by me to set up a direct contact with the Lucy group. . . . Your telegram was handed over to Paul. . . . Again he boasted in such a way that I had a hard time of it controlling myself. He refuses to come to Geneva for meetings. . . . Again I beg you to release me from further contact with Paul . . . (who) tried to establish contact for the transmission of his material through Pierre and Ignatz . . .

In other words, Sissy and Paul still had no radio operator of their own but did not want to turn over their encoded messages to Dora for transmission by Edward (Edmond Hamel) and Maud (Edmond's wife Olga), by Rosa (Margarete Bolli) or by Jim (Alexander Foote). One report identifies Pierre as Roger Vauthey of Lausanne, supposedly a courier or cutout between Rado and Mario in France. Foote, however, in a private interview held in 1953, said that Pierre and Vita were Pierre Nicole and his wife. Our own view is that Pierre was indeed Pierre Nicole, but that Vita was Tamara Vigier. Pierre Nicole, born in 1911, served as a cutout between the Rote Drei and the Swiss Labor Party, which was extremely left-wing, though not officially Communist. The head of this party was Pierre's father, Leon, born in 1897 in Montcherend, Vaud. Leon Nicole had recruited several members of the Rote Drei on behalf of the GRU. He and Pierre were in touch with Dora, Sissy, and Jim. The identity of Ignatz is not known. He could have been any one of several other Swiss Communists.

By 5 November 1943 the danger signs had multiplied, and Moscow feared that Rado might be arrested, leaving the Center cut off from Lucy's information. It therefore repeated the proposal that Sissy and Jim be placed in direct contact so that if anything happened to Dora, Jim could still maintain the flow of intelligence. On 10 November Dora replied that Jim was in serious danger. The reason, although the cited message does not say so, was that Edmond and Olga Hamel had been arrested by the Swiss police on or about 8 October 1943, as had another W/T operator, Margarete Bolli. (Sissy, Paul, and Vita were arrested later—in May 1944.)

On 28 November 1943 the Director instructed Dora to tell Sissy and Pakbo to work independently for a time. The most important information was to go through Jim. What Moscow obviously did not know was that Jim had been arrested eight days earlier.

VI. DORA

The fourth key personality in the Rote Drei was Alexander Rado, the Hungarian cartographer who took over the direction of the net from Maria Poliakova and who assumed contact with Ursula Hamburger's sources after she left Switzerland for England at the end of 1940. Rado's story is well known and is retold here only in the barest outline. He was born 5 November 1899 in Upjest, Hungary. It is almost certain that he was working already for Soviet military intelligence when he left Paris for Geneva in 1936. Rado and Ursula Hamburger worked independently of each other until the fall of France in June 1940 because Rado had been able until then to send his reports to Moscow via microfilm carried by couriers to Paris. When the Germans occupied France, Moscow ordered Hamburger to make contact with Rado and place the transmitter of her new husband, Leon Charles Beurton, at Rado's disposal. Hamburger had trained both Foote and Beurton in operating a transmitter, and they in turn trained the Hamels and Margarete Bolli. In 1941 Moscow resolved a struggle for power by subordinating Duebendorfer to Rado. (One report has Poliakova going to Switzerland for the purpose.) But Rado's authority was not absolute, and the fact that the Center gave Duebendorfer a code of her own and sometimes by-passed Rado when communicating with her shows that the Soviets did not intend to let Rado consolidate his position completely.

Dora, a simple anagram for Rado, is the sender or recipient of almost all the Rote Drei messages. The main exception are those sent or received directly by Sissy, and those sent by Albert or by the Center but mentioning Albert in the text. There is no doubt that Albert, like Dora, is Rado; but efforts to find a pattern or significance in Rado's choice of cover name for a particular message have not been successful. Albert, like Dora, sends standard OB messages. The shift in names does not indicate a parallel shift in transmitters, because both "Dora" and "Albert" messages were found at their flat when the Hamels were arrested. The possibility that Dora is Rado as chief of the Rote Drei, and Albert is Rado as an individual, disintegrates when checked against the traffic. Flicke postulated a secretary who, as Albert, signed messages for Rado when he was away; but no one else ever heard of such a secretary, and "Dora" and "Albert" messages were sometimes transmitted on the same day. So the mystery is unsolved.

Rado's story has been told by Foote (and others) and is not repeated here, although all concerned should be aware that Foote—who disliked Rado—minimized his role in the Rote Drei, attacked his personal integrity on dubious grounds, and erroneously believed him executed in the USSR, whereas in fact Rado is flourishing as a cartographer in Hungary and Foote is dead.

By the beginning of 1941, then, Ursula Beurton, nee Hamburger, was in England; the desk chief for the operation, Poliakova, was in Moscow; Rado was in Geneva as the chief Rote Drei member in Switzerland; and Sissy and her friend Paul were in Bern (not Geneva, where Foote erroneously places them).

Dora had two other key sources who, like Sissy, provided him with intelligence from sub-sources. They were Long and Pakbo, identified and described at a later point in this study. But Sissy was more important than either of them, for one reason only: Lucy and his sub-sources.

The cutout between Lucy and Sissy was Taylor, whose true name was Christian Schneider and whose story is well known.

VII. LUCY AND TAYLOR

The Center thought highly of Taylor, chiefly because Moscow misunderstood his role. The first reference to him in our holdings is in a message sent by the Director to Dora on 8 October 1942. The message terms him a new source, although in fact he was merely a go-between. On 20 October 1942 the Director told Dora to identify Taylor's sources, not knowing that the sources "belonged" to Lucy, not Taylor. Another Moscow-to-Dora message, sent the same day, refers to "Taylor's information" about OKW (German High Command) plans. A week later Moscow again asked for the identities of Taylor's sources. In December 1942 and January 1943 the Center began to speak of Taylor and Lucy jointly. By February 1943 the Center's follow-up questions were directed to Lucy, with scant mention to Taylor. That the Soviets continued to overestimate Taylor's importance is nevertheless evident in a Director-to-Dora message of 6 October 1943, which suggested that the work of the Lucy-Taylor group might be continued after the war ended and which promised Taylor an income for life if he agreed. Perhaps Sissy misrepresented to Moscow the insignificant role that Taylor actually had; perhaps she merely kept stubbornly silent about such facts; or perhaps she misunderstood the true situation because she was in touch only with Taylor and not with Lucy.

In only one sense was Lucy important. If Rudolf Roessler had not been living in Switzerland during the Second World War, his sources in Germany might have found it troublesome or even impossible to get their reports into Soviet hands. In fact, they might not have cared much one way or the other about Soviet reception of their material, as long as it went to the Western Allies. But as was pointed out in the recent review of Accoce and Quet, the widely accepted story that Lucy was a master spy is nothing but a myth. As we have seen, the Center tried to eliminate Sissy and put Dora in direct contact with Taylor and Lucy. If this maneuver had succeeded, it is probable that Dora would have been instructed to pressure Lucy to divulge his sources, whose identities Moscow had already requested again and again. And if Lucy had yielded, then the truth would have been apparent—Lucy's true function was no different from that of Taylor. Both were mere cutouts. What made Lucy and Taylor important, what made Sissy important, and to a large extent what made the Rote Drei important was a small band of Germans—allegedly live men—Lucy's sources.

VIII. LUCY'S SOURCES IN WORLD WAR II

The record clearly shows that Lucy had four important sources: Werther, Teddy, Olga, and Anna. Of the three hundred thirty-two messages from Dora to the Director of which there are copies in our holdings, Werther is the source of sixty-nine (21 percent); Teddy, of thirty-one (10 percent); Olga, of twenty-six (8 percent); and Anna, of eleven (3½ percent). These four were probably not the only sources reporting to Lucy; Lucy was not the only source reporting to Sissy; and Sissy was not the only principal agent funneling reports from a network into Rado. Yet these four persons produced 42½ percent of the total traffic from Switzerland to Moscow. (Assuming as we do that our holdings are large enough so that projections are mathematically sound.)

We do not know the identities of any of them. We can, however, dismiss the theory of Foote and some other writers that these cover names merely referred to the source's access rather than his identity, so that Werther stood for Wehrmache; Olga, for Oberkommando der Luftwaffe; Anna, for the Auswertige Amt (Foreign Office); etc. There is nothing in the traffic to support this theory, which seems to be based on speculation only. All Rote Drei code names for which true identities have been established were designators of individuals *per se*, not of types of cover or access.

Despite the printed assertions to the contrary, Rudolf Roessler *did* divulge the identity of his sources, or at least of some of them. Three and a half years before his death, he provided identifying information about four of his chief sources to a trusted friend. They were, said Lucy, (1) a German major—whom he did not name—who had been the chief of the Abwehr before Admiral Wilhelm Canaris assumed command; (2) Hans Bernd Gisevius; (3) Carl Goerdeler; and (4) "General Boelitz, deceased."

IX. GENERAL HANS OSTER

Lucy's confidant garbled the first identification and may have done the same with the fourth. Canaris took charge of the Abwehr on 1 January 1935. His predecessor was not a major but another admiral, Conrad Patzig. But Hans Oster was a major in the Abwehr at that time, and he remained in the service, in which he served as the chief of staff and also as the heart of the twentieth of July group which conspired to overthrow Hitler and, finally, to assassinate him.

Hans Bernd Gisevius said that he first met Oster some time between August 1933 and April 1934. "At that time he was . . . setting up the war ministry's counterintelligence organization . . . known . . . as the Abwehr." (*To the Bitter End*, Houghton Mifflin Co., New York, 1947, p. 142)

A number of sources have noted how well-informed Oster was. His knowledge of state secrets extended even to those held by the bitterest enemies of the Abwehr: the Gestapo and the Nazi security service, called the SD (for Sicherheitsdienst).

> Oster was able, generally speaking, through his contacts with Graf (Wolf Heinrich von) Helldorf, the Berlin Prefect of Police, and with (Arthur) Nebe, the Reichskriminaldirektor . . . to learn quickly what was going on in the entourage of Hitler and Goering and also in the Gestapo headquarters in the Prinz-Albrecht-Strasse.

(Karl Heinz Abshagen, *Canaris*, English edition, Hutchinson and Co. Ltd., London, 1956, p. 122)

The fact that Oster was prepared to provide Germany's enemies with information which was of crucial importance, even though they lacked the power to make full use of it, is also well established. Even Accoce and Quet, despite their denigration of the twentieth of July group, concede that Oster told Colonel J. G. Sas, the Dutch Military Attache in Berlin, that Germany intended to invade Norway. Abshagen reported he gave Sas this warning on 3 April 1940 for relay to Norway and also told Sas of the invasion of Holland before the event, In fact, Oster had begun to send specific, factual warnings to the West as early as 1938.

The man who had become a major in 1929, a lieutenant colonel in 1935, a colonel in 1939, and a major general in 1942 was unswerving in his detestation of German fascism and in his conviction that morality necessitated action. As time passed and Hitler's power grew, Oster became convinced that the plots to eradicate the Nazis through the internal intervention of German armed forces would fail because of the waverings of the German generals. He warned the West because he recognized that Hitler could not be brought down inside the Reich until he had been defeated on the battlefields.

Most contemporary German historians boggle at this point. They write in detail about the twentieth of July conspiracy but gloss over the fact that from 1938 until his discharge from the Abwehr on 31 March 1944, when he was placed under house arrest in Schnaditz, near Leipzig, Oster was furnishing vital information to Germany's foes and was therefore—at least in Nazi eyes—engaged in high treason.

How did Oster obtain information? Gisevius said,

> Oster . . . had formed a circle around himself
> . . . he utilized the potentialities of the Abwehr
> so cannily that he was able to establish a whole
> network of confidential agents. . . . Oster
> seemed to be organizing an intelligence service
> of his own, within the counterintelligence serv-
> ice. . . . One of the most important of his activ-
> ities was to install his own confidential agents in
> the most diverse positions.

And Oster was on intimate conspiratorial terms with such persons as General Ludwig Beck (who, with Oster, sent Dr. Josef Mueller to the Vatican for peace negotiations with the British, negotiations at which the Pope presided); General Georg Thomas, head of the Economics and Armaments Branch of the OKW; Generals Fritz Thiele and Erich Fellgiebel, respectively chiefs of communications for the Army and the OKW; and General Friedrich Olbricht, chief of the Allgemeine Heeresamt and permanent deputy to the commander-in-chief of the Home Army. These men, and others like them, were active members of the conspiracy; most of them were executed by the Nazis. And they were in a position to have direct access to precisely the kind of information reported by Lucy's sources.

How did the information reach Lucy? Here too we can only speculate. A biographic summary of Oster in the International Biographic Archives includes the following:

> In addition to his military duties, Oster was si-
> multaneously the technical center of the anti-
> Hitler resistance in the Army. He spared neither
> effort nor risk to set up connections between
> military and civilian resistance groups.

Gisevius adds,

> He once described to me in one sentence his
> own conception of his function within the Re-
> sistance movement. He was standing at his desk

> looking down pensively at the four or five tele-
> phones whose secret circuits connected him with
> the most diverse authorities. "This is what I
> am," he said. "I facilitate communications for
> everyone everywhere."

Oster had the entire communications network of the Abwehr at his disposal, and he used it to support the anti-Nazi cause. Abshagen comments,

> The so-called "A-net" (consisting of independ-
> ent lines of communication at the disposal of
> the Abwehr only) would ensure that the "con-
> spirators" only would be able to transmit news
> and orders.

He adds,

> The Abwehr organization was the nerve center
> from which lines led to the General Staff, to
> General (Erwin) von Witzleben . . . to Goer-
> deler, to Beck . . . to (Baron Ernst von) Weiz-
> saecker (the Under Secretary of State and for-
> merly Minister in Bern), and through him to a
> group of diplomats abroad. . . .

As was noted earlier in this study, the timing of Rote Drei messages would have permitted sending almost all of the traffic through Abwehr courier channels from Germany to Switzerland. We know that Gisevius had access at least twice and sometimes three times a week to a courier pouch from the Foreign Office in Berlin to the German Embassy in Bern. At least every other day Gisevius was also serviced by an OKW courier as the result of a procedure instituted by Oster. And for urgent messages Oster or a cohort could safely use an Abwehr telephone. How the Abwehr's lines were shielded against Gestapo and SD monitoring is not known, at least by this writer; but that they were so shielded is demonstrated by the conspirators' uninhibited use of telephones and the survival of the group until 20 July 1944.

In brief, even if Lucy had not listed "Canaris' predecessor," Gisevius, and Carl Goerdeler, all key figures in the twentieth of July group, as having been among his sources, the characteristics of the Lucy messages and of their transmission from Germany to Switzerland suggest that Werther and the others probably had Abwehr communications channels at their disposal. There seems to be no plausible alternative theory.

X. HANS BERND GISEVIUS

Gisevius has told much of his own story in *To The Bitter End*, but like other Germans he stresses the resistance activity of the underground and says little about espionage. (There are a few exceptions. Speaking of the twentieth of July conspiracy, Gisevius says, "We had our spies everywhere—in the war ministry, the police headquarters, the ministry of the interior, and especially in the foreign office. All the various threads came together in Oster's office." But comments in this vein are rare.) He entered the Abwehr in 1939 or 1940; and when Paris fell, Canaris and Oster sent him to Zurich with the cover of a vice consul.

But even before the war started, Gisevius had started to make trips to Switzerland to meet with representatives of the Western Allies. He says,

> We had decided to meet in Switzerland after the "March madness." (The term is a reference to Hitler's seizure, with Western acquiescence, of the Sudetenland in March 1939.) We wanted to establish closer connections with the British and French, and it no longer seemed advisable to do this in Berlin. (Hjalmar) Schacht had business in Basle in any case. I was glad of the opportunity to complete my notes on the French crisis. Goerdeler intended to stay around Berlin until the end of the Czech crisis; then he planned to follow us as soon as possible.

In Ouchy, Gisevius met Goerdeler and an unidentified companion who is mentioned only as a person of considerable influence in London and Paris circles.

XI. EX-CHANCELLOR JOSEF WIRTH

Gerhard Ritter tells of another, similar meeting which occurred some months later, in February 1940. He says that the ex-Chancellor of Germany, Josef Wirth, had emigrated to Switzerland and had offered to act as an intermediary between the British and the German anti-Fascists.

In a document which Dr. (Reinhold) Schairer

> took to London, he called Chamberlain's atten-
> tion to the existence of an important opposition
> group. . . . In mid-February two Foreign Office
> representatives, friends of (Sir Robert) Vansit-
> tart, met Wirth at Ouchy and another man,
> well known in London, who had, since war
> broke out, lived in Lucerne and from there had
> kept up his connections with friends in Britain.

The other man could have been Inchel, Freiherr von Godin, or
Lucy himself, or any of several other Germans who, like Wirth, were
living in Lucerne.

Wirth also appears in Rote Drei traffic. On 14 January 1943 the
Center sent the following message to Dora:

> (a) Request reply about exact substance of
> talks between Long (George Blun, a French
> journalist and important member of the Rote
> Drei) and Wirth. Especially interested in con-
> tents of Wirth's negotiations with the USSR.
> What does he plan to do, as a practical matter,
> to establish contact?
>
> (b) What opinion does Long now have of
> Rot's statements? Does he believe that they are
> true? Long absolutely must report clearly about
> the intent of Rot's group to orient itself toward
> the Soviet Union. Is it possible that at the pres-
> ent time there exists an organized opposition of
> commanding officers against Hitler?
>
> (c) Rot should report the location from which
> Germany sent thirty divisions to Italy. What is
> the picture in respect to reserves in Germany?
> How does the OKW react to the Russian offen-
> sive? What are the plans and intentions of the
> OKW for the next few months?
>
> (d) Repeat, what documents does Rot intend
> to publish? Because of their great importance,
> request a good check on all these questions and
> a prompt answer.

Six days later the Director asked some questions about the intentions of the OKW, the German High Command. Moscow directed the requirements be levied upon Lucy's group and added, "if
feasible, Long should try to get relevant information from the Wirth
group."

On 20 April 1943 the following message from Dora was transmitted:

> From Rot.
> Through the Director General coming here
> . . . Mayor Goerdeler from . . . Bendlerstrasse
> (OKW Headquarters):
> (a) The first fixed day for the German attack
> on the East Front is 14 June. Only operations of
> modest proportions are planned.
> (b) The General Staff expects the event by
> the end of April at the earliest; it could snowball.
> The so-called second echelon of generals (literally, generals in second-best uniforms), who already wanted to take action against Hitler in
> January, has now decided to liquidate Hitler
> and also his supporters. An earlier attempt failed because Hitler was warned by Manstein.

On 5 October 1943 the following went from Dora to the Director:

> On 27 September Salter talked with the former
> German Chancellor Wirth in Lucerne. Wirth
> rejects the German Liberation Committee (the
> reference is to the "National Committee of Free
> Germany," created by the Russians) in Moscow
> because it hinders instead of hastening the disintegration of the Nazi regime. Those who feel
> partially responsible for the establishment of
> that regime will cooperate more closely with the
> Nazi leaders. Bourgeois German Democrats are
> prepared to collaborate with German Communists but not under Soviet guidance. Therefore,
> they reject the Moscow Committee. According
> to Wirth, the German Embassy in Bern is extremely interested in Sokolin. Krauel, a former
> German consul in Geneva, serves as the intermediary in this matter.

On the basis of these messages and of the scanty information about the movements and activities of Gisevius in Switzerland, it is suggested that Gisevius may have been Rot. Gisevius knew Roessler, which may well explain why Lucy identified him correctly as a source but failed to list Oster, whom he had never met, by name. Gisevius also knew Wirth, whose link to the twentieth of July group had been sanctioned by Generals Oster and Beck. He obviously knew Carl Goerdler, one of the most important of the conspirators. Gisevius was sympathetic toward the Soviet cause, a fact which became more apparent after the war than it was during it. He was thoroughly trained in clandestinity as a result of his role on the twentieth of July group, his three and a half years as an agent of British intelligence, and his work for OSS in Switzerland. It seems probable that people like Goerdeler and Beck, who themselves favored the Western solution—i.e., a postwar Germany oriented toward the United States and the U.K.—believed that Gisevius felt as they did and that those members of the twentieth of July who favored the Eastern solution, people like Count Klaus Philip Schenk von Stauffenberg and Adam von Trott zu Solz, thought that Gisevius shared their views.

There is one difficulty inherent in the theory that Rot was Gisevius. As was said earlier, Lucy named Gisevius as one of his sources. Rot, however, seems to have been a source of Long rather than Lucy. But there may be no real contradiction here; Gisevius could have been in clandestine contact with both Roessler and Blun, just as he was in clandestine contact with many other people. Because Lucy and Sissy succeeded in concealing the identities of the Lucy group from the Russians, the dual role of Gisevius in the Rote Drei, if he did in fact play such a role, could not come to light.

XII. CARL GOERDELER

The third man named by Roessler as one of his sources was Carl Goerdeler, who had been Lord Mayor of Leipzig from 1930 to 1936, when he resigned and broke with the Nazis. A conservative visionary, a Protestant monarchist, a headstrong philosopher, Goerdeler remained a civilian all his life. All of the information provided to Moscow by Lucy could have been obtained more readily, more securely, in greater detail, and at a higher level from leading military figures in the resistance than from Carl Goerdeler. It seems probable that Roessler named him just because he knew him personally as he knew Gisevius. Whatever information Goerdeler provided, he must have obtained it from fellow conspirators, not from direct access. It is therefore not possible to draw any logical inferences about which cover name, if any, referred to Goerdeler.

XIII. THE UNKNOWN BOELITZ

The fourth source named by Lucy was "General Boelitz (deceased)." Unfortunately, no record of a general named Boelitz has been discovered. There was a Dr. Otto Boelitz, born a pastor's son in Wesel in 1876, who became the Prussian Minister of Art, Science, and Education. In 1934 he was a *Culturrat* (advisor on cultural matters) and a member of the German Foreign Institute. He was also the first director of the Ibero-American Institute in Berlin. Some time during 1934 Dr. Boelitz fell into the bad graces of the Nazis and was replaced as head of the Ibero-American Institute by a general named Faupel. Thereafter, one report suggests, the Institute was used by the Nazis in support of espionage and subversion in Latin America. Dr. Otto Boelitz died in Germany on 29 December 1951.

No record linking him to Roessler on the one hand, or to Oster, Goerdeler, or any other member of the twentieth of July group on the other, has been found thus far. There remains, however, the possibility of another garble. A Colonel Friedrich (Fritz) Boetzel was head of the German military intercept office in Munich before 1933. From 1934 to 1939 he headed the ciphers department (Chiffrierstelle) of the OKW. Thereafter he was commanding officer of the intelligence evaluation office of the Southeast Army group, Athens, where he remained until 1944. He had ties to Canaris and Oster. And a German First Lieutenant of the Signal Corps, interrogated in April 1945, described Colonel Boetzel as an anti-Nazi.

To summarize: We have Werther, Teddy, Olga, and Anna as Lucy's principal sources and as the principal sources in the Rote Drei network. We have Oster, Gisevius, Goerdeler, and Boelitz identified by Roessler as having been among his sources during World War II. We have no basis for matching true and cover names, although Oster seems the likeliest candidate for Werther.

XIV. SISSY'S OTHER SOURCES

Let us next consider who worked for Sissy (Rachel Duebendorfer) besides Lucy and Taylor. Foote lists Isaac and one "Hofmeier" of the Swiss Communist Party as contacts of Duebendorfer. Isaac, who does not appear in any Rote Drei message at our disposal, worked where Sissy had also been employed, at the International Labor Office in Geneva. Foote lists him as Alexander A_____. The first name is correct; the true last name is Abramson. Apart from playing a minor part in Sissy's ill-advised attempt to get help from the RIS in Canada after Rado went into hiding, Isaac's chief contribution to the Rote Drei was to provide safe storage for sensitive materials, a side benefit that resulted from his diplomatic status at the ILO. He either did not function as a source or was insignificant in that capacity. Karl Hofmaier, born 17 May 1897 in Basle, a Swiss citizen and a journalist, was the leader of the left wing of the Swiss Communist Party. He had been in the USSR in the early 1920s, had spent eight years in a prison in Italy, and was in Moscow in 1939. He came into conflict with Julius Humbert-Droz, leader of a more moderate faction of the Swiss CP. Both had Rote Drei contacts after the war started, but we lack particulars about the reasons for Hofmaier's contacts with Sissy and Dora.

Several reports have linked Sissy with Maurice Emile Aenis-Haenslin, a Swiss citizen born in St. Denis, France, on 30 February 1893. These reports allege that Aenis-Haenslin, a Communist of long standing, served as a courier between Henri Robinson of the Rote Kapelle and Sissy. (We have found no substantiation for this assertion and are disinclined to accept it.) As best they could, the Soviets avoided contaminating one network through contacts with another. Exceptions seem to have occurred when Moscow tried to transfer money from one country to another. But if Aenis-Haenslin was used to bring funds to the Rote Drei from France, his contact would logically have been with Rado or Foote rather than Sissy.

The assumption that Aenis-Haenslin was in contact with Duebendorfer seems to rest chiefly upon an exchange of traffic in May 1943. Sissy reported the arrest of Maurice in France. Maurice knew Sissy's true name, and she feared that the Gestapo would learn of her role in espionage. Aenis-Haenslin was arrested in Paris by the Gestapo, but conflicting dates—1942 and 1943—have been reported for this event.

It has been established that Tamara, the daughter of Sissy, and a former husband named Curt Caspari served her mother in some espionage capacity, probably as a courier. The first reference to her in the traffic is a message from Gisela (Maria Josefovna Poliakova) to Sissy. The message, sent in Sissy's code and dated 23 April 1943, ended with the following: "How are you? What is Mara doing? Greetings to her and both of you from Gisela." Mara is Tamara.

"Both of you" means Sissy and Paul.

Tamara had married a French Army captain, a militant Communist named Jean Pierre Vigier; and either Tamara or her mother seems to have brought the young man into the net. Some commentators, including Dallin, have maintained that Vigier was alias Braut, who appears in Rote Drei traffic in July, August, and September 1943. The claim seems weak. On 16 August 1943 the Center told Sissy, "Give us an exact account of Braut. Is he truly a comrade?" But Jean-Pierre Vigier, like his father Henri, was well known as a Communist. It seems likelier that he and Tamara are the Pierre and Vita of the following message from Moscow, sent on 22 August 1942 to Dora:

> Is Mario firm? Would he betray Pierre and Vita
> if interrogated? Are you sure Pierre and Vita, if
> they have a talk with the Swiss police, would
> not betray Dora?

The best guess about Mario is that he was Otto Manning, a Communist Party leader in Biel, Switzerland.

In addition to Mario, Sissy was linked to a Rote Drei source called Marius. On 8 October 1942 the Director, in a message sent through Dora to Sissy, said, "Your new people, Marius and Taylor, do not work badly. One must always control them, however, and keep them active." And a message of 5 July 1943, sent directly to Sissy, referred to the arrest of Marius in France. The fact that Mario, Marius, and Maurice were all arrested has caused some analysts to guess that two of them or all of them were identical, but no basis for such an assumption has been found. We do not know who Marius was, and lack even a clue, but the dates of arrest indicate that he was not the same person as Mario. Moreover, both names appear more than once in the traffic, so that the likelihood of error is not great.

As was noted earlier in this account, the Paul who appears in the radio traffic could hardly be anyone except Paul T. Boettcher, Sissy's common-law husband. Born on 2 May 1891 in Leipzig, Germany, Boettcher had been a member of the Central Committee of the German Communist Party, a Minister of Finance in Saxony, and the chief editor of the *Arbeiterzeitung* in Leipzig. He fled to Switzerland after the Nazis came to power. Whether he began living with Rachel Duebendorfer before or after the Spanish Civil War, in which Boettcher served in the International Brigade, she gave him her husband's identity papers, probably in 1941, when the Swiss authorities ordered his expulsion from the country. He remained in Switzerland illegally. He and Sissy were arrested on a charge of espionage in December 1943 but escaped on 23 July 1945 and fled to France. Both were sentenced *in absentia* to two years. Boettcher went from France to East Germany, where he again edited a Leipzig newspaper and where he also became a professor of Russian at Halle University. Sissy apparently remained in France. But in 1947 she vanished. Dallin maintains that she was "arrested, tried, and severely punished in Russia."

Although Foote maintained that Boettcher was not part of the Rote Drei network, the traffic clearly indicates the contrary. A message from Moscow, dated 23 April 1943 and transmitted in Sissy's own code, was addressed to "Sissy and Paul." In a lengthy warning of 4 July 1943, the Director warned that as a result of the arrest of Maurice, Sissy was to "keep her apartment absolutely clean" and added, "It is best that Paul not sleep in the apartment." Referring to the same event, Rado referred to "Sissy and her man."

Rado apparently found Boettcher hard to take. On 22 September 1943 Dora sent to Moscow a long lament which included the following:

> Your telegram was handed over to Paul . . .
> Again he boasted in such a way that I found it
> hard to control myself. He refuses to come to
> Geneva for meetings. . . . Again I beg you to
> release me from further contact with Paul . . .
> After I had made S (presumably Sissy) under-
> stand that I would not receive him, he tried to
> establish contact for the transmission of his ma-
> terial through Pierre and Ignatz.

(As was noted earlier, there are grounds for thinking that Pierre was Jean-Paul Vigier, Sissy's son-in-law. It has also been asserted, however, that Pierre was Pierre Nicole, a Swiss Communist and the son of Leon Nicole, who headed the far-left, pro-Communist Swiss Labor Party. Both father and son were deeply involved in Rote Drei work. They served as spotter, recruiters, couriers, fund raisers, and in various other capacities. If Pierre is the son, then Ignatz could well be the father. The conjecture is somewhat strengthened by a message, date unknown, to the Director and almost certainly from Dora:

> Re: Pierre and Noel.
> I have often pointed out that contact with
> Pierre is dangerous for me. Therefore meetings
> have been confined to those for the purpose of
> transfer of money.

Both Pierre and Leon Nicole were associated with Noel Field during the 1942-1943 period. If this theory is right, then the likeliest cover name for Jean-Paul Vigier is Braut, a French source who worked for Sissy.)

Some confusion has resulted from an assumption by Flicke and others that Paul was not Boettcher but rather a W/T operator working for Sissy. That this assumption is incorrect is shown by a message sent from the Director to Dora on 5 November 1943:

> In addition, Jim must immediately take care of
> the training of a second W/T operator, and you
> may also use the one working for Paul. We can
> give him (Paul) an order that he is to place his
> S/T operator at (your) disposition.

This message is also significant because it shows that the Hamels, Margarete Bolli, and Foote were not the only radio operators working for the Rote Drei. On 28 June 1943 the Director granted permission for the training of Harry as a radio operator. There are also references to an operator or trainee whose cover name was Roger. Harry is believed to have been Henrietta Bourgeois, an unmarried Swiss stenographer born in Canton Vaud in 1917 and recruited in 1943 by Pierre Nicole. She was to have been trained by Foote as a W/T operator, and after a quarrel with her parents she gave up her job in Geneva. But Foote was arrested before the training could start. Roger may have been a Swiss citizen, Jean Jacques Roger Spiess, born 15 or 16 September 1916. Spiess and his wife, Josette, lived in Lausanne during the war. He was a Communist or a sympathizer and was associated with Foote. At last report, in 1965, he was a manufacturer of woodworking machinery in Renens, Switzerland, and was making frequent business trips to the Congo.

Another of Sissy's sources was her cousin Walter Fluckiger, whose Rote Drei name was Brand. He was born in Bern in 1906, travelled to the USSR, and married a Russian. During the war, or part of it, he lived at the Richmond Hotel in Geneva. When he was arrested is not known to us, but it has been reported that in December 1953 he was in prison in Switzerland because of espionage performed for the Soviets. The similarity in cover names of some of Sissy's sources (Mario, Marius, Maurice as noted above) reappears in "Braut" and "Brand," erroneously considered identical by some commentators. Braut's information came chiefly from France; Brand's, from Italy and Switzerland.

Sissy was also in touch with an unidentified person whose cover name was Charly. On 5 May 1943 Moscow asked, "Why is Sissy against recruiting Charly? He is an honest and good co-worker, but we do not know his wife. A third station (i.e., transmitter) is necessary." This last sentence is mysterious because three Rote Drei transmitters were functioning when the message was sent—unless there had been a temporary breakdown.

A Rote Drei source who is thought to have been a member of Sissy's group was Diener, whose true name was Francois Lachenal. In our holdings Diener appears but once in the following message of 30 July 1943 from Dora to the Director:

> Diener from Vichy:
> On 14 July de Brinon tried, with the help of
> Berlin military circles, to overthrow Laval and
> form a new fascist government including Deat,
> Doriot, Benoist, and Mechin. The plot failed
> because Petain is now protecting Laval.

Francois Lachenal, born 31 May 1918 in Geneva, was a Swiss citizen who spent much of World War II in Vichy. It has been reported that he passed his information directly to Sissy's son-in-law, Jean Pierre Vigier, and that he remained a Soviet agent after the war ended. He worked in the Political Department (Swiss Foreign Office) where he copied documents on behalf of the Soviets before he was dismissed.

Rachel Duebendorfer's Rote Drei contacts fell into three categories. By far the most important group was Lucy's quartet of Werther, Teddy, Olga, and Anna—all in Germany. Sissy resisted strenuously every effort of Moscow and Rado to determine the identities of the members of the Taylor-Lucy team, and it is fair to conjecture that a major reason for her resistance was that, had she lost this remarkable asset, she would have had little enough left. For the second group was composed of peripheral people like Brand and Diener, probably turned over to Sissy by Vera Poliakova before the war. And the third element was made up of Sissy's own family: the man with whom she was living, Paul Boettcher; her daughter and the daughter's husband; and a cousin.

XV. LONG

Alexander Rado had two other principal agents. One of them, George Blun, was a French journalist whose sub-sources could not match the production of Lucy's group in quality or quantity, but who was nevertheless a valuable asset for the Soviets.

Blun, born on 1 June 1893 in Alsace-Lorraine, was married to another reporter, Marthe Kentzel. During World War I he worked for the British and French intelligence services. He was expelled from Switzerland in 1920 for Communist activities. In addition to the Rote Drei activity described below, his services as a World War II agent were reportedly extended to the British and the Poles. He also had Swiss intelligence contacts. He was in close contact with the leadership of the Swiss Communist Party well before World War II; in fact, this relationship began in 1925. He came to know many of the key members of Swiss intelligence and the Rote Drei during World War II. Like many other spies working in Switzerland at that time, Blun served several masters. Among them were the Swiss, the Soviets, the Poles, and the French.

Blun's alias for W/T purposes was Long. As such, he appears in the Rote Drei traffic (or at least in our holdings) twenty-eight times between October 1941 and mid-November 1943.

Blun spent much of this period in Berlin, although he also travelled to Switzerland and France. His contacts ranged from key Rote Drei personnel to the Swiss G-2, German journalists like Ernst Lemmer of the *Neue Zuercher Zeitung*, the director of a Swiss airline, Swedish industrialists and engineers, German nobility and captains of industry, Hungarian diplomats, French resistance circles, an SS Lieutenant General, prelates of the Vatican, Austrian financiers, and at least two German anti-fascists who play significant parts in this story—Hans Bernd Gisevius and Josef Wirth.

This wide range of contacts at high levels seems at first blush to be at odds with Long's performance. The explanation is that his sources were mostly unwitting and his contacts casual. The following were probably witting, because they had radio aliases and because the traffic so suggests.

XVI. AGNES

Agnes, whose true name was Ernst Lemmer, represented a Zurich newspaper in Berlin and traveled to Switzerland repeatedly. He was in contact with one Burckhardt, the Swiss military attache in

Berlin who also had contacts in the twentieth of July group and who served as a communications channel to Switzerland. He first appears in our holdings in a message of 22 October 1941, Dora to Director. Long is listed as the source and Lemmer, who is said to have obtained the information from the Foreign Ministry, as the sub-source. The information concerned the siege of Moscow. The message ends with, "In the future I shall call him (Lemmer) Agnes." Our files, however, contain only two more messages citing Agnes. The dates are 13 August and 18 September 1943, and the messages are merely reports of the lack of morale at the German home front. Lemmer is nevertheless important because he served as a source for Lucy during the second, post-war phase of Lucy's career in espionage. Lemmer was born on 28 April 1898 in Remscheidt, Germany (although Dallin, for some unknown reason, thought he was born in Odessa and lived in Russia for seventeen years). He attended the Universities of Marburg and Frankfurt am Main. He joined the German Democratic Party (DDP), became chairman of the Young Democrats, and was also secretary-general of a trade union. In 1924 he was elected as a DDP representative to the Reichstag and thus became the youngest member of the body. He lost three posts when the Nazis seized power, and he was forbidden to write for any newspaper published in Germany. He became the Berlin correspondent for the *Pester Lloyd* of Budapest and the *Neue Zuercher Zeitung*, as well as a reporter in occupied Belgium for the Brussels *Soir*. After the war Lemmer was accused in West Germany of having collaborated with the Nazis. He settled immediately after the war in the Berlin suburb of Klein-Machnow, in the Soviet sector, where he owned a house. In October 1945 he became the deputy chairman of the Christian Democratic Party (CDU) in the Soviet Zone and a member of the board of the Free German Trade Union Federation, the Communist FDGB. He was also deputy mayor of Klein-Machnow. He was in close and cordial contact with leading members of the Soviet military occupation. On 20 December 1947, however, the Soviet authorities removed Lemmer from the vice-chairmanship of the CDU, ostensibly because of policy conflicts. He moved to West Berlin in 1949 and became editor of the anti-Communist Berlin *Kurier*. In 1950 he was elected to the five-man executive of the CDU in West Berlin. In January 1952 he was elected as a CDU representative to the Bundestag, and in December 1955 he became chairman of the West Berlin CDU. In November 1956 he was appointed Minister of Postal and Telecommunications. In October 1957 he became Minister for All-German Affairs. (One report of that period stated innocently, "Lemmer . . . is said to be opposed to the work of the Allied and German intelligence networks in West Berlin.") In 1966 Lemmer was a special representative of Chancellor Erhard in Berlin. He is currently listed as a retired Cabinet Minister who last held public office in 1965.

The same source who repeated the identities of the four World War II sources whom Lucy had named to him also said that Lemmer was a source of Lucy's during the 1947-1953 period when Lucy and Xaver Schnieper worked for Czech intelligence.

The postwar charges of collaboration with the Nazis, which Lemmer denied and outrode, seem to have been true. During his interrogation after the war, Walter Schellenberg said that Lemmer had been an agent of Amt VI.

XVII. KURZ

Another source for Long was an agent whose cover name was Kurz (German for "short"). His true name was Clemens Bernhard Alfermann. He was born on 25 January 1907 in Oberhausen, in the Rhineland. He attended the Universities of Cologne, Paris, and Berlin. In 1935 he emigrated to Switzerland. He settled first in Lausanne and then in Zurich, at Seefelderstrasse 257; and he became an editor of *Europa Press*. He also served as a reporter for *Transocean* of the German Press Agency, the DNB. He became a leading member of the Free Germany Committee, which was Soviet controlled. In December 1943 an intercepted Polish message referred to Alfermann as "a good man," and Clemens Alfermann was suspected of being a Polish agent.

Several reports list him as having been an agent or representative of the Abwehr and specifically of Ast Breslau (of Amt III-F, counterespionage). At the same time, however, he was closely linked with Hans Daufeld, who worked for Amt VI of the SD (Walter Schellenberg's intelligence service) in Lausanne from 1942 to 1945 with cover as a consul. According to Daufeld, Alfermann was eligible for the draft but Daufeld intervened in his behalf, and in exchange Alfermann wrote comprehensive reports for Daufeld.

It is possible that Alfermann served as a communications link between the twentieth of July conspirators in Germany and the Rote Drei network in Switzerland. Abwehr packages brought sealed from Berlin to Geneva by courier were regularly received by Alfermann.

Some time during the war Alfermann approached the U.S. Consulate General in Zurich through George Blun, who served as his intermediary in offering to exchange information about Germany for a guarantee of postwar protection. The offer seems to have been rejected.

In August 1944 Alfermann asked an unidentified Abwehr representative in Geneva whether he would be willing to meet a member of the Deuxieme Bureau. The Abwehr man agreed. The Frenchman turned out to be George Blun, who quickly said that he had nothing to do with the Second Bureau but worked instead for the IVth Section of the Red Army Staff. He accused the Abwehr officer of being partly responsible for the arrests of some Rote Drei members in Switzerland and suggested that the arrests be stopped. He asked the Germans to provide information about the Abwehr and told him that doing so would stand him in good stead after the war. The officer refused.

Soon after the war ended, Alfermann became involved with Josef Wirth in a project whereby packages of food and clothing were mailed to East Germany. He made frequent postwar trips to the British zone of Germany, trips which were facilitated by the British authorities. On 31 March 1948 he returned to Germany, taking up residence first in Duesseldorf and then in Bonn, but making frequent trips to Belgium and Switzerland. In 1952 he was considered for the post of press attache at the West German Embassy in Bern, but the Swiss refused to accept him. He became the liaison representative of the Public Service and Transport Workers Union (OeTV), which held meetings with representatives of Communist countries. In March 1966 he was scheduled for a trip to the USSR.

The portion of traffic that we hold contains only two references to Kurz. The first, dated 28 December 1942, directs Dora to ascertain from Dux why the Swiss police issued a summons to Kurz and searched his house. (We do not know the identity of Dux. He was probably a Swiss police officer in touch with Pakbo.) The second message, 27 January 1943, is Dora's reply. The police told Kurz that the house search had resulted from the fact that a British agent working in Switzerland had been using Kurz's true name. Dora said that the explanation was "obviously untrue." Since the search, Kurz had been under surveillance. Kurz also reported that no one had appeared for a meeting with Georg on 12 December 1942. Although the identity of Georg is not known, it is possible that the reference may have been to George Blun, despite his having a well-established cover name.

XVIII. GRAU

A third source for Long was Grau, whose true name was Manfred von Grimm. Born in Vienna on 30 December 1911, von Grimm fled to Switzerland on 19 March 1938. Before the war he had worked as a sub-source for a French agent, Rudolf Lemoine (alias Korff-Koenig). Von Grimm, whose information was going to the Poles, used the cover name Schmidt. When Lemoine was arrested by the Germans in October 1942, he identified von Grimm, whom the Poles promptly dropped. In Switzerland von Grimm lived in Davos. His work for the Rote Drei apparently began after his tie to the Poles was severed. There are also reports that he was associated with British intelligence during World War II. In 1947 he was living in Holland.

Grau makes eight appearances in the messages included in our holdings. The first of these, dated 22 January 1942, was from Dora to the Director and read thus:

> Long wants to use Manfred von Grimm, a partisan of the Austrian Schuschnigg, who lives here, and pay him one hundred fifty francs monthly. Von Grimm's father was an Austrian general and consul in Holland. Request your approval.

Another message, dated 8 October 1942, concerned a Finnish Lieutenant named Aminoff, a relative of Marshal Mannerheim, who was bearing a message from Mannerheim to the Pope. Grau, who was a baron, was also a friend or associate of the Prince of Lichtenstein, who in 1943 appeared in the radio traffic as Axel but who was probably unwitting.

XIX. ROT

A fourth source was Rot. Although the true identity of Rot has not been determined definitively, a case can be made for the hypothesis that he was Hans Bernd Gisevius. Our holdings contain only three messages which mention Rot. The first, from the Director to Dora, is dated 14 January 1943. It reads in part as follows:

> (a) Request reply about exact substance of talks between Long and (Josef) Wirth. Especial-

ly interested in content of Wirth's negotiations with the USSR. What does he think, practically speaking, about how to establish contact?

(b) What opinion does Long now have of Rot's statements? Does he believe that they are true? Long absolutely must report clearly about the intent of Rot's group to orient itself toward the Soviet Union. Is it possible that there exists at the present time an organized opposition by commanding officers against Hitler?

Paragraph (c) concerned OKW plans. Paragraph (d) asked about some documents which Rot intended to publish.

These comments and queries dovetail with the Gisevius theory. Gisevius' group, the twentieth of July, seems clearly meant; and it was, as has been mentioned earlier, split into pro-Soviet and pro-Western factions. Gisevius knew Wirth, whom Goerdeler and Beck had accepted as a confidant and representative in Switzerland. In fact, both Gisevius and Wirth conducted wartime negotiations with the British, although whether they did so jointly is not known to this writer. The twentieth of July group did, of course, number commanding officers, including generals and marshals, among its members. As for publication, Gisevius was assembling documents by the date of this message, as well as earlier, with the intent to publish what later appeared in his book *To the Bitter End*.

The second message, 20 April 1943, Dora to the Director, mentions Goerdeler by name and says that he or his information is coming from the Bendelerstrasse, the location of the OKW headquarters in Berlin. Gisevius knew Goerdeler well, of course, because both were members of the small inner circle of the twentieth of July. He also knew in advance when Goerdeler was coming to Switzerland. The message includes the following:

The so-called second rank of generals (literally, generals in second-best uniforms), who already wanted to take action against Hitler in January, has now decided to liquidate Hitler and all those who support him. An earlier attempt failed because Hitler was warned by Manstein.

The third message went to Moscow on 22 July 1943. It is sourced to Rot via courier. It is chiefly concerned with a serious German defeat on the East Front and the OKH reaction to that defeat.

Another Rote Drei source believed to have reported through Long was Fanny, an unidentified journalist whose information concerned military developments on the West Front.

XX. FELD

Still another source, Feld, was claimed after the war by Otto Puenter, Rado's third major source, as an unidentified sub-source who lived in Feldkirch, Austria, and repeatedly crossed illegally into Switzerland on courier missions. But Puenter is more than unreliable; as will be explained later, he has confused the record through a series of misstatements which he must know to be untrue. There is a chance, though it is rather slim, that Feld was Karl Forstmann, who lived in Feldkirch during the war and who did serve as an illegal border-crosser into Switzerland, but who apparently served Blun's network, not Puenter's. The French arrested Forstmann as a Nazi in 1946, but Gisevius intervened in his behalf. He indicated that Forstmann carried out important courier missions for Henry Goverts, a Swiss publisher in Hamburg, but made no mention of the Rote Drei.

Feld appears in three messages, in August and September 1943, which relayed low-level OB obtained mostly from soldiers on leave.

To repeat: The sources who had aliases and who are known to have been members of Long's group were Agnes, Kurz, Grau, Rot, Fanny, and possibly Feld. With the exception of the last-named, a courier, the members of the group have a certain homogeneous quality. They were not military professionals, like Werther, Teddy, and the rest. Three of them, including Long, were professional journalists. Most of them worked for two or more intelligence services. Their policital views and their motivation often seem ambiguous and devious, if not opportunistic.

XXI. THE BACKGROUND OF JOSEF WIRTH

Apparently Dr. Josef Karl Wirth was not a witting Rote Drei source, because he appears in the traffic by true name rather than alias. The Soviet interest in him, however, and in establishing contact with him, as well as other indications, strongly suggests that whether he ever worked within the Rote Drei framework or not, Wirth did maintain a clandestine relationship with the Soviets. During a postwar interrogation Flicke said that by the beginning of

1943 Wirth had sources who gave him information that he, in turn, passed to George Blun, and that Moscow was much interested.

Wirth's career in World War II is still somewhat enigmatic. Without the "government of fulfillment," which he headed as Chancellor of Germany from May 1921 to November 1922, there might not have been a Treaty of Rapallo, which re-established German-Russian diplomatic relations after World War I. And without the Treaty of Rapallo there might not have been "the spirit of Tauroggen," the friendship between the Soviet and German military establishments which was vital to Germany's evasion of the restrictions of the Versailles Treaty through training given its nascent armed forces on Soviet soil. Wirth is worth a longer look.

He was born on 6 September 1879 in Frieburg in Breisgau, where he taught school for seven years and served as a town councillor. By 1913 he was a member of the Baden Landtag as a member of the Catholic Center Party. From 1914 to 1918 he served in the Reichstag; from 1920 to 1921 he was the Federal Minister of Finance; and during his 1921-1922 period as Chancellor he also served (except for five months) as Foreign Minister. He resigned and withdrew from public service for seven silent years. In 1930-1931 he served as Federal Minister of Interior. When the Nazis seized power in 1933, he left Germany and established residence in Switzerland. He travelled, chiefly to Paris and Washington, but usually stayed in his adopted hometown of Lucerne, where he lived at Haldenstrasse 7. (Rudolf Roessler also moved to Switzerland, in early 1934, and also settled in Lucerne.)

Wirth's Minister of Finance, Walter Rathenau, was assassinated in June 1922. A speech which Wirth made at that time caught in one sentence the essence of his political views: "Der Feind steht rechts"—The enemy is on the right.

What was Wirth doing in Switzerland during the war? Mr. Dulles noted in *Germany's Underground*:

> After the attack on Norway (9 April 1940) but before the invasion of the Lowlands (10 May 1940) and France, the military conspirators, on the initiative of General Beck, communicated with the former Chancellor Josef Wirth, a convinced anti-Nazi who was living in Switzerland, and asked Wirth to make use of certain Anglo-French contacts he had to ascertain the intentions of the Western powers in the event that a

> military putsch succeeded in overthrowing Hit-
> ler. An ambiguous, noncommittal answer ar-
> rived just as the offensive in the West began.

As was noted above, Wirth met with British representatives in Ouchy a little earlier, in February 1940. He also had some contact with Allen Dulles, both directly and through Gisevius.

But his role was by no means limited to serving as an emissary of the twentieth of July group to the Western Allies. He was also in touch with Walter Schellenberg's Sicherheitsdienst, the Nazi Security Service, through Schellenberg's agent Richard Grossmann, whose aliases were Director and Ludwig. Grossmann, whose V-Mann (agent) number was 144/7959, was born in Pforzheim on 29 September 1902. From 1941 to late 1943 Grossmann worked in Switzerland, ostensibly as a representative of a firm in Stuttgart called Pintsch and Col. His duties included serving as a link between Schellenberg and Wirth. In a statement of 23 November 1943 Grossmann termed Wirth a double agent but did not explain further. Grossmann's major target was the very church circles in Germany with which Wirth was in contact. There is no reason, however, to conclude that Wirth was informing the SD about them or that he was betraying the plans and personalities of the twentieth of July group. It is likelier that Schellenberg saw in Wirth the same potential discerned earlier by Oster and Beck: the capacity to serve as a peace emissary. (By 1943 Schellenberg had concluded that Hitler's Germany was finished and was seeking to persuade an ambitious, crafty, and yet foolish Himmler that he should replace the Fuehrer.) Wirth's contact with Grossman ended some time in 1944, when the latter was arrested by the Gestapo.

Wirth, then, had contacts in Germany with both Nazis and anti-Nazis, as well as ties to the Americans, French, and English. But Grossmann suspected him of being a double agent (as Grossmann himself seems to have been), and he may well have meant that the Soviets were at the other end of the line, because he made the remark to a British intelligence officer.

Wirth's postwar career clearly marked him as a henchman of the Soviets. During the war he led in Switzerland a left-wing clique which was planning for a postwar Socialist government which would gain power in Germany through the defeat of the German armed forces followed by assistance from the USSR. A paper written by Wirth on 3 July 1945 contrasted the American, British, and French zones of Germany unfavorably with the Soviet zone. He argued that the Soviet zone had a great appeal (Anziehungskraft) for the patient German people because it permitted the establishment of political parties, whereas the Western Allies had thwarted his efforts to found his own party, Democratisches Deutschland, in West Germany. He was also engaged in a plan to send food packages to East Germany. (This Hilfspakaetchen operation is interesting because when Lucy and his colleague Xaver Schneiper went to work for Czech intelligence after the war, they microfilmed their reports and enclosed them in food packages sent to a cover address in Duesseldorf. The procedure seemed safe because thousands of food packages were going from Switzerland to Germany.)

On 1 May 1951 an anti-Communist group called "The Committee for the Liberation of Victims of Arbitrary Totalitarian Acts" launched an attack on Wirth, as well as Martin Niemoeller and others. The group was under the leadership of Margarete Buber-Neumann, who had suffered at both Communist and Nazi hands. On that day, the Communist Labor Day, the group sent to the office of the Federal Chancellor a telegram demanding "ruthless measures against former Reich Chancellor Dr. Josef Wirth, Hesse Church President Niemoeller, and all henchmen of Moscow who are no longer persons of good faith." The telegram, calling for the expulsion of Wirth and the others from West Germany, added:

> The Soviet intention to establish a counter-parliament against Bonn with Wirth as federal chancellor, and thereby to realize by force the holding of All-German talks on Ulbricht's orders from Moscow, endangers security and order . . .

Undeterred, Wirth went to East Berlin in December 1951 for the first of a series of meetings with important Soviet functionaires. During this initial visit he telephoned Ernst Lemmer, whose earlier work for the Rote Drei has already been discussed. Although he had been invited to East Berlin by Fritz Ebert, the mayor, and Karl Schirdewan, Chief of Section West of the SED (Communist Party), he reportedly spent more time with the Russians than with the Germans. One report states that during another trip, made one year later, Wirth held a secret meeting in Berlin with Lavrentiy Beria.

XXII. PAKBO

Rado's third principal source, Pakbo, was of less value to him and the Soviets than was Long, just as Long and his group did not measure up to Sissy and hers. Pakbo's true name was Otto Puenter. Born 4 April 1900 in Staefa, Switzerland, Puenter was a lawyer and a journalist who worked for the Socialist press in Bern. Reportedly he was a secret member of the Swiss Communist Party. He was in contact with the Swiss military intelligence service which used him as a channel to pass to the Soviets selected items of intelligence.

Dallin has devoted an entire chapter to Puenter, but much of what appears therein is false. Puenter has, in fact, made many false statements. He said that information about the German General Staff which he obtained during World War II came from General Alfred Jodl. He asserted that he kept in a monastery in Switzerland the entire plan for the German attack upon Stalingrad in October 1942, which he himself encoded before passing it to Rado. He alleged that Werther stood for Wehrmacht and Lucy for Luftfahrt-ministerium (Ministry of Air). He said that Lucy was a Czech. He wove a complex and fascinating tale about a young Austrian radio operator who came from Dornbirn, near the Austro-Swiss border. He had promised the home folks that he would transmit his location every night just so that they would know where he was. He chanced to be assigned to Hitler's headquarters, with the result that Pakbo always knew the Fuehrer's whereabouts. The implausibility of this fable is, however, no greater than that inherent in his explanation of his cover name. He claimed that he had teams of agents in Pontrezina, Aarau, Kreuzlingen, Bern, and Orselina—hence PAKBO. Actually, it is unlikely that he had teams of agents anywhere, and certainly improbable that they would be located at the unimportant places named by Puenter. By his own account, one of his teams was at Feldkirch/Dornbirn, but his cover name contains neither an "F" nor a "D." As a matter of fact, most of his contacts lived in Bern and Geneva.

Puenter has alleged that early in 1941 a de Gaullist reported to him that the Swiss service had received accurate information about Hitler's plan to attack the USSR in a month or a month and a half. The de Gaullist said he was looking for a contact with Moscow to pass on the information. Pakbo went to Rado to deliver the story—i.e., the attack was scheduled for 15 June 1941. Rado asked who was the source. Pakbo in turn inquired and was told the man's name was Roessler. Rado then decided to get in direct contact with Roessler, and that connection continued thenceforth.

This is Pakbo's genius for fabrication at its best. In 1941 neither Lucy nor Pakbo himself had any connection with the Rote Drei. A Dora-to-the-Director message of 15 July 1942 included the following: "At the beginning of April a new source of information appeared; he has the cover name Pakbo . . ." As was noted earlier, Lucy also joined the net in 1942. Secondly, Puenter has said in writing that he had never been in contact with Roessler and did not know his true name. Thirdly, Lucy did not meet Rado through Puenter for the simple reason that he never met Rado at all, as the traffic shows.

The question that naturally arises, then, is this: If Pakbo has told lies about important matters after the war, did he also lie to the Soviets during the war? Apart from a challenge on 7 October 1942, the Soviets seem to have accepted Pakbo's reports as valid and to have found them useful. The chances are that Pakbo, like Jim, merely tried to exaggerate the importance of his role after the war had ended.

Pakbo appears in twenty-two known messages, but only six of these contain any substantive information. The time span is from 15 July 1942 to 8 January 1944. Apparently he learned something about the Rote Kapelle arrests in Germany and reported accordingly, because on 5 October 1942 the Director asked for more information. And he also reported the arrest of Paul Boettcher, because on 8 January 1944 Moscow said, "As far as we know, Pakbo has never heard of Paul. How does it happen that he has heard so certainly about Paul's arrest?"

Like Lucy and Long, Pakbo had direct contact with the Swiss G-2. His chief sub-source was Salter, whose identity has not been firmly established but who may have been Louis Suss, born 6 October 1890 in Beblenheim, Alsace-Lorraine. A French citizen, Suss died in Switzerland on 25 April 1955. As of May 1968 his widow, Friedel, nee Kirschbaum, lived in Chene-Bourg, Geneva. There were two children, Christiane and Louis Michel. Christiane married an American ILO employee named Thompson. She was observed in 1955 at a meeting with a Soviet representative to the UN who is also a suspected intelligence operative.

Salter appeared in ten messages. He was in contact with former chancellor Josef Wirth and with British intelligence. He also knew Long and Kurz; in fact, compartmentation was often breached in the Rote Drei network.

One report says that a Professor Andre Oltramare and his son Dr. Marc Oltramare both passed intelligence to Puenter during the war and that he relayed their information to the Soviets. Andre Oltramare was a professor at the University of Geneva, where he lived with Jeanne Hersch, a philosopher much younger than he. At one time he was president or vice-president of the Geneva chapter of the Socialist Party. In 1933 he was a member of the Geneva Relief Committee for Political Prisoners, on which Pierre Nicole also served. Among his associates in 1942 were Jean Vincent, Max Horngacher, and Maurice Ducommun, all of whom were suspected of being Soviet agents.

One Mario Bodenmann, a Swiss socialist and journalist, has also been reported as a sub-source for Pakbo.

A probable Pakbo source was Bruder, who appears in only two messages, both from Dora to Director, dated 27 January and 10 May 1943. Both messages provide information about the production at the Oerlikon Arms Factory in Switzerland. The president of Werkzeugmaschinenfabrik Oerlikon, Buehrle, and Company was Emil Georg Guehrle. In middle and late 1943, as Foote has also related, the network was extremely short of funds. Pakbo and others solicited funds from Swiss businessmen, promising profitable postwar commercial orders from the USSR in exchange. Pakbo approached Buehrle, who did business with the USSR, on this basis; and Buehrle contributed eighty thousand francs. After the war the Soviets refused to honor the obligations incurred on behalf of the Rote Drei. Most of the businessmen complained bitterly, and Pakbo has alleged that he made some effort to repay the loans that he had personally solicited. Buehrle, however, merely wrote off the loss.

Whether Buehrle passed money to Pakbo or to Sissy, we have solid grounds for surmising that he was the Bruder of the Rote Drei traffic.

Despite published claims to the contrary, there is no reason to believe that a source called "Lilly of the Vatican" ever existed. Pakbo has denied that he had a line to the Vatican.

XXIII. JIM

Foote claimed in *Handbook For Spies* that he and Rado were equals, or nearly equals, each having his own network, code, and communications system. The truth, however, is that Foote, like

Puenter, grossly exaggerated his wartime importance. The traffic does not bear out Foote's claim that he had sub-sources of his own. On the contrary, Moscow clearly regarded him primarily as a W/T operator, although the most senior member in that category, and secondarily as a support man expected to give Rado help in problems of funding. Foote, whose cover name was Jim, appears twenty times in the messages in our possession. The time span is 31 October 1942 to 14 April 1944. These messages contain no new information, but they are of value in reducing Jim's self-portrait to its true, minor dimensions.

XXIV. The Structure of the Rote Drei

Now, that part of the Rote Drei structure which has been partially excavated and cleansed of distortions can be delineated. Alexander Rado is at the apex of the network, having inherited the leader's role from Maria Poliakova and Ursula Beurton. Rado had three principal sources: Rachel Duebendorfer, George Blun, and Otto Puenter, listed in order of decreasing importance. Each of these had a network of sub-agents. Through Christian Schneider and Rudolf Roessler, Duebendorfer was in touch with the most important sources in the entire network: Werther, Teddy, Anna, and Olga. Others of Sissy's known contacts, by code name, were Paul, Pierre, Vita, and Mario. Probable additional, though minor, members of her net were Bill, Bircher, Brand, Diener, Fanny, Fernand, Schwerin, and Stefan. Among his sub-sources Roessler listed, by name or description, General Hans Oster, Hans Bernd Gisevius, Carl Goerdeler, and an unknown general named Boelitz.

The second principal agent, George Blun (alias Long), directed a network which consisted chiefly of Agnes, Kurz, Grau, Rot, Fanny, and perhaps Feld.

The third principal agent, Otto Puenter (alias Pakbo), headed a net that included Salter and Bruder, as well as others whose cover names are not known.

Alexander Foote (alias Jim) was the most important of the radio operators. The others were Edmond and Olga Hamel (Eduard and Maude), Margarete Bolli (later Bolli-Schatz, cover name Rosa), probably Harry and Roger, and possibly others.

XXV. The Role of Karel Sedlacek

To this point we have viewed the Rote Drei network chiefly as an apparatus which produced intelligence for the Soviet military service. But Lucy's information, some or all of Long's, and probably Pakbo's also went to the West. The vital product, Lucy's, reached the Allies through a Czech colonel whose true name was Karel Sedlacek and whose alias was Uncle Tom. We have his story from General Frantisek Moravec, who, as Sedlacek's superior, had sent him to Switzerland in the first place. In 1935 Sedlacek was working in southern Bohemia as an intelligence officer whose targets were in Bavaria. His talents and skill caught Moravec's eye, and Sedlacek was sent to Prague for a year's training in operating a W/T set, secret writing and encoding, and decoding. He was already fluent in German. In June 1937, his training completed and his cover prepared, Sedlacek left Czechoslovakia as Karl Selzinger, a correspondent of the Prague newspaper *Narodni Listy*. For more than a year he built his cover in Zurich; then, by the fall of 1938, his first reports, military and political, arrived in Prague. By then the Czech officer was a friend of Major Hans Hausamann, the Swiss intelligence officer who directed the conveniently unofficial "Bureau Ha." In fact, it was Hausamann who provided Sedlacek's information.

By the spring of 1939 Sedlacek had begun to feel uneasy in Zurich, which was swarming with German agents. He moved to Lucerne, where Lucy was living. The two met because both used journalism as cover. Beginning in September 1939, Sedlacek was reporting by W/T to the London Czechs on German OB, movements, weapons, etc. His information came from Hausamann, who got it from Lucy, who in turn decided what information would go to which recipients. From 19 May to 6 September 1944 Lucy was under arrest, charged with passing intelligence to the Soviet and British services. From the date of his arrest, the flow of Lucy's information from Sedlacek to London stopped completely and finally. (It is thus established that information from Lucy to both the East and the West had ceased before the twentienth of July 1944 and that therefore Lucy's sources could have been among the conspirators.) Sedlacek did continue to transmit other information to London after the war ended, but after Lucy's arrest Sedlacek's reporting deteriorated rapidly in both quality and quantity. Promoted to lieutenant colonel after the war, Sedlacek became the Czech military attache in Bern, where he remained until recalled to Prague in early 1947. How he was instrumental in launching Roessler upon the second phase of his career in espionage is reported below.

Because of the clear identification of "Karl Selzinger" as the alias under which Karel Sedlacek appeared in Switzerland, it was somewhat surprising to find a number of derivate references terming Selzinger an alias used by Rudolf Roessler. In *The Secrets of a Soviet Spy*—a French translation by Edition de la Paix in 1951, and based upon the first edition of Foote's *Handbook For Spies* (1949)—the claim is made that Lucy was Selzinger. Foote then mixed up Roessler and Sedlacek so thoroughly that confusion has persisted ever since. He said that Selzinger was a "man of the theater, probably a director," which is fairly accurate for Roessler but not for Sedlacek. He said that Selzinger was never a German but rather had been born a Czech national, a statement that is false for Roessler but true of Sedlacek. He added that Selzinger was allowed by Swiss authorities to remain in Switzerland in exchange for intelligence from Germany with which he provided the Swiss, a statement that was true of both men. Finally, Foote said, "Until the annexation of Czechoslovakia, Lucy worked for the General Staff of Czechoslovakia; hence it is possible that the secret of his mysterious sources is to be found in Prague." (p. 86—translation by the author) There is no reason to believe that Roessler worked as an agent for Czechoslovakia until World War II had ended, whereas Sedlacek was a staff officer of Czech military intelligence.

One confusion was created not by Foote but by those who cited him, with or without attribution. Foote did not say, in 1949-1951, that Selzinger was an alias used by Roessler. It appears that at that time he did not know or did not remember Roessler's name. What he said was that Lucy was Selzinger, with the clear implication that Selzinger was Lucy's true name. Before the second edition of *Handbook for Spies* came out in 1964, Foote or his editors knew that the true name of Lucy was Rudolf Roessler. But instead of correcting the earlier errors, the 1964 edition compounded them by printing exactly what the French version had said except for the substitution of Roessler for Selzinger throughout. Thus Roessler now was called a Czech national and a member of the prewar Czech service, errors picked up even by German newspapers.

Corroboration for General Moravec's identification of Selzinger as one of the aliases used by Sedlacek appeared in an article by R. Stroebinger, "The Man Whom No One Knows," *Lidova Demokracia*, Prague, 23 July-17 September 1967. Stroebinger's account is partially distorted by repetition of false statements made by Pierre Quet and Pierre Accoce, whose unreliability the Czech writer does, however, recognize. Stroebinger quotes an unidentified intelligence colleague of Sedlacek's as saying that he began his intelligence work on the Czech-German border in southern Bohemia. A very successful operative, he had in both countries an agent network that included a German Catholic priest and a member of the Abwehr, living in Dresden, whose name was Paul Thummel and whose designator as a Czech agent was A-54. (Comment: It appears possible that Stroebinger is here attempting to play down the role played by General Moravec. Thummel was his agent and not Sedlacek's as far as we know.) According to Stroebinger, Thummel sent his valuable information to a letter drop—Josef Jursa, Willa (Villa?), Canton Zurich, Rosengarten, Switzerland. Thummel used as an alias the name Josef Koehler. It is not clear whether Jursa was a separate person used as a mail drop or was an alias under which Sedlacek picked up this mail.

According to Stroebinger, Sedlacek functioned as a cutout between Roessler and Major Hans Hausamann, both of whom knew him as Uncle Tom. In fact, Stroebinger asserts that after Munich, Hausamann "invited a close collaboration . . . with the Czechoslovak intelligence service, the Second Department of the Ministry of Defense." Sedlacek, however, had his own lines not only to London and France but also to Prague. He had, according to Stroebinger, a shortwave transmitter with which he maintained regular contact from Zurich. His cover name for this traffic was Kazi.

Stroebinger's assertion that Sedlacek served Roessler as a cutout to Hausamann, for reasons of security, clashes with his claim that Sedlacek and Roessler met at the Villa Stutz, Kastanienbaum, near Lucerne. The Villa Stutz was the headquarters of the Bureau Ha (for Hausamann).

There are records of several cover names for Karel Sedlacek: Uncle Tom, Kazi, Selzinger, Charles, and two others of particular interest.

First the files consulted contain several references to a Karel Balecek or Palecek, who has been confused with Sedlacek but who is probably not the same man. There are also references to Karel Sedlacek, born 24 August or 24 September 1894, who does not seem identical; but these items add that as early as April 1953 the subject used the alias Charles Simpson. A report of 1960 lists Sedlacek as a former journalist (correct) and former military attache in Bern (correct) and adds that during World War II he lived in Switzerland (perhaps at St. Gallen during part of this period) with a British passport and under the name of Charles Simpson. Clearly, more work will be required to establish whether the Sedlacek who arrived in Zurich as a Czech correspondent named Selzinger also appeared in Switzerland at a later date as a British subject named Charles Simpson.

Also intriguing is a 1946 report that says that a Colonel Sedlacek, the military attache in Bern, had then been identified as an intelligence officer who was "presumably working for the Russians." This report added, "He came to Switzerland during the war as a British agent, bearing a British passport in the name of Simon." Obviously Simon could be a garble for Simpson. The Center in Moscow, moreover, would be unlikely to use as a radio cover name an alias appearing on a British passport. Therefore, several references to Simon in Moscow-Paris traffic between July and September 1945 are probably coincidental. Such a conclusion, however, would by no means exclude a working hypothesis that Sedlacek collaborated not only with the Swiss and British but also with Soviet intelligence. Many people who worked inside the Rote Drei did the same.

Stroebinger's piece contains several references to Rote Drei traffic but, unfortunately, does not include the text of any of these messages. Here are examples:

> On Wednesday, 11 June 1941, Roessler brought to Rado a sensational message received from Dr. Ch. Schneider: a general assault on the territory occupied by Russia will start on Sunday, 22 June, at 3:15 a.m. Rado sent this message immediately to the Director, his superior . . . in Moscow, via Foote's transmitter. Several days later—14, 16, 17, and 18 June 1941, Alexander Foote sent to Director all information received from Lucy. It was exhausting work. Moscow's answer was short: We heard you clearly. Over.

This message, which is not in our holdings, is spurious, an invention possibly based upon Foote's account. Schneider was the cutout, not Roessler. And Schneider took Roessler's material to Sissy, not to Rado. The clincher, however, is the fact cited near the outset of this report. The holdings that we do have establish that Sissy's tie with Taylor began in the fall of 1942. A message of 8 October 1942 from Director to Sissy includes the sentence, "Your new people Marius and Taylor do not work badly." There is a theoretical possibility that Lucy's information was going to Moscow much earlier, through a different channel, and that Sissy was not cut in until late 1942; but the possibility seems remote and contrary to what we know of the practices of Soviet military intelligence.

Stroebinger does cite two messages correctly, or nearly so. But both were sent in February 1943, and both have appeared in overt publications.

XXVI. VLADIMIR SOKOLIN

Earlier in this account, in a section dealing with Dr. Josef Wirth, a message of 5 October 1943, Dora to Director, was cited. Included therein was this statement: "According to Wirth the German Embassy in Bern is extremely interested in Sokolin." The remark appears in a context chiefly concerned with the Free Germany Committee, conceived in and directed from Moscow.

Vladimir Sokolin (spelled Sokoline in some accounts) may have been the alias of one Vladimir Shapiro or Schapiro, or Shapiro may have been the alias and Sokolin the true name. We shall call him Sokolin. The records which concern him are extensive but have not been summarized here because all available information indicates that he was not a part of the Rote Drei. Born in Geneva of Jewish parents, the father a White Russian and the mother Scottish, Sokolin became in 1937 the Under Secretary of the USSR's Permanent Delegation of the International Labor Office, League of Nations, Geneva, as well as the Assistant Secretary General of the League of Nations. There was a seeming break with Moscow after the USSR was dropped from the League of Nations in December 1939 as a result of the invasion of Finland. But either the split was unreal, designed to strengthen cover, or it was patched up and healed, because the reports of Sokolin's wartime activities clearly indicate espionage conducted on behalf of the USSR. He was in touch with Leon Nicole, Alexander Abramson, and perhaps others who were associated with the Rote Drei. It was also reported that through one of these contacts he asked Rado if he could be of service and that Rado relayed the suggestion to Moscow, where it was rejected. There are clear indications that Sokolin was engaged in economic espionage for the USSR after the war ended. It appears then that in this instance, as in others, Soviet intelligence tried not to mix their networks, the security of which required separation.

XXVII. PHASE II—LUCY'S POSTWAR OPERATION

Here our account would have ended if Karel Sedlacek had not known Xaver Franz Josef Schnieper, a Swiss citizen born on 6 January 1910 in Emman, Lucerne Canton. He had attended the Universities of Koenigsberg, Berlin, and Vienna, majoring in drama and intending to direct plays, an ambition which he had to abandon when the Nazis seized power. He first met Rudolf Roessler, who was equally interested in drama, in Berlin in 1933. By the beginning of the following year, he had persuaded Roessler and his wife to move to Lucerne. Schnieper also went back to Switzerland and found employment in Lucerne as a librarian. By October 1936 he was a member of a leftist Catholic group which twice a month published a newssheet called *Entscheidung*.

Sedlacek knew Schnieper well. He also knew that by the time the war ended, both Schnieper and Roessler were plagued by financial problems. Both were struggling to make ends meet as free-lance journalists. Some time before his departure for Prague, Sedlacek introduced his successor as Czech military attache to Schnieper. The successor, in turn, introduced Schnieper to Captain Rudolf Wolf of Czech intelligence.

In the summer of 1947 Wolf asked Schnieper to ask Roessler whether he was willing to resume intelligence work. Lucy agreed. With Schnieper serving as intermediary, Roessler supplied the Czechs—and thus the Soviets—with information, mostly military, on the forces, dispositions, weapons, etc., of the United States, England, and France in West Germany, as well as the budding West German military force. They were sentenced by a Swiss court on 5 November 1953 to a year and nine months, respectively; but the time already spent in detention, nine months for each, was counted. Released in early 1954, Roessler died in 1958.

This bald account sounds mundane—a trivial, almost irrelevant epilogue to the glamorous days of World War II. Yet a moment's reflection shows that such a view is unjustified. Lucy's first phase lasted for only a little more than two years, his second for six. The second phase lacks the high drama of the first, but the fact remains that Roessler and Schnieper delivered valuable classified information to the Soviets, via the Czechs, in the postwar period as well. And the intriguing question of sources looms as large in both phases.

Moreover, it is not likely that the two periods are unconnected. Lucy obviously had human sources for his 1947-1953 reporting, even though his defense heavily stressed the amount of information that he had gleaned from the newspapers. If we can unearth some of these people, we can expect to find links to the sources of 1941-1944.

One contact, according to newspaper accounts of the trial, was a Mrs. Theresa Hildebrand of the staff of a Chicago magazine called *Common Cause*. Roessler asked the Czechs if they wanted to add 1500 francs monthly to his pay so that he could extend his coverage to the USA through Mrs. Hildebrand and her contacts. The indictment of Roessler said, however, that he had merely copied the names of Mrs. Hildebrand and others from *Common Cause* and that they were not implicated.

A professional source who examined some of the microfilmed reports prepared by Roessler and Schnieper for passage to Prague concluded that part of these had come not only from the Blank Office (Federal Ministry of Defense, then headed by Theodore Blank) but specifically from the office of Joachim Oster, the son of General Hans Oster.

Joachim Oster, usually called Achim, was born on 20 February 1914 in Dresden. He entered the army in 1933 as an officer candidate with the Second Artillery Regiment. He was promoted to first lieutenant in 1938, to captain in 1941, to major in 1943. He attained general's rank during the postwar years.

In 1949 he began work as secretary to Dr. Josef Mueller, who was a friend of his father's and a member of the twentieth of July group. Oster held this position for at least six years. During this period Mueller reportedly headed a group which worked for a neutralist, pro-USSR Germany. Other members of the group, besides Mueller and Oster, included Otto John and George Blun, whom we have already mentioned as Long of the Rote Drei.

In 1950 Joachim Oster was appointed to the Blank Office. He served as chief of the security section of Amt Blank (Department IV/A6) and in this capacity conducted liaison with the British, French, and Americans, as well as with other Germans. In January 1956 he was transferred to other, presumably less sensitive, duties in the Ministry of Defense. About September 1958 he was posted to Madrid as the military attache. There he reportedly established contact with the old Spanish Loyalist, Gil Robles.

XXVIII. THE RETURN OF AGNES

The unidentified contact of Roessler, who reported in 1955 that Goerdeler, Gisevius, "General Boelitz," and "the predecessor of Canaris" were World War II sources of Lucy's, also said that as of the reporting date Roessler was still in contact with one Lemmer, who was either in the Blank Office or who had a contact therein. Other Phase II sources were said to be one Thormann and a man named Borchheimer, who was a professor at the University of Heidelberg.

There can be little doubt that the first of these is the same Ernst Lemmer who, as Agnes, was a Rote Drei source during World War II.

XXIX. DR. WERNER THORMANN

Thormann is believed to be Dr. Werner Thormann. He was born in Germany, acquired Austrian citizenship through naturalization, but until 1933 remained mainly in Germany, where he was chief editor of the weekly *Deutsche Republik* and the *Rhein-Mainische Volkszeitung*. At an undetermined time he served Dr. Josef Wirth as his secretary, probably during Wirth's 1921-1922 period. After the Nazis' seizure of power, he moved to Paris, and from September 1939 to May 1940 he was an editor and speaker on the German Freedom Station there. In July 1940 the U.S. Government granted him an emergency visa, and he spent the war years in the United States and Switzerland. As of April 1947 he was the editor of *Zukunft* (Future). He died some time before 1958.

XXX. PROFESSOR MAX HORKHEIMER

"Borchheimer" appears to be a garble for Professor Max Horkheimer, born 14 February 1895 in Stuttgart. About 1928 he became head of the Institute for Social Research, founded at the University of Frankfurt to disseminate Marxist Studies. When Hitler came to power, the Institute moved to Geneva. In 1934 Horkheimer came to the United States and there established the main offices of the Institute under the sponsorship of Columbia University. By 1948 he was attempting to re-establish a branch of the Institute in Frankfurt am Main, and by the following year he was a member of the faculty of the University of Frankfurt.

There are reports that he is or was a fellow-traveler, once closely associated with the Lenin Institute of Moscow; that he has or has had Soviet intelligence ties; and that he had been considered for the position of psychological advisor to the West German Defense Ministry (Amt Blank) although he was an opponent of the Bonn Government.

There is no proof that Horkheimer provided Lucy with information after World War II. And if he did so, the system of communication remains unknown. It is noted, however, that one Emile Siegmund Grunberg was the son of Karl Grunberg, the first director of the Institute for Social Research. He and his brother Karl were translators for the International Labor Organization in Geneva. Emile and his wife knew Alexander Abramson (alias Isaac), Rachel Duebendorfer (alias Sissy), and Paul Boettcher, as well as probably other members of the Rote Drei network.

There is, however, a difficulty, a blur in the logic, inherent in the assumption that Josef Wirth, Joachim Oster, possibly Josef Mueller, Ernst Lemmer, Werner Thormann, and Max Horkheimer were Lucy's sources, or among those sources, during the period of 1947-1953. During this period the Soviets could have established contact with any of them much more simply and directly than through a procedure whereby they met with Roessler in Germany or Switzerland, Roessler passed reports to Schnieper and thus the Czechs, and the Czech service gave the product to the Soviets. Lemmer, in particular, was far better placed than Roessler to serve as the central collection point.

The question may be partly resolved by one of Roessler's major courtroom arguments in his defense. He maintained that almost everything that he sold to the Czechs was compiled from overt sources, chiefly newspapers, and that the information given him by his German friends was much less important. The claim may be true, for people who knew Lucy considered him a truthful man. The remainder of the answer is that the act of providing Lucy with intelligence would in no way have precluded the direct provision of the same or other information by the same sources to Soviet intelligence officers, or to both German services, East and West, or to practically anyone else. For these men, Lucy included, were great equivocators, adept, as the German phrase has it, at carrying water on both shoulders.

XXXI. LUCY THE MERCENARY

There can be no doubt that Lucy himself was motivated chiefly, if not entirely, by mercenary considerations. Here are a few excerpts from the traffic flowing between Moscow and Rado:

> 12.3.1943 . . . Agree to buy Plan Ostwall for 5000 francs. Does Lucy know whether these documents are genuine and reliable?
>
> 10. and 11.11.1943 . . . Sissy states that Lucy group no longer works when the salary stops.
>
> 14.11.1932 . . . Please tell Lucy in our name that . . . his group will surely be paid according to his demands. We are ready to reward him richly for his information.
>
> 9.12.1943 . . . Inform Lucy not to worry about the money situation.

During the postwar phase Lucy submitted somewhat more than one hundred reports. He and Schnieper were paid a total sum of between thirty-three thousand and forty-eight thousand Swiss francs. Lucy kept three-fourths of this sum.

XXXII. THE PEDDLERS

During his career Roessler provided intelligence to services of the USSR, Czechoslovakia, Switzerland, and England at a minimum.

Malcolm Muggeridge commented in *The Observer*, 8 January 1967, on Lucy's cupidity:

> I seem to detect a professional touch in the assiduity with which Roessler, when the Russians at least realized his worth, screwed out of them seven thousand Swiss francs a month by way of retainer and a lot of generous supplementary bonuses besides—by Red standards, a very high rate of remuneration.

And Wirth? His record suggests that he became a Soviet agent of influence in the early 1920s. A year or two after the signing of the Treaty of Rapallo, he made the first of several trips to the USSR, where he conducted financial negotiations involving forestry rights and the construction of a railroad. He was pleased that German men and officers were being trained on Russian soil, in evasion of the Versailles Treaty, even though his own regime was called the "government of fulfillment" because it was supposedly carrying out all of its obligations under that treaty. The Rote Drei traffic itself shows that Moscow at times directed Rado to obtain intelligence from Wirth during World War II.

Yet he was also in contact with Walter Schellenberg, through Richard Grossmann and perhaps in other ways as well. Was he, then, withholding from the SD his relationship with the Soviets as well as what he knew about the twentieth of July conspirators? The answer to the first part of this question is probably yes, but the same cannot be said about the second, at least not with much assurance. Himmler was prepared to listen to proposals that were treasonable from a Nazi point of view whenever he deemed the circumstances secure. There are clear indications in the record that he envisaged himself as Hitler's successor. He once told Canaris that he knew perfectly well the identities of all the anti-Hitler plotters. In short, if Wirth and others were betraying the conspiracy to Schellenberg, they were also being doublecrossed by a Himmler who hoped that the plan to assassinate the Fuehrer would succeed.

The Soviets, the SD—anyone else? Wirth's major Rote Drei contact appears to have been the French journalist, George Blun. In 1940 he made a trip to Paris in order to inform the French government personally of the military situation in Germany after the invasion of Norway. He made similar trips after the war. There is a report of contact with the Deuxieme Bureau. And there was some contact on the record, unproductive, with the OSS during the war.

Ernst Lemmer's intelligence contacts were discussed earlier— USSR, Swiss, and SD as a minimum.

Hans Bernd Gisevius joined the Nazis, worked in the German police and the Ministry of the Interior, yet joined the twentieth of July plotters. He supplied the British with intelligence for three and a half years before the war and during its initial phase. Then he became a major OSS contact.

There are only uncertain indications that he was linked to the Rote Drei. One source reported that Gisevius had contact with Rado. His relations with the Swiss police were excellent, and he was on good terms with quite a few Swiss businessmen, one of whom was Emil Georg Buehrle of the Oerlickon Machine and Tool Works. His ties to the courier Karl Forstmann have been noted earlier in this account.

We know that Gisevius had intelligence contacts with the Western Allies. Roessler listed Gisevius as a source. There are indications that he knew some members of the Rote Drei net and may himself have been alias Rot of that group. But there are also valid indications that despite the confidence which Hans Oster, Goerdeler, and others in the twentieth of July group seem to have accorded him, he may have been an RSHA agent too. One report stated that Himmler's secretary had so identified him. Some postwar interrogations of German intelligence officers include their comments that Ernst Kaltenbrunner, RSHA chief and Schellenberg's superior, received reports from Gisevius as late as April 1945. The record contains other references to links between Gisevius and Heydrich as well as Gisevius and Schellenberg. Such reports, however, are likely to be unreliable. All twentieth of July participants became unpopular with most Germans. When Gisevius went to the Nuremburg War Crimes Trials in 1946 as a witness for Hjalmar Schacht, he became also a highly effective witness for the prosecution, hence doubly unpopular in postwar Germany. That some denunciations were inspired by rancor therefore seems highly probable. At first blush it appears odd that he was allowed to remain a German intelligence officer in Switzerland after the RSHA assimilated the Abwehr, despite the fact that the Gestapo issued an arrest order for him in August 1944. But it should be recalled that Goerdeler, sentenced on 8 September 1944, was not executed until February 1945 because Himmler hoped that the contacts of such men with the Western Allies might save his own skin later. On balance, then, it is considered that Gisevius had intelligence contacts with the Americans, the British, the Swiss, and probably the Soviets, but not with Nazi Germany, except for his major role in the resistance.

XXXIII. THE STAGE AND THE ACTORS

This account has said next to nothing about the Swiss role in the drama of the Rote Drei. Today Switzerland tends to seem just the scenery of the story—the picture-postcard, snow-frosted backdrop against which the action was played out. But this aura of passivity, of being uninvolved, is really illusory. The fact is that certain Swiss officers were very directly a part of the activity of the Rote Drei. Understandably, this involvement remains a source of some concern to the Swiss, even today, because it is at odds with that strict neutrality which Switzerland has proclaimed for centuries as buckler and breastplate.

The traffic, however—that obdurate record on which we have tried to base as much of this account as possible—plainly reveals Swiss involvement. When arrests were made, Moscow asked why Rote Drei members in contact with the Swiss authorities—Lucy, Pakbo, Long—did not get more information from them. The Swiss General Staff was a sufficiently valuable source to have been given the Rote Drei cover name of Luise. Lucy's contacts with the Swiss military intelligence preceded his work in the Rote Drei, and the same is very likely true of Pakbo and certain others.

At least two Swiss officers should be mentioned here. The first is Brigadier Colonel Roger Masson, now dead, who was the chief of Swiss wartime intelligence. The second is Major Hans Hausamann. Before World War II began, Hausamann had recognized that Switzerland, already teeming with the spies of other nations, was itself sadly lacking in military intelligence and in sources to provide it. In Teufen, near St. Gallen, he established an unofficial intelligence center, funded actually or nominally by himself and certain friends. When war came, this office, known as the "Bureau Ha," was linked to the official Swiss Army intelligence structure. Quite deliberately, however, the Swiss chieftains did not incorporate the office into the Army but left it largely autonomous. It is reasonable to conjecture that this preservation of unofficial or only semi-official status resulted chiefly from the significant fact that Bureau Ha outside the official framework could be far freer of the shackles imposed by neutrality than any part of the government could be.

Dr. Xaver Schnieper worked as a junior officer in the Bureau Ha. He introduced Lucy to Major Hausamann. Only the Swiss know today whether the vital information coming from Germany went first to Lucy and then, via Hausamann, to Masson, or whether the Swiss received the bulk of the information from their sources in Germany and passed it to Sedlacek for relay to the British and to Lucy for relay to the Russians. What we can be sure of is that Switzerland was not just part of the World War II scenery; it had a small piece of the action.

The story of the Rote Drei remains nevertheless the tale, in essence, of two firm camps, between which shuttled ambiguous and uncommitted men. On the one side stood the anti-Hitler German conspirators. There was an East-West schism in their ranks, but they were united and unwavering in their resolve to rid Germany and the world of Hitler. On the other were the Soviet armed forces and intelligence services, also committed to Hitler's destruction but only as a step toward the same domination of the earth that Hitler had longed for. Both groups, the tiny and the vast, were made up for the most part of dedicated activists. Between the two forces were Roessler and certain of his associates: Wirth, Mueller, Lemmer, Gisevius, Horkheimer, probably Thormann, perhaps Joachim Oster. These are a different breed from such twentieth of July figures as Hans Oster, Goerdeler, and Beck. During the 1943-1945 period, at least, Lucy, Lemmer, et al., were psychologically much more akin to Himmler, Kaltenbrunner, and Schellenberg than to the heroes of the resistance, the Soviets, or even such Rote Drei figures as Rachel Duebendorfer.

Lemmer is the pure type, and his postwar tenure as Deputy Chairman of the Christian Democratic Union in East Germany is its perfect symbol.

These are the men who posed as arbiters, as intellectuals who had preserved their integrity by being above it all. But the truth is that they did not say, "A plague on both your houses." They dickered. They sought advantage—private material advantage—from many quarters.

Roessler, Blun, Lemmer, and the rest could have been replaced by any others willing and able to live well in wartime Switzerland; their roles were essential, though not very important; but they themselves, as individuals, were not of consequence.

The true heroes of the tale are those few men who lived in an age of appalling complexity, of rottenness at the highest levels of their government, so that they were forced not only to risk a barbaric death (some of them were executed by being strangled with piano wire) but to deal unequivocally with the fact that what morality demanded of them was treason.

A few of them were Lt. General Ludwig Beck, suicide; Lawyer Hans von Dohnanyi, hanged; General Erich Fellgiebel, hanged; Dr. Carl Friedrich Goerdeler, hanged; Reichskriminal-direktor Arthur Nebe, hanged; General Friedrich Olbricht, hanged; Major General Hans Oster, hanged; General Fritz Thiele, hanged; Field Marshal Erwin von Wilzleben, hanged.

Lucy and his Rote Drei associates lived on.

THE ROTE KAPELLE ELSEWHERE

The agents of the Rote Kapelle did not confine their activities to Belgium, France, Holland, Germany, and Switzerland. There is evidence that the Rote Kapelle organization extended its operations into several other countries as well. The following is a country by country summary of the contacts known to have existed between these countries and the main networks of the Rote Kapelle. Specifically, Soviet intelligence operations in Bulgaria, Rumania, Yugoslavia, Czechoslovakia, Italy, Austria, Poland, Portugal, Scandinavia, and Canada had ties with the Rote Kapelle. Most of these connections were used as channels for financing and communications, but there was also some operational interaction. This section of our study is very thin. The fact that our accounts of Soviet espionage in Western Europe are far more detailed than our records of such activity elsewhere will permit should not be construed as an indication of the extent of operations but solely as a reflection of the extent to which records of the operations have been available.

AUSTRIA

Manfred von Grim, an Austrian broker residing in Vienna, established contact with Alexander Rado, probably in Zurich. Von Grim suggested to Rado that they use von Grim's friend, Prince von Lichtenstein, and the latter's high connections, for intelligence purposes. Von Grim was given the code name Grau and from then on was frequently mentioned in the Dora traffic to Moscow. Von Grim made frequent trips to France and Italy, during which he engaged in espionage under cover of some kind of business undertaking. In Austria he developed a wide circle of contacts from whom he elicited information.

Margarethe Seidler was the cousin of Manfred von Grim and worked closely with him. Margarethe Seidler maintained an intimate relationship with Otto von Habsburg. It is not clear whether von Grim had prevailed upon her to contract this relationship for intelligence purposes. Von Habsburg was probably an unwitting source.

Schneiderin was the code name of an unknown agent who probably operated in Austria and had contact with the Rote Drei in Switzerland. A message from Moscow to Dora on 20 December 1942 stated that one or two transmitters for the Swiss group could be left with Schneiderin, who presumably lived near the Austrian-Swiss border.

BULGARIA

Germaine Schneider probably served during 1937 as a courier to an unknown agent in Bulgaria. The establishment or reorganization of a network in the Balkans was part of the agenda of discussions attended by Trepper in Switzerland in 1937. By the autumn of 1940 the Stoinoff-Mirtscheff group was operating effectively in Bulgaria. In the autumn of 1941 the Germans achieved their first interceptions of the Stoinoff-Mirtscheff W/T traffic between Bulgaria and Moscow, but they were unable to decipher the messages.

Leopold Trepper told one of his German interrogators that news of the compromise of Wenzel's cipher was sent from Bulgaria to Moscow, presumably in July 1942. Since it was Germaine Schneider who first brought the news to Trepper, it is possible that her old courier connections with Bulgaria may have been used, though she does not seem to have gone there herself. It seems likely that any intelligence traffic from Trepper's contacts in Western Europe would have been handled in Bulgaria by the Stoinoff-Mirtscheff network or by the Russian Legation in Sofia, to which this network was linked. The Stoinoff-Mirtscheff network was becoming progressively stronger during 1942, and by November 1942 the Germans had detected twelve separate W/T links running from Bulgaria, some to Moscow and some to Tiflis.

In January 1943 the Germans succeeded in deciphering the code used in the Stoinoff-Mirtscheff traffic from Bulgaria to Moscow and Tiflis. It is not known whether they were helped by the discoveries they had made in the Low Countries and France during 1942. In February 1943 they seized the Stoinoff-Mirtscheff W/T station at Varna in Bulgaria, but their follow-up was so slow that warning reached Moscow from at least one of the several other lines.

Seven other Stoinoff-Mirtscheff stations were captured during 1943, and the Germans believed that the only remaining W/T contact of the group with Moscow was through the Soviet Legation at

Sofia. Despite their belief that this line had survived, the Germans attempted a W/T playback through Milka Stoinoff. At a later date, but perhaps still in 1943, one agent of the Stoinoff-Mirtscheff group escaped to Russia.

CANADA

In 1940 Hermina Rabinowitch left Europe via Portugal to work at the headquarters of the International Labor Organization, which had been transferred to Montreal. She had worked for the ILO since 1929, and from Igor Gouzenko's documents and her unwilling evidence in the Canadian case it seems clear that she also qualified as a member of "Gisela's family." ("Gisela" was Maria Josefovna Poliakova.)

In November 1943 Rabinowitch received from Rachel Duebendorfer an appeal for help in a letter sent under cover of the ILO pouch. Duebendorfer asked for six thousand seven hundred dollars. Following the arrest of the W/T operators Foote, the Hamels, and Bolli, Duebendorfer appealed to Hermina for money through Alexander Abramson, who also used the ILO pouch.

In January 1944 Duebendorfer again cabled Hermina for help, and in March 1944 Duebendorfer sent Hermina another letter. Only in April 1944 did Hermina finally get the interest of Nikolai Zabotin, the Soviet Military Attache. On 5 May 1944 Hermina was visited in Montreal by Sergei Kudryaytsev, who had been detailed by Motinov to handle the contact with her. She was shown a letter addressed to her signed "Gisel." This letter reads as follows:

> Dear Hermina,
>   Thank you very much indeed for your care in our affairs and we hope that you will help us in future. It is important for us to send a letter to Geneva for Sissy. Can you send this letter with a a reliable man whom you trust? All expenses will be paid. Please let us know about your proposals in this connection as soon as possible. Please inform us about delivery of your service mail to Geneva and why are you sure that it is not censored? Please wire to Rachel or Alexander that Gisel's parents are interested about the health of Sissy and Paul and that they will help

them. We ask you to forward ten thousand dollars to that watch company according to Sissy's
instructions. Make arrangements with our representative about forwarding this sum of money
to you in USA. All your personal expenses will
be paid.

With best regards,

Gisel.

Rabinowitch understood this letter to mean that she was authorized by "Gisel" to arrange for the payment of ten thousand
dollars to the Helbein Watch Company in New York. Hermina admitted to the Royal Commission that she had made a trip to New
York in order to have the money conveyed to Geneva. On this occasion, while in New York, Hermina was in touch with Rachel P. Pregel, the wife of Alex Pregel, with Lydia Zagorsky, who lived with
the Pregels, and with Mrs. Jacques Sherry.

In 1946 Igor Gouzenko testified at the trial of Edward M. Ma-
zerall, who was charged with violation of the Canadian Officials Secret Act. Gouzenko stated that Hermina Rabinowitch, an important
Soviet agent, travelled in 1944 to New York, where she received ten
thousand dollars from Pavel Mikhailov, acting Soviet Consul in New
York City and a Soviet Army Intelligence officer. He also testified
that Rabinowitch then transmitted this money to "Sissy" (Rachel
Duebendorfer) in Geneva, Switzerland, using as an intermediary
the head of a watch company in New York.

CZECHOSLOVAKIA

The organization or reorganization of an RIS network in Czechoslovakia was apparently on the agenda of discussions attended by
Leopold Trepper in 1937 or 1938 in Switzerland. It is possible that
the RIS network known as the Oskol group began its existence in
Prague during 1939, and Victor Sukolov may have visited the group
about the time of his visit to Berlin in April 1939. Very little is
known about the Oskol group, but it is presumed to have been connected with the Soviet Embassy in Prague. During 1940 the Oskol
group was probably developing sources in Czechoslovakia and communicating with Moscow through the Soviet Embassy.

On 3 October 1941 the Germans captured a W/T station in

Prague and made seventy-three arrests. There seems little doubt that this was the Oskol service, of which nothing more was heard. Although Schulze-Boysen is reported to have had intelligence connections in Prague, the Germans do not seem to have found any evidence of a link between the German and Czechoslovakian groups.

Towards the end of 1943 the Germans captured a Soviet W/T agent in Bohemia. They claimed to have followed this arrest with a successful W/T playback.

In an August 1941 radio message from Moscow Sukolov was instructed to deposit two thousand RM with Brantischeck and Wojatscheck or through them to contact and deliver the sum to Rudi. Brantischeck and Wojatscheck were art dealers who operated a shop in Prague. This shop served as an agent contact point and as a depository for funds for other agents attached to the net. Rudi was the cover name of an individual whose true name has not yet been ascertained. Rudi's mission was to bribe persons around von Neurath, the Reich Protector for Czechoslovakia, and to recruit or exploit them for espionage purposes.

In early November 1941 Sukolov visited Czechoslovakia and made contact with Maria Rauch in Raudnitz, Machagasse 1414, and with Fnu Urban, a hops dealer, in Prague. Sukolov is known to have delivered a parcel to Maria Rauch, the wife of Heinrich Rauch, who was an agent of Sukolov's network in Belgium.

Margarete Barcza, the mistress of Sukolov, was a Czech national. When Sukolov and Barcza went to Marseilles in January 1942, they formed or reactivated a group of Czech agents under the cover of a Simex branch office.

Bogdan Kobulov, a Soviet intelligence officer stationed in Berlin from November 1940 until June 1941, probably distributed transmitters to agents in Czechoslovakia and Poland.

ITALY

Henri Robinson paid two visits to Italy from France, via Switzerland, in 1936 and possibly was managing a Red Army agent somewhere in Italy. In 1937 or 1938 Trepper was scheduled to discuss the reorganization of a network in Italy. Rado may have been conducting operations against Italy as early as 1937. In 1942 there were clear signs of operations against Italy in which Rado may have been involved. It is known that on one occasion in 1942 information was passed to him via the Italian and Swiss Communist parties. At another unknown date in the same year Foote received from Italy a false passport in the name of Schneider. This was a Swiss confection, and it was Foote's task to renew it through Anna Mueller. According to Foote's recollection, it had been renewed once before at Marseilles. The owner of the passport seems to have had no connection with Christian Schneider or with Franz Schneider. Some time later Foote identified the photograph in the Schneider passport with the face of a man pictured in the Italian press because of his arrest for espionage in Italy.

There is an unconfirmed story that a diplomat in the German Embassy in Rome was detected as a Russian agent as a result of the arrests and interrogations in the Schulze-Boysen group.

According to another source, the 4th Section of the RU had in 1940 in Italy an illegal resident called Grigoriyev (Grigori), who was arrested there in 1940, sentenced to thirty years, and may still have been in jail in 1950.

POLAND

Rudolf von Scheliha, who had worked as a secretary in the German Legation at Warsaw since 1930, was recruited as an agent for Soviet intelligence in 1936 or 1937. His first case officer, if not recruiter, was Rudolf Herrnstadt, a journalist employed on the *Berliner Tageblatt* in Warsaw. Because Herrnstadt was a Jew, direct contact with von Scheliha became unsafe under the Nazis; and Ilse Stoebe, employed in Warsaw as a foreign correspondent for German and Swiss newspapers, acted as a cutout. Herrnstadt passed von Scheliha's information to the Soviet Embassy in Warsaw, and von Scheliha continued to supply valuable information through Ilse Stoebe until September 1939, when war broke out between Germany and Poland.

PORTUGAL

At the end of October 1940 money was passed through Portugal to Rado in Switzerland; three thousand five hundred dollars of the total was intended for Ursula Hamburger. Trepper told his German interrogators that during June 1941 an RU agent passed through Paris on his way to Portugal and relieved him of certain responsibilities in the peninsula. The story is reasonable because the withdrawal of Soviet embassies at that time and the consequent scarcity of communications disturbed much of the RU organization in Western Europe. But there is no evidence in Trepper's earlier career of a Portuguese or Spanish connection, and it might be suspected that here, as elsewhere, he exaggerated his importance in order to deceive the Germans.

There are indications in 1944 and 1945 that Pannwitz, the leader of the Sonderkommando which exploited the arrests of Trepper and his friends in 1942, extended his interests into Spain and Portugal.

RUMANIA

In the spring of 1940 Moscow proposed to Ursula Hamburger that her group should be transferred to Rumania and that Foote should go there as a forerunner to establish Rumanian contacts. The proposal was not approved and seems to have been abandoned when the Germans moved into Rumania.

Maria Ghiolu, a Rumanian national residing in Bucharest, was in close contact with Alexander Foote. At one point she maintained an intimate personal relationship with him.

Ghiolu's sustained contact with Foote through Marius Antoine Chamoutet, the official courier for the Swiss government's foreign affairs office. Ghiolu passed to Chamoutet information about Marshall Ion Antonescu's closest associates. As a relative of highly-placed personalities in Antonescu's entourage, she moved about freely in these circles.

In all probability Ghiolu used a second transmission channel to Foote. This channel ran through her sister Grazia de Rham, nee Ghiolu, who lived in Switzerland.

SCANDINAVIA

Leopold Trepper may have visited Sweden in December 1936 on a special mission to assess intelligence obtained there. The agents he met may have been working for either Red Army intelligence or the GUGB. Trepper is likely to have used his 1936 contacts in Scandinavia as part of a long term operation which he planned against the British Isles in later years.

Trepper told his interrogators he took part in discussions with a Russian, a Swede, and a Norwegian in 1937 or 1938 on the establishment or reorganization of a network in Scandinavia. The discussions were held in Paris.

In 1938 Trepper passed through Denmark, Sweden, and Finland on his way to France from Moscow. He may have been able to announce to his contacts in these countries the plans for the establishment of the Foreign Excellent Raincoat Co. and its proposed export business with Denmark, Finland, Norway, and Sweden.

Leon Grossvogel toured all four Scandinavian countries in the spring of 1939, ostensibly for the Foreign Excellent Raincoat Company. In Stockholm Grossvogel set up fnu Boellens as an agent for the company, but it is not known whether Boellens was even willingly engaged in espionage.

From January to August 1942 Arvid Harnack passed the collected intelligence of his group through Bernard Baestlein of the German Communist Party in Hamburg via Flensburg and Denmark to the Soviet Embassy in Stockholm. It seems probable that the Danish and perhaps the Swedish Communist parties were intermediaries on this line. It is possible that this link was also used by Schulze-Boysen after his courier service to Belgium failed at the end of June 1942. There is some support for this possibility in Schulze-Boysen's claim that he succeeded in passing certain vital information to Stockholm just before his arrest. The Germans believed, however, that this story was an attempt by Schulze-Boysen to postpone his execution. He seems to have implied that the material could only be recovered if he were given liberty to visit Sweden himself.

In 1942 branch offices of Simex were opened in Oslo and Copenhagen.

In 1942 Alexander Foote received a message from Moscow requesting his help in the delivery of a W/T set to a girl in the Swedish Red Cross. Foote was unable to make the first contact for this transaction in Switzerland, and the plan came to nothing.

YUGOSLAVIA

In the early spring of 1941 Alexander Rado was given an address in Yugoslavia, but it is not known whether this was intended to be an extension of Rado's service or an emergency link.

According to German reports branch offices of Simex were set up in Belgrade and Sofia in 1942.

PART TWO

MODUS OPERANDI
OF THE ROTE KAPELLE

I. GENERAL

The exodus of large numbers of political and religious persecutes from Germany and Nazi-controlled areas of Europe provided the Soviets with an unexpected operational bonanza—the rapid and non-attributable extension of Soviet IS capabilities into Europe through the relocation of trained Soviet agents migrating as refugees.

The Soviets began the expansion of their intelligence networks in the 1930s. The preparations had been made even earlier. Although the intelligence organization had developed experience by 1939, only after the beginning of World War II did it develop its operational methods and techniques to the point of competence. Even then the Soviet intelligence nets in Europe showed the weaknesses of extemporizing, of patchwork, that rarely characterize Soviet operations today.

The following information about operational methods and techniques is based on details from Rote Kapelle cases. On many subjects the available information is inadequate. For example, very little is known about how agents were spotted and recruited or about couriers—their cover stories, how they carried their information or what security measures they took. We have practically no information about the day-to-day operations of the cover firms or how they were intertwined with the espionage activities.

The Soviets considered most of the networks of the Rote Kapelle as deep cover operations. Therefore, the support functions performed by official Soviet installations and local Communist parties were very important. The official installations, such as embassies, consulates, military missions, and trade delegations supplied directions, communications, equipment, passports, visas, and other documentation. They also served as cover and transmitted funds. Association with local Communist parties involved serious security risks and was therefore avoided whenever possible. As this record has shown, however, Soviet intelligence was ill-prepared for World War II. The experiences of the times forced the leaders of the European nets to solicit help from Party members quite frequently despite the risks.

Some general characteristics of Soviet intelligence methods and techniques are worth emphasizing. The first concerns the availability of personnel for the Soviet intelligence services. Recruitment is well described in an Abwehr report dated 24 March 1943, which reads in part:

> The arrests of December 1941 made us realize for the first time that we had come to grips with the Soviet intelligence services in the West. The method of recruitment of the agents arrested after the first coup of 12-13 December 1941 differed so essentially from that of other foreign agents that all previous experience in the West was valueless. It soon became clear that the Russians had been using skilled labor and had drawn their recruits from politically trained Communists, or at least from among persons of the extreme left. It was therefore necessary for the German officer concerned to acquaint himself with the theories which underlay the training and establishment of Russian agents and which were then unknown to Abwehr officers.
>
> It is impossible to separate Communist ideology from the work of the Soviet intelligence service. The Comintern has no difficulty in recruiting suitable agents, even in the West. Professed Communists are well-accustomed to clandestine work since their activities and even their residence are illegal in most Western European countries. Tolerant laws and lax frontier controls have also been to their advantage ... As a result, the USSR and the Russian General Staff have concentrated particularly on sending agents to the West.

There is an interesting parallel between the operational covers used by the Soviets in the espionage operations of the Rote Kapelle and those of Soviet espionage operations in other parts of the world and under varying conditions—war or peace, cooperative or uncooperative populations. Since the days of the Cheka, a far-flung complex of reputable firms, banks, trusts, and holding corporations has been used operationally by the Soviets to cover, to support, and to control their agents throughout the world.

The final point concerns the shortcomings of the RU in the

handling of the Rote Kapelle networks and the resultant weakness in operations. While Moscow was reasonably energetic in the provision of money and material and gave sound security warnings from time to time, on the whole it showed an academic attitude. Moscow made little allowance for field problems or for the personalities of the various agents.

II. COVER AND SECURITY

According to a German interrogation report of Leopold Trepper, the "Grand Chef" made a distinction between two types of intelligence agents and described the cover each should have:

> The first type has an assignment for a certain time and must live completely illegally in order not to leave behind personal traces. This type lives without auxiliary aid. The Grand Chef recommends living in a boarding house as a tourist for not longer than three months.

> The other type of intelligence agent lives legally and arrives with allegedly lawful papers. If he plays the role of a merchant, then he really must have a business knowledge. If he plays the role of an architect, then he must be proficient in that profession. In his professional circles such a man must have a good reputation. The name to be chosen for the forged identification papers must be familiar in the country in question.

> He has to know the land and people of his alleged birthplace well, so that he can answer all possible questions, should that become necessary. He also has to speak the dialect of his birthplace and must not attract attention when speaking his mother tongue. Acquaintances from the country of his birth, as well as restaurants and social gatherings where he might meet people from his mother country, are to be avoided.

Trepper was of the opinion that an espionage agent should not use official cover. He felt that persons in official positions, because of their restricted social life, were not well-placed to inform themselves thoroughly about military events or political movements. An independent agent, on the other hand, could live with any group of people and discover the views of every section of the population. Trepper's opinion to the contrary, the evidence seems to indicate that official Soviet establishments were consistently used to support the Rote Kapelle, and there was a definite need for their assistance. Their primary function was to aid the operation of the deep-cover networks, and the Soviet intelligence agents assigned to these establishments served as contacts between the deep-cover agents and Moscow.

Apparently at one point it was thought that official cover should be in the guise of commercial representation, such as a delegate to a trade commission, and that the covers of military attaches and diplomatic officials should not be used. If a commercial representative were compromised, his activities could be dismissed as an isolated instance without reflecting on the diplomatic staff. And there are many indications that the Soviet intelligence services did use the cover of official commercial representatives. But there seem to have been as many or more Soviet intelligence agents who used military attache cover and other Soviet Embassy cover. Until the outbreak of the war between the USSR and Germany, one of the most important support functions rendered by Soviet agents in official positions was to assist the deep-cover agent with his communications.

A noteworthy characteristic of Soviet intelligence during World War II was its dread that its organization and operations had been penetrated. This dread was frequently extreme, and in some cases it definitely prejudiced the efficiency of Soviet intelligence operations. There were numerous examples of this fear in the Rote Kapelle. The Soviets thought that Alexander Foote was working for the British, and in Moscow he was flatly accused of having collaborated with Rachel Duebendorfer in betraying the Rote Drei organization to the British. The Soviets feared that Trepper had betrayed his country and that Sukolov was working for the Gestapo. They believed that Robinson was working for the French and that Ozols was working for the Germans. These fears were justified, of course, in the case of Sukolov, but in the other cases they were groundless.

The Soviets seem to have had a genuine fear that the "Anglo-Americans" would become privy to Russian intelligence operations anywhere and use this knowledge to disadvantage the USSR. When the Swiss police started to roll up the Rote Drei and Rado asked Moscow's permission to seek sanctuary at the British Embassy, not only for his safety but also as a means of restoring communications, the

Center's response was vehemently—almost vituperatively—negative. At the war's end, when Allied good faith had been demonstrated, the Soviet Government continued to plug the propaganda theme that the British and Americans had tried to conclude a separate peace with Hitler, but this charge was levelled as part of the calculated Soviet distortion of history. It is doubtful that knowledgeable members of the Government and intelligence services of the USSR ever believed this myth.

Despite their fears the security measures directed by the Soviets were often incredibly lax and actually jeopardized operations. On 28 August 1941 Moscow wired Sukolov:

> An important agent known as Ilse will in the future
> be designated under the cover name Alte . . .

It did not take long for the Germans to identify Ilse Stoebe and then to round up the Rudolf von Scheliha group. In the Robinson papers, the Rado traffic and other intercepted Soviet communications, there were numerous clues—including true and cover names for the same person appearing in the same message—which produced useful counterintelligence leads on the identities of Soviet agents.

When Trepper returned to Moscow in 1945, he had several complaints to make about the Center's administrative blunders during the war. He thought that Moscow had broken all the rules and made an unforgivable error in sending messages to Sukolov ordering him to Berlin and giving the addresses of the three chiefs of the German networks. When Trepper first heard about this mistake, he reportedly exclaimed: "It's not possible. They have gone crazy!" Trepper's grievances were not treated sympathetically by the Director, and he was imprisoned.

Before the war the networks controlled by trained and experienced Russian agents and staff personnel were kept isolated from one another and were successful in maintaining the necessary level of compartmentation. As the difficulties of operations, administration, and communications in wartime increased, many of the security measures were sacrificed.

It should be noted that the agents and the radio operators stationed in the various European countries were usually not identical. Although frequent overlaps and parallel operations did exist even on the lower levels, the organizations merged at the top under one chief. As a rule, a radio operator, technician, or other member of the radio organization would know nothing about the overall organizational structure. Sometimes members of a radio team and members of an agent team lived on the same street and even in the same building without ever coming into contact. There were of course exceptions, especially 1943 and 1944, a rather critical period for the Rote Kapelle, when more and more often dual functions pertaining to both spying and communications were assigned to the same person. Hence it could happen that a member of the radio organization was also employed as an agent, and vice versa. This situation was brought about by the fact that the loss of important personnel somehow had to be compensated. Replacements for the technicians, radio operators, and other specialists were difficult to arrange.

The chief of a network was responsible for the smooth operation of both the agent and radio organizations within a defined area. This chief was almost invariably a specially trained intelligence officer of the Red Army with many years of experience, like the "Grand Chef" or "Kent." The obvious exception was in Germany, where all three of the group leaders—Schulze-Boysen, Harnack, and von Scheliha—were amateurs and received very little guidance from professional intelligence officers.

In addition to the agent and radio organizations, various auxiliary units were at the disposal of the Rote Kapelle for support and collaboration. Some of these units were subordinate to the Comintern and the Party leadership in the various countries, while others were activated and guided directly from Moscow.

III. FINANCES

According to information furnished by Foote, the head of a network was responsible for paying the entire network and submitting his accounts to Moscow once a year. He also had to send an estimated budget for the next year's expenditures. This yearly grant was seldom paid in one lump sum. At least twice a year, as a rule, an agent from the network was sent to meet a courier from Moscow, who handed over the money, usually in United States dollars.

The network chief could not put his money into a bank. He kept the entire sum in dollars hidden and, from time to time, removed what was necessary and changed it into local currency for immediate expenses. Sometimes he was permitted to put the money into a safe-deposit box.

It is interesting to note that a ten thousand dollar payment frequently figured in the financing of the Rote Kapelle operations. When Mikhail Makarov reached Paris from Moscow in 1939, he was given a Uruguayan passport in the name of Carlos Alamo and ten thousand dollars, probably to set up a cover firm. Grossvogel's participation in Le Roi du Caoutchouc in 1939 and 1940 started with ten thousand dollars, which Trepper had received from Moscow. Norman Stein gave Alexander Rado ten thousand dollars in 1943 in France. Hermina Rabinowitch was given ten thousand dollars in New York in July 1944 to transmit via Helbein to Duebendorfer in Switzerland. The figure of ten thousand dollars became a standard sum in major RU financial transactions.

It seems that the Soviets were generous in financing their intelligence operations. But some of the networks were essentially self-sustaining. Simex and Simexco became thriving concerns, and the agents behind those cover firms helped to support their espionage activities by their business earnings.

IV. Motivation

The organizational structure of the Rote Kapelle was bound together by the motivation of its agents. In view of the hardships they endured and the risks to which they were subjected, it is obvious that the agents of the Rote Kapelle were very strongly motivated. Motivation is a difficult factor to assess because it is typically a complex *melange* of emotions, beliefs, convictions, and hatreds. Some general remarks, however, can be made about the reasons for which the members of the Rote Kapelle risked their lives and, in more than a hundred instances, sacrificed them.

Most, but not all, of the key figures in the Rote Kapelle were ardent Communists. Comintern agents like Henri Robinson and Daniel Gouwlooze were loyal to the "workers of the world" and gladly offered their services for Soviet intelligence activities. Leopold Trepper, Victor Sukolov, Konstantin Jeffremov, and the other Soviet intelligence officers were loyal to the Center and to Stalin. Their commitment was not so much to Marxist-Leninist theory as it was to their service (the RU) and to their country. (Trepper was born in Poland but claimed Soviet citizenship.) Sukolov at one time believed in the "cause," but he became "soft," as Trepper said, and developed bourgeois tastes in cigars, shoes, and the comfort and pleasure of Margarete Barcza's company.

The ideological motivation was probably most fervent, though also most muzzy, in the German networks of the Rote Kapelle. Although it is difficult in many cases to distinguish between a loyalty to Communism and a resistance to Hitler, it is clear that the common tie in all of the German groups was a profound sympathy for Communism. Schulze-Boysen and Harnack recruited exclusively on the basis of a commitment to the Communist cause. Ilse Stoebe, who was probably just as important as von Scheliha in that group, was a convinced Communist as early as 1930.

A number of German and some non-German writers have grappled with the problem of whether those Germans who worked as spies for the Soviets were heroes or traitors. For the most part these ruminations bog down in legalisms (*Landesverrat* vs. *Hochverrat*), abstractions, or emotionalism. In no case could those who opposed the Nazis and actively sought their downfall be considered traitors to the German heritage or peoples. But there is a clear moral distinction between those whose goal was the restoration of a representative indigenous German government and those who sought to exploit anti-fascism for the benefit of the Soviet Union.

Many of the members of the Rote Kapelle were Jewish and had an intense hatred for Nazism. Although most of the Jews were also Communists, like Trepper, Grossvogel, and Gouwlooze, there were some who were probably motivated more by being Jewish than by being Communists. This distinction seems especially valid for the Sokols in Paris and probably for Anna and Basile Maximovitch. Abraham Rajchmann was described in German reports as a "greedy, sniveling Jew"—a sterotype repeated in all German reporting—but he claimed in his interrogation by Belgian authorities after the war that he was recruited because he had lost relatives to the Nazis and not because of the money Grossvogel offered. According to Trepper "the Jews had no other means to fight and they undoubtedly gave Nazism its deadliest blows."

Very few members of the Rote Kapelle were motivated primarily by monetary considerations. The most striking figure in this small category, however, was Rudolf von Scheliha, who was recruited in Warsaw after he had become hopelessly in debt through gambling. Vlademar Keller of Simex, who made a fortune before his arrest by dealing in industrial diamonds with the Todt Organization, may have been another agent who worked mainly for money. And the record clearly shows that Rudolf Roessler of the Rote Drei had a wide mercenary streak.

Some of the members of the Rote Kapelle became implicated through family ties or through affection. Georgie de Winter, the mistress of Trepper, had no political convictions but followed Trepper because she loved him. Germaine Schneider recruited her two sisters,

Renee Blumsack and Josephine Verhimst; Henri Robinson prepared his illegitimate son Victor Schabbel for a career in espionage. Margarete Barcza was passionately attached to Victor Sukolov, and the German spinster Margarete Hoffmann-Scholz provided information to Basile Maximovitch after he showed a romantic interest in her and proposed marriage. It is likely that these persons became involved in intelligence activities chiefly because of their romantic or family connections.

V. DOCUMENTATION

The Soviets used various methods to obtain passports and visas. They tried to use only first class papers and preferred not to forge them. Whenever possible, they attempted to obtain actual documents through fraudulent means and, if necessary, to alter the information to fit the person who was going to use them. That they did not always manage to meet professional standards is shown, however, by the clumsy Canadian documentation with which Trepper and his family arrived in Belgium.

Those agents who traveled from the USSR arrived at their stations with passports, although they were not necessarily the ones with which they started their journeys. In many instances the agent stopped off en route for a pre-arranged rendezvous with a contact who would pick up his original passport and exchange it for another. The new passport was usually in a different name and contained the visas necessary to continue the trip.

In arranging for the use of false papers and a false identity, Trepper insisted that the documents should be in a name which was native to the country of origin and in common use, such as Smith, Miller, or Schulz. Police investigations and inquiries were thereby made more difficult. He also insisted that as far as possible agents should avoid being photographed or giving specimens of their handwriting. If his agents had to resort to forged papers, Trepper insisted that care be taken to insure that the impress of the stamp was not too clear. He maintained that a genuine stamp was always worn and left a blurred impress.

VI. CONTACTS AND PERSONAL MEETINGS

In the course of his interrogation by the Germans, Trepper theorized on some points to be remembered in arranging contacts and personal meetings. He had gleaned these theories from his many years of operational experience. His observations included the following:

> For making a first contact with an agent, Sundays and holidays are best since on those days the police are generally less alert. The most satisfactory method of introducing two agents to each other is as follows—the agent who is to meet the new members arrives at the site of the rendezvous first. The person making the introduction walks past with the second agent but without approaching or pointing out the first agent to him. A later meeting is then arranged, which the two agents concerned attend by themselves, the first agent now being in a position to recognize and to approach the second. The purpose of this arrangement is that any third party who may be watching the initial meeting cannot know with whom the contact will be made.

Trepper recommended several types of places for holding personal meetings. Post offices, churches, museums, and race courses are good for personal meetings and for initial contacts. Railway stations, he said, should never be used because the police are always active there. Theaters make good meeting places, if the proper arrangements are made. If the meeting takes place in a theater, Trepper suggested that the agents obtain adjacent seats so that they could see each other. There is no need for conversation. This technique is excellent for initial meetings. It is also a secure rendezvous for the handing over of reports. Of course, care must be taken to reserve adjoining seats or, if reservations are unnecessary, to attend the theater at a time when it is not crowded.

The regular meeting place should be changed frequently. The time and place should be such that the meeting appears natural. A summer resort, for example, would not be selected for a meeting in the winter. If a permanent rendezvous or cover address is required for the delivery of reports, it should be in a place like a bookshop, newspaper stand, or ticket office. It is not secure to select a place where either of the agents is too well known.

The principal agent should always be as inconspicuous as possible and, if feasible, should not appear at a rendezvous at all. If he must appear, the rendezvous area should be selected as far as possible from where he lives. The principal agent should be able to contact his agents regularly through pre-arranged meetings. Members of the network routinely attended these meetings, but the head agent went only if he felt it necessary. The network agents should not be able to contact their chief in any way. They should have no address or telephone number where he could be reached. Thus the principal agent can maintain control and yet avoid unnecessary contact. In this manner the risk of vertical compromise can be reduced.

Fruitless trips to the rendezvous site can be avoided by a system of advance signals. The signal might be the placing of a mark in a telephone book after a particular name if the meeting is to be held. If the mark is not there, the meeting is cancelled.

Telephones, and especially private telephones, should not be used in arranging personal meetings. They may be used, however, to give warnings through either a ringing system or a conversation in double-talk. In the former system no conversation takes place because the warning consists of the ringing of the telephone bell a stated number of times. In the other system the wording of the conversation gives the warning.

One example of the telephone warning was used by Spaak in Paris in 1943. He phoned his house, and his housekeeper replied, "Bonjour, monsieur," if the police were there and "Bonjour, Monsieur Spaak," if they were not. This system enabled Spaak to escape arrest, even though the Germans occupied his house for many days.

The principal agent should arrange with Moscow for an emergency rendezvous procedure that could be resorted to at any time. (Trepper used to arrange emergency meeings with Moscow about once a year.) The site of the proposed meeting should be described in detail to Moscow. Trepper supplied picture postcards to pinpoint the exact spot. Passwords and safety signals should be arranged. Certain days of each month should be selected on which to make contact. These arrangements are made so that if ordinary contacts are broken off, contact can be re-established at one of the pre-arranged emergency meetings. This arrangement also enables Moscow to put *anyone* in touch with the principal agent by sending him to the emergency rendezvous.

Accommodation lodgings should be selected with great care, preferably in the suburbs. If a boarding house is used, it should be one having few boarders. The agent should make friends with fellow lodgers in order to use such people as references in case he needs them. Correspondence should be directed to the address, even if the agent has to write cards and letters to himself, to suggest a reasonable amount of normal correspondence. The principal agent and his sub-agents should identify several hotels and other places in which they can, if necessary, spend a night without being questioned. The names of these places should be relayed to Moscow so that they can be referred to and used.

Emergency meetings sites should never be used more than once. (This precaution is apparently theoretical and was not followed by all the networks.) For example, when Foote first became involved with the Hamburger network, he was told he would be given a fixed emergency rendezvous spot in a nearby country, probably Belgium or Holland. He would be given certain days and hours, passwords and safety signals to be used by him and by his contact. He was to use the same meeting site whenever he lost contact with his group leader or on orders from Moscow.

VII. COMMUNICATIONS

Until the outbreak of war with Germany, most communications between the Rote Kapelle networks and Moscow were directed through the official Soviet installations. Couriers and postal links connected the networks with these installations. From there the information went by wireless or by pouch to Moscow. Trepper used the Soviet Embassy and the Soviet Chamber of Commerce in Belgium. Later, when he went to France, he made use of the Military Attache's office in Paris and then Vichy. Robinson used the communications services of the Soviet Embassy in Paris. Von Scheliha's information was transmitted through the Soviet Embassy in Poland and later through the Soviet Embassy and the Tass representative in Germany. Schulze-Boysen and Harnack communicated through the Soviet Embassy in Germany and the Soviet Trade Delegation. Rado sent his microphotographs by courier or by post to the Soviet Embassy in Paris for onward transmission. When the official installations were withdrawn, however, and wireless communications had to be used almost exclusively, the transmitters proved to be inefficient and required constant adjustment.

The wireless transmitters were the most vulnerable aspect of all the Rote Kapelle operations. There were numerous problems: the recruitment and training of operators, the procurement and maintenance of W/T sets, the selection of suitable sites for transmitting, and the delivery and concealment of codes and call signals.

The Germans began intercepting messages from the Rote Kapelle transmitters in late 1940 or early 1941. With the aid of their D/F equipment, they succeeded in locating the sites used for transmission. In almost every series of apprehensions, the initial arrests were of the W/T operators. This was the case of Makarov and Wenzel in Belgium, the Sokols in France, the Hamels and Foote in Switzerland, and many others. Some of the captured W/T operators offered to collaborate with the Germans; others refused to talk and broke down only after intensive interrogation.

Sometimes, and particularly during the war years, such a mass of information was submitted for wireless transmissions that it had to be cut down and edited. Only the barest essentials of the material could be sent. Otherwise all of an operator's time would have been spent on communications work. Such lavish use of time was not feasible because operators sometimes worked in other capacities as well. Foote, for example, whose primary assignment was as a W/T operator, acted as a cutout for at least two of the agents in the network. He picked up messages at the agents' villas, reviewed the information, and with the agents' aid tried to reduce it to a manageable length.

Contact with Moscow was usually made late at night or early in the morning. Trepper's operators contacted Moscow between the hours of 2300 and 0200. Foote contacted Moscow at 0100, and if conditions were satisfactory and the message short, he finished transmitting in a couple of hours. If he had long messages and atmospheric conditions were bad, he was often at the transmitter until 0600. Messages that passed between England and France were sent before noon, usually between the hours of 1000 and 1200. Some of the frequencies were used on even-numbered days and others on odd-numbered days, according to a schedule.

Schedules detailing the time that a particular operator was to transmit were arranged by Moscow and submitted to the operator. In addition to the regular schedules the networks were given special schedules and special wave lengths for emergency traffic. These schedules were to be used in case messages had to be sent during the daytime. Trepper, for example, had a wave length which could be used every day at a particular time. Over this wave length he also received special messages from Moscow for Robinson. Robinson had no direct contact with Moscow because his transmitter had insufficient power, but he did have a special wave length for transmitting to England. Foote, too, had an emergency schedule. This included several days of each week when Moscow would be listening at prearranged times for his call. On other days Foote would be required to listen for a message from Moscow.

Call signs were usually fixed but did change from time to time for security reasons. The signal for the change of call signs came directly from Moscow. When Foote wished to call Moscow, he tapped out his call sign in Morse on the assigned frequency. Moscow acknowledged on the same frequency. On hearing Moscow's reply, Foote switched to another wave length and different call signs to send his material. Moscow, of course, also changed wave lengths and call signs. This system somewhat minimized the possibility of radio monitoring.

The messages were always in cipher. The cipher—in theory—could be read only by Moscow and the agent in the field who held the cipher. Moscow regarded its ciphers as unbreakable unless the key were known. The process of enciphering messages was divided into two parts. The first was based on a keyword which had six letters and was changed at intervals by Moscow. The second stage involved the "closing" of the first simple encipherment against the text of a code book. The enciphering phrase could be taken from anywhere in the book starting at any word in the line. The process for deciphering was the reverse procedure. It involved determining the passage in the key book and subtracting the necessary number of letters.

According to Trepper the codes used for enciphering and deciphering messages were referred to as the "Talmud." They were taken exclusively from literary works, and the series of letters was selected at random. In all agents' messages and in all enciphered texts, only cover names were supposed to be used to refer to sources, sub-agents, and others. The messages were couched in a jargon which made them difficult to interpret and readily comprehensible to the people in the networks only. Even if the gist of the message could be made out, the agent's identity was ordinarily concealed by the use of a cover name.

Another link for transmitting messages to Moscow was the Communist Party. This emergency channel was used only after the other links had been disrupted. The Communist Party used couriers as well as wireless transmitters. The networks of the Rote Kapelle used the services of at least three Communist Parties—the Dutch, the French, and the German. It is possible that the Swiss Communist Party was also used.

Postal links were another means of communication. Very frequently open codes were used. Sometimes operational or administrative matters, such as making or confirming meeting arrangements, were handled in this way. At other times actual intelligence was passed through the mails.

The chiefs of the networks usually sorted out, evaluated, and edited the information that came to them. In some instances the documents were microfilmed and then given to couriers in microfilm rolls. In this connection it is interesting to note that Henri Robinson on 20 December 1940 received a message from the Center in Moscow advising him that RU headquarters was sending instructions on "micro-appareil." Whether this refers to microphotography as a whole or only to microdots is not known.

After 1941 all Soviet Military Intelligence officers posted to the field were well grounded in the technique of microphotography prior to their departure from RU headquarters in Moscow.

Sometimes secret writing was used in an effort to insure greater security in transmitting messages. When Trepper was planning his operations for Western Europe, he arranged with the military attache in Paris that reports be written in secret ink betwen the lines of a simple message and sent through the diplomatic pouch. In 1938 the RU sent an agent from the USSR to the Military Attache's office in Paris as a clerk to be responsible for the proper handling of secret ink communications. After the outbreak of war, this plan was discarded, and the agent went to Brussels to be trained as a wireless operator for Sukolov.

Trepper did not like to send secret writing through the regular post, and, as a matter of fact, he told the Germans he never used this technique. He indicated, however, that if secret inks were used, they should be confined to preparations which could form part of an ordinary medicine chest.

Rado probably made arrangements for communicating by secret writing. In the spring of 1941 Moscow sent him an address in Yugoslavia with which messages in secret writing could be exchanged. There is no indication, however, that the link was ever established or used.

Alexander Foote's first espionage assignment took him to Munich. It was by means of secret writing concealed in a book that his Munich address was sent to a contact in England.

Couriers were used very extensively in the Rote Kapelle networks. Most of the couriers were aware of what they were carrying, but some were used as "dummies." The chief of the network would usually send a courier or one of his trusted cutouts to a fixed rendezvous in a neighboring country to make contact with a courier from Moscow. The courier system, though slower than most of the other means of communications, was more secure for the transmission of bulky documents and equipment.

Many techniques were used to camouflage the appearance of intelligence material so that it could be delivered securely to the proper parties. When Trepper was interrogated, he stated that an agent should never appear to be handing over anything unusual to his contact but should use some everyday object as camouflage. He suggested the following articles as convenient for this purpose: fountain pens, cigarettes, cigarette packets, coat buttons, compacts, medicine bottles, pocket and wrist watches, match boxes, and so forth. Some of these articles could also be used to store material. Reports could be hidden between the pages of a newspaper which had been pasted together, in the soles of shoes, underneath labels on trunks, or in jam jars in their original packing. Small objects, when kept at home, could be hidden in a flour bin or among vegetables. Members of the Rote Kapelle networks used many of these concealment techniques.

During his interrogation by the Germans, Trepper gave the following additional information about couriers and cutouts. Reports should always be passed through a cutout and not by the agent himself. Couriers and cutouts should not return directly to their own or new lodgings after attending a meeting. They were to keep away for at least six or seven hours to reduce the risk of being followed. When the cutout received the report, he was to delay for at least twenty-four hours before delivering it in order to be certain that the original agent had not been followed. Under no circumstances was the agent to carry the intelligence reports on his person during this period; he was to put them in safekeeping until the time for further transmission. If records had to be made, the documents were to be taken to the proper person at the indicated safe address to be photographed or microfilmed.

Trepper found it convenient to use married couples as cutouts and couriers. One could receive the original report, and the other could hand it over twenty-four hours later. The Girauds, for example, were used in this way. Mme. Giraud picked up Kathe Voelkner's reports, kept them for about a day, and then passed them to her husband. Trepper found that women were very useful for courier work. He used them for contacts between the Belgian and French networks and in his dealings with the French Communist Party.

VIII. CONCLUSION

The Rote Kapelle had too many agents. Its most important sources were, of course, in Germany. Most of them volunteered their services or accepted recruitment after Germany attacked the USSR. Until then, Soviet intelligence apparently lacked highly placed penetrations of the Germans and therefore had to quickly build large clandestine structures that transmitted such a quantity of data that the sheer bulk of traffic became a hazard of itself. In general, Soviet methods of operations, skills, and equipment were on a par with those of the other major powers in World War II. But Stalin's deep distrust of the Western Allies, a peculiar Soviet paranoia, permeated the Russian intelligence services as well. Consequently, the Soviets deeply distrusted any information not supplied by their own agents through their own channels. This attitude inevitably magnified the workload of the Rote Kapelle. A structure built too late and in haste, a structure in which only some of the parts had been skillfully formed and adequately tested, a structure that was then overloaded, was bound to show cracks in the walls and come tumbling down.

PART THREE

PERSONALITIES

KURT ABRAHAM

(alias V-Mann Abbe) penetrated first the Belgian and then the French Rote Kapelle organization on behalf of the Germans. In 1947 he was under interrogation by the Belgian authorities.

ALEXANDER ABRAMSON

(alias Issak, in W/T traffic; aka Sascha, nickname; aka Ali-Us, pen name) was born 12 January 1896 in Koenigsberg, Lithuania. A Lithuanian Jew, he chose Soviet nationality after the occupation of Lithuania.

Characterized as a social snob, scholarly, very intelligent, a qualified lawyer and economist, he was an employee of ILO, Geneva. He married Eugenie Auerbach (also called Greta Goldschmitt). He is a first cousin of Hermina Rabinowitch and Dr. Robert Kempner.

In 1937, at Russian insistence, Abramson replaced M. Cortet in the Russian information section of ILO. The author of pseudoscientific pamphlets which were actually Communist propaganda, Abramson was a candidate, with Vladimir Sokolin, for a position in the Russian Legation in Bern; but he was refused because he was Jewish and remained at his ILO post.

In June 1941, according to letters which Rabinowitch wrote to the Gruenbergs, Abramson, who was getting along well with the Soviets, was all set to go to Russia. Then the Russo-German war broke out, and he was forced to remain in Switzerland.

In October 1941 Carter of the Institute for Pacific Relations tried to get him an emergency visa for America. In December 1942 Rabinowitch wrote:

> Abramson is stuck in Switzerland. The charming Vichy officials have refused to grant transit visas to Jews. Something must be done, so I proposed to Stein, Assistant Director of the ILO in Montreal, that he go to New York and Washington and gather the necessary documents.

Previously the ILO in Geneva had obtained an Argentinian visa for Abramson with the idea that thereafter he could get to the USA or Canada. But Rabinowitch wrote that she did not know "how he will get all the other visas. It seems that some persons in the U.S. Government are interested in his history; perhaps he will be able to come on the clipper." The "persons . . . interested" were thought by the Gruenbergs to be John Winant and Frances Perkins, both of whom knew Abramson in Geneva.

In the summer of 1944 Abramson was involved in a payment to a Swiss network by Russian military authorities in Canada. When Abramson's role in these financial transactions was revealed in the Canadian spy trial in 1946, he lost his job with the ILO.

In the autumn of 1944 Abramson was advisor to the Russian Military Mission investigating internment camps in Switzerland. After the breakup of the Rado network, most of the important Lucy material was stored in his safe. It was picked up by Foote and taken to Paris in November 1944.

In the autumn of 1946 Abramson attended a Geneva conference as Economic Affairs Officer for the UN and was reported to be one of the key Soviet agents in Western Europe for "Russian directives which he passed to Tamara Vigier when he is in Paris." In Paris in 1947 Abramson was in constant touch with Jean Pierre Vigier and Bernard Bayer. In the fall he claimed to be working for the Federation Syndicale Mondiale. He used Vigier's apartment for headquarters in the fall of 1947.

Later in 1947 he tried to get a job with the ILO in Geneva. As the result of the Royal Commission Report, Abramson was interrogated. He admitted nothing, denied all personal knowledge of William Helbein, Mulvidson, and Puenter, and claimed that his knowledge of Max Horngacher, well-known Swiss Communist in Geneva with whom he was reported friendly, and of Edmond Ferenczi, was very slight. He claimed he did not know the real nature of his work when he was connected with Duebendorfer.

Some time prior to 1947 Abramson also served as liaison between the International Labor Office and the USSR when the Soviet Union was a member of this organization. Abramson was in direct contact with Zabotin and Sokolin, both Russian agents, and allegedly used Tamara Vigier for his contact with the French Communist Party.

Henri Vigier, who lived very near Abramson in Geneva, received frequent visits from his son, Jean Pierre Vigier. It was reported that Abramson also received frequent visits from Captain Vigier.

He lived in Geneva for more than thirty years. He speaks French, German, English, and Russian.

In 1947 Abramson was reported to be assistant and advisor to Leon Jouhaux, General Secretary of the CGT.

Alexander Abramson is probably not identical with Alexander Abramovitch Abramson, head of a Tientsin intelligence network prior to 1932, and a Jewish CP member who started intelligence work in 1927 as an organizer of a women's spy ring. This mission was to observe activities of Chinese and U.S. forces through their nationals and to gather minute details and report conversations. He disappeared in southern China in 1932, and no further traces of him have been found.

In 1950 Leon Jouhaux, the veteran trade union leader and president of the French Economic Council, intervened on behalf of Abramson, Rabinowitch, and Norman Stein.

MAURICE AENIS-HANSLIN

(alias Maurice, alias Robin) was born 20 February 1893 in St. Denis (Seine), France. He is a Swiss national living in France at Savigny-sur-Orge. A long-standing Communist, he was once an official of the Central Committee of the Swiss CP. He is an engineer employed by the business enterprise Unipectine of Switzerland.

Aenis-Hanslin was a sub-agent of Duebendorfer and was Henri Robinson's man in Paris for the RIS network. He also assisted Robinson financially. He was involved in the Trepper network as the liaison man for transferring funds between Robinson in Paris and Duebendorfer in Switzerland from 1940 to 1942. He made frequent courier trips between France and Switzerland before and during World War II for the Soviet Military IS and had some knowledge of the Swiss network. In 1942 and 1943 he may have supplied intelligence to Tamara Vigier for Duebendorfer. He is believed to have had an important role in the Rote Kapelle and is linked with Hans Schauwecker, Karl Hofmaier, and Franz Schneider.

Aenis-Hanslin maintained a lavish apartment in Paris which was a safehouse with many secret hiding places. It served as an office for Robinson as well as a meeting place.

Aenis-Hanslin married Gabrielle Schneider in 1928 and was separated in 1933. He remarried after the war, but his second wife died at an unknown date. He was arrested with his mistress, Edwige Couchon, by the Gestapo on 12 April 1943 and sentenced to death. Couchon subsequently died in the Ravensbrueck camp, but the Swiss intervened in Aenis-Hanslin's behalf, and he was released.

Before the war, on Comintern instructions, Aenis-Hanslin established a small factory in the outskirts of Paris and was used as a channel for the distribution of Comintern funds to Western European CP's. After the war he moved to Paris as chief engineer for Swiss financier and businessman Hans Schauwecker, who is co-owner of Unipectine, a dried fruit company with headquarters near Zurich. Unipectine is a suspected cover enterprise because Schauwecker has contributed large sums of money to local Communist organizations and Aenis-Hanslin is probably a liaison agent between Swiss and French Communist Parties and a distributor of secret Communist funds for intelligence purposes.

In 1945 he attended the funeral of Germaine Schneider in Zurich.

In 1948 Aenis-Hanslin was reportedly sending the publications of *Mundus Verlag* to Germany in collaboration with Hans Schauwecker and Karl Hofmaier, once Secretary General of the Swiss CP. Aenis-Hanslin is a member of the board of Intertechnica AG, and Hofmaier is a technical advisor for that firm.

Aenis-Hanslin also reportedly had several contacts with Franz Schneider, who acted as a courier for the Rote Kapelle network in Western Europe.

RITA ARNOULD

(nee Bloch, alias Juliette or Julia) became Isidore Springer's mistress while a university student in Brussels. She was married to (fnu) Arnould, who died before the outbreak of the war.

She was a courier and W/T operator for Sukolov's organization in Belgium and acted as a courier for Springer. It was Rita who had rented the house at 101 Rue des Attrebates at Etterbeeck to accommodate Makarov and Sofie Posnanska. She had received instructions in W/T from Wenzel and Danilov and attended two meetings with Augustin Sesee, another W/T operator.

She was arrested on 12 December 1941 and immediately turned informant for the Germans. She was reportedly executed.

OTTO BACH

was a member of the German Chamber of Commerce in Paris during the war. In the summer of 1944 he was closely connected with Pannwitz, whose views on cooperation with Russia he shared.

He was supposed to go to Stockholm in July or August 1944 to contact Russian representatives with a memorandum proposing collaboration among France, Germany, and Russia.

He was threatened with expulsion from Paris by the Nazi Party. Well known as a former Socialist, he was formerly at the International Labor Office in Geneva and a friend of Winant, later U.S. Ambassador to London.

He accompanied Pannwitz to Constance in August 1944. In Berlin from September to December 1944 he worked for Auslands Organization on economic inquiry. Later he was a driver at an Army depot in Rathenow.

He was a contact of Duebendorfer.

BERNARD BAESTLEIN

was a leading Communist functionary in Hamburg and maintained an active intelligence group there before World War II. Born in 1894, he belonged to the illegal Saefkow group.

He supplied information to Wilhelm Guddorf, who ran a courier service to Moscow. Both Arvid Harnack and Harro Schulze-Boysen made use of Baestlein's service. In May 1942 Baestlein assisted Erna Eifler and Wilhelm Fellendorf. Eifler, a Russian agent, was dropped by parachute into Germany with a W/T set and was instructed to find Ilse Stoebe and to re-establish communications with Rudolf von Scheliha. Eifler was accompanied by Wilhelm Fellendorf, also equipped with a W/T set. Both took shelter with Baestlein in Hamburg and were arrested as a result of the capture of Wilhelm Guddorf by the Gestapo.

In October 1942 Heinrich Koenen was parachuted into Germany with similar instructions and provided with incriminating documents with which to blackmail von Scheliha, should this prove necessary. Koenen was arrested shortly after his arrival, and neither he nor Eifler succeeded in getting into contact with Ilse Stoebe. The Germans operated both as W/T deception agents and were thus able to capture von Scheliha and Ilse Stoebe in the autumn of 1942. The Germans continued the playback until about 1943.

MARGARETE BARCZA

(nee Singer, alias La Blonde) was born 14 August 1912 in Saaz, Czechoslovakia. She was Sukolov's "great love" and had a son by him (Michel, born in April 1944 at Neuilly). Her mother, Elsa Singer, lives in New York City. During World War II Sukolov sent her money via Maurice Padawer.

Margarete married Ernst Barcza 7 April 1932 and lived in Czechoslovakia, where her first son Rene Josei was born 22 December 1932. Her husband made a fortune in hops, and she herself had come from a wealthy family. The Barczas emigrated from Saaz to Prague in 1938 and then entered Belgium as refugees on 24 April 1939. Margarete met Sukolov (alias Sierra) in 1940 in Brussels, where he had a lot of money and lived in grand style. Ernst Barcza died 16 March 1940, and Margarete became Sukolov's mistress in May 1940.

Sukolov fled to France in December 1941; but before he left, he made arrangements for Margarete and her son Rene to go to France also. There are two accounts available of how this trip was made. Abraham Rajchmann, the forger, told his story to the Belgian authorities after the war. (See Rajchmann's statement which appears earlier in this study.) Gilles Perrault, who visited Margarete in Brussels in December 1965, provides a graphic account in *L'Orchestra Rouge.*

Margarete and Sukolov were arrested together at Marseilles 12 November 1942.

Margarete saw Sukolov for the last time in 1945, and despite several attempts since then to locate him, she has not been able to do so.

Margarete was tall (noticeably taller than Sukolov), well-built, blonde, elegant, and attractive. She spoke Czech, French, and German.

According to a 1960 NATO Special Committee report, Margarete was remarried in 1953 to Simon Brogniaux, born at Roux on 8 September 1895. In 1954 they were domiciled at 136 Rue de Ribaucourt, Molenbeek-St. Jean. Margarete had not been reported to the Belgian authorities for political activities. She is still residing in Belgium.

Margarete has an older brother, Bedrich Jaroslav Singer (alias Fritz) who was engaged in Soviet intelligence activities in France during World War II. In 1946 Bedrich Singer was reportedly living in New York City with his mother Elsa.

WILLY BERG
(alias Huegel) was born on 1 March 1891 in Biesellen, Kreis Osterode. He was a Kriminalinspektor and had been von Ribbentrop's bodyguard in Moscow at the time of the Soviet-German pact. He worked for Karl Giering and then for Pannwitz and had the job of surveilling Trepper and Sukolov.

British reports indicate that Berg was also in contact with the Soviets. Undoubtedly, Trepper and Berg trusted each other, and it is possible that Berg permitted Trepper to escape German custody in September 1943.

In 1954 Berg was living at 31 Luebeckerstrasse, Berlin.

HELENE BERGER

(nee Lieser) was born 16 December 1898 in Vienna, Austria. She is an Austrian national. She was formerly of Yugoslav nationality by virtue of her marriage to Charles Berger, born 28 March 1901 in Munich, Germany, of Yugoslav nationality.

She resided at 52 Boulevard Malesherbes, Paris, and was employed as a secretary and economist with the Organization for European Economic Cooperation (Marshall Plan). She is the bearer of an Austrian passport issued 17 September 1948 by the Austrian Consulate General at New York City. She has made trips to Switzerland and Italy in connection with her employment with the OEEC. Her passport carries an extension of her visa pending the issuance of a Consular Card by the French Foreign Office at the request of the OEEC.

Prior to April 1947 she resided at 68 Rue Montchoisy, Geneva, Switzerland, during which time she was employed by the Unitarian Service Committee, with headquarters at 37 Quai President Wilson at Geneva, and Paris headquarters at 61 Rue Jouffroy, Paris. This organization deals with the purchase and distribution of relief supplies.

She was a contact of Duebendorfer.

At the time of her arrest, Duebendorfer carried important documents concealed in the soles of her shoes. After release on bail she took a flat in 135 Rue de Lausanne, and through her fellow lodger, Helene Berger, attempted at Roessler's instigation to pass portions of the Lucy reports to the British.

Helene Berger also assisted Duebendorfer financially to the extent of three thousand dollars on promise of repayment of Berger's sister, Annie Berger, in the United States.

Duebendorfer met Foote for the first time after his release in October 1944 and introduced him to Berger.

MAURICE ROBERT BEUBLET

was a Belgian lawyer who acted as legal adviser for Simexco in Brussels. Before World War II he had been an important Communist leader in Brussels, but he publicly resigned from the Party. Beublet was arrested in November 1942. He may have turned informant against other members of the Belgian network while in St. Gilles prison, where he was reportedly found hanged in his cell.

LEON CHARLES BEURTON

(alias John William Miller, alias John, alias Fenton) was a British subject, born 19 February 1914 in Barking, London. His father was a naturalized British subject of French birth. He was in the International Brigade in Spain. When Foote was asked by Ursula Hamburger to name a suitable assistant, he suggested Beurton. However, Beurton's actual recruitment was done by Brigitte Lewis (Long), sister of Ursula. Beurton was turned over to Hamburger in Vevey, Switzerland, on 12 February 1939.

During the summer of 1939, after a briefing, Beurton was sent to Frankfurt/Main to observe the IG Farben works at Offenbach. In August, after the signing of the Russo-German pact, and because war was imminent, he was recalled with Foote to Switzerland where both men were given W/T training by Ursula. In 1940 Beurton married Ursula Hamburger, thus giving her British citizenship.

It was thought by Moscow that Hamburger was compromised by her maid. She was directed to leave Switzerland and to go to England, as she did in December 1940. She left her code with Beurton and at the same time gave Foote a new code, together with instructions and a new timetable that she had received from the Center.

After the spring of 1941 Beurton did little work, but he remained with Rado's group until the summer of 1942. Then, with the help of Captain Farrell, Eleanor Rathbone, and possibly Marie Ginsberg, he obtained a British passport in the name of Miller and went to the U.K. via Spain. In July 1942 Beurton arrived in the U.K. from Lisbon. In 1948 he was employed as a machine fitter in Chipping Norton and was active in the local CP.

DR. MARIO BIANCHI

was born on 27 April 1909 in Chiasso, Italy. His wife was Germaine, nee Lienhard. Bianchi was an ear, eyes, nose, and throat specialist. In 1949 he lived in Geneva and may have lived there during the war as well. His wife was the sister of Leon Nicole. Bianchi served the Rote Drei as a safehouse keeper, as a point of contact for Leon Nicole and his son Pierre as well as the Vigiers, and as a transmission point for contacts with Italy (perhaps by way of his brother Emilio in Lugano).

Soon after the arrest of the Hamels in October 1943, Bianchi hid Alexander and Helen Rado for two or three weeks.

JOSEPH BLUMSACK
was the husband of Renee Blumsack. He was recruited by Germaine Schneider, his sister-in-law, for the courier service between Brussels and Paris. In March 1929 he was listed as a member of the foreign workers' section of the Belgian Communist Party. In June 1942 he sought refuge in the home of Yvonne Poelmans at Ixelles. He was arrested in Brussels on 7 January 1943 and deported to Germany. He escaped from the Birkenau Camp, and his ultimate fate is unknown.

RENEE BLUMSACK
(nee Clais, alias Nora) was recruited by her sister Germaine Schneider for the courier service between Brussels and Paris. She was born 2 January 1907 at Anderiecht. After Germaine's arrest and interrogation by the Germans in June 1942, Renee, with her husband Joseph Blumsack, took refuge in Yvonne Poelmans' house at Ixelles. She was arrested in Brussels on 7 January 1943 and deported to Germany. In 1945 she died in the Mauthausen Concentration Camp.

GEORGE BLUN
(alias Long, aka Andre Choisy, pen name) was born 1 June 1893 in Alsace-Lorraine, son of George and Lucie Corvisard (French). He is married to Marie Kentzel, a journalist. He speaks French and German fluently.

Blun worked for the British and French IS during World War I. In 1920 he was expelled from Switzerland for his Communist activities. He had been taken into the Comintern and was thought to be directing Soviet espionage against Germany.

From 1925 through the 1930s he was in Germany, primarily in Berlin, working as a correspondent for various papers, including Paris' *Le Soir* and *Journal*.

In 1939 he moved his office to Zurich, where he was supposed to have some good German contacts and was suspected of being in the employ of both the French and Polish intelligence services. Later documents show that Blun's first loyalty was to Russia, for whom "on his own confession" he worked continually in connection with the Rote Drei.

Just when Blun started to work for the Russians is not known, although he was permitted in Switzerland in 1939 only under observation. His reports to the Swiss were mainly on political matters, although they contained some military information. He gave reports to the Swiss from January to September 1943. In 1942 Blun was involved in the establishment of the Vorarlberg cache from which Russian parachute agents in Austria were paid. At this time he was denounced by a fellow agent at an unspecified place, interrogated by the Gestapo, and subsequently released.

In 1943 Blun is said to have offered his services to the French, but they could not afford to pay him what he wanted; and they also suspected that he was working for the Russians.

While Allen Dulles was in Switzerland during World War II, he was in contact with George Blun and a newspaper colleague of Blun's named Walter Bosshard, both of whom were close to Dr. Josef Wirth.

Blun, according to the Flicke material, is reported to have had a source—"Agnes"—in Ribbentrop's office. He also supplied information to the Rote Drei from "Bruder," "Fanny," "Feld," "Rot," and "Luise," the latter being a W/T name for the Intelligence Department of the Swiss General Staff.

In 1946 Blun left Switzerland and eventually found his way to the Russian Zone of Berlin where he worked for the Russians. In the autumn of 1947 Blun was reportedly in touch with Japanese diplomats in Berlin. He then went to Geneva, where he wrote for the *Gazette de Geneve*.

Fnu BOELLENS

was appointed by Grossvogel as the agent for the Foreign Excellent Raincoat Company in Stockholm in 1939. He had been recommended for the post by the Belgian Consulate in Stockholm. Boellens established an advertising and business agency for the company. He may not have known of Grossvogel's actual purpose in establishing this office in Sweden. Boellens was of Belgian nationality.

PAUL BOETTCHER

(alias Hans Saal-Bach, W/T cover name "Paul") was born 2 May 1891 in Leipzig. His common-law wife was Rachel Duebendorfer. In 1920 he was the editor of *Sozial Demokrat*, a USPD organ, and in 1922 editor of the *Leipziger Volksleitung*.

In May 1923 he went to a secret conference of German factions called by the Politburo at Leipzig. Present were Heinrich Brandler, Ruth Fisher, Arcadi Moslov, and Ernst Thaelmann. On 10 October

1923 Boettcher became Minister of Finance of Saxony and a member of the Saxon Cabinet. He was expelled about 1929.

In 1934 he went to Switzerland from Leipzig and lived underground for a year. He appeared in Switzerland as Duebendorfer's husband, whose identity he had assumed, and remained there illegally, although he was the subject of a Swiss expulsion order.

In 1936 or 1937 he joined the International Brigade and fought in the Spanish Civil War, at which time he had one Madeleine, a French journalist, as his mistress. In 1938, proposing to set up business in the U.K., he got a loan of five thousand pounds from Christian Schneider.

Communications difficulties necessitated the amalgamation of the Duebendorfer net with the Rado group. It appears that in the early part of the war Moscow was thinking of having Boettcher set up a W/T station by the summer of 1943 and sent him a cipher for that purpose. He was to have had at least one W/T operator. The Rote Drei traffic indicates that Paul was sick in the early fall of 1943. Later in the year he appears to have had a strained relationship with Rado, as did Duebendorfer.

Boettcher was arrested by the Swiss for espionage on 6 April 1944 and on 31 May was transferred to a refugee camp at Siehem. On 23 July 1945 Boettcher escaped from this camp and fled with Duebendorfer to France. In August they were in Paris. On 23 October 1945 he was sentenced *in absentia* by the Swiss to two years' imprisonment, ten thousand Swiss francs fine, and fifteen years' expulsion from Switzerland.

SUZANNE BOISSON
(nee Schmidt or Schmitz) was born 22 January 1918 at Pongkaton, Dutch East Indies. In 1940 and 1941 she was probably used as a courier for the Sukolov group. She was introduced by Guillaume Hoorickx to Mikhail Makarov, whose mistress she became. She was a friend of Hoorickx' mistress, Anna Staritsky, and of Anton Danilov. She was arrested 13 December 1941 after Makarov's capture but was subsequently released for lack of evidence.

Suzanne Schmidt was arrested when she went to 101 Rue des Attrebates, Brussels, the day after Makarov's arrest.

In 1944 Suzanne Schmidt married Pierre Georges Prosper Boisson, born 8 May 1919 in Brussels. He is by profession a doctor and from 1950 to at least 1960 was employed by the Brussels Education Department as a school inspector. The Boisson's last known address

(1960) was 26 Rue Paul Lauters, Brussels.

According to a 1960 NATO Special Committee report, neither Suzanne Boisson nor her husband were suspected of Communism. They did not appear to be maintaining contacts with former members of the Rote Kapelle.

MARGARET BOLLI

(alias Rosa, aka Schatz-Bolli and Schwarz-Bolli) was born 15 December 1919 in Basle. (Another report states she was born 29 May 1912 in Beringen, daughter of Adolphe and Luise Schenk.)

She became acquainted with Alexander Rado in October 1941 while she worked as a waitress at a cafe in Bern. Rado advised her to learn French and to study typing. Later, when living with relatives in Lausanne, she met Foote, who taught her Morse code and the operation of a transmitter. When Bolli became proficient, Rado employed her for four hundred francs a month.

In September 1942 she settled in Geneva, ready to carry out the instructions of Rado, whom she knew as "Albert." From October 1942 to March 1943 Bolli transmitted from 4 Rue Soleure, Geneva. In March 1943 she was established in an apartment on 8 Rue Henri Mussard, where Rado sent her a transmitter via Hamel. The set was cleverly hidden in a portable gramophone, and Bolli transmitted the encrypted texts of messages between midnight and one in the morning two to three times a week. Her salary was increased to six hundred sixty francs a month plus expenses and maintenance.

Around the middle of 1943 she fell in love with and became the mistress of Hans Peters, a German penetration plant and member of Abwehr III, to whom she disclosed the name of the book *Es Begann im September,* used in the encipherment of Rado's traffic. She was arrested with Peters on 13 October 1943 by the Swiss police but pleaded that she had accepted work with Rado in full faith that she was working against the Nazis.

Bolli was defended by Jacques Chamorel, a lawyer from Lausanne, and was sentenced by the Swiss Military Tribunal to ten months' imprisonment and five hundred francs fine. Otto Puenter put up her bail, and the sentence was suspended.

In September 1947 she was reported to be visiting in Rome, accompanied by her husband, Arthur Schatz, a merchant. In 1956 she and Shatz were living in Basle.

Fnu BOLLINGER

was an electrical engineer arrested in the Simexco roundup of November 1942. He reportedly died at Dachau.

ERNST ALEXANDRE JULIEN BOMERSON

was born 11 October 1899 in Verviers, Belgium. He was an employee of the firm Lever Brothers in Brussels and there made the acquaintance of Franz Schneider, a department head. Bomerson was sympathetic to Schneider's political opinions, and the two became close friends. Bomerson also met Schneider's wife, Germaine.

During the German occupation Bomerson, at the request of Schneider, did bookkeeping for Jean Janssens, who was the lover of Germaine Schneider's sister Josephine Verhimst.

After the arrest of Johannes Wenzel, Franz Schneider asked Bomerson if he could find lodgings for a certain Hofman without registering with the police. Bomerson agreed to let Hofman stay at his home in Forest. Hofman was actually Jeffremov, who was arrested before he was able to move to Bomerson's house.

When Franz Schneider was repatriated to Belgium in 1945, he returned to Brussels and found that all his possessions had disappeared. He thus accepted the hospitality of his friend, Bomerson, with whom he stayed for about two weeks.

Schneider has visited Bomerson in Brussels several times since 1945, and they apparently correspond regularly.

HENRIETTE BOURGEOIS

(alias Harry) was born in 1917 in the Canton de Vaud, Switzerland. She was unmarried and a stenographer. In 1943 Bourgeois was recruited by Pierre Nicole to be trained as a W/T operator by Foote. She gave up her job in Geneva, thereby precipitating a quarrel with her parents.

Rado used this quarrel as an excuse to set Bourgeois up in a flat so that her training could start. Foote was arrested before the training began, and after his release Nicole asked if something could be done for her. Foote believes nothing was done. In November 1947 she was still living in Geneva.

MARCELLE CAPRE

(nee Lambert, alias Martha) was born 2 August 1914 in Paris. She was the secretary and assistant to Henri Robinson at least from October 1940 and probably a cutout to Robinson's agent "Jerome."

In the spring of 1941, apparently under Robinson's instructions, she recruited agents from among French laborers to be deported to Germany.

She controlled a source of intelligence on French aircraft. Although she was arrested in December 1942, she was unbroken in March 1943.

She was married to fnu Capre, a French Communist Party leader who was arrested probably on the outbreak of the war.

According to an Abwehr report dated 19 January 1943, Marcelle Capre had hidden Germaine Schneider in her house.

ROBERT JEAN CHRISTEN

was a shareholder in Simexco and a personal friend of Sukolov. He may have provided help for Sukolov and Trepper in Brussels in 1940 and 1941. Christen was born on 22 May 1898 in St. Imier, Switzerland. He was the proprietor of the Florida nightclub in Brussels. At the time of the general roundup of Simexco employees and officers in November 1942, Christen was arrested and deported to Germany. In March 1945 he was repatriated to Brussels.

After the arrests of December 1941 Sukolov went to see Christen at his home. He told Christen that he was leaving immediately for France and asked him to keep a box for him. Christen agreed. A few weeks later Nazarin Drailly came by to pick up the box. Christen claims that it was not until then that he learned the box contained a radio set.

According to a 1960 NATO Special Committee Report, Christen was the husband of Rolande Bertha Luckx, born 23 October 1910 in Bruges. He was described as a cafe proprietor, and his residence was given as 675 Chaussee de Jette, Jette-St. Pierre. He had not been reported for subversive activities or for contacts with former members of the Rote Kapelle.

Christen is still residing in Belgium and in 1965 he was interviewed by Perrault.

HANS KARL COPPI

(alias Strahlmann) was born 25 January 1916 in Berlin. His father was Robert Coppi, born 16 December 1882 in Leipzig. His brother Kurt was born 14 May 1919. His wife Hilde Coppi, nee Raasch, was born 30 May 1919 in Berlin. They had a child, Hans Robert Coppi, born 14 May 1938.

The entire Coppi family was involved in Communist activity,

and Hans was one of the principal agents and radio operators of the "Coro" group, using the cover name "Strahlmann." Hans Coppi was the lover of Erika von Brockdorf, nee Schoenfeld.

Coppi and his wife were arrested 12 September 1942. He was executed on 22 December 1942. She was executed on 5 August 1943.

ALFRED VALENTIN CORBIN
(alias Belleme) was born 26 February 1916 at Clichy (Seine), France. A French national, he was married to Marie-Louise Dubois, born 11 January 1900 at Arcueil (Seine).

He was the director of Simex in Paris and was in contact with Trepper and Grossvogel. He had probably been recruited by Hillel Katz. He lived at 15 Rue Carnuschi, Paris.

In January 1942 he went to Marseilles to found a branch of Simex and provide cover for Sukolov, who built an intelligence group covering the south of France. He was able to undertake courier missions between Marseilles and Paris by virtue of his business cover.

He was arrested on 19 November 1942 and reportedly executed in Berlin on 28 July 1943. His wife died in a concentration camp.

His brother, Robert Albert Corbin, born 10 October 1904, probably was not involved in clandestine activity but knew several of the Simex group, notably Waldemar Keller.

BUNTEA CRUPNIC
(alias Irma Salno, alias Irene Sadnow, alias Andree, alias Yvonne) was a member of the Jeffremov network and responsible to Elizabeth Depelsenaire for the provision of safehouses for agents in the Brussels area. She was probably concerned primarily with Communist resistance workers, but in June 1942 she was responsible for providing John Kruyt with accommodations. Kruyt was parachuted into Belgium to reinforce the Jeffremov network and had two meetings with Crupnic (alias Salno).

Buntea Crupnic is a Rumanian Jew born 22 or 28 February 1911 at Soroki, Rumania. She is the widow of Oscar Smesman, born 19 March 1888 in Merelbeke, Belgium. Crupnic acquired Belgian citizenship, presumably through her marriage to Smesman.

In 1946 Crupnic was on the staff of the newspaper *Clarte*, Boulevard d'Anvers, Brussels. Her last known address (1960) was 167 Rue des Pommes, Liege. She was at that time employed as a social worker.

A 1960 NATO Special Committee report states the following

about Crupnic:

> Although it cannot be definitely stated that she works for an intelligence service, she is considered capable of doing so on behalf of a service behind the Iron Curtain.

Buntea Crupnic has been described as having fair hair, dark eyes, a short, thin build, and teeth widely separated in the upper jaw.

CHARLES FRANCOIS DANIELS

acted as a courier for Sukolov between Simexco in Brussels and Simex in Paris. He was a business associate of Guillaume Hoorickx and Heinrich Rauch. Daniels was born on 30 December 1911 in Schaerbeck. He was married to Denise, nee Deuly, who, until March 1941, was in touch with a member of the Soviet Embassy in Paris. From early 1941 Daniels ran in Antwerp a factory called Atea dealing in household and telephonic equipment. About July 1941 Hoorickx and Rauch withdrew from Simexco and joined forces with Daniels in a business venture. Their offices were at 192 Rue Royale, Brussels, in the same building as that of Simexco.

According to a 1960 NATO Special Committee report, Daniels was remarried to Anna Catharine de Greef, born at Tourneppe on 21 January 1925. His employment was shown as a company director. His domicile was at 9 Place du Petit Sablon, Brussels. The Daniels/de Greef couple was at that time attracting no attention from the Belgian authorities for intelligence activities.

ANTON DANILOV

(alias Antonio, alias Desmet [s], alias de Smet [s], alias de Smith [in Belgium]) was a secret writing specialist and radio operator for the Sukolov group from the summer of 1941 until his arrest in Brussels the night of 12-13 December 1941. He was a Red Army Lieutenant and had been posted in 1938 from the USSR, via the Balkans, to the Soviet Military Attache's office in Paris. He later served at Vichy under Captain Karpov. In June or July 1941 Danilov was sent by Trepper to reinforce Sukolov's organization in Brussels, specifically to assist Makarov with the radio transmissions. His false identity papers in the name of de Smets were provided to him by Hoorickx, who obtained them through de Reymaeker.

In his statement to the Belgian authorities, which appears earlier in the study, Abraham Rajchmann described the arrangements made for Danilov's trip from France to Belgium.

On 12 December 1941 Danilov was arrested while transmitting at 101 Rue des Attrebates, Brussels. He resisted strongly and was seriously injured during the course of the struggle. The Germans attempted to use Danilov in their radio playbacks, but he apparently cooperated very little. In 1943 he was deported to Germany and subsequently executed.

Much of Perrault's information concerning Danilov is incorrect. Perrault did not know, for example, that it was Danilov who was arrested with Makarov at the Rue des Attrebates in December 1941. He mistakenly believed that the radio operator arrested that night was Hesekil Schreiber (alias Camille) who worked first for Trepper in Paris and then in Lyons with Springer. Perrault is also wrong with respect to the date of Danilov's arrival in Belgium. According to Perrault, Danilov arrived in Belgium in 1939, whereas the actual date was 1941. Perrault himself recognizes that some of his statements regarding Danilov are contradictory.

ELIZABETH (BETTY) DEPELSENAIRE

(nee Sneyers) is a Belgian Communist of long standing. She worked for the Jeffremov group in Brussels during 1941 and 1942. In 1942 she was associated with Irma Salno and others in the provision of accommodation and facilities for Soviet agents parachuted into Belgium. Elizabeth is the widow of Albert Depelsenaire, who in 1940 was *auditeur-militaire* in Brussels. In November 1941 he was arrested and executed by the Germans for assisting Communists. Elizabeth is by profession a lawyer. She was born 23 August 1913 at Bonheyden. At one time she was an employee of the firm Philips, Rue d'Anderlecht, Brussels, but she was dismissed because of her Communist sympathies. In the autumn of 1941 she recruited Jean Otten, Jeanne Otten, and others to provide safehouses for partisans in hiding. Depelsenaire was arrested by the Germans in early July 1942, after the arrest of John Kruyt, Sr. She allegedly was betrayed by Marth Vandenhoeck. Depelsenaire was associated with Franz Schneider during the war, and in 1946 and 1947 she lived with him in Switzerland as his mistress. On 2 August 1947 they were married, but they have since separated. In 1960 Depelsenaire had contacts in the top circles of the Belgian Communist Party. Her address was 234 Rue du Trone, Ixelles. Elizabeth Depelsenaire is the authoress of *Symphonie Fraternelle,* an account of Miriam Sokol's experiences in Breendonck.

RACHEL DOBRIK
was born 1 May 1908 in Warsaw. She is Swiss by marriage to a Swiss
dentist named Jentet. Later she got a divorce. This marriage was for
the purpose of obtaining Swiss citizenship and concealing her origin
and past.

   She helped Rachel Duebendorfer with funds via her sister, Berta
Helbein, in New York. Berta Helbein was married to Jacques Helbein, the brother of William Helbein.

   During the war large U.S. credits were placed in Berta Helbein's
account with the Swiss Bank Corporation in Geneva. This money was
said to be profits from the sale of watches exported from Switzerland
to the USA. At an unknown date Rachel Duebendorfer approached
Berta Helbein with a request for money, the equivalent of which
would be paid to Wilhelm Helbein in New York. Berta Helbein
agreed and carried out the transactions after hearing from William
Helbein that the money was in his possession. Sums paid were 21
June 1943: three thousand four hundred Swiss francs; 6 November:
five thousand Swiss francs; 3 January: twenty-eight thousand Swiss
francs.

   It was Rachel Dobrik who warned Rado that the Swiss were
going to arrest the Rote Drei suspects in Switzerland.

CHARLES VICTOR EDGARD DRAILLY
born 1 December 1901 in Gilly (Belgium), was the brother of
Nazarin Drailly. He was employed in a bank and became a director of
Simexco in March 1941. He was probably aware of the activities of
the Belgian network, but he did not actively participate in them.
Charles Drailly was the husband of Lucienne, nee Carlier, who in
1946 sought Georgie de Winter to learn the fate of her family. Drailly was arrested 25 November 1942 and deported to Germany. He
died of typhus at Mauthausen concentration camp 4 January 1945.

NAZARIN ADOLPHE EDOUARDE LEOPOLD LEON DRAILLY
had been a Brussels acquaintance of Grossvogel since 1934. He was
born 29 April 1900 at Gilly (Belgium). In May 1940, after the German invasion, Drailly and his family fled to France. Early in 1941 he
was persuaded by Trepper to return to Belgium to collaborate with
Sukolov in the establishment of Simexco. According to the articles of
incorporation, Drailly's investment in Simexco amounted to two
hundred eighteen thousand five hundred Belgian francs.

   After Makarov's arrest in December 1941, Drailly hid Sukolov in his home for a few days. When Sukolov went to France, Drailly became the managing director of Simexco. He was fully aware of Simexco's real purpose and he collected military and industrial intelligence from certain of Sukolov's agents, such as Jean Passelecq. At the time of the roundup of Simexco employees in November 1942, Drailly managed to evade capture. He took refuge in the house of a woman friend, Jeanne Ponsaint. According to Perrault, Ponsaint was arrested by the Germans on 11 December 1942, when she was sent by Drailly to deliver a package to his wife.

Drailly was arrested 6 January 1943, tortured at Breendonck, and deported to Germany. He was executed in Plotzensee, Berlin, 28 July 1943. (Perrault states that Drailly died in Dachau of bubonic plague.) Nazarin was the brother of Charles Drailly.

Drailly was married to Germaine, nee Temmermann, born 20 February 1899. She was arrested 26 November 1942 and eventually deported to Germany. Madame Drailly was liberated 8 May 1945 and repatriated to Brussels. In the summer of 1946 she and her sister-in-law, Lucienne Drailly, sought out Georgie de Winter to learn the fate of their family. In 1947 she was living in Anderlecht. She is a known Communist.

The Draillys had a daughter, Solange Eva, born 1 February 1926 in Ixelles. She too was arrested in November 1942 in the Simexco roundup. She was later released for lack of proof. In May 1946 Solange left Belgium, ostensibly for her health, but she stated privately that she hoped to make fresh contact with the organization for which her father worked. Solange has been described as an ardent Communist.

MARCEL VINCENT DROUBAIX

(alias Hector) was born 16 May 1893 in Antwerp. Educated in England, he had been a captain in the British Royal Horse Artillery in the 1914-1918 war. He died in the Buchenwald Camp in February 1945.

He was a member of the French resistance network Mithridate, operated by Colonel fnu Bressac. This network incorporated a group run by Ozols and was penetrated by Sukolov, working under German control. Droubaix became aware of the German penetration of the Mithridate network in June 1944.

He was arrested in Paris on 18 July 1944 at a pre-arranged rendezvous with Sukolov.

His son, Marcel Marie Droubaix (alias Achilles) was also involved in the Mithridate network.

RACHEL DUEBENDORFER

(nee Hepner) was born 18 July 1901 in Warsaw, Poland, daughter of Arcadi Abraham Hepner and Regina Pines. She has a sister named Rose Reudi Luschinsky, nee Hepner. Her first marriage, circa 1921, was to Kurt Caspary, a German lawyer by whom she had a daughter, Tamara, who later married Jean Pierre Vigier (alias Braut). She divorced Caspary, who went to Australia, and then married Henri Duebendorfer, a Swiss mechanic, circa 1932, in order to get Swiss citizenship. They separated almost immediately.

Her common-law husband was the German newspaperman Paul Boettcher (alias Hans Saalbach, alias Paul) and she has been known as Mrs. Paul Boettcher. She lived with Boettcher, who assumed the name of Paul Duebendorfer, from 1934 until their arrest in 1944.

From 1934 to 1944 she was employed in the translating section of the ILO in Geneva. She and Boettcher frequented a cosmopolitan social circle, openly expressing anti-Nazi views; but they were not aggressively Communist in their speech, although known to their friends as pro-Russian.

She lived at a standard far beyond her ILO salary, although when she first settled in Geneva she was noticeably impoverished. While working at the ILO, she paid frequent visits to her sister Rose in Zurich and also travelled frequently to France, visiting her parents in Nice.

During 1934 she was the recipient of correspondence for Boettcher from the U.S. Communist Jay Lovestone, through whom Boettcher sought assignments for left-wing U.S. journals.

In 1941, on orders from Moscow, Alexander Rado established contact with Duebendorfer. In August 1943 Rado was warned by Rachel Dobrick, sister of Berta Helbein, the wife of William Helbein of New York, of the impending roundup of the Rote Drei.

With her lover Boettcher, Duebendorfer was arrested by the Swiss police on 2 June 1944, but she was released or escaped shortly thereafter. In July 1945 she escaped to France, but she was sentenced *in absentia* to two years' imprisonment, a fine of ten thousand francs, and fifteen years' expulsion from Switzerland.

Paul Tillard, the novelist and former *L'Humanite* correspondent in Peking, published a novel, *L'Outrage*, Juilliard, Paris, 1958, which is reportedly based on the life story of Duebendorfer and Paul Boettcher. According to the story, Franz (Boettcher), after working in Geneva as a Soviet agent during World War II, returned to Moscow after the war accompanied by his wife (Duebendorfer) "in order to get a few things straightened out about his work." The hero was arrested and sentenced to Siberia for fifteen years. After Stalin's death all foreigners were freed. He found that his wife had gone mad. They were put face to face; she recognized him, but the look she gave him was one of hatred, and she spat in his face. The known facts indicate that this account is entirely false.

Duebendorfer was described by friends as untidy in appearance and habits, and not highly cultured. She was openly opposed to the Nazis but cautious in displaying the Communist sympathies she undoubtedly held.

Duebendorfer's radio code name was "Sissy." Her closest associates were:

Irene and Emile Grunberg, fellow employees at ILO, who now live in the United States.

Lorre and Karl Kapp, who worked at ILO with Duebendorfer. According to the interrogation report of Lorre Kapp, Rachel, Rose, and Lorre were children together in Danzig.

Christian Schneider, an employee of ILO who is the Taylor of Rote Drei traffic and who served as cutout between Lucy (Rudolf Roessler) and Sissy.

Leon Steinig, born 6 June 1898 at Trembowla, Austria. Former ILO and UN employee.

Horace Glickman, a Lithuanian, radio engineer, 131 Blvd. Brune, Paris. Childhood friend. Duebendorfer lived at his house when she escaped from Switzerland. Rabinowitch also stayed with the Glickmans.

Otto Bach, who introduced the Kapps to Rabinowitch in Geneva, was a former ILO employee who knew Pannwitz and Winant.

Henri Vigier (father of Jean-Pierre Vigier), who was in Rhodes as personal representative of Dr. Ralph J. Bunche of the U.N.

Tamara and Jean-Pierre Vigier, daughter and son-in-law, who knew many underground people in Switzerland, including Noel Field.

The European press reported the death of Rachel Duebendorfer in East Germany in 1973.

ALEXANDER ERDBERG

was the Russian who recruited Arvid Harnack around December 1940 in Berlin. Harnack introduced Schulze-Boysen to Erdberg, who recruited him for active work early in 1941. Erdberg acted as a contact between Moscow and the Harnack and Schulze-Boysen groups in Berlin. About May or June 1941, shortly before the Soviet Embassy was withdrawn from Berlin, Erdberg, of the Soviet Trade Delegation, took steps towards the independent operational establishment of both the Harnack and Schulze-Boysen groups. He gave Harnack two thousand reichsmark and Adam Kuckhoff, five hundred reichsmark. These funds were for financing the groups and the payment of agents.

Erdberg was particularly interested in secret war production of the firm Auer at Heiligensee Henningsdorf near Berlin. According to Roeder, the husband of Rose Schloesinger was connected with Erdberg. So were both the Schumachers and Johannes Sieg.

It is possible that Erdberg is identical with Sergei Kudrayavtsev, who was involved in the Corby case in Canada in 1946 and who in 1969 was Soviet Ambassador to Cambodia.

GRETE FALK
(aka Mrs. Friedrich Bernard Hermann Lenz; Margaret Charlotte Luise Falk; Margaret Charlotte Luise Lenz; Dr. Grete Lenz, nee Oevel) was born 5 March 1899 in Siegen, Germany. She married Dr. Fritz Falk, who was born 24 July 1898 in Cologne, on 10 August 1932. He committed suicide in 1933. Dr. Falk was a Jew and was persecuted by the Nazis.

After her first husband's death, Mrs. Falk left Germany with the help of the Quakers. She proceeded to London in order to work with the Society of Friends. Later she immigrated to the U.S. through the assistance of the Society of Friends. She was employed in Pittsburgh, Pennsylvania, for about one year and then moved to Washington, D.C., where she was employed in social welfare research.

She originally entered the U.S. on 29 June 1934 in New York, and the records of the INS reflect that she was destined to Dr. Ludwig Bernstein, 17 Fernando Street, Pittsburgh, Pennsylvania. She filed a declaration of intention to become a U.S. citizen on 5 April 1935 and was naturalized on 7 May 1940 in the District of Columbia.

For several years Mrs. Lenz worked for the Council of Social Agencies (USPHS). She left the U.S. about 25 October 1940 for Germany in order to be with her husband, who was refused an extension of his visitor's visa and was obliged to return to Germany.

While Mrs. Lenz was in Washington, D.C., she and Professor Hertha Kraus of Bryn Mawr College arranged for Max Adenauer, one of Konrad Adenauer's six children, to visit the United States. Max Adenauer visited the U.S. on a tourist visa in 1936 and saw Mrs. Lenz several times in her office.

On 24 November 1946 Mrs. Lenz wrote to her friend Professor Hertha Kraus that she had been a member of the German underground movement and had also worked with the twentieth of July group. She claimed that she and her husband had a number of narrow escapes from the Gestapo.

> I was on friendly terms with Dr. Mildred Harnack-Fish (wife of Arvid Harnack) and have worked for Dr. Adam von Trott, one of the leading men of July twentieth; I was supposed to accompany Trott to the Peace Negotiations.

Fnu FEYS

was the name of a W/T operator in Ostende working under Makarov in 1941. According to Piepe's information, Feys was responsible for transmissions to London. He was tall, good-looking, and employed by the Police Commissariat in Ostende.

It is probable that Feys is identical with Augustin Sesee, known to have been Makarov's assistant W/T operator in Ostende.

WILHELM FRANZ FLICKE

was born in Odessa, Russia, on 22 January 1897 of German parents. He first entered the German army in 1915.

During World War II he did cryptographic work against Rote Kapelle—chiefly Rote Drei—targets.

Although Flicke posed as an expert and wrote a book on the subject (*Die Rote Kapelle,* Kreuzlinger, 1949), his information is sometimes inaccurate if not misleading. After the war, doubts arose about his reliability, mainly because his sister and his estranged wife were both living in the Soviet Zone of Germany. Flicke died on 11 October 1957.

ALLAN ALEXANDER FOOTE

(alias Jim, alias Alfred, alias Major Granatow, alias Alfred Feodorovich Capidus, alias Alexander Alexandrovich Dymov, alias John South, alias Albert Mueller) was born 13 September 1905 at Kirkdale, Liverpool.

In December 1936 Foote went to Spain as a volunteer in the International Brigade. His experiences are described in his book,

Handbook for Spies.

From 1938 to 1940 Foote was an agent of the RIS sabotage group intended to operate against Germany. From 1941 to 1943 he lived in Switzerland and operated a W/T transmitter as a member of the Rote Drei network, first under the direction of Ursula Beurton, formerly Hamburger, nee Kuczynski (alias Sonia, sister of Mrs. Bridget Lewis), and then under Alexander Rado. Ursula Beurton was responsible for training Foote in the use of his W/T transmitter. In addition to enciphering, deciphering, receiving, and transmitting traffic with Moscow, Foote instructed other recruits in W/T. From the summer of 1941 he utilized his social contacts in order to obtain Swiss currency for the network against repayment of dollar sums in the USA and South America.

In November 1943 Foote was imprisoned by the Swiss, who had picked up his transmissions by D/F equipment. He was released in September 1944 and shortly thereafter made his way to France, where he contacted the Soviet Military Mission in Paris.

Given a cover name and story, Foote travelled from Paris to Moscow in January 1945. His story was that he was a former Estonian national, now a Soviet citizen, who had been deported from Tallin to France by the Germans. Now, posing as a POW, he was being repatriated to the USSR on the first plane to leave France.

In Moscow Foote was given new documentation, which represented him as Alexander Alexandrovich Dymov, a Russian born in Madrid. That birthplace was used to explain his faulty Russian.

After he had spent about eighteen months in the USSR, RU headquarters finally decided to return Foote to the field on a new mission. This time he was to pose as a German named Albert Mueller and was to operate from Argentina against the United States. It was planned that he should arrive in Berlin, ostensibly as a repatriated POW, and take up his new identity from there. In March 1947 Foote presented himself to the British authorities in Berlin, a very sick man, and declared that he had become disillusioned and wished to abandon his career as a Soviet agent.

He died in London in 1956.

SELMA GESSNER-BUEHRER

(alias May) was born 6 March 1913 in Switzerland. She was a bookseller. She had married and divorced a certain Winter and then married Robert Gessner-Buehrer (also spelled Buhrer), a designer, in 1939.

She had been active in Communist circles in Germany in the early 1930s. By 1936 she was in Switzerland and working for Soviet Military Intelligence as an agent under Maria Josefovna Poliakova (alias Vera). In 1940 Gessner-Buehrer was operating a book store in Zurich with Theodore Pinkus. The Runa office (newspaper agency thought to have been in the service of the Comintern), with which Pinkus had been associated, had been closed in late 1939.

She was recalled from retirement by Moscow in 1941 for the purpose of giving assistance to Rado. She acted as a cutout between Foote and Julius Humbert-Droz, to whom she handed a W/T set around 1939. Her associates were Poliakova, Anna Mueller, Rachel Duebendorfer, Pinkus, and Hans Jurgen Holm.

KARL GIERING,

born circa 1890, was the first head of the Sonderkommando in Paris and a friend of Willy Berg. He was Kriminalrat in Amt IV, Abteilung II, RSHA. He had worked on the Rote Kapelle investigation in Belgium before coming to Paris.

Giering of the Gestapo and Piepe of the Abwehr were ordered to collaborate in the investigation of the Rote Kapelle.

In August 1943 Giering was dying of cancer and was replaced by Heinz Pannwitz, rather than Heinrich Reiser, who was in line to replace Giering.

Trepper has advised that he was glad to see Giering leave and replaced by Pannwitz because, "Giering, with his great skepticism of a policeman, thought that the Jews were not worth more than the others. Pannwitz believed they were worth less than the others."

SUZANNE GIRAUD

was born 18 November 1910 at Pierrepont (Aisne), France. She is probably identical with Lucienne Lenoyer, who was married to Pierre Georges Giraud (alias Robert, alias Lucie) born 13 February 1914 in the Rhone Department.

The Girauds were the custodians of a W/T set located at Le Pecq (S & O). They were recruited by Grossvogel for the communications section of Trepper's organization in France.

At first, in 1942, Suzanne shared with her husband the position of Trepper's courier to the French CP, carrying reports for transmission over the CP line to Moscow. She then became a cutout for Trepper to Kathe Voelkner. She picked up reports and other materials Voelkner had assembled. Giraud had been selected for this purpose by Trepper because she spoke no German, and Voelkner's French was very bad. They met in the evening, outside Metro stations, and were instructed not to speak to each other. In case her link through Giraud should break down, Voelkner also had an emergency rendezvous with another cutout for every two months.

Giraud was arrested in 1942 and may have been executed.

HANS BERND GISEVIUS

was born on 6 June 1904 in Arnsberg, Westphalia. In October 1940 he was assigned to the German Consulate in Zurich as a vice consul. This position was cover for his work for the Abwehr. However, some postwar statements by German intelligence personnel indicated that as late as April 1945 he continued to send in reports to Ernst Kaltenbrunner, who was then the head of the SD. In so doing he may have acted as a double agent for OSS, Switzerland.

General Hans Oster, deputy to Admiral Canaris, had instituted a courier service which functioned at least every other day between the OKW (General Staff) headquarters in Berlin and the German Embassy in Bern. Gisevius had access to this pouch at least twice and usually three times a week.

Gisevius had excellent relations with the Swiss police and, through his mother, with British intelligence. But he also had connections with at least two members of the Rote Drei. One of these was Georges Blun (alias Long). The other was Rudolf Roessler (alias Lucy), who after the war identified Gisevius to a confidant as one of his (Roessler's) four sources. Because three of the four were key members of the twentieth of July conspiracy (the fourth being unidentified), it appears that General Hans Oster and others may have sent to Roessler the information that the Rote Drei sources were "Werther," "Teddy," "Anna," and "Olga."

DR. CARL FRIEDERICH GOERDELER

was born on 31 July 1884 in Schneidemuhl, West Prussia. For a number of years, until 1936, he was Oberbuergermeister (lord mayor) of Leipzig. In the Nazi period he became Reichschancellor for Price Control.

After he fell out with Hitler, Goerdeler joined the twentieth of July conspiracy. He was hanged on or about 16 October 1944.

He is one of the four Rote Drei sources in Germany named by Rudolf Roessler.

DANIEL GOULOOZE
(alias Daan) was born 28 April 1901 in Amsterdam. His name is also spelled Gouxlooze and Gouwlooze. A Dutch Jew, he was originally a carpenter, later became a publisher, and in 1930 served as manager of Pegasus, publishers of Communist literature in Amsterdam.

He received his training at the Karl Marx School in Moscow and returned as a contact man for the Comintern, covering Western Europe. His work at Pegasus was his cover. He became a member of the Executive Committee of the CP in 1932. In 1934 he was arrested in connection with a plot to assassinate Queen Wilhelmina.

During the occupation he was a contact man, and at one time he had four W/T sets and one in reserve. He had contact with KPD members in Berlin and with Comintern members in Belgium, France, and Great Britain. He rendered considerable assistance to Johann Wenzel's communications service in the Low Countries, providing recruits from within the CP and W/T links with Moscow when Wenzel's own lines failed.

His reports were presumably only political in nature. Goulooze was therefore not charged by the Germans as a "terrorist" but as a spy. This fact apparently saved his life after his arrest in Utrecht on 15 November 1943. Before this date some of his contacts in Germany had already been arrested by the Gestapo. The arrests resulted in the liquidation of Goulooze's organizations in Amsterdam around July 1943. After "crazy Tuesday," Goulooze was sent, along with other prisoners, to Oranienburg. He claimed that he was able to avoid any further consequences in Oranienburg by using an alias in the camp. After the liberation he returned to the Netherlands, where he was not fully trusted by national Communists.

In 1957 Goulooze was working at De Vrije Katheder, and his job there was considered a cover. In view of his training and his political tendencies, the Dutch suspected that he was still working for Moscow. Goulooze died in September 1965.

In the 9 September 1967 issue of *Vrij Nederland* (Socialist, circulation 46,000) appeared a review by Igor Cornelissen of the book by Ger Harmsen on Goulooze. According to his book Goulooze was "in the service of the Comintern (1930-1945)" and was charged with the protection of the Communist movement against infiltration attempts by the police and with the maintenance of illegal ties. Not only was the CPN involved, but also the Communist Party of Indonesia, "which was violently persecuted by the Dutch Government." Harmsen states that, following the non-aggression pact, the organization of the Comintern, the KPD, and the French Communist Party broke down; so the Central Office of the Comintern in Moscow became still more dependent on Goulooze's organization. Only through him could contact be maintained with the Communists in Western Europe. For example, through his lines of communication advice could be given concerning the liberation of the Italian Communist leader Togliatti from a Paris jail. On 10 May 1940 Goulooze's organization did not need to go under cover; it had never been anything but illegal. In Chapter III of his book Harmsen deals with the period 1945-1965 and paints a not very stirring picture which runs parallel to this history of the CPN during this period. Goulooze came in conflict with de Groot and other Communist leaders, was eliminated, and in fact came to stand outside the Party. Goulooze kept quiet. "He did not want to wash dirty linen in public and, moreover, did not think it would benefit the movement if he revealed what he really had done. It was the period of the Cold War!"

MANFRED VON GRIMM
(alias Grau, alias Schmidt), an Austrian, was born in Vienna on 30 December 1911. He went to Switzerland on 19 March 1938 and some time thereafter began working for Polish intelligence under the alias of Schmidt. He also worked for the French; he was a sub-agent of Rudolf Lemoine (alias Korff-Koenig). Lemoine was arrested by the Germans in October 1942 and betrayed von Grimm, who the Poles then dropped. During that same year he was picked up by or for Alexander Rado. His Rote Drei cover name was Grau. Von Grimm lived in Davos during the war. In 1947 he was living in the Hague.

ADOLF GRIMME
was born 31 December 1889 at Goslar-Harz, Germany. He was an associate of Arvid Harnack and had been involved with the Neues Beginnen group with Hans Hirschfeld and Paul Hagen, a friend of Alfred K. Stern.

In 1927 Grimme was Minister of Culture and was still in the same post in 1930-1933 in the government of Braun. After Hitler came to power, Grimme served several terms of imprisonment for Communist activities.

He took part in illegal Communist meetings with Harnack and Kuckhoff. Adam Kuckhoff gave Grimme money for safekeeping. Grimme was arrested in September 1942 and was sentenced in January 1943 to three years' imprisonment.

In 1948 Grimme was Minister of Cultural Affairs in Land Niedersachsen, British Zone.

MEDARDO GRIOTTI

was born circa 1902. An Italian national, he was an engraver by profession. He was an agent of Robinson's at least from 1940 and possibly before the outbreak of war. As soon as he was settled in France, Trepper arranged for Medardo Griotti, who operated a safehouse in France, to start producing false documents. Robinson and Trepper had their first meeting at his house, which remained a rendezvous for these two key figures until Robinson's arrest at Griotti's house in December 1942. Trepper and Robinson used Griotti's services for the provision of false papers and stamps.

Griotti's wife Anna was also an agent of Robinson's. She was used as a courier within Robinson's group in France and also assisted in the illegal work of her husband.

According to a 1968 report, Griotti, who is now dead, had been a much more important agent than was originally thought, and in effect one of Robinson's main assistants. His wife, who in February 1968 was living in Italy, was Robinson's personal secretary and liaison agent with numerous illegal assets.

JEANNE FERNANDE GROSSVOGEL

(nee Pesant, or Johanna Ferdinanda) was born 16 September 1901 at Bevere-Audenarde (Belgium). She became French by her marriage to Grossvogel, but also retained her Belgian nationality. The Grossvogels were married at the Holborn Registry Office (London) in May 1938. She was the former wife of Robertus Ernstus Schouls, from whom she was divorced. Until Makarov took over in the spring of 1939, Jeanne Grossvogel was the manageress of the Ostende branch of "Le Roi du Caoutchouc." In late October 1942 at Uccle, she gave birth to a daughter, Nicole Germaine Grossvogel. Jeanne was arrested 25 November 1942 and taken to Moabit Prison in Berlin. In the spring of 1943 she was transferred to Ravensbrueck Camp.

LEON GROSSVOGEL

(alias Pieper, alias Grosser, alias Andre) was born 27 November 1904 in Lodz, Poland. He also used the aliases Leo, Xavier, and Suchet. He was a French Jew of Polish origin. By occupation he was an electrician and business manager.

He entered Belgium from Strasbourg in 1926. He first lived

with his sister in Gand. In 1928 he spent a month in Luxembourg and then settled definitely in Belgium. On 2 June 1928 he was tried for complicity in an adultery suit. He received as penalty a two hundred and sixty franc fine or eight days in prison with three years' probation. At the same time he was fined seven hundred francs or thirty days in prison for aggravated assault and battery. As early as 1929 he was known in Belgium as an active Communist. From 1929 to 1938 he was employed by the Brussels firm "Roi du Caoutchouc," and in December 1938 he became the general manager of the Foreign Excellent Raincoat Company, a subsidiary firm. He travelled to Norway, Sweden, Denmark, and Finland for this firm, which was used by Trepper as a cover.

Trepper had known Grossvogel in Palestine during the 1920s. Under Trepper's direction Grossvogel established Makarov as manager of the Ostende branch of the Excellent Raincoat Company. In 1939 Grossvogel utilized Abraham Rajchmann's services on Trepper's behalf and arranged a meeting between Rajchmann, Trepper, and Makarov.

Before the war Grossvogel was paid by Russian intelligence the equivalent of one hundred seventy-five dollars per month. Later this was raised to two hundred twenty-five dollars monthly.

After the outbreak of war and abandonment of Trepper's campaign against the U.K., Grossvogel probably ceased working for the expansion of the raincoat company's overseas business. In 1940 he retreated with Trepper to France, and in the fall of 1940 Grossvogel laid the foundations of Simex in Paris. Grossvogel functioned as one of Trepper's most trusted assistants and even organized his own small group responsible for logistics and communications. In December 1940 he visited Sukolov in Brussels. In 1941, after Simex was well established, Grossvogel began to withdraw, handing over management to Alfred Corbin. While in Paris, Grossvogel resided in a house occupied by the film actor Georges Milton.

Grossvogel's assistants included Germaine Schneider, the Sokols, Otto Schumacher, and the Girauds. His mistress, Simone Pheter, used the mail of the Belgian Chamber of Commerce, in which she was employed, for communications between Paris and Sukolov in Brussels. In June 1942 contact was established between Grossvogel in Paris and Jeffremov and Wenzel in Brussels. In August 1942 he visited Rajchmann in Brussels to procure false identity papers for Germaine Schneider and another agent of the group.

In December 1942, following the German penetration of the

Belgian groups and the arrest of Rajchmann, Grossvogel himself was arrested at a rendezvous with Rajchmann, Malvina Gruber, and Mme. Griotto in the Cafe de la Paix, Paris. During 1943 he was interrogated by the Gestapo and was possibly used by them for further penetration of French groups.

At the time of the Allied invasion, Grossvogel was probably still held by the Gestapo in Paris. Grossvogel may have been evacuated to Germany or executed in Fresnes Prison in July 1944, but another source claims he was still alive somewhere in France at the end of 1946.

Grossvogel was married to Johanna, nee Pesant. Simone Pheter was his mistress from about 1939 to 1942. He was the father of a daughter born to Johanna Grossvogel in October 1942.

Grossvogel was the brother of Sarah Kapelovitz, whose husband, Leon Kapelovitz, was the director of the "Roi du Caoutchouc" and the Foreign Excellent Raincoat Company.

MALVINA GRUBER

(nee Hofstadterova) was born 6 December 1900 in Jamborkretz, Czechoslovakia. She was the wife of Adolf Gruber, a Czech of Hungarian background, resident of the U.K. since 1938. She has six children. One of them, Eugene Gruber, was arrested circa 1949, at Frankfurt, for being in possession of forged U.S. passports and visas.

She was the mistress of Abraham Rajchmann, the forger.

From 1938 to 1942 she was the assistant and courier for Rajchmann and cutout between Rajchmann and Trepper; she acted as a courier between Paris and Brussels, conducting illegal frontier crossings. According to Perrault, Malvina also acted as a courier to Switzerland. In 1938 she visited Antwerp to get false passports for Rajchmann from Rosenberg, who is possibly identical with Victor Rosenberg, the brother of Helen Zubilin. Victor Rosenberg worked for Ignace Reiss in a photo laboratory used by the Soviets.

After the occupation of Belgium she worked as a courier for Trepper and Rajchmann in the south of France. In June or July 1941 she escorted Anton Danilov from France to Belgium. In October 1941 she took Anne Marie van der Putt from Rajchmann to Trepper in Paris and escorted Sofie Posnanska back to Brussels. In December 1941 she took Margarete Barcza and her son Rene from Brussels to Paris.

She was arrested by the Abwehr in Brussels on 12 October 1942 and was used along with Rajchmann for penetration purposes by the

Germans in Brussels and Paris until 1944. She was protected from deportation and execution by the Sonderkommando and allowed to return to Belgium, but after the war she was ordered deported by the Belgian authorities. She left for Czechoslovakia via Germany in October 1945 but was arrested in Germany in August 1946. In August 1947 she was in prison in Belgium, and in February 1949 she was sentenced to ten years' imprisonment by a court martial in Brussels. She was released in December 1951, and on or about 23 December 1951 Malvina Gruber arrived at the Jewish Home for the Aged sponsored by the Juedische Kulturgemeinde, Munich, and requested admission, stating that she was temporarily without funds. She said she was Jewish, a former KZ inmate, and therefore fully entitled to be given shelter there. She stated also that she had six children, all of them in Israel, three of them serving as soldiers in the Israeli army. She remained at the home until about 10 February 1952.

She reportedly left Belgium for Israel in order to rejoin her children.

A 1952 report stated that Malvina Gruber was still engaged in RIS activities.

MAX HABJANIC

(alias Cobbler Max), a Swiss citizen of Balkan extraction, was employed for thirty-one years in the Department of Justice and Police of the canton of Basle.

About 1937 and 1938 Habjanic provided Anna Barbara Mueller with several illegal but genuine passports, all of which eventually landed in the hands of Henri Robinson, who received them from Franz Welti, a Basle lawyer. Habjanic "created" these passports by filling them out on valid blanks and sending them to an unsuspecting police chief for signature. Welti, whose mistress was Anna Mueller, became acquainted with Habjanic during a lawsuit in 1926.

Habjanic was arrested at his home in Basle in October 1948 but was provisionally released because of bad health.

URSULA HAMBURGER

(nee Kuczynski, aka Ursula Beurton, alias Sonia) was born 15 May 1907. She was originally Polish but became a German through marriage with Rudolf Hamburger (alias Rudi). She became English by marriage to Beurton. Her father, Rene Robert Kuczynski, German born, became a lecturer at the London School of Economics. She has four sisters, one of whom is Brigitte Lewis (Long), and a brother,

Juergen Kuczynski, who introduced Klaus Fuchs to Soviet intelligence officers.

Prior to 1930 Ursula Hamburger worked for the Ullstein Press in Berlin. From 1930 to 1935 she worked for Soviet military intelligence in Shanghai, together with her first husband, Rudolf Hamburger. In 1938 she was sent to Switzerland on an espionage assignment against Germany, having worked earlier for the KPD under the alias Sonja Schultz.

Hamburger told Foote that she was entrusted to build up her own espionage net in Switzerland and was left to her own resources. She maintained that the only direct contribution which the GRU made to her was money, a wireless apparatus, and one agent. She gave Foote the impression that she selected and recruited her own agents. In March 1940 she was visited by Rado with an agent from Belgium—probably Sukolov.

In May 1940 she was instructed to move with Foote and Beurton to Rumania, but Italy's entry into the war prevented this move from materializing. Early in 1940 she divorced Rudolf Hamburger, and on 23 February 1940 she married Leon Beurton (supposedly a marriage of convenience).

In February 1941 Ursula Hamburger arrived in the U.K. The Beurtons left England for East Berlin in 1947.

Associates of Ursula include Foote, Franz Obermanns, Alexander Rado, Leon Nicole, Edmond Hamel, Olga Hamel, and Ilona Suess.

EDMOND HAMEL

(alias Eduard) was born 20 April 1910 in Noiremont, Switzerland. A long-standing Communist, he was trained in 1926 in Paris as a wireless specialist. In 1930 he went to Geneva and shortly thereafter returned to Paris, where he received a radio electrician's certificate. In 1933 Hamel returned to Geneva and opened a radio shop, building up a prosperous business. During this period he became active in Nicole's political circles.

In the summer of 1940 Nicole recommended Hamel to Moscow for recruitment. In August 1940 Hamel started W/T training under Foote and Beurton. It was carried on by Beurton when Foote left for Lausanne in December.

In March 1941 Hamel, having become proficient in W/T operations, began transmitting to Moscow from his shop on Rue de Carouge. Everything went well until late in 1942, when the Swiss Cantonal Police, searching for Communist literature, raided Hamel's shop. They uncovered a spare transmitter, but the operating set passed undetected. Hamel was imprisoned for a few days, although his real activities were not suspected at this time by the Swiss. Upon his release he transferred his set to Chemin de Conches, where he operated until his arrest in October 1943.

In April 1943 Hamel started his transmissions for Rado and at the same time was teaching his wife Olga the Morse code. Apparently, when Hamel started transmitting for "Albert" in 1941, he was unaware of the identity of his employer. Even after meeting Rado, Hamel was probably unaware that he had been working for Rado for almost two years.

Upon his arrest, Hamel pleaded that he transmitted blindly messages which were given to him, but he was sure they were not prejudicial to the Swiss. The October 1943 arrest of Hamel also resulted in a search of his house, which revealed to the Swiss police a partial record of Rado's accounts.

In October 1947 Hamel presented himself to the Swiss Military Tribunal for trial. He was sentenced to nine months further imprisonment, but he was released six months later.

OLGA HAMEL

(nee Delez, alias Maud) was born around 1907 in Valais or Noiremont, Switzerland. Her brothers were militant Communists. She assisted her husband in the transmission of W/T traffic and received large sums of money from Rado in 1942 and 1943 for her work. She was sentenced by a Swiss court in 1947 to seven months' imprisonment.

ARVID HARNACK

was born in 1901 in Germany. He was the son of Otto Harnack, the noted historian, and the nephew of Adolf von Harnack, a famous theologian.

In the 1920s he studied economics at the University of Wisconsin at Madison and there met and married Mildred Fish. They returned to Germany, where they both studied and taught economics and philosophy. A doctor of philosophy and economics, he lectured at Giessen University in 1929.

Leader of an intelligence group based in Berlin, Harnack worked for Alexander Erdberg at least from the early summer of 1941 until his liquidation in the autumn of 1942. It is possible that Harnack and his circle of Communists and left-wing sympathizers were exploited by Erdberg for the GRU for some years before the outbreak of the Russo-German war. Through Harnack, Erdberg obtained control of the Schulze-Boysen group.

In anticipation of the withdrawal of the Soviet Embassy, Erdberg supplied Adam Kuckhoff with a wireless transmitter for Harnack's service and attempted to organize the group into an independent network having direct W/T communication with Moscow. This aim was not achieved, however, and in August 1941 Victor Sukolov visited Berlin to assist Harnack and the other groups in Germany. The transmitter which he supplied for Harnack's group proved unusable, and Harnack's only line to Moscow appears to have been through Wilhelm Guddorf and Bernard Baestlein's courier service.

Eventually Harnack arranged to communicate by courier from the German Communist Party in Hamburg, through Denmark, to the Soviet Embassy in Stockholm, whence messages would be relayed to Moscow. Harnack also must have had some communications link with Sukolov and later Jeffremov when the latter took over from Sukolov.

Harnack is known to have employed the following agents in his network:

Herbert Gollnow, an Abwehr officer at OKW headquarters;

Wolfgang Havemann, a lieutenant in German naval intelligence;

Adam Kuckhoff and his wife;

Leo Skrzypczynski, proprietor of a firm manufacturing W/T components for the Luftwaffe;

Adolf Grimme;

Johannes Sieg, the *Rote Fahne* journalist who was born in the United States;

Karl Behrens and Rose Schloesinger, who were used as couriers to Hans Coppi; and

Dr. Friedrich Lenz, who acted as a cutout between Harnack and the Soviet Embassy in 1941.

Harnack was executed on 22 December 1942.

MILDRED ELIZABETH HARNACK

(nee Fish) was born about 1902 in the United States. An American citizen, she was in the 1920s a student at the University of Wisconsin when she met Harnack. She returned with him to Germany, where they both taught economics and philosophy. She was in sympathy with her husband's devotion to Communism. In 1939 she lectured at Berlin University and the Foreign Office. She participated in her husband's clandestine activities and was executed on 16 February 1943.

On page 352 of her book, *Treason in the Twentieth Century,* Margret Boveri writes:

> Louis Lechner . . . came into contact regularly—at the meetings of the German-American Chamber of Commerce, of which he was president—with Arvid von Harnack, who had the American desk at the Ministry of Economics and whose wife, Mildred Fish Harnack, was one of the most prominent American women in Berlin society.
>
> She helped Martha Dodd (Mrs. Alfred K. Stein) organize those now legendary tea parties which were such social events in Berlin in the 1930s. The assumption that one of the codes which Lochner bore concealed on his person upon his return to the U.S. originated from the Rote Kapelle is far from fantastic. . .

HORST HEILMANN

(alias Wilder) was born in 1923. He joined the Hitler Jugend in 1937 and the NSDAP in 1941. He was a student of Foreign Affairs in Berlin until his enlistment in the Wehrmacht, where he worked in the cipher section of the OKH. He was able to inform Schulze-Boysen of the breaking of Wenzel's traffic. He was executed with Schulze-Boysen.

Heilmann hid some of Schulze-Boysen's documents in the home of the theater manager Oscar Ingenohl, who lived at the time with Reva Holsey (real name Emma Holzey, now married to Ingenohl) in the same house in which Horst Heilmann lived. Both Ingenohls subsequently worked in the Rote Kapelle.

Hans Heilmann, brother of Horst, was also suspected of having participated in the Rote Kapelle. Hans was a radio operator during the war and served in France with the Wehrmacht.

Ingenohl and Guenther Weisenborn were in close contact in 1954. Ingenohl's wife was in contact with Michael Tschesno and Greta Kuckhoff in 1954.

WILLIAM HELBEIN

(alias Gelmars, alias Helmars) was born 7 November 1888 at Berdit-scheff, Russia. He is a naturalized U.S. citizen. He is married to Pearl Helbein, nee Coleman. He is the brother-in-law of Berta Helbein and the director of Helbros, a watch firm, 6 West 48th Street, New York City, and the biggest individual buyer of Swiss watches in the U.S.

In the summer of 1944 Helbein admitted receiving ten thousand dollars from "an unidentified foreign woman" which he forwarded to Abramson in Switzerland.

RUDOLF HERRNSTADT

an editor and journalist, was born 17 March 1903 in Gleiwitz. By origin he was a German-Jew and came from a trilingual family (Russian, German, and Polish). His father, a deputy and a lawyer in Gleiwitz, died in the gas chambers at Auschwitz in 1939. He had defended in the courts numerous cases of accused Silesian and Polish miners who were persecuted for participating in strikes.

Herrnstadt had had contacts in the KPD since 1925, although he was a non-registered member. He was a collaborator of the AM *Apparat* and worked in this matter with Susi Drechsler and Ilse Stoebe, who both worked for the *Berliner Tageblatt*. In 1926 Herrnstadt worked for the *Berliner Tageblatt* in Prague and in 1932 in Warsaw. In 1933 he was foreign correspondent in Moscow.

In 1928 or 1929 Herrnstadt was recruited by the Soviets and has been working for them since that date. In 1933 he became a Soviet citizen by naturalization. During his Warsaw activity he established a number of important intelligence contacts. Among them were Rudolf von Scheliha and Ilse Stoebe, who was executive secretary to Theodor Wolff. Stoebe was the foreign correspondent for various Swiss newspapers in Berlin from 1933 to 1939. From 1939 to 1942 she worked at the Foreign Ministry and collaborated with von Scheliha.

Herrnstadt worked mostly for Red Army intelligence and used journalism as a cover, participating in the reorganization of numerous foreign groups. In 1942-1943 he was political instructor and operational head of Soviet parachute groups. (The majority consisted of Communist emigrants.) In 1943 he was co-founder of the NKFD (National Committee, Free Germany). In 1945 he returned to Berlin, founded the *Berliner Verlag,* and became chief editor of the *Berliner Zeitung*. In 1949 he became chief editor of *Neues Deutschland* and was put in charge of surpervising the press in the East Zone of Germany. In 1950 he became a member of the Central Committee of the SED and a candidate for the Politburo (elected by the Third Party Congress of the SED) and a member of the People's Chamber.

Important Soviet officials consider Herrnstadt to be extremely valuable and well informed (1958). He is regarded as unusually intelligent, skillful, and loyal to the Kremlin. His current intelligence activities are reportedly directed against West Germany.

ALBERT HOESSLER

(alias Helmut Wiegner, alias Stein, alias Franz) was born 11 October 1910 in Muhlau, Sachsen. He was a long-time KPD functionary and served in the Loyalist Army in Spain. In 1938 he returned to the Soviet Union where he was trained as an intelligence agent and parachutist.

In August 1942 Hoessler dropped into Germany and became active in the Rote Kapelle. On 9 October 1943 he was arrested by the Gestapo in Berlin.

Hoessler was introduced by Kurt Schumacher to Coppi, with whom he attempted to establish a W/T link with Moscow, first from the shelter of Erika von Brockdorff's house and then from that of Oda Schottmueller. He was instructed to keep in touch with Robert Barth, with whom he had been parachuted and who may have been intended to render a similar service to Harnack's group.

He reportedly died at the end of the war, although this statement is unconfirmed.

KARL HOFMAIER

(aka Hoffmaier) was born on 17 May 1897 in Basle, Switzerland. A Communist and a journalist, he was in the USSR in the early 1920s. He was imprisoned in Italy from 1927 to 1934, when his fifteen-year sentence was commuted. He then went back to the USSR, lived in Moscow, and survived the 1936 purges. He returned to Switzerland about 1939 and began work for the Rote Drei in 1939. He became a leader of the left wing of the Swiss Communist party. He and Humbert-Droz were bitter rivals until Hofmaier was expelled from the CP for financial irregularities in 1946. During the war he was in touch with both Rachel Duebendorfer and Alexander Rado.

He had three brothers and a sister. One brother died in 1934; another committed suicide in 1946. The sister, Karoline, married. The third brother, Emil, born 21 March 1901, was also involved in espionage on behalf of the Soviets but was not a member of the Rote Drei network.

CAROLINE HOORICKX

(nee Sterck) was the wife of Guillaume Hoorickx. She gave assistance to the Belgian network from 1939 to 1941. Even though Caroline had been separated from Hoorickx since before the war, she introduced him to Makarov, by whom he was recruited as a courier for Sukolov. Caroline Hoorickx was the mistress of Makarov in 1939 and 1940 at Ostende while he was there in charge of a branch of the Excellent Raincoat Company.

Caroline and Guillaume Hoorickx were the parents of a son who was brought up by Hoorickx' mistress (and later wife), Anna Staritsky.

GUILLAUME HOORICKX

(alias Bill) was born in Antwerp on 12 April 1900. He was an agent of the Sukolov network in Belgium from the autumn of 1940 until the end of 1942. He was married to Caroline, nee Sterck, from whom he was separated before the war. In 1940 his wife introduced him to Makarov, by whom he was recruited as an informant and as a courier on his visits to France for the Red Cross. In February or March 1941 Sukolov took him into Simexco as a buyer, a position which enabled him to become a regular courier to Simex in Paris, carrying intelligence material between Sukolov and Trepper. Hoorickx and his friend Henri Rauch withdrew from Simexco about July 1941, probably on Trepper's instructions to provide extra cover. Hoorickx, Rauch, and Charles Daniels then joined forces in a new business venture with offices at 192 Rue Royale, Brussels, in the same building as Simexco. Late in 1941 Hoorickx was in touch with Reymaeker, who supplied him with identity cards for members of the organization.

Anna Staritsky, a Russian, was the mistress of Hoorickx during the war; they later married.

Hoorickx was arrested in Rixensart with Rauch on 28 December 1942. He was deported to Mauthausen, where he worked as a doctor. He was repatriated to Belgium 2 June 1945. After the war Hoorickx tried to reorganize Simexco and was trying to recontact Trepper. About April 1946 he collected from Claude Spaak the identity documents left in his possession by Hersz and Miriam Sokol. In November 1946 he was visited in Brussels by Georgie de Winter, Trepper's former mistress. In April 1947 Hoorickx was using a Nice address for mail and was in touch with Charles Daniels in Brussels.

Hoorickx was apparently sought in 1947 by the Soviet Embassy in Brussels through Waltraud Heger, the step-daughter of Henri Rauch.

In 1954 Belgian authorities were informed that Hoorickx and his wife (Staritsky) were living at 150 Avenue Emile Zola, in Paris and also had a flat at 14 Rue Cafarelli, in Nice, where they often went to stay because of his bad health. They made frequent trips to Belgium, where they were in contact with various White Russian families. They often stayed at the home of Nikita Koussoff, a known anti-Communist. The 1954 report indicated that Hoorickx was suspected of being engaged in some kind of intelligence activity.

JULES FREDERIC HUMBERT-DROZ
(alias Droll) was born 11 January 1872 in Chaux de Fonds, Switzerland. He was a Swiss citizen and a journalist. He lived at 153 Albisstrasse, Zurich. His wife was Jenny Humbert.

In the early 1920s Humbert-Droz was said to be a collaborator with Willi Muenzenberg and Henri Robinson in the founding of the Comintern Youth International in Switzerland. In 1924 he was editor of *Communist International* and was political secretary of the Communist group in 1924, 1926, and 1928. In 1928 he was also the member of the Western European Bureau of the Comintern. He was imprisoned for a brief period in the late 1920s for his Communist activities in Switzerland. In 1926 he visited Moscow and in November 1927 was arrested by Swiss authorities for implication in the recruitment of volunteers for the International Brigade.

Thought to be one of Poliakova's agents before the war, Humbert-Droz took over a transmitter and wireless parts from Mme. Gessner-Buehrer, probably in 1939 or 1940. From May 1939 to the spring of 1942, he was president of the Swiss CP. At this time he approached an RIS agent (probably Alexander Rado) with an offer to organize economic espionage in factories producing goods for Germany. At the time he was a talent spotter for Rado.

Humbert-Droz was instructed by Dimitrov in Moscow to help Foote, but the Swiss police arrested him (Droz) in Winterthur shortly thereafter (June 1942) for illegal Communist Party activity, and he was able to do little for Foote because he served a six-month sentence.

In 1942 Humbert-Droz was reputedly expelled from the Swiss CP. In August 1946 he was in Zurich for the Swiss Socialist press, his work not having been approved by the Communist Press. The same year he was again imprisoned by the Swiss for his Communist activities.

In 1948 Humbert-Droz was sued by Karl Hofmaier for having libeled him concerning his Gestapo connections during the war.

HERMAN ISBUTSKY

(alias Bob, alias Lunettes), a Belgian Jew, was born 19 May 1914 in Antwerp. He resided at 144 Langeleemstraat, Antwerp.

Isbutsky was an agent of the Trepper-Sukolov group as early as 1939 and was trained in W/T by Wenzel. In 1941 he was also performing services for the Jeffremov group. He was to have built up his own network in the summer of 1942, but he was prevented from doing so by his arrest in late July 1942. His arrest resulted when Jeffremov, under German control, arranged a rendezvous with Isbutsky and Peper in Brussels. Isbutsky was executed.

JEAN BAPTISTE JANSSENS

was recruited by Germaine Schneider to act as a courier between Brussels and Paris for the Jeffremov network. He was born 9 December 1898 in Brussels and was by occupation a shoemaker. He was divorced from his wife, nee Croyssaerts. He was the lover of Josephine Verhimst, nee Clais, the sister of Germaine Schneider.

In 1942 Janssens provided lodging for Johannes Wenzel at 97 Rue Artan, Schaerbeek. When Wenzel was arrested on 30 June 1942, while transmitting from a building in the Laeken district, Janssens and his mistress, Verhimst, were immediately taken into custody and interrogated. They were released by the Germans a few days later.

In January 1943 Janssens and Verhimst were arrested. Janssens died in Breendonck Concentration Camp.

JULES JASPAR

was born 1 March 1878 at Schaerbeek, Belgium. He was a former official of the Belgian Foreign Office. His brother was once Prime Minister of Belgium. At one time Jaspar was Belgian Consul in Indochina. In 1939 he became associated with Grossvogel as a director of the Foreign Exccllent Raincoat Company and probably became aware of its use as a cover for Soviet espionage. Jaspar fled to France in May 1940 following the German invasion. In December 1941 Jaspar moved to Marseilles, and in January 1942 he assited Sukolov in the establishment of the Marseilles branch of Simex. Jaspar became a director of the firm. In the summer of 1942 Trepper proposed to send Jaspar to North Africa on Simex business as cover for an intelligence mission. This plan was not put into execution.

Jaspar was arrested 12 November 1942 in Marseilles and deported to Germany. In June 1945 he was liberated and repatriated to Belgium.

Jaspar either married or lived with Georgie de Winter after the war, probably in southern France. According to one source, he was in Brussels in November 1947, living with his widowed sister, Madame Lacroix, at 77 Avenue Theodore Roosevelt, Brussels.

Jaspar was married to Claire Jaspar, who was arrested by the Gestapo in November 1942 and subsequently died in prison. She may have assisted her husband in his Simex work and possibly in undercover activities for Sukolov.

Jaspar propably died circa 1948-1949, but according to one report he was still living in 1954.

KONSTANTIN JEFFREMOV

(alias Eric Jernstroem, alias Pascal) was born 15 May 1910 in Sawotzki, Russia. His name is also spelled Yeffremov. He was a Soviet army captain, an expert in chemical warfare, and an engineer. An RU operative, Jeffremov may have been active in Western Europe at least since 1936, when he may have recruited Franz and Germaine Schneider in Belgium on behalf of Henri Robinson. His activities at that time were, therefore, probably directed at least in part against the United Kingdom. Jeffremov may also have lived in Switzerland some time during the period 1936-1939, perhaps in Zurich.

In September 1939 Jeffremov arrived in Brussels, posing as a Finnish student named Jernstroem. His prewar intelligence function was alleged to have been the collection of technical information on chemicals, and he may have been intended to operate quite independently of Trepper and other RU agents in Western Europe. On the outbreak of war he was instructed to build up a network in the Low Countries for the collection of military, political, and economic intelligence. He utilized the services of his former recruits, the Schneiders, and of Wenzel, whom he may also have known personally. Jeffremov organized and ran this network independently of Trepper and Sukolov, although such agents as Wenzel, Isbutsky, and Peper worked for both groups simultaneously. Using Wenzel and Peper as his intermediaries, Jeffremov also played a leading role in the organization and direction of the Dutch network of the Rote Kapelle.

Wenzel may not have established a W/T service with Moscow on Jeffremov's behalf until the end of 1940, when contact was probably made through Winterink. During 1940, however, Jeffremov may have used the services of an operator in Ostend. Before the war Jeffremov had a contact in Switzerland and used a certain "Chimor" as his courier. "Chimor" was probably Franz Schneider.

In May 1942, under RU instructions, Jeffremov met Trepper at the Schneider house in Brussels and took over the Low Countries network of Sukolov. This new task entailed the transmission to Moscow of Schulze-Boysen's material. Wenzel agreed to become the W/T operator for the new group.

Following Wenzel's arrest 30 July 1942, Franz Schneider asked Ernst Bomerson to hide Jeffremov in his house at 25 Rue Alfred Orban, Forest, introducing Jeffremov as "Hofman." Jeffremov was arrested 22 July 1942 before he could move into the Bomerson house. He was attending a rendezvous arranged by Rajchmann with a German contact man to obtain false identity papers.

Apparently Jeffremov offered little resistance and was almost immediately used by the Germans for penetration and W/T playback. He arranged a meeting with Isbutsky and Peper, at which time they were arrested.

From October 1942 Jeffremov operated the W/T line "Buche-Pascal" to Moscow under control, being held in Breendonck Prison Camp until April 1944 when he was moved to Paris. There he was housed with Sukolov at 63 Rue de Courcelles, but they were not permitted to associate. The transmitter was run from Paris in July 1944. In August 1944 Jeffremov was taken to Berlin, and the playback was continued from Schoeniche, near Potsdam.

One good source of information concerning Jeffremov reported that when Jeffremov was interrogated after his arrest, he tried to adhere to his Finnish cover story but gave contradictory statements and spoke a broken Finnish. A search of his quarters resulted in the discovery of a number of postal cards from the United States. Apparently he had been communicating with Soviet contacts in the United States. Jeffremov's Finnish passport was issued in the United States, where he received a visa prior to his entry into Belgium. His passport was genuine. Jeffremov's intelligence activity could not be proven, but his Russian origin was verified. He was confronted with Wenzel, who was also under arrest. Jeffremov then admitted that he knew Wentzel, who described Jeffremov as his superior.

According to this same source Jeffremov had been a member of the Komsomol and had studied chemistry in Moscow. He then did service with the Soviet army as an officer. For several years he was assigned to a technical staff of the Far East Army and was stationed at the Soviet-Manchurian border. He was then ordered to Moscow, where he was trained for intelligence work. After his training was completed, he travelled via Odessa to Bucharest, where he received new identity cards and an airplane ticket to Belgrade. There he received his Finnish passport. He continued via Italy to Switzerland, where he remained for a few weeks. He went on to Paris and stayed for a short time before he left for Brussels.

Jeffremov regularly received funds from the United States. The payments were at a normal, moderate level for a student and therefore did not cause any suspicion. The postal cards which were found during the search of his quarters were communications to Jeffremov from RU representatives in the United States. In addition, Jeffremov received money from the Soviet trade representative in Brussels. The latter brought him in contact with a Belgian industrialist who provided him with important espionage material concerning Belgian industry. His name has not been determined.

> There are three conflicting versions of his (Jeffremov's) downfall:
>
> 1. According to one veteran of the Rote Kapelle Kommando, persuading Jeffremov to turn traitor was the simplest of tasks. He was a Ukrainian and therefore prone to anti-Semitism. It was pointed out to him that all his superiors were Jews and that he would be a real fool to sacrifice himself for such riffraff; he agreed.
>
> 2. According to Fortner (Henry Piepe), Giering's team of torture experts arrived in Brussels and set to work on the prisoner. He held out for a few days; then he was broken.
>
> 3. According to another Abwehr officer, Jeffremov succumbed to a more subtle maneuver. His whole family was in Russia—including his young wife, whom he adored. She was an engineer, specializing in railway engines, and she was deeply patriotic. Jeffremov was told that unless he cooperated, the Center would be informed that he had betrayed Wenzel— which was, of course, quite untrue. This story would cost him his wife's love and esteem, and she herself would be exposed to reprisals by the Soviet authorities. Jeffremov decided that love came before duty. (It is known that Jeffremov had a wife and mother living

in the Soviet Union and that he was very devoted to them.)

According to some sources, Simexco (raided in November 1942) was the victim of Jeffremov's treachery, not of . . . Henry Piepe's professional flair. When Trepper had handed over control to Jeffremov, he told him about Simexco, but he urged him to keep away; after Kent's (Sukolov's) long spell as head of the firm, the situation was extremely risky. (There is evidence also that Trepper's warning to Jeffremov was based on his lack of complete confidence in Nazarin Drailly's loyalty.) It is argued that Jeffremov exposed Simexco when he gave away all his other secrets.

Jeffremov's ultimate fate is not known, but according to one source he escaped at the end of 1944 and eventually reached Moscow by way of Switzerland.

JOJO
was about thirty years old in 1942 and was probably of Spanish origin. His true identity is unknown. He belonged to the French Communist underground network and had been sent by Moscow to Trepper during the end of 1942. He was a radio repairman.

His parents owned a restaurant in St. Denis, a suburb of Paris. He was arrested shortly after Trepper but managed to escape from the Germans in June 1943, and his whole family then disappeared.

HEINZ ERWIN KALLMANN
was born 10 March 1904 in Berlin-Charlottenburg. He is a physicist. From 1929 to 1934 he lived in Berlin and worked as a research engineer in C. Lorenz, A.G., Berlin-Tempelhof. In March 1934 he went to London, where he worked as a research engineer in Electrical and Musical Industries with Hans Gerhardt Lubszynski.

It appears that in England Kallmann was an unwitting source of the "Professor," who provided information regarding television and related subjects to Henri Robinson.

He went to the United States in 1939 and has lived at 417 Riverside Drive, New York City.

LOUIS KAPELOWITZ
(alias Kapel or Capel) was a director of the Foreign Excellent Raincoat

Company and may have been involved to some extent in his brother-in-law Grossvogel's activities for the RU in Belgium. Kapelowitz' wife Sarah was Leon Grossvogel's sister. Kapelowitz was born 13 July 1891 in Kassa, Czechoslovakia. In June 1936 he became a director of the Excellent Raincoat Company, and in December 1938 he became a director of its subsidiary, the Foreign Excellent Raincoat Company, used by Trepper for cover purposes. Kapelowitz fled to France in May 1940 following the German invasion of Belgium. He subsequently returned and lived underground in Brussels for two years. In 1943 he reportedly went to Switzerland, but in November 1944 he returned to Belgium to resume his business. At the beginning of 1947 Kapelowitz was in Palestine with his wife, who returned to Belgium 10 January 1947. Kapelowitz himself left Palestine for Belgium 21 April 1947, but at the end of 1947 he was attempting to return to Palestine.

Maurice Padawer and Adolf Lerner, co-directors of the Foreign Excellent Raincoat Company, were both married to sisters of Louis Kapelowitz.

Sarah Kapelowitz in 1947 was reportedly living at 89 Herzl Street, Tel Aviv.

Kapelowitz has a brother, Maurice, who was interviewed by the FBI in 1947:

> Maurice Capel (brother of Louis Kapelowitz) was interviewed . . . He advised that Leon Grossvogel was known as an outright Communist in Brussels all during the 1930s, and he stated that Lerner, Padawer, and Louis Kapelowitz were aware of this fact and for this reason were very wary of Grossvogel.

Kapelowitz is reportedly the cousin of Harry Gold, the convicted Soviet agent.

CAPTAIN NIKOLAYEVICH GENADIY KARPOV
was born 21 March 1906 in Moscow. In 1939 he was a clerk at the Soviet Embassy in Paris and later at Vichy. He may have been concerned with the welfare of Trepper's organization and probably arranged on Trepper's behalf the transfer of Danilov from Paris to Brussels in the summer of 1941. In April 1943 Karpov was at the Soviet Embassy in Teheran as an attache and NKVD representative. Karpov was reportedly engaged in the recruitment of agents from among Polish Jewish refugees. In July 1945 he was in Moscow. In April 1948 Karpov was in Berlin; but by August 1948 he had moved to Brus-

sels, where he was First Secretary in the Soviet Embassy, specializing in problems of displaced persons.

HILLEL KATZ

was born 24 September 1905 in Chenzin, Poland. He used the aliases of Andre Dubois, "Rene," and "Le Petit Andre." He was either married to or lived in a common-law relationship with Cecile Fichtenweg (alias Cecile Dubois).

A Polish Jew, he had been a member of the Communist Party in Palestine and in contact with Syrian revolutionaries. During the occupation of France he became one of the most important agents of the French network of the Rote Kapelle as well as secretary and assistant to Trepper. He was in charge of liaison between Grossvogel, Robinson, and Simex.

His brother Joseph Katz (aka Mayer ben Josef Katz) was part of the Lyon network. Hillel Katz has also been known under the name of ben Mordechai.

In December 1942 Hillel Katz was arrested during the Simex roundup and was used for further penetration by the Germans into other Soviet groups in France and into the French Communist Party.

There has been considerable confusion as to the identity of the various Soviet agents named Katz. For example, Joseph Katz, born 15 March 1912 in Vilna, Lithuania (who is now in Israel), is not related to Joseph Katz, born 17 September 1910 in Grodzick, Poland. The latter was the brother of Hillel Katz; the former was Elizabeth Bentley's superior. Alexander Katz, born 6 May 1887 in Odessa, was a contact of the Joseph Katz who is now in Israel. Otto Katz (alias Andre Simon), born 27 May 1895 at Jistenbnice, Czechoslovakia, the Comintern agent who was executed in 1952, is not identical with Simon Katz, born 12 August 1902 in Paris.

In 1957 the French DST interrogated Cecile Fichtenweg (alias Cecile Dubois), born 20 May 1904 in Czestokow, Poland. She was the mistress or wife of Hillel Katz (alias Andre). Cecile advised that during 1941-1942 she had contacted Georgie de Winter. Again in 1944 or 1945 she became interested in the state of health of the son of Georgie and Trepper, who was being cared for by the Queyries at Suresnes. Cecile claimed she wanted to contact the son of Georgie and through him to recontact Georgie so that she could get news of Hillel Katz.

Cecile never admitted to the French services that she knew what Katz was doing. The Germans claimed that in the course of time she discovered it:

and her husband then used her for the maintenance of contacts. She has not been arrested but is in hiding with our help so that we can use her in our further operations as a contact woman, which would enable us to get more information on replacement circles. (Abwehr report, 24 March 1943)

HEINRICH KOENEN
(alias Heinz Koenen, alias Henrich Ludwig Koester, alias Karl Ludwig) was born 12 May 1910 in Koenigsberg. He was a German Jew but claimed Russian citizenship since 1940. His father, Wilhelm Koenen, was a member of the Communist International in 1919. His sister is Johanna Beker.

He belonged to the NPD and fled Germany in 1933. He went to the USSR where he was trained at the intelligence centers in Moscow and Kuibyshev (1934-1940). Before being dropped into Germany, he had been trained at a Russian parachute school and in W/T. The Gestapo had advance notice that Koenan was to be dropped. They gained this knowledge from a message intercepted from Moscow. Koenen was arrested by the Gestapo on 26 October 1942. Ilse Stoebe, whom he was supposed to contact, had already been arrested by the Gestapo in Hamburg.

Koenen was dropped by the Soviets over Osterode in East Prussia and was intended for the Stoebe-von Scheliha group. He was supposed to meet Erna Eifler and Henri Robinson's son, Victor Schabbel. He was also to do some work with the Schulze-Boysen and Baestlein groups. The password which Koenen was to use in contacting Stoebe was "greetings from Rudi" (meaning Rudolf Herrnstadt). It was from Koenen's papers captured after his arrest that the dollar transaction, via Bank Julius Baer in Zurich, of seven thousand five hundred dollars to von Scheliha was discovered.

Heinrich Koenen was reportedly executed toward the end of the war, but according to another report he was in a concentration camp at Sachsenhausen in 1945. According to an even later report, he was SED Secretary for Saxony.

JOHN WILHELM KRUYT, SR.
(alias von Krumin, alias Henri Depotter) was a Soviet agent dropped by parachute in Belgium 24 June 1942. He was equipped with a radio set and was intended as a reinforcement for the Jeffremov network. Kruyt's accommodation was to be the concern of Elizabeth Depelsen-

aire, and he had two meetings with one of her agents, Irma Salno. Kruyt was born 8 September 1877 in Amsterdam and by occupation was a Protestant minister. He was at one time a member of the Dutch Second Chamber. In 1922 he was a member of the Third International. In 1923 Kruyt went to Russia and for a time was a professor of Scandinavian languages at Moscow University. In the early 1930s he was attached to the Soviet Trade Delegation in Berlin, and from 1939-1942 he was back in the Soviet Union. Kruyt's wife committed suicide in the USSR. He reportedly had an English mother.

His son, named after him, was parachuted into Holland on 22 June 1942.

Kruyt, Sr., was arrested by the Gestapo on 20 June 1942 after his denunciation by Charles and Marie Bocar of 56 Avenue Charles Quint, Bercheur-Ste-Agathe, an accommodation address recommended to Kruyt by the RU, which had also supplied him with the emergency postbox Stig Lindel, Bondegaten 60, Stockholm. After his arrest Kruyt was successively detained in St. Gilles, Breendonck, and Moabit (Berlin) prisons.

There is evidence that Kruyt was dropped into Belgium by the British and that the British High Command may not have been aware of Kruyt's true role. He may even have lived for a while as an immigrant in England, working for the RIS.

JOHN WILLIAM KRUYT

(alias Schouten), the son of John Wilhelm Kruyt, born 25 August 1926, was dropped in Holland with a W/T set and made contact with Goulooze. According to one report, Kruyt, Jr., was dropped for the Soviets by the British SOE. He spoke fluent Dutch, German, and Russian.

ADAM KUCKHOFF

was born 30 August 1887 in Aachen, Germany. He was executed on 5 August 1943. He was married the first time to Marie Viermeyer, born 10 September 1891 in Wolfenbuettel. This marriage was dissolved on 6 June 1937 in Berlin. By his first wife he had a son, Armin-Gerhard Kuckhoff, born 13 March 1912 in Munich.

A family relationship exists between Adam Kuckhoff and the woman Rote Kapelle agent Gertrud Viermeyer, nee Kuckhoff, born 7 May 1895 in Wolfenbuettel. The husband of the latter is the brother of the first wife of Adam Kuckhoff (Marie Viermeyer).

A philosopher and writer on Communism and Marxism, Kuckhoff was a producer at Prague Films, A.G. His illegal Communist activities dated back to 1932, and his intelligence work may have begun during the prewar Nazi regime.

MARGARETE KUCKHOFF

(nee Lorke, aka "Greta"), born 14 December in Frankfurt/Oder, was Adam Kuckhoff's second wife. They were married 28 August 1937 and divorced—date unknown. Adam Kuckhoff's divorce from his first wife, Marie, nee Viermeyer, apparently occurred because Margaret Lorke was awaiting the birth of his child. Adam Kuckhoff had a son by Margarete Kuckhoff, named Ula Hans Georg Kuckhoff, born 8 January 1938 in Berlin.

An economist, Greta Kuckhoff studied at the Universities of Berlin, Wurzburg, and Wisconsin. In the United States she and her husband had known William Dodd and his daughter, Martha (Mrs. Alfred K. Stern).

Arrested in 1942, Greta was sentenced to death in February 1943, but the sentence was commuted to ten years in the penitentiary. She remained in the prison at Waldheim until May 1945.

From 1948 to 1949 Greta was a member of the Secretariat of the Economic Commission, the German *Volksrat,* the *Kulturbund,* and other Communist organizations, including the SED.

From 1949 to 1950 Greta was chief of a division in the Ministry of Foreign Affairs and member of the provisional Volkskammer (Parliament). Since 1950 she has been president of the Deutsche Notenbank, and as of 7 January 1957 she was still president of the Notenbank with the rank of minister.

Greta was a very good friend of Schulze-Boysen and his wife, as well as of Arvid Harnack and his wife. She also had contact with Guenther Weisenborn and other Rote Kapelle members.

Greta reportedly contacted the NKVD immediately after the occupation. She was able to make immediate contact with Staff Section IV of the Soviet army. Since then she has been doing work in her spare time for this section and has constantly tried to revive old contacts in West Germany and other countries of the West. She has been extremely active in "peace" groups and has frequently attended international conferences, including Vienna (1961), Moscow (1962), Frankfurt (1963), Stockholm (1963), New Delhi (1964), and Helsinki (1965). In 1964 she became a vice president of the German Peace Council and in 1968 a vice president of the League of Friendship among Peoples. In 1968 she was awarded the "Star of International

Friendship." She became a member of the World Council of Peace in 1969.

HANS KURFESS

was born 3 October 1915 at Wohlau, Silesia. After studying law and economics at the Universities of Munich, Koenigsberg, Geneva, and Berlin, he practiced law in Linz in 1938. He obtained his doctorate in February 1939 and began his official career as assistant magistrate at Bergen, Ruegen. After war broke out, he moved to Breslau in September 1939, becoming a Referendar (junior attorney). In March 1940 he was legal advisor to the German-Hungarian Chamber of Commerce in Budapest. In 1941 he had to return to Germany to do his military service, and in January 1942 he was transferred to the Interpreters' School at Meissen, where he received instruction in English.

At the Interpreters' School he made the acquaintance of Otto Lentz; and in June 1943, when Lentz was sent to Funkabwehr Aussenstelle in Paris for work with the Sonderkommando, Kurfess followed him there and worked as a cryptographer attached to the Aussenstelle. He eventually replaced Lentz, who had acquired good business connections and wished to leave.

From October 1943 to April 1944 Kurfess worked with the Sonderkommando. His chief function was to encipher the texts prepared by "Fritz" (Sukolov) for transmission. This work became more and more a formality and was eventually taken over by Pannwitz's secretary. In April 1944 Kurfess accompanied Pannwitz to Madrid.

With the decrease of his duties (never onerous), Kurfess established various small business connections and eventually worked in the black market. In the course of visiting various firms and reporting on their activities, he got to know Otto Bach, a former Socialist in Paris who knew Pannwitz through Lentz.

From Bach, Kurfess heard various items of information about the Sonderkommando and occasionally met Pannwitz socially. Kurfess helped Lentz in his business enterprises in the south of France by maintaining liaison with various firms and negotiating deals.

Kurfess left Paris on 17 August 1944 for Nancy, where he attached himself to the Sonderkommando on Pannwitz. He then went to Colmar and from there to Constance. He and Lentz were finally picked up by Italian partisans in Milan in the summer of 1945 and were turned over to CIC at Sondrio.

FRANCOIS LACHENAL

may have been a Rote Drei agent (alias Diener) who was a sub-source for Rachel Duebendorfer. He was born on 31 May 1918 in Geneva. He became a lawyer, diplomat, journalist, and publisher. From 1942 to 1946 he served as an attache, first in Vichy, then in Berlin. He reportedly passed his information directly to Jean Pierre Vigier, the son-in-law of Rachel Duebendorfer. He also maintained close contact with Leon Nicole and passed him secret information too. Lachenal spoke some Russian.

MADAME Fnu LAMBERT

was used in 1940 as a contact point for meetings between "Clement" (probably Sukolov) and Gouwlooze in Brussels. In the autumn of 1940 von Proosdy was sent to her house in Brussels to train a W/T operator for Clement's service. Madame Lambert was the widow of a Belgian sculptor who was killed during the war.

Fnu LEBENTHAL

is mentioned in the Rajchmann interrogation as the individual who supplied Rajchmann with documents in the name of "Gilbert," to be used by Trepper. This took place in approximately late May or early June 1942.

The pertinent portion of Rajchmann's statement is as follows:

> [H]e (Trepper) asked me to establish for him an identity in the name of "Gilbert" and insisted that the card and the seals be authentic. For this purpose I went to Antwerp to a shop on Rue Pelican run by a certain Lebenthal, who had been recommended to me by Malvina (Gruber), I think. The shop was a candy store or a pastry shop. Lebenthal promised to furnish me authentic documents as well as certificates of good morals and conduct. He kept his word, and I had Malvina take the documents to Uncle (Trepper), who was at that time in Paris.

PAUL LEGENDRE

(alias Victor, alias Gros, alias Colonel Fernand) was born 29 April 1878 at Sens (Yonne). A French national, he was a retired army captain. He belonged to the Mithridate group in the French Resistance and was recruited into the Ozols network, which was controlled by the Germans.

Even after the liberation Legendre continued to furnish information to the Germans concerning the morale of the American troops. Arrested by the French in 1944, he was freed upon the intervention of Colonel (fnu) Novikov.

The whereabouts of Legendre are unknown, but his son Jacques lived at last report at 5 Villa Chanex in Paris.

ERNST LEMMER

(alias Agnes) was born on 28 April 1898 in Remscheidt, Germany. He attended the Universities of Marburg and Frankfurt. After the Nazis seized power in 1933, Lemmer was denied permission to appear in any newspaper published in Germany. He became a foreign correspondent for *Pester Lloyd* in Budapest, *Neue Zuercher Zeitung* in Zurich, and *Le Soir* in occupied Belgium. He appears in a 22 October 1941 message from Rado to Moscow. The message identifies him as a subsource of "Long" (Georges Blun), a member of the Ribbentrop Bureau, and a Berlin correspondent who telephoned reports to the *Neue Zuercher Zeitung*. This message also gave his true name and said that in the future he would be called "Agnes."

After the war ended, Lemmer became one of the founders of the Christian Democratic Union (CDU) in the Soviet Zone of Germany. He held various official positions until he defected, actually or nominally, to West Germany in 1949.

It has been reported that when Rudolf Roessler and Xaver Schnieper embarked on postwar espionage for Czechoslovakia, 1947-1953, Lemmer was one of Roessler's sources. Our records contain indications of clandestine work for other services as well. For example, Walter Schellenberg said during interrogation that Lemmer had been an agent of Amt VI (foreign espionage) of the RSHA (main security office in Nazi Germany).

OTTO HERMAN WALDEMAR LENTZ,

whose name is also spelled Lenz and Lencs, was born on 2 December 1909 at Darmstadt. He worked in Koenigsberg monitoring broadcasts from the USSR from 1936 to 1938. His father, who was in the Soviet Consulate at Danzig, was involved with the Schulze-Boysen group in Berlin. Both father and son were suspected of RIS activity before the war.

In 1942 Lentz was arrested, then released and sent to work under Heinz Pannwitz, the chief of the Sonderkommando in Paris. He was involved in Funkspiel (W/T playback) operations with Trepper and

Sukolov.

At the end of the war Lentz was again suspected of RIS activities. He was in contact with Johannes Haas-Heye, the brother-in-law of Harro Schulze-Boysen, in 1947. Weisenborn told Lentz that the Soviets wanted him to keep in touch with Germans who were former members of the Schulze-Boysen group.

Lentz and Hans Kurfess were picked up by Italian partisans in Milan in the summer of 1945 and turned over to CIC at Sondrio. They were then interrogated by CSDIC, CMF, OC Army Section, Allied Group, Rome, in October 1945. They furnished detailed information on the Rote Kapelle, the work of the Sonderkommando in Paris, the OKH deciphering department, OKW intercept stations France, Radio Mundial, and numerous personalities in the Rote Kapelle.

In 1950 a report was received indicating that Otto Lentz, born 2 December 1909, was working as a journalist and radio reporter and living in Italy. He was blacklisted on 17 February 1955 by the French IS, which considered him a "dangerous adventurer, swindler, and multiple agent who will work for the highest bidder."

In 1966 Lentz was collaborating with Pannwitz in producing a book on the Rote Kapelle. It appears that Lentz also collaborated with Perrault. Oscar Reile advised that Lentz had previously written on the Rote Kapelle. Reportedly, Lentz has also been in contact with the BND through the Bundespresseamt in Bonn. According to Reile, Lentz was not employed by the BND, but he allegedly worked for the French and tried to sell his services to most of the intelligence services of the West.

FRIEDRICH BERNARD HERMANN LENZ
was born on 8 December 1885 at Marburg-Lahn, Germany. A German national, he is a sociologist and author. His residence in 1954 was Bismarkstrasse 15, Bielefeld, West Germany.

Prior to 1933 Lenz was a professor at the University of Giessen. At that time he was in close contact with Arvid Harnack. His Soviet principal was Sergei Bessonov, a functionary of the Soviet Embassy in Berlin (who was at that time also the principal of Gunther Lubszynski). According to an official French source, Lenz himself was in contact with Lubszynski.

After the rise of Hitler, Lenz continued his special activity for some time and then went first to England, later to the United States. He was reportedly sent there by the Soviet intelligence service. In 1940, on orders from his employers, he returned to Germany, where he immediately resumed his liaison activity between groups of intelligence agents and the Soviet Embassy. During this same period, as camouflage, he wrote some Nazi brochures.

After 1945 Lenz joined the German Communist Party and resumed his activity in East Berlin. In addition he became a member of the Kulturbund Zur Erneuerung Deutschlands, a pro-Soviet organization.

Prior to 1933 Lenz was president of the Arbeitsgemeinschaft Zum Studium Der Sowjetischen Planwirtschaft (Society for the Study of Soviet Economic Planning). This society had been created on order from the Soviet service to serve as a cover for them. Under this cover Harnack, Friedrich Lenz, and others recruited technicians of high standing under the pretext of studying the planned economy of the Soviet Union. They later organized a trip to the USSR, the alleged purpose of which was to study. While in the USSR, these technicians were put in contact with the Soviet intelligence service through the intermediary of WOKS (Association for the Maintenance of Cultural Relations Abroad). Upon the advent of Hitlerism, these individuals hastened to liquidate this association in order to work individually or in small groups until the time the Rote Kapelle network was organized.

A German *Who's Who* published in 1948 lists Friedrich Bernhard Hermann Lenz as a professor, doctor of laws, and doctor of philosophy. The listing indicates that Lenz received his education at the Bismarck Gymnasium in Berlin, at the Universities of Lausanne, Munich, Bonn, and Berlin, and at the American University of Washington, D.C., where he was granted an M.A. degree. It is likewise noted that his wife, Dr. Grete Lenz, received her education in Koeln, Germany, and in Washington, D.C.

An investigation of Lenz and his wife was conducted in the United States, and a report dated 26 July 1954 reflects that Lenz lived in Washington, D.C., as a temporary visitor from October 1938 to July 1940. While in the United States, he reportedly conducted research at Washington, D.C., and wrote a book. He enrolled at American University in September 1939 and in June 1940 received an M.A. degree. He married Grete O. Falk on 18 March 1939. Mrs. Falk had been in the United States from June 1934 and remained until October 1940. She was employed by a welfare agency and was naturalized as an American citizen on 7 May 1940. She returned to Germany via Japan and the USSR on a German passport. Mrs. Lenz in 1951 was in charge of social affairs for the Foreign Office, German Federal Republic, Bonn. Friedrich Lenz has a brother who in 1954 was a judge in Hamburg—British Zone of Germany.

ABRAHAM ISAAC LERNER

(alias Adolf) was born 13 September 1891 at Dukla, Poland. Lerner had been a director of the Excellent Raincoat Company since June 1936 and a director of the Foreign Excellent Raincoat Company, used by Trepper for cover purposes, since December 1938. Lerner escaped from Belgium to France during the war, probably in May 1941, and made his way to the United States via Portugal. By April 1946 he had returned to Brussels and was still a director of the Excellent Raincoat Company, also known as "Le Roi du Caoutchouc." His address in 1946 was 80 Avenue Boetendaal, Uccle. Lerner was married to Livia Kapelowitz, the sister of Louis Kapelowitz.

Lerner, Maurice Kapelowitz, Maurice Padawer, and Harry Gold were partners in the Lecap Rainwear Company, 27 East 21st Street, New York City, which company was dissolved in 1948.

HANS GERHARDT LUBSZYNSKI

was born 30 August 1904 in Berlin. He is the first cousin of Gunther Lubszynski, who lives in Paris. His mother lived at "Les Terrasses," Territat, Laud, Switzerland. Before Melinda Maclean disappeared behind the Iron Curtain, she reportedly was in contact with Mrs. Lubszynski. Hans was a member of the German CP and was employed by the Telefunken Company. A radio engineer, he arrived in 1934 in England, where he was closely associated with Dr. Heinz Erwin Kallmann, both as a business colleague and personal friend.

ROSE LUSCHINSKY

(nee Hepner) was born 20 January 1903 in Danzig. She became Swiss by virtue of a sham marriage with a man named Reudi, divorced him, and married Dr. Heinz L. Luschinsky.

She and Rachel Duebendorfer, nee Hepner, her sister, made their way together from Poland through Germany to Switzerland; both erased the traces of their origin and their activity on behalf of Moscow by contracting mock marriages.

Luschinsky has a medical background, and in 1937 she was on the medical faculty of the University of Paris. In 1938 she took part in the Spanish Civil War and was with the French Army in North Africa in 1939.

ANTONIA LYON-SMITH

(alias Marie Cormet, alias Antoinette Savier) is the daughter of an English brigadier and reportedly a distant relative of the British royal family. She was born 20 September 1925 in Toronto and is a British subject.

A cousin of Ruth Peters, who became Jean Claude Spaak's second wife, Lyon-Smith resided in France during World War II and was acquainted with Claude Spaak, who procured false papers for her.

She was arrested by the Germans on 21 October 1943 and thereafter became the mistress of Karl Gagl, a member of the Sonderkommando.

With respect to Antonia Lyon-Smith, Pannwitz writes as follows:

> Antonia Lyon-Smith lived in my villa with the Kommando, sharing a room with one of the secretaries for more than three months. I did not allow her to be brought to court, as stated above, because she would have received a fairly severe sentence for helping the enemy. Purely humane motives lead me to arrange this, without Berlin's knowledge but with the approval of the head of the military court which was handling all Rote Kapelle cases. My motions were inspired, by neither an effort to obtain Lyon-Smith's collaboration in an espionage operation nor by a sexual interest in her. She had become involved in the war machine through an unfortunate series of circumstances, and as the daughter of an English general, she simply could not refuse to do whatever was asked of her to assist, allegedly, the Allied cause. Her relatives in Paris with whom she lived were extremely bitter and filled with hatred (presumably against the Germans). She, on the other hand, did not share their bitterness, although they did not conceal their feelings from her. She ate breakfast every morning with me and those of my staff who worked most closely with me. I undertook various psychological tests to determine exactly what her attitudes and feelings toward Moscow were. By instinct she was definitely hostile to the Soviets. She had never known the true nature of the group she met through Mme. Spaak. I once offered, joking but pretending to be very serious, to have

her put over the Spanish border so that she could report to the English Consul in Spain, who would arrange for her transportation back to England. She begged me not to do this because, she said, she would immediately be imprisoned in England as a German spy; no one would believe the truth. I then asked her if she would report what good treatment she had received in my Kommando. She replied that she would certainly not make any such report during the first three years because she would be imprisoned if she did. I released her to her relatives toward the end of 1943 or early 1944 on her word of honor that she would not leave Paris. We checked on her regularly, and I know that she kept her word. She had made such a good impression on me that I never doubted that she would keep her word. We left her in Paris when we withdrew. She is reported to have been treated much worse by her own people than by us, the enemy. There were various indications of this. Later in Berlin I explained the entire case and was never reprimanded for my actions.

MIKHAIL MAKAROV

(alias Carlos Alamo, alias Chemnitz) was born 2 January 1905 in Leningrad. He was a Russian national and had a Soviet passport issued 14 December 1933 in Moscow. He also had a Uruguayan passport issued at New York 16 October 1936 in the name Alamo, born in Montevideo 12 April 1913. He was married to Alexandra Petrova, nee Firfarova, but he lived with Suzanne Boisson, nee Schmitz or Schmidt, while in Brussels. An engineer by profession, Makarov was a lieutenant in the Red Army and received intelligence training in Moscow, with special instruction in the preparation of false papers.

In March 1939 Makarov was sent to assist Trepper, travelling from the USSR via Stockholm, Copenhagen, and Paris, where he was supplied with false identity papers in the name of Alamo and given ten thousand dollars. After Rajchmann's recruitment, Makarov was relieved of the responsibility for producing forged documents and concentrated on W/T communications. He probably received training from Wenzel. His cover was provided by Trepper, who arranged for him to be placed as proprietor of the Ostende branch of the Excellent Raincoat Company. He was directed to establish a transmitter in

Ostende, probably for communications with England. While in Ostende, Makarov lived with Caroline Hoorickx, the wife of Guillaume Hoorickx. After the bombing of Ostende in May 1940, which caused damage to the business premises, Makarov moved back to Brussels. Trepper decided that Makarov was not qualified to recruit and handle agents; so Makarov henceforth served primarily as the W/T operator for the network. He succeeded in establishing a W/T link with Moscow.

In the summer of 1941 Anton Danilov became an assistant W/T operator in Brussels under Makarov. The transmitter was housed in 101 Rue des Attrebates, an establishment run by Rita Arnould and Josefa Posnanska. The Germans arrested Danilov in the act of transmitting on the night of 12-13 December 1941, and the next morning they captured Makarov. According to Belgian police records, Makarov was imprisoned at St. Gilles, sentenced to death, and executed at Plotzensee (Berlin) in 1942.

According to another report, Makarov had been sentenced to death by a German court-martial, but his execution was deferred because he was a nephew of Vyacheslav Molotov. In August 1944 Francois Saar-Demichel of the DGER supposedly negotiated the release of Leon Blum, Kurt von Schussnig, and Molotov's nephew from a prison castle near Worgl, where they had been held.

It is probable that Makarov (alias Alamo) is identical with a Makarov who entered Belgium for the first time 11 January 1934—en route for the United States—under his own name, changed his identity while there, and returned to Belgium five years later as Carlos Alamo.

CHARLES EMILE MARTIN

(alias Lorenz or Laurenz, alias Dubois) was born 29 July 1889 in Petrograd. He was a Swiss of Soviet origin and spoke fluent German, French with a Marseilles accent, and Russian. He and his wife Elsa had two children, Erich and Galja. He was an engineer and photographic expert, supposedly from St. Croix, canton of Vaud.

Martin and his wife Elsa were RIS agents of long standing and were almost certainly under NKVD control. He worked in the Far East in China and Japan with his wife before the war. In 1939 he entered Switzerland.

After the German attack, Martin lost contact with Moscow and worked through Louis, a former agent of his in San Francisco, to reestablish connections with Russia. In the summer of 1942 he was in touch with Foote and gave low-grade intelligence on Western operations.

In July 1943 he refused a transmitter which Foote had been told to give him. Foote thought Martin was an NKVD agent and not GRU. He also suspected him of being a double agent on behalf of the Germans.

When Foote returned to Moscow, he was closely questioned about Martin by an NKVD official who appeared to be going to Switzerland to gain further information about Martin's activities.

Martin lived at 32 Chemin de la Fauvette, Chailly, near Lausanne, and had a well-equipped laboratory in his villa. He had connections with two sources of information in Germany whose cover names were Barras and Lambert. Barras was in southern Germany. Both supplied mainly information regarding troop movements and measures in France. Martin supposedly had sources which extended to the French Deuxieme Bureau. He also established a connection with Marius Mouttet and acted as a go-between on this line.

ELSA MARIE MARTIN

(nee Maeder, alias Lora, alias Laura) was born 31 March 1899 in Leningrad. She was the daughter of Bartholomeo and Marie Nuenuksela. She married Charles Emile Martin on 31 December 1931. (Further information about her appears in the sketch of her husband, which precedes.)

According to one report Martin and Laura claimed they were Swiss but both came from Russia. Before 1937 they had worked as Soviet agents in Manchuria, where they made considerable money.

In 1937 they left Manchuria via Moscow, were "allowed out," and then came to Switzerland.

In 1953 they were both still in Switzerland, though Russia was bringing pressure to send them back to Russia. Laura had become psychotic under strain and attempted suicide. The Martins were investigated by the Swiss and interrogated in 1955 and 1956. Reportedly, they refused to talk.

On 11 January 1956 Mr. and Mrs. Martin were sentenced to three months' imprisonment at Lausanne. Afterwards, they were deported to the USSR.

CHARLES MATHIEU

(alias Le Cousin, alias V-Mann Carlos) was a chief inspector in the Belgian State Police. On behalf of the Germans he penetrated the Belgian networks of the Rote Kapelle, supplying Rajchmann with false papers for various members of the network. In July 1942 Jeffremov was arrested at a rendezvous with Mathieu. Early in 1943 Rajchmann gave Mathieu a reserve W/T set to be concealed in the latter's house. In 1947 Mathieu was interrogated by the Belgian authorities.

Mathieu's present whereabouts are unknown, but it is almost certain that Piepe's statement that Mathieu had been executed was erroneous.

ANNA MAXIMOVITCH

was born 8 May 1901 in Tchernikoff, Russia, of Paul and Aglaide Friedman. A Russian refugee and a nerve doctor, she was the unmarried sister of Basile Maximovitch. With the help of her brother she directed a clinic at Choisey-le-Roi and later established a camp at Vernet, near the Pyrenees. Her father was a Czarist general, and Anna was a real Russian and Czarist.

She entered France in 1922 and resided at 12 Rue de Viatau, Colombes, and in the Chateau de Billeron at Lugny-Champagne (Cher).

In 1941 Anna and Basile Maximovitch recruited Kathe Voelkner for Trepper's service in Paris. Anna Maximovitch was arrested on 12 December 1942 and probably later deported and executed.

The Countess de Rohan-Chabot was a patient of Maximovitch and was on very friendly terms with her. She rented the Chateau Billeron, which she owned, to Dr. Maximovitch for a relatively low price. The Rohan-Chabot family regarded itself as the future dynasty in Bretagne, with the husband of the Countess as the pretender to the throne. The husband was an active French officer and had contacts with officer circles in Limoges. The Countess reiterated the statements of monarchist French circles that with the approval of Marshal Petain, France would again become a monarchy after the latter's death.

BASILE MAXIMOVITCH

was born 22 July 1902 in Tchernikoff, Russia. He was a civil engineer and the brother of Anna. He arrived in France with his sister in 1922. Reportedly he volunteered his services to Trepper and got the reputation of being the "Casanova" of the Rote Kapelle.

Margarete Hoffman-Scholz, who was secretary to Colonel Hans Kuprian and also the niece of Heinrich Stulpnagel, Commander of Greater Paris, fell in love with Basile. Margarete gave him German intelligence data. She became secretary to Otto Abetz.

Basile and Anna Maximovitch were very important to Trepper.

Basile, through Margarete, was at the heart of the Wehrmacht. Anna, through Bishop Chaptal, was inside the Vatican. Anna wanted to poison the German High Command with curare. Kathe Voelkner was a friend of Margarete at the Chateau de Billeron. Kathe had been a dancer recruited by Soviet intelligence. Basile proposed Kathe to Trepper but did not know that she had already been recruited by the Soviets.

Maximovitch was arrested with his sister on 12 December 1942 and was probably executed.

MARIUS MOUTTET

(alias Marius), a Frenchman, was a former Socialist Minister who took refuge in Switzerland after the German occupation of France. He lived in Montreux from 1942 to 1943. His services had been recommended to Moscow by his son Gustave in London.

He was a war-time informant of the Swiss group through Charles Martin. His intelligence was passed by Martin to Foote for transmission to Moscow. Foote, as a Soviet agent under Moscow instructions, established contact with Mouttet through Martin, who posed as a British agent and deceived Mouttet. Rado dropped Mouttet, who does not appear in the Rote Drei traffic after 1942.

After World War II Mouttet was a senior member of the French Senate, and circa 1959 he became vice president of the Senate Committee for Foreign Affairs, Defense, and Armed Forces.

ANNA BARBARA MUELLER

(alias Anna, but not identical with the Rote Drei source "Anna" in the German Foreign Office) was born 9 April 1880 in Basle. A Swiss citizen, she was at one time the proprietress of an appointments agency and reportedly "the Burgess of Basle since 1920."

Mueller began working for the RIS shortly after the Russian revolution, at which time she started helping persons cross the Swiss border at Basle. In 1936 she was working for Maria Josefovna Poliakova, engaged in attempting to get Russian agents across the Franco-Swiss frontier by obtaining false papers from the Swiss police officer Max Habjanic. She also acted as a link between Robinson and Rachel Duebendorfer.

Several of Mueller's relatives were implicated in the Schulze-Boysen network in Germany. In 1943 she was enticed into Germany to try to help her brother Hans. She was arrested, kept in custody, and used in the interrogation of Robinson. The Germans sentenced her to death, but the Swiss intervened, and she was given only a two-year sentence. Liberated by the Soviets, she returned to Switzerland.

HANS MUSSIG

(alias Jean Varon, alias Rueff) was born 18 January 1904 in Mannheim, Germany. He was married to Ilse Bach. In February 1939 Mussig was recruited by the French Intelligence Service. During the occupation he was surveilled by the Gestapo and was arrested in Grenoble. Indicted for espionage, he was interogated thirty-five times by the Germans, and in order to save his life agreed to collaborate with the Sonderkommando.

Pannwitz explained to Mussig that the Germans had succeeded in penetrating the French Resistance, and Mussig reportedly helped the Sonderkommando in operating the Mithridate network for the benefit of the Germans.

LEON NICOLE

was born 10 April 1887 in Montcherend, Vaud, Switzerland. He married the sister of the wife of Dr. Mario Bianchi. In 1932 he was president of the Swiss Socialist Party. He later became a prominent member of the Swiss Labor Party (Communist). He maintained close contact with Noel H. Field, Alexander Rado, and Louis Dolivet. He was also in touch with Rachel Duebendorfer. He served the Rote Drei network as a spotter and recruiter. After World War II he maintained open contact with the Soviet Embassy in Bern. In early 1952, however, the Swiss Labor Party received orders from Moscow to expel him. He died on 28 June 1965.

PIERRE NICOLE

the son of Leon, was born in Switzerland in 1911. He served as a cutout between his father (and the Swiss Communist Party) and both Alexander Rado and Alexander Foote. Pierre Nicole may have been the alias Paul (not Paul Boettcher) who was trained as a W/T operator but arrested in December 1943 before going on the air. This identification, however, is far from firm.

ERICH NUTIS

(alias Andre) was born 16 December 1918 in Frankfurt am Main of Russian refugee parents. His nationality was probably German. He became a secretary at Simexco in January 1942. He was arrested in the roundup of November 1942 and deported to Germany. In April 1945 he was released and returned to Belgium. His last known address was Avenue de la Seconde Reine, Uccle (1947).

FRANZ OBERMANNS

(alias Eeriki Noki, alias Alex) was born 29 October 1909 in Elberfeld. A German national, he spoke German, French, and Italian. His wife Alice, nee Ruesch, was born 27 November 1917.

He had received his intelligence training from the Red Army in Moscow and arrived in Switzerland shortly before the war to reinforce Ursula Beurton's network. He had a Finnish cover and passport as Eeriki Noki, born 8 July 1906, in Somere, Finland.

After his arrest by the Swiss for carrying false documents, he was held in a Swiss labor camp. The lawyer, Herzl Theodore Sviatsky, protected his interests and reported on his welfare to Beurton and subsequently to Foote.

Repatriated to Germany in 1945, he was appointed a KPD official in the French zone. In 1947 he visited Switzerland and sent a message to Moscow through Sviatsky.

SARA HEYA ORSCHITZER

(nee Broide, alias Anna Mikler, alias Beila Yerushalmi, alias Luba Alexayevna Brikson) was the wife or mistress of Leopold Trepper. She was born in 1904 of Polish parents at Radzilficor, Poland. Trepper first made the acquaintance of Orschitzer in 1924 while he was in Lemberg (Poland). She was then working in a chocolate factory and attending evening classes with the object of training as a teacher. She remained in Warsaw after Trepper's emigration in 1924 but subsequently followed him to Palestine. She arrived there in 1925 as a domestic servant. In Poland she had been active in Jewish leftist circles, and she was in complete sympathy with Trepper's political views. In Palestine in February 1927 she took part in an illegal Communist demonstration, was arrested, and served two months in prison. In June 1928 she was again arrested while soliciting funds for the International Red Air and served a further prison sentence in Jaffa. Trepper and Orschitzer probably began living together as man and wife in Palestine in 1927 or 1928. She was subsequently recommended for deportation; but on 7 July 1929 she announced her marriage to Josef Orschitzer, a Palestinian citizen, with the result that the deportation order was stayed. During 1929 she was reportedly active as an illegal Communist worker under the name Beila Yerushalmi, but she evaded arrest. In 1930, in the name Orschitzer, she applied for and received a

Palestinian passport in order to travel abroad for her health. In the summer of 1930 Trepper and his wife arrived in Paris together. In April 1931 their elder son was born. A birth certificate provided by the hospital was not registered in France, but it was registered later in Moscow. In 1931 Orschitzer returned to Palestine and resumed her Communist activities. In November 1933 she was again arrested and sentenced to two months' imprisonment. An attempt was then made to set her Palestinian citizenship aside on the grounds that she had been continuously engaged in seditious activities and that she had never lived with or been supported by her nominal husband. The application failed because there was no method of revoking a wife's citizenship independently of that of her husband.

Orschitzer probably rejoined Trepper early in 1934 in Moscow where he was undergoing intelligence training. Orschitzer herself attended Kumns University for a year and also attended a school of languages to learn French. In 1936 she gave birth to a second son.

In March 1939 Orschitzer, using the alias Anna Mikler, a Canadian national, accompanied Trepper to Belgium. She was aware of Trepper's intelligence activities and assisted him in them. In August 1940, following the German invasion of Belgium, she returned to Moscow. She took with her the younger son. The other boy had been left in Moscow to continue his schooling. Orschitzer reportedly welcomed Trepper on his return to Moscow in April 1945. He apparently showed a great deal of pleasure in the reunion, bringing her a present from Cairo, where the plane had stopped en route.

An unconfirmed report states that Orschitzer "divorced" Trepper some time after 1945, when she learned the circumstances of his relationship with Georgie de Winter.

GENERAL HANS OSTER

was Canaris' deputy, a key figure in the twentieth of July group. General Oster's story has appeared in several published works. Although Rudolf Roessler did not name Oster or identify him correctly, it seems likely that it was Oster whom Roessler had in mind when he divulged the identities of certain principal sources, as recounted in the body of this study.

JEAN OTTEN

was recruited by Elizabeth Depelsenaire in 1940 or 1941 for Communist or partisan activities in Belgium. He and his wife Jeanne, nee Wynants, were part of the group responsible for the provision of safehouses for agents. In June 1942 he was involved in the arrangements for John Kruyt's protection. Arrested 13 July 1942 after Kruyt's capture, he was imprisoned at St. Gilles, Brussels; but on 31 December 1942 he was released on payment of one hundred thirty thousand Belgian francs. He was re-arrested 2 October 1943 and taken to Fresnes Prison, Paris. In November 1943 he was sentenced to three years in prison and was deported to Germany.

Otten was born 3 June 1911 in Koekelberg. By occupation he was a salesman.

According to a 1960 NATO Special Committee Report, Otten and his wife were residing at 108 Avenue Brigade Piron, Molenbeck-St. Jean. The report states: "The Ottens can be regarded as having abandoned intelligence work owing to all the misfortunes they have experienced and their bad state of health."

JEANNE OTTEN

(nee Wynants) was born 23 October 1914 at Molenbeck-St. Jean, Belgium. She is the wife of Jean Otten. Jeanne Otten, like her husband, was recruited by Elizabeth Depelsenaire to provide safehouses for the Jeffremov network. In June 1942 she was involved in the arrangements made for John Kruyt's welfare. With her husband she was arrested by the Germans 13 July 1942. She was interned at St. Gilles Prison but was released 28 August 1942 on the payment of fifty thousand Belgian francs. She was re-arrested by the Gestapo 2 October 1943 and was taken to Fresnes Prison, Paris. She was sentenced to death 3 November 1943 and was deported to Germany. She was subsequently liberated by the Allies.

Jeanne Otten at one time was a secretary for Phillips Radio Company in Brussels.

According to a 1960 NATO Special Committee Report, Jeanne Otten was then living with her husband at 108 Avenue Brigade Piron, Molenbeck-St. Jean.

MAURICE PADAWER

(alias Moses Meier Padawer) was born 5 November 1897 at Mielic, Poland. He is a U.S. citizen and the husband of Theresa, nee Kapelowitz.

Padawer became a director of the Belgium firm, the Excellent Raincoat Company (Le Roi du Caoutchouc) in 1924, and in 1938 he was a director of its subsidiary, the Foreign Excellent Raincoat Company, used by Trepper for cover purposes. In the summer of 1940 he fled to France, later returning to Belgium. In March 1941 he returned to France, and from there he went a year later to the United States. During the war Sukolov used Padawer to send money to Margarete Barcza's mother, who was living in New York.

Padawer was the subject of an investigation in the United States, and pertinent excerpts from a report dated March 1951 follow:

> The Foreign Excellent Raincoat Company was established in Belgium in 1938. This company had a network of outlet stores throughout Europe which were set up as fronts for members of a Soviet espionage network described by the Germans as "Rote Kapelle."

> On 20 September 1950 Maurice Padawer's wife was interviewed in New York. She reported that Subject (Maurice), Adolph Lerner—aka Abraham Lerner—and Louis Kapelowitz, all brothers-in-law, had organized the firm, Le Roi du Caoutchouc, in 1924 in Brussels, Belgium. Mrs. Padawer stated that the Subject (Maurice) presently holds the position of office and manufacturing manager of Le Roi du Caoutchouc and that this makes it necessary for him to spend considerable time in Belgium. She further advised that Subject had no investments of any type in the United States at the present time.

> Maurice Kapelowitz, Adolph Lerner, Maurice Padawer, and Harry Gold were partners in the Lecap Rainwear Company, 37 East 21st Street, New York City, which company was engaged in the manufacture of raincoats . . . Kapelowitz, Lerner, and Padawer were all brothers-in-law, and Harry Gold was a cousin of Maurice Kapelowitz.

> On 15 August 1950 . . . Harry Gold, official of Pago Originals, Inc., 222 West 37th Street, New York City, advised that he was a former partner of Maurice Padawer and other relatives in the Lecap Rainwear Company which was dissolved in 1948.

> Gold stated that he left the Lecap Rainwear Company in 1946, later forming the Pago Originals Company. He advised that Maurice Padawer had been at one time associated with Pago Originals but had had no connection with that company since December 1949.

The extent of Padawer's involvement in intelligence activities is not known, but he probably knew or at least suspected that Grossvogel was using the Foreign Excellent Raincoat Company as a cover for Communist or espionage activities.

ARMAND PALIVODA

was born 28 September 1906 in Bedzin, Poland. He was director of RKO in Geneva. He has two brothers—Henri, a Swiss citizen; and Josef, a U.S. citizen. His sister, Ann Palivoda, is married to Howard Charles Newton.

Investigations of the Rote Drei disclosed that he was involved in a transfer of funds from New York to Geneva for the Soviets.

Palivoda was denied Swiss citizenship because he was suspected of being an MVD agent. He was also denied a French visa for the same reason.

HEINZ PANNWITZ,

whose true name is Heinz Paulsen, was born on 28 July 1911 in Berlin. As a youth he belonged to the Evangelical Church, and he once studied theology. He gave up his studies for the ministry because of divisions in the Evangelical Church regarding its attitude toward Hitler. He is married to Hannah Bailer and has four children.

In 1937 he was appointed to the criminal police services through the influence of Martin Mauck, and in June 1939 he passed his examinations and became a criminal police commissioner with the Berlin Kripo.

In 1940 he was posted with the Gestapo, and in 1942 he was responsible for investigating the assassination of Reinhard Heydrich in Prague (27 May 1942). Pannwitz had trouble in the Heydrich case. He allegedly told his superiors: "Do you want retaliation or do you want the facts?" He was reportedly against retaliation and was transferred to the Finnish-Russian front.

For unexplained reasons he was transferred to Paris to take over the Sonderkommando (a combined counterintelligence unit) in March 1943. He was in charge of combatting Soviet military espionage nets in Western Europe. He commanded the Paris Sonderkommando until the last days of the war. He claims that as a result of his work "the entire Rote Kapelle network lay in German hands."

On 2 May 1945 he became a prisoner of war, having surrendered in accordance with Soviet orders, and was flown to Moscow, where he was interviewed by Abakumov of Smersh. Victor Sukolov accompanied him. Abakumov was not convinced that Pannwitz had the ability to play back Soviet agents against Moscow for two and a half years. Other Soviet interrogators later told Pannwitz that it was impossible to believe that he had unearthed Soviet nets and doubled them. According to the Soviets, there must have been a German penetration of the NKGB at the highest level. Pannwitz admitted he willingly became a Soviet prisoner through his fear of what would happen to him if he fell into U.S. hands.

Pannwitz was sentenced to twenty-five years in a Soviet work camp but was released in 1954. Dr. Eugen Steimle, who was once Pannwitz's boss, believed that Pannwitz was an RSHA penetration of the Rote Kapelle. Steimle reported that Richard Grossman and Pannwitz were brainwashed and given cover for future espionage on behalf of the RIS.

Since his return to Germany from Russia, Pannwitz has lived at 23 Kreuzaecker, Ludwigsburg bei Stuttgart. From time to time he has worked for West German intelligence services.

JEAN CLEMENT GHISLAIN PASSELECQ

was born in Mons, Belgium. Before the war he was a member of the Rexist Party in Belgium. In March 1941 he became a registered shareholder of Simexco, through his association with Nazarin Drailly. As a member of Simexco, Passelecq became an active agent in the Sukolov network, supplying military intelligence to Sukolov himself, to Isbutsky, and to Drailly. He was probably assisted in his clandestine work by his secretary, Jeanne Ponsaint.

Passelecq was arrested 25 November 1942 and deported to Germany. In April 1945 he was liberated and returned to Brussels. He tried to get in touch with Georgie de Winter in the summer of 1946.

Passelecq divorced his first wife, Madeleine, nee Marendaz, and later married his former secretary at Simexco, Jeanne Ponsaint.

According to a 1960 NATO Special Committee report, the Passelecqs were then living at 120 Avenue van Volxem, Forest. He was a travelling salesman. The report concluded that "No longer engages in any activities connected with an intelligence service. Jean Passelecq should be regarded as an anti-Communist."

MAURICE PEPER

(alias Wassermann, alias Hollander) was a member of the Belgian network under Sukolov in 1940. He later became active in Jeffremov's group, acting as liaison between Brussels and Amsterdam. Peper also served as a cutout between Jeffremov and Rajchmann.

Peper was born 12 December 1899 in Amsterdam. He was Jewish. Until 1940 Peper was a wireless operator for a commercial steamship company. He was a member of the Dutch Maritime Union and the then illegal International Seamen's Union. For the Rote Kapelle his primary duties were as a courier and liaison man, but according to one source he supervised three sending and receiving stations. Peper worked closely with Wenzel, and it is possible that he was originally recruited by him.

Peper was arrested approximately 25 July 1942 as a result of information given by Jeffremov. Peper and Herman Isbutsky were instructed by Jeffremov to attend a meeting; and when they appeared, they were arrested. Peper was induced to speak and revealed that he was the liaison officer with a network in Holland and that he had a rendezvous in a few days with the leader of the Dutch network, Anton Winterink. He was therefore escorted to Amsterdam by a III F officer (Henry Piepe). Peper was allowed to attend the meeting under close surveillance, but he did not meet his contact and returned. Further interrogation of Peper showed that he was also in a position to get in touch with the leader through a Dutch family, the Hilbollings. It was decided to send him to the house of this family, which was also one of his contact's cover addresses, so that he might arrange a meeting for the evening. Peper went to the house and arranged a meeting for 8:30 p.m. in a restaurant. The meeting took place as arranged, and both men were arrested. At the time of his arrest, Winterink shouted out a name to a crowd which had collected, and it was clear that he had been followed to the meeting and was thus warning off his followers. The Hilbollings were then arrested.

After his arrest Peper also furnished to the Germans information which led to the arrest of Augustin Sesee in early August 1942.

According to a 1960 NATO Special Committee report, Peper was living at 60 Lange Kievitstraat, Antwerp, with his wife, Clemintina Pelagia, nee De Cock. His nationality was given as Dutch and his occupation as waiter. The Belgian authorities had no knowledge of political activity by Peper.

MARCEL PERRAULT

(or Perrot, alias Paul) was an agent in the Ozols network. He lived at 86 Rue du Cherche-Midi in Paris in 1940-1941. His present whereabouts are unknown.

RENEE PETITPAS

(alias Blanche; alias Biquette, CP cover name) was born circa 1912.

She was in the Soviet Union in 1932 and had worked for the French CP for some years before the war.

A French national, she had been recruited from the ranks of the French CP by Robinson to serve as a link with the French CP sources and to provide a safehouse for the accommodation of a W/T transmitter.

She was an associate of Maurice Aenis-Hanslin. Her arrest by the Gestapo at the beginning of 1943 followed that of Robinson.

PETROV

was a Bulgarian engineer and business contact of Grossvogel in Brussels in 1940. In May 1940, through the Bulgarian Consulate, Petrov obtained a car for Trepper to make a journey through Belgium, ostensibly on business. The real purpose of the journey was to collect information on the German advance.

HENRY FRIEDRICH WILHELM PIEPE

(alias Harry, alias Dr. Pieper) was born 25 July 1893 in Uelzer, Germany. He was a captian in the German Army, having been in command at Ghent under the occupation of Section III F of the Abwehr. When on 10 May 1940 the Wehrmacht attacked the West, Piepe was a lieutenant in the armored division. He fought at Verdun in World War II.

In the course of 1941 a radio location service working in Berlin reported the existence of a secret radio transmitter operating in contact with Moscow. Around October or November 1941 Piepe was ordered to take charge of the investigation in view of the fact that the transmissions were originating in the Ghent sector. As a result of Piepe's D/F activities, the Abwehr located the Soviet transmitter at 101 Rue des Attrebates in Etterbeek, and there Piepe in December 1941 found Sukolov's transmitter and arrested Danilov and Makarov. Other arrests followed, including Johannes Wenzel.

Soon after the arrest of Wenzel, orders were received from Berlin directing Piepe to turn over the case of the secret Soviet transmitters to a Special Commission created in Berlin for this purpose, and soon thereafter Karl Giering arrived in Brussels and introduced himself to Piepe in the name of the Special Commission. Piepe was ordered to give up the documents he had collected regarding the case, to maintain contact with Giering, and to keep informed about the affair.

According to Piepe, Wenzel was taken to Berlin and after a short period of time agreed to divulge the key which he used to encode and decode the messages. In the back traffic was a message to "Kent" which contained Schulze-Boysen's address in Berlin.

Piepe reported that he was not ignorant of the fact that the Gestapo made some of the captured radio operators transmit under control. He did not know a great deal about the controlled transmitters managed by the Special Commission. Instructions in this regard came exclusively from Berlin.

After the operations appeared to have been completed in Belgium, the Special Commission was transferred to Paris. Piepe was sent to Paris after the arrest of Trepper with the aim of attending the interrogations as an observer. According to Piepe, Trepper quickly confessed and agreed to reveal to the Germans all the details of his organization. Based on Trepper's information many transmitters were discovered, and most of Trepper's colleagues were arrested.

According to Piepe, Trepper was never incarcerated by the Germans. He was placed under surveillance by the Special Commission in Paris. He was, however, authorized to take walks under surveillance. Trepper had requested permission to have sexual relations with a woman for his health. This permission had been refused, and one day in the course of a promenade with Willy Berg of the Special Commission, Trepper disappeared. A few days later he wrote to Berg explaining that he had fled because they would not allow him to have relations with a woman.

Piepe has furnished the American services with detailed information concerning his investigation of the Rote Kapelle, but what he has said does not coincide with what he reportedly told Perrault. Perrault attributes much of his information to a non-existent Franz Fortner, a former Abwehr official, who is surely Piepe.

JOHANN PODSIADLO
was born 8 January 1894 at Danzig. He was an artist and art teacher. He was Kathe Voelkner's lover.

Podsiadlo was almost certainly aware of, and implicated in, the work of his mistress for Trepper's organization in Paris.

A German national, he was employed as an interpreter in the labor recruiting section of the German Kommandantur in Paris.

He resided with his mistress at 5 Impasse Rolleboise, Paris. The Gestapo arrested him on 13 January 1943, and he was later executed.

An Abwehr report dated 19 January 1943 states as follows:

Podsiadlo, the Reich's German who fled, was discovered in a cafe on 13 January 1943 and arrested. To date, he denies that he betrayed his country intentionally . . . (he) admits the charge of having seen the typewriter of his mistress Voelkner in their common dwelling . . . He also admits that on the request of his mistress he stole blank forms from his German office and handed them to her.

YVONNE CLEMENCE FANNY POELMANS
(alias Mouni) worked in a minor capacity for Jeffremov's group in Belgium, under the direction of Germaine Schneider, by whom she was recruited.

Yvonne Poelmans was born 21 November 1910 in Ixelles. She was a qualified gymnast and masseuse. Following Germaine Schneider's escape into France in June or July 1942, Yvonne Poelmans sheltered Joseph Blumsack and his wife, Renee, also agents of Germaine. She was arrested 7 January 1943 at the same time as the Blumsacks. Detained in Mauthausen Concentration Camp, she was later transferred to Belsen, where she died.

Poelmans and the Blumsacks were betrayed by Franz Schneider, who revealed to the Germans where they were hiding.

MARIE JOSEFOVNA POLIAKOVA
had the code names "Gisela," "Mildred," "Vera," and "Meg." She appears in the Rote Drei traffic as "Vera." She was an RU officer who played the principal role in organizing the network in Switzerland before World War II.

She was born about 1910 of Russian Jewish parents. Her place of birth is not in our records. Her father served for years as a representative of the People's Commissariat for Foreign Trade. He worked in various European countries, including England, Germany, and France. She lived abroad with her family. She acquired a knowledge of foreign countries and languages; she was fluent in English, German, and French.

In 1931 the Central Committee of the Komsomol recommended Poliakova to Soviet Military Intelligence. She attended the Higher Intelligence School of the RU on Arbatskaya Ploschad in Moscow. The course lasted nine or ten months. One of her classmates was Ivan Alekseyevich Bolshakov, who had been taken into the RU about 1935 or 1936. They became close friends, and perhaps more than friends.

She spent much time abroad in responsible assignments during the 1930s. She was at one time an Illegal Resident from the Technical Intelligence Unit (which until 1940 was a part of Section I of the RU's Office of Operations). As such she served in Switzerland and France. She also served as the Illegal Resident in Germany and Belgium under the direction of Section I (Europe) of the RU.

About 1937 Poliakova returned from Switzerland to Moscow. While in Europe she had had interests not only in Switzerland but also in France and possibly in Italy. Her connections in France had included Henri Robinson, and in Switzerland her contacts had included Rachel Duebendorfer, Anna Mueller, Selma Gessner-Buehrer, and perhaps Julius Humbert-Droz.

Recalled to Moscow about 1937, Poliakova survived the purges; but her father was liquidated. Her brother, who was studying at the Zhukov Military Academy of Aviation, was arrested and may have been executed. As a result she was embittered against Stalin's regime and the State Security Service.

At an unknown date, probably earlier than 1940, Poliakova married a fnu Dobritzberger, a Hungarian Comintern agent who had been active as such for several years. About 1940 he was transferred to or recruited by military intelligence and was placed in the Special Duties Section (Section V) of the Office of Operations. He had been a leading member of the Schutzbund in Florisdorf/Vienna.

During the fall of 1940 Ismail Akhmedov arrived at RU headquarters and was made deputy chief of Section IV (Technical Intelligence, Office of Operations, RU). Chief of Subsection I (Western Europe) of Section IV was fnu Meleshchnikov. He was then on assignment in Europe, and Poliakova was the acting chief. She was considered exceptionally able.

Early in 1941 Meleshchnikov left Moscow on another assignment, and Poliakova was confirmed as the chief of Section I. Filip Ivanovich Golikov had been appointed RU chief in 1940. He distrusted old-line officers like Poliakova, who had been recruited in the time of General Ian Berzin and who had served under Uritski, Yezhov, and Proskurov (who had been dismissed because of failures that occurred during the Russian-Finnish War). Poliakova had been Proskurov's closest friend and adviser. She was too useful, however, to be dismissed. She gave lectures in RU training programs. She was said to know by heart the files of illegal agents all over the world who worked for Section I (Europe), Section IV (Technical), and Section VI (Research, Development, and Training). She also knew some of the files of Sec-

Personalities of the Rote Kapelle   329

tion III (Far East and America). In 1940 and 1941 Akhmedov was her superior officer.

Among Poliakova's contacts were the following: Akhmedov; Andreyev, former chief of Section I; Aseyev, Boris Pavlovich, chief engineer of the NIIS RU RKKA; Arshansky, Section IV officer; Berzin, General Ian, former RU chief; Baranov, Petr Ivanovich, Section IV officer; Bolshakov, Ivan Alekseyevich, chief of Section VI and later of Section I; Golikov, General Filip Ivanovich, RU Director from 1940 to mid-1942; "Hans," illegal agent at RU headquarters in 1941; Epshtein, Commissar, later colonel, Section I officer; Keane, Dorothea, wife of Arthur A. Adams; Konovalov, Dmitri, chief of Section IV; Krutikov, Aleksei Dmitriyevich, chief of Personnel Directorate, NKVT; Kuznetsov, Chief of Section I after Andreyev; Malenkov, Georgi; Mansurov, Section V officer; Melnikov, Section V officer; Mikoyan; "Papa"; "Pikurin"; "The Seven Brothers"; Shaw (Show, Boyle); Vinogradov, Section VII, male.

In February 1941 Poliakova went to Riga to help one fnu Arshansky, a case officer of Section IV, to recruit one or more agents. Two Jewish girls, names unknown, were recruited in Riga in early 1941 by an espionage agent named Arshansky. They were to be dispatched to New York by way of the USSR, Japan, and San Francisco. In New York they were to work for alias Faraway. They spent a week in training with Poliakova in Moscow. They were then dispatched, although Poliakova had not completed her work with them, because alias Faraway was expected to complete their training in the United States.

In 1941 the deputy chief of Section IV (from 1940 to the autumn of 1941) was alias Pavel Petrovitch Mikhailov. (Comment: The true name was something like Menshikov.) At the end of 1940 or early in 1941 he left for the United States. His work was taken over by Poliakova.

At some time in 1941 Poliakova, who in Moscow was the responsible officer for the Rote Drei, went to Switzerland to deal with problems there. On her orders Rachel Duebendorfer was subordinated to Alexander Rado. She inspected an agent net in Germany while en route to Switzerland.

By 1944, if not earlier, Poliakova had been promoted from captain to major. At the end of 1944 she succeeded Lt. Colonel fnu Artiomenko as chief of an RU subsection working against Spain.

Poliakova received Alexander Foote and Leopold Trepper in Moscow in January 1945. She interrogated Foote and met him twice a week until she fell seriously ill in April 1946.

She remained active in Department IV until at least 1953.

JEANNE EMMA MADELEINE PONSAINT

worked in Simexco beginning in the spring of 1941 as a secretary to Jean Passelecq. She was actively engaged in intelligence activities for the Sukolov group.

Jeanne Ponsaint was born 15 January 1921 at Ixelles. Before the war she was a member of the Rexist Party. At the time of the general roundup of Simexco employees in November 1942, she escaped arrest; and from 25 November 1942 until her arrest on 11 December 1942, she provided accommodation for Nazarin Drailly, who was also being sought by the Gestapo. According to Perrault, she was arrested while attempting to deliver a package to Drailly's wife, who was in prison. Jeanne Ponsaint was first detained at St. Gilles. In April 1943 she was deported to Germany, where she was imprisoned at Mauthausen. She was repatriated to Belgium 8 May 1945.

Jeanne Ponsaint is the authoress of a book, *Je Suis une Condamnee a Mort (I Am Condemned to Death)*.

In the summer of 1946 Ponsaint attempted to contact Trepper's mistress, Georgie de Winter.

In 1960 Ponsaint was the wife of Jean Passelecq, for whom she had worked at Simexco in 1941-1942, and they were living at 120 Avenue van Volxem, Forest.

LOUISE MARIE PAULINE PONSART

(nee Houvenaeghel) was born 23 January 1907 in Ixelles. From the spring of 1941 until July 1942 she was employed as a secretary at Simexco. There is no evidence that she engaged in intelligence activity.

Louise Ponsart was arrested 25 November 1942 during the general roundup of Simexco employees. She was imprisoned in Brussels but was released 16 April 1943.

Louise Ponsart is not identical with Jeanne Ponsaint, another secretary at Simexco during the same period.

SOFIE or JOSEFA POSNANSKA or POTZNENSKA

(alias Anna Verlinder, alias Annette, alias Sara) was a Jewess from Poland who worked for Trepper in Paris in 1940 and 1941. She may have received training in cryptography in Moscow before the war. In October 1941 she was sent to Brussels to serve as an encipherer for Makarov. She was escorted across the Franco-Belgian frontier by Malvina Gruber. Posnanska lived with Rita Arnould at 101 Rue des Attrebates, where Makarov's transmitter was housed.

Sofie Posnanska was arrested the night of 12-13 December 1941. She committed suicide in St. Gilles Prison, Brussels, in September 1942.

According to one report Sofie had a husband, Joseph Posnanska, who was a member of the Lyons group of the Rote Kapelle under the direction of Isidore Springer. Joseph Posnanska was reportedly arrested in November 1942.

MARCEL PRENANT

French biologist and Communist leader, was born circa 1893. A well-known political agitator in France, he was a member of a Bolshevik group of Bessarabian emigres. Subsequently he became a professor at the Sorbonne in Paris.

In 1933 he was associated with anti-Fascist congresses and other left-wing movements. In 1940 he was staff officer in the French army and subsequently a Franc-Tireur in the French resistance. Arrested by the Gestapo in February 1944, he was deported to Neuengamme, Germany, in June. In 1945 he was a deputy member of the Central Committee of the French CP.

Prenant was a friend of Jacques Soustelle, who was attached to de Gaulle's staff in England.

OTTO PUENTER

(alias Pakbo, aka Dr. Otto) was born 4 April 1900 in Staefa to Gottfried and Maria Bangerter. He is a Swiss citizen. A lawyer and journalist (head of INSA Press and Agence Puenter) and very wealthy, he is married to Giacomina-Martina Neuroni.

As Pakbo he headed a Rote Drei group consisting of Salter, Long, and a clandestine Communist organization in southern Germany known as "Rot." He had liaison with the Swiss General Staff (probably General Masson).

Most of Puenter's traffic was sent to Moscow through Bolli, for whom he provided the bail when she was arrested.

At the time of Foote's arrest, Puenter was preparing to have his own transmitter under Bourgeois. Upon Rado's departure for France, he is thought to have taken over the Swiss net and allegedly transmitted a message from Rado to Moscow after Foote's arrest, using the Chinese MA in Bern.

Puenter is an accredited parliamentary reporter for the left-wing of the Socialist Party, writing reports from the Bundeshaus for *Volksrecht* and other papers.

Puenter has published articles about Soviet wartime espionage in Switzerland, has granted a number of interviews, and has appeared on Swiss television. His version of events magnifies his own role and seriously distorts the record. He has not even told the truth about his code name. He has ascribed its origin as an anagram of the first letters of towns in which he had networks of sources, whereas Rado has described Pakbo as a phonetic form of *paquebot* (steamship), a name given Puenter because he was fat. Puenter's persistent muddying of the waters appears to serve Soviet purposes as well as his own.

HERMINA RABINOWITCH,

a Lithuanian Jewess, was born 5 October 1890 or 5 October 1891 in Kaunas, Lithuania. Her name also is spelled Germina Rabinowitz, Rabinovitch, Rabinowicz, and Rabinovicius. She has used the alias of "Hermann." She is the daughter of Ephraim Rabinowitch and Sophia Trachtenberg. Her father was a wealthy gynecologist who died in a German concentration camp.

Her sister, Larissa, is the wife of Miguel de Echegary, a Spanish diplomat who was once assigned in Washington, D.C.

Rabinowitch as a child was seriously crippled in both legs by infantile paralysis. She walks with the aid of two canes. About 5 feet tall with brown eyes, dark hair, fair skin, and a stout build, she is morbidly introverted and emotionally unstable. She speaks fluent Russian, French, German, and English. She has a Ph.D. in economics and social science from Heidelberg. She also has studied economics in Paris and Geneva. She is unmarried.

Paul Massing recalled the name of Rabinowitch, a crippled woman who used crutches and worked for the Soviet Trade Delegation in Berlin in late 1929 or 1930.

From 1929 to 1940 she was employed as a research assistant in the ILO, Geneva, and was an intimate friend of Rachel Duebendorfer and Paul Boettcher. In 1927 she visited Moscow and was probably interviewed by GRU officials.

On 21 August 1940 she left Geneva by car for Barcelona and Lisbon and sailed from Lisbon to New York in September 1940. From 1941 to 1945 she was employed in the ILO, Montreal, paying frequent visits to New York.

The publicity she received as the result of the Gouzenko disclosures has been described in detail in Dallin's book. Dallin's version of Rabinowitch's role in the Corby case, however, may not be completely accurate. He has written:

> Even after the Director authorized the funds, the mighty apparat could find no better way to transfer the money to Switzerland than through the amateurish Hermine. It was July 1944 before Hermine finally received $10,000, which she handed over to William Helbein. It was not until 3 November (approximately a year after the urgent request had first been made) that the Helbein's branch in Geneva paid 28,000 Swiss francs to the Soviet network.

As a result of the Corby case, the ILO asked Hermina to resign. She had to leave Canada. After failing in her attempt to get U.S. citizenship, she went to France, where in October 1947 she worked for the Office Nationale D'Immigration in Paris. In May 1948 she was working for the American Joint Distribution Committee, 118 Rue St. Dominique, Paris.

On 4 April 1950 the French services advised her orally that her papers were no longer valid in France, and on 7 September 1950 she and Norman Stein were deported from France. They went to Israel.

In 1959 it was learned that Rabinowitch was using the Hebrew name Hermina Ron and was then employed in the Beilinson Hospital, Petahtkva, Israel, and resided in the same town. Reportedly, she led an extremely secluded life in Israel but managed to travel frequently to Europe to visit friends.

Among her contacts have been:

Charles Becker, an employee of the Economic Section of ILO, Geneva. He is the "Confiseur" (alias Kuchenmann) of the Robinson case. Robinson sent "Confiseur's" address in Mendoza, received from Rachel Duebendorfer, to Moscow. Since 1940 he has been in Argentina.

Itshak Cysin, born 16 December 1885 in Russia. A businessman, he resides in Israel and has made frequent trips to France and the U.S. He is a cousin of Esther Glickman, 131 Boulevard Brune, Paris, the address given for Cysin in the address book of Jacob Albam.

Jacques Sherry, owner of the Compass Travel Bureau.

Marie Ginsberg, who attempted to contact Abramson and Rabinowitch in Paris in 1949.

George Rabinowitch, who lives in South America. He is a cousin of Hermina.

Otto Stein, Vice Director of ILO; probably a relative of Norman and Ronald Stein.

Leon Steinig, U.S. citizen since 1948. From 1926 to 1930 he was with ILO, Geneva. He, his wife, and Hermina were frequent guests at the home of Dr. Ludvik Vitold Rajchman, a suspected Soviet agent.

Lydia Zagorsky, a good friend of Hermina. She lived with the Boris Pregels in New York.

Leon Jouhaux, the veteran trade union leader and president of the Economic Council who intervened for Abramson, Rabinowitch, and Norman Stein.

Joseph Haden, former OSS employee and later interpreter at the UN. He worked at ILO, Geneva, and was suspected of being a Communist. He is known to have been a close friend of Abramson and Rabinowitch, particularly the latter, who was frequently a guest at his home in Montreal and, in fact, lived there for a while.

ALEXANDER RADO

was born in Ujpest, Hungary, on 5 November 1899. A Hungarian Jew, he was the oldest child of Gabor and Malvina Rado. His father was a wealthy merchant and prominent figure in Budapest. The son has used the aliases of Dr. Sandor Rado, Weber, Ignati, Koulicher, and Dr. Schmidt. His radio names in Rote Drei traffic were Dora, an obvious anagram, and Albert.

He has a brother, Francois Rado, who was probably an agent of the RU in Budapest during World War II and who now lives in Paris. He also has a sister, Elizabeth Klein, who now lives in Stockholm.

His wife, Helene Rado, nee Jansen, was an important Soviet agent in her own right, and her case will be discussed separately. They had two sons who now live in Paris. Helene died in Budapest on 1 September 1958 and Rado married Erzebet Bokor in 1959.

While a student, reportedly a brilliant one, Rado became a member of the Hungarian Communist Party in 1919 during the dictatorship of Bela Kun. Reportedly Rado got to know Rosa Luxemburg and Karl Liebknecht, founders of the German Communist movement, and through the influence of Hungarian and German Communists, he went to work in the Secretariat of the Comintern and became a friend of Zinoviev. While in Moscow, Rado met

Helene Jansen, who worked as a secretary for Lenin. The Rados were married in Moscow in 1923 or 1924.

Rado studied geography in Jena, Germany; and while he completed his studies, it seems he received financial support from the USSR.

The Rados made a trip to Moscow in 1931, presumably for briefing and orientation. Upon returning to Germany in 1932, Rado accepted employment as a geographer for the Almanac de Gotha in Berlin, a position he held until 1933. On 28 March 1933 Rado entered Vienna, after escaping the Nazi purge of Communists in Berlin. On 9 June 1933 he went to Paris with Kurt Rosenfeld and established the Agence Impress.

In 1933 Rado was a member of the Communist group headed by Willy Muenzenberg, and together with Dr. Kurt Rosenfeld, the late Prussian Minister of Justice, Rado established an anti-Nazi news agency under the name of Impress (Independent News Agency). He was in touch with professors at the Sorbonne and also worked in the Geographic Society of France.

In 1936, because Impress had not proved very successful, he moved with his wife to Geneva and established Geopress, a news agency which distributed maps and geographical data illustrative of political and, later, military events. This business was very successful. In Geneva the Rados lived at 113 Rue de Lausanne, and Geopress was housed at 2 Rue Gustave Maymier.

From 1936 to 1943 Rado directed a Soviet intelligence network in Switzerland. His activity during this period will be discussed hereinafter.

In August 1943 Rado was warned by Dobrick of the impending roundup by the Swiss police. From May to September 1943 Alexander Rado is reported to have received ten thousand dollars from Norman Stein, who is alleged to be a second cousin of Lazar Kaganovich.

With his wife Rado arrived in Paris in September 1944 after fleeing Switzerland to avoid arrest. Rado got in touch with the Soviet Military Mission as soon as it arrived in Paris. Rado claims that he approached the Soviet Mission with the intention of reporting, as known to him, the condition of the organization known as the Rote Drei in Switzerland. Rado was put in contact with Colonel fnu Novikov, to whom he told his story; it was suggested that he go to Moscow where a full inquiry could be made. He agreed to go, and accordingly on 6 January 1945 he embarked on a Russian plane in

Paris with false papers under the name of Ignati Koulicher. Also on board this plane were Alexander Foote and Leopold Trepper, both under assumed names.

During the plane trip Rado got into a conversation with his fellow passengers. As a result he decided to get off the plane in Cairo, where he tried to commit suicide.

Rado was ultimately persuaded or induced by the Russians to continue his journey and on 29 July 1945 finally left Egypt en route to Russia accompanied by a Russian official.

In support of claims that Rado had actually been sincere in his request for British aid in Cairo and that his turnover to the Soviets by the British and subsequent forced transfer to the USSR were against his wishes, there is considerable documentation available reflecting extensive efforts on his own part, and on the part of his wife and sister-in-law, to enlist help in his behalf. There is also evidence that Mrs. Woolley, nee Jansen, wrote to the British Embassy in Moscow, asking for intervention on behalf of Rado. Also available are copies of Rado's will and his own letter of 1945 from Cairo, addressed to Frederick Kuh, United Press correspondent in London, wherein he made the following appeal:

> Miss Martha Rajchman (now Mrs. Cranowski, aka Czarnowski), who collaborated with me as a cartographer, and her father, Ludwik Rajchman, would help me if they were informed of my destiny and whereabouts.

In his letter Rado provided Kuh with the Bethesda, Maryland, address of Mrs. Czarnowski.

In 1946 Rado was sentenced by a Soviet Court for treasonable activities against the state, and everyone thought he had been executed. In August 1955 Helene was thinking of marrying a Swiss named Alfonso Arnaud; but just before she could get married, she got a message that Alexander was still alive and that "Grandfather has confidence in him now and he will be sent West in six months." Shortly thereafter, Rado appeared as a professor in Budapest, and in March 1956 Helene joined her husband in Budapest.

As resident director of the Swiss network, Rado is said to have held the secret Red Army rank of Major General. He was awarded the Order of Lenin in 1943. The apparatus he directed—the Rote Drei—made significant contributions to the success of Soviet forces. The hostile attitude of Beria may have figured importantly in the handling of Rado's case. During World War II Beria sent his son to Switzerland to work in Rado's network, a move intended to keep young Beria from frontline army duty. The son, a playboy type, wasted network funds, jeopardized security, and did no useful work. Rado had him recalled to the USSR. Young Beria was eventually killed while serving in the Red Army, and for this his father blamed Rado.

A majority of the reports that deal with Rado since 1956 picture him as a devoted Communist who goes out of his way to deliver map-illustrated lectures on the spread of Communism, who teaches formal university courses in Marxism-Leninism, and who zealously monitors the political reliability of Hungary's younger generation of cartographers and geographers. He has been the prime mover behind the Bloc 1:2, 500,000 World Map program, and there are indications that he views this project as the crowning achievement of his professional life.

Although he is now in his seventies, he continues to travel all over the world in connection with his profession. He visited Mexico City in 1966.

Alexander Rado's case is unique because he is among the few living Soviet agents whose memoirs have appeared. They were published in Hungary in 1971 and in the Soviet Union in 1972.

In an article entitled "Code Dora," by V. Chernyshev, special *Komsomolskaya Pravda* correspondent, dateline Hungary, 20 February 1968, Rado is identified as the "war chief of the Soviet intelligence center in Switzerland, and presently a prominent Hungarian scientist."

The last paragraph of the article included this praise for Rado:

> The Rado group dealt much damage to the enemy . . . Soviet troops completed the job for which anti-fascist intelligence agents fought. Europe was liberated. Today, in recalling this, one must render what is due to all those who did their part for the victory over fascism.

HELENE RADO

(nee Jansen) was born 18 June 1901 in Frankfurt, Germany. As a young girl Helene Jansen worked as a secretary to Lenin. She met Alexander Rado in Moscow and married him there in 1923 or 1924. Alexander Rado was a prominent member of the CP of Hungary in 1919, before and during the Bela Kun regime. Helene and Alexander

Rado are the parents of two sons: Imre, born in 1925; and Alexander, Jr., born 1930. Both sons are French citizens.

From 1933 to 1936 Helene Rado and Hertha Tempi, nee Sommerfeld, worked for the Rassemblement de la Paix and for the Unitarian Service Committee in Paris. She had been appointed by Noel Field.

In 1936 Alexander Rado moved to Geneva, where he headed a Soviet intelligence network in Switzerland. Geopress was his cover for espionage work. Helene assisted him in this work.

In January 1945 Alexander Rado departed for Moscow, but Helene stayed in Paris and continued to work for the Unitarian Service Committee with Hertha Tempi. Helene also worked—at some point during her stay in Paris, and while Alexander Rado was in Russia—with Vladimir Pozner. They were close friends and had been since their days in Germany and with Impress in France. Pozner had worked with the maquis during the war and Helene, Alex, and Pozner were together in the same resistance group. Helene translated some books for Pozner. They also published together and translated some German and French literary works. In 1948 Elsa Bernaut, the former wife of Ignace Reiss, advised Paul Massing that she had gotten a letter from Helene, who reported that Alexander Rado had disappeared in Russia.

In 1949 Mrs. Rado lived with Johannes Adolph Holm in Garches, France. Later she planned to marry Alfonso Bruno Arnaud, a Swiss, but just before her intended marriage she was advised that Alexander was still alive. She joined her husband in Budapest in 1956, where she died of cancer during the summer of 1958.

ABRAHAM RAJCHMANN

(alias Adam Blanssi, alias Kartenmann, alias Arthur Roussel, alias Fabrikant, alias Max) was born 24 September 1902 in Dziurkow, Poland. He was married to Esteva Fiedler, and Malvina Gruber, nee Hofstadterova, was his mistress. Esteva Fiedler was born 28 September 1912 in Lodz; she died 6 June 1956 at Bordet Institute, Uccle.

An expert forger and engraver, Rajchmann had a long criminal record. He had contacts in the Brussels and Antwerp passport offices.

Rajchmann admitted working for the RIS since 1934 or 1935, and he had known Grossvogel since 1934. Grossvogel in 1939 introduced him to Trepper, who took him over as forger for the Belgian group. In the summer of 1940 Rajchmann fled to France, where he was interned; but in September or October 1940 he returned to Belgium on Trepper's instructions to work for the Sukolov group. Following Makarov's capture in December 1941, he was introduced by Isbutsky to Jeffremov, for whom he obtained false papers. From approximately the summer of 1941 Rajchmann had been in close contact with the Belgian police inspector Mathieu, who was working for the Germans as a penetration agent. Jeffremov was arrested in July 1942 while attending a meeting with Mathieu. The meeting had been arranged by Rajchmann. Rajchmann himself was arrested 2 September 1942. Willy Berg of the Gestapo stated that Rajchmann immediately offered to cooperate with the Germans and rendered "excellent services." Rajchmann was used with his mistress, Malvina Gruber, in penetrating and capturing further agents of the Brussels and Paris groups.

In January 1943 Rajchmann was provided by the Germans with false papers in the name of Arthur Roussel for residence in Brussels. Rajchmann was arrested 23 July 1946 by the Belgian authorities and sentenced by the Military Tribunal 18 February 1948 to twelve years in prison for espionage. He was released 7 June 1956.

According to a 1960 NATO Special Committee report, Rajchmann was living at 32 Avenue Jean Voiders, St. Gilles. His nationality was given as "stateless." He was said to be suffering from heart trouble. His occupations were listed as film operator, journalist, and tailor. He had not been reported to the Belgian authorities for further political activities.

JINDKICH HEINRICH "HENRI" RAUCH

was born 26 October 1891 in Vienna. He was a member of the Sukolov group in 1940-1941 and may have continued to collaborate with the survivors of the group under Jeffremov.

Rauch was married to Marie, nee Forster, formerly Friedrich, born 23 July 1894. He had a step-daughter, Waltraud Heger, nee Friedrich, and a step-son, Helmuth Friedrich. Rauch's mistress was Renee Schwing, an employee at Simexco.

From 1925 to 1939 Rauch lived with his wife and children in Aussig, Czechoslovakia, with a family named Singer. (Margarete Barcza, nee Singer, the mistress of Sukolov, reportedly told Gilles Perrault that Rauch had been a friend of her family in Czechoslovakia.) Rauch, a Czech Jew, left Aussig for Brno 8 August 1938 after the annexation of the Sudetenland. As the Czech representative for the Belgian firm "Poudrerie Royale de Wetteren," Brussels, he obtained a visa for Belgium 20 July 1939. In September 1939 he was joined by his wife and daughter at 259 Avenue Albert, Forest. Rauch at this time became active in giving assistance to Jewish refugees from Germany.

Rauch was arrested by the Belgian authorities 10 May 1940 but was immediately released. He left with his family for France to live in the Czech colony at Ayde. At the end of September 1940 he returned to Belgium, c/o Claesen, 108 Rue Rodenbeck, and began to work for Sukolov.

At the beginning of December 1940 Rauch's wife and daughter were repatriated to Prague.

In April 1941 Rauch became an employee of Simexco in Brussels. In July 1941, however, he became associated with Guillaume Hoorickx and Charles Daniels in a separate business at the same address as Simexco—192 Rue Royale, Brussels. This was probably done at Trepper's direction to improve the cover of the group.

Early in November 1941 Marie Rauch, the wife of Henri, was visited at Raudnitz, Czechoslovakia, by Sukolov, under cover as a hop merchant.

In late 1941 Rauch obtained false documents from de Remaeker for Danilov and other members of the network.

Pierre de Soete was an agent of Rauch and acted as a courier for him to France.

Rauch was arrested with Hoorickx at Rixensart 28 December 1942. In April 1943 he was transferred to Mauthausen, where he died 7 January 1944.

HEINRICH JOSEF REISER

was born circa 1895 and fought as a German soldier in World War I. He was a POW in England. He became an engineer in North Germany after World War I and at one time worked in South America.

Reiser was in line to replace Karl Giering of the Sonderkommando in Paris in 1943, but Pannwitz arrived to replace Giering. Reiser was then transferred to the Gestapo post in Karlsruhe during the summer of 1943.

Reiser and Piepe arrested Robinson. In the interrogation of Robinson, the Sonderkommando did not want the Abwehr to learn of the "Grand Jeu" and the real meaning of the Funkspiel.

According to Pannwitz, "Kriminalkommissar Reiser was apparently a typical Gestapo type, interested only in arrests and with little or no imagination." Under Pannwitz the work of the Sonderkommando entered a new phase and became more subtle, steadily developing the political side at the expense of the operational.

Reiser is probably the author of a study entitled *Rote Kapelle— Ruckblich Auf Aufbau Organisation Taetigkeit Bis Zum Zusammenbruch 1945.*

HENRI JOSEPH DE REYMAEKER

(alias Rik, alias Rik van Janneke) was an agent of Sukolov's network in Belgium, supplying information chiefly on the Flemish Nazi Party. In late 1941 he obtained false identity cards on behalf of Rauch and Hoorickx for Danilov and other members of the network. De Reymaeker was born 6 April 1907 at Tervueren, Belgium. In August 1942, after two earlier interrogations, he was arrested and imprisoned by the Germans. He was released about eighteen months later. In the summer of 1944 after the liberation of Brussels, de Reymaeker was arrested by the Belgian authorities but then released. In August 1945 he was rearrested. In August 1946 de Reymaeker was again at liberty, holding a post in the local administration at Schaerbeek, Brussels. In 1960, still a municipal employee, he resided at 9 Jezus-Eiklei, Tervueren.

HENRI ROBINSON

was probably a German Jew and identical with Henri Baumann, born 8 May 1897 in Frankfurt am Main, Germany. According to Gestapo files, Robinson (whose name is spelled Robinsohn by the Germans) was born in St. Gilles, Brussels. Among his aliases were Otto Wehrli, Albert Gottlieb Bucher, Alfred Merian, Harry Leon, Giacomo, Alfred Duyen, Harry Merian, Andre, Lucien, and Leo. His father was reportedly David Robinson, born at Vilna, Russia; and his mother was Ann Cerhannovsky, born in Warsaw.

He lived with Klara Schabbel during the 1920s and 1930s and had an illegitimate son by her, Victor Schabbel, born in 1921 in Berlin.

Reportedly he could speak fluent German, English, French, Italian, and Russian. He was about 5 feet 8 inches tall with a dark complexion, black greying hair, a high forehead, deep-set eyes, a big curved nose, full lips, wore glasses and pince-nez, dressed well, had a quiet appearance, and frequently carried an umbrella and briefcase under his arm.

During World War I Robinson studied in Geneva, and after the war he was associated with the German Communist Willy Muenzenberg and the Swiss Communist Jules Humbert-Droz in the International Communist Youth Movement. In 1923 he was in charge of the AM Apparat for military-political work in the Rhineland and chief of the youth movement in the Ruhr. He was a member of the KPD and in the 1920s made several trips to the USSR with Klara Schabbel. He was also head of the Communist Youth International in the Comintern.

In 1924 he was technical chief of the AM Apparat for Central and Eastern Europe, and in 1929 he was an assistant under the Russian General Muraille, responsible for the administration of the Soviet intelligence services in France. In 1930 he became chief of BB Apparat with the IV section of Red Army intelligence in France, did courier work and acted as liaison officer among the Russian espionage organizations in France, Switzerland, and the U.K.

In 1936 he worked with the Military Attache of the Russian Embassy in Paris, and in 1937 he took over Harry II's networks in England and France. In 1940 he was head of the AM Apparat for Western Europe, and until his arrest by the Germans on 21 December 1942 he directed an espionage network in France.

Not much older than Trepper, he was already the assistant to the chief of Soviet espionage in France three years before Trepper came to that country to learn his business with the "Phantomas." During the 1920s and 1930s Robinson had continued to improve and increase the number of his contacts in France, while during the same period Trepper had lived in Russia and Belgium. Nonetheless, it was Robinson who became a subordinate to Trepper, and not the reverse, when war broke out.

Trepper belonged to Red Army intelligence, which was then in the forefront, whereas Robinson was a member of the Comintern apparatus, which had lost prestige, was suspected by Stalin of deviationism, and was regarded by the young technocrats of the Center as inefficient and soft. In ordering Trepper to join forces with the Comintern group, the Director had warned that Robinson had been in ideological conflict with the Kremlin, that he was politically untrustworthy, and that he was suspected of being an informant of the Deuxieme Bureau. Therefore, the order was to use him with the greatest prudence.

General Sousloparov arranged a meeting between Trepper and Robinson on the eve of "Barbarossa," the German attack upon the USSR. (Actually "Operation Barbarossa" was the subject of Hitler's directive ordering the attack. The directive was issued on 18 December 1940.) Hiding his bitterness, Robinson obediently turned his

French and Belgian agents over to the disposition of the Rote Kapelle, giving the "Grand Chef" his roster of informants. Robinson had then many good contacts in French officialdom and sources in the German High Command. His agents furnished Trepper with detailed and precise information concerning the escape of General Giraud, the Dieppe raid, the results of the Allied bombardments on France, the preparations prior to the disembarkation of the Anglo-American forces in North Africa, and other information.

Robinson did not always obey Trepper. After Hersch Sokol and Johann Wenzel were arrested, Robinson refused to use his transmitter to relay messages.

Trepper, according to Perrault, assisted in the arrest of Robinson in Paris. Apparently they disliked each other intensely. Trepper thought that Robinson and the Comintern were amateurish and that Robinson was poorly documented. Robinson was arrested by Reiser and Piepe. In the interrogation of Robinson the Kommando did not want the Abwehr to know about the "Grand Jeu" and the real meaning behind the Funkspiel or radio playback.

Robinson's arrest probably resulted from information provided by Trepper. Robinson, like Trepper, quickly agreed to work for the Germans. But when Trepper escaped from the Sonderkommando in June 1943, Robinson was rearrested and transferred to Berlin. His ultimate fate is uncertain, but there are numerous reports that he is still alive.

According to Horst Kopkow of the RSHA, AMT IV A2, Robinson was held in France for six months, was then transferred to Germany for interrogation, and was finally brought before the same court martial as was Schulze-Boysen. He was then condemned and executed. Admiral Manfred Roeder, chief prosecutor at the Schulze-Boysen trials, believes, however, that Robinson was tried before a Feldgericht in June or July 1943, probably in Paris. According to Willy Berg of the Sonderkommando, Robinson, after his arrest, was kept in Paris in a villa on the Boulevard Victor Hugo, where he worked for the Sonderkommando, and it was through his efforts that other Rote Kapelle agents were drawn in by the Germans.

Robinson's mistress, Klara Schabbel, was reportedly executed with members of the Schulze-Boysen network in 1943. Their son, Victor Schabbel, also played a role in Soviet intelligence in Germany during World War II.

Although he worked under the name of Robinson in France, he also made use of three Swiss aliases: Alfred Merian, Otto Wehrli, and

Bucher. The last two identities belonged to real people. One of them, on instructions from Karl Hoffmaier, a Swiss Communist leader who was in touch with the espionage operation, applied for a passport that he did not need. That was the passport Robinson used.

According to the French IS, Robinson's chief agent was Maurice Aenis-Haenslin, a citizen of Gelterkinden, Switzerland, and director of the Schauwecker Unipektin Company in Paris. The French maintain that the agent triumvirate of Hans Schauwecker, Maurice Aenis-Haenslin, and Franz Schneider is still operating on behalf of the Soviets.

At the time of Robinson's arrest the Germans found in his possession four false passports and the famous "Robinson papers."

RUDOLF ROESSLER

(alias Lucy) was born in Kaufbeuren, Germany, of German parents on 22 November 1897. (The frequent references to his alleged Czech origin and links to Czech intelligence before World War II are false.) He was discharged from the German army without rank or decorations in 1918. He went to Augsberg, where his family was then living, and there he edited a newspaper for some ten years before becoming general secretary of the Buehnenvolksbund (Alliance of Stage People) in Berlin.

In 1933 he left Germany as a political refugee and moved to Lucerne, Switzerland, where he founded a publishing company, the Vita Nova Verlag, the following year.

In the summer of 1939 Dr. Xaver Schnieper invited Roessler to work for Swiss intelligence. Roessler accepted on the condition that the offer was official. Schnieper then turned to Captain Hans Hausamann, who headed an unofficial Swiss intelligence organization known as the Buero Ha. Hausamann had ties to Brigadier General Roger Masson, chief of the Swiss (military) intelligence service. Hausamann sent one of his people, Dr. Franz Wallner, to deal with Roessler. (Later, in July 1943, Hausamann broke off his contact with Wallner, whom he suspected of doubling for an unidentified service.)

At the beginning of 1942 Roessler complained to a Swiss captain of the general staff, Dr. Bernhard Mayr von Baldegg, that the work for Hausamann was not very interesting. Von Baldegg was the deputy to Captain Max Waibel, chief of Noehrichtenstelle I, who also reported to Masson. Both officers paid him. Noehrichtenstelle I gave him two hundred fifty to four hundred francs a month. The Buero Ha gave him one thousand a month initially and two thousand later. The

RU also paid him, initially seven hundred a month but later three thousand, supplied by Rachel Duebendorfer via Christian Schneider. These facts and the radio traffic show that Roessler was mercenary.

A number of published accounts claim that Roessler was among the Soviet agents who warned Moscow about the German invasion of the USSR, Operation Barbarossa, before its launching on 22 June 1941. Both the Rote Drei traffic and such informed sources as Hans Rudolf Kurz (Nachrichenzentrum Schweiz, Huber and Co., Frauenfeld, 1972) have shown, however, that Roessler's first contact with the Rote Drei network was made in the late summer or early fall (probably September) of 1942, more than a year after the invasion.

The Czechoslovakian government-in-exile had in Switzerland a representative named Karel Sedlacek (alias Simpson) aka "Uncle Tom," who received information from Hausamann and sent it by radio to the London Czechs. Sedlacek lived in St. Gallen in the home of Hausamann's mother-in-law. He and Roessler were cronies, and it appears that they exchanged information. Two years after the war ended, Sedlacek reactivated Roessler as a spy, this time for the Czech intelligence service. The Swiss arrested Roessler and his partner in the undertaking, Xaver Schnieper, at the beginning of March 1953, because this time Roessler had been operating without the knowledge of the Swiss authorities. Roessler drew a sentence of one year.

Roessler's value to the Rote Drei and the Center in Moscow derived entirely from his extraordinary sources in Germany. (In this context the word *his* is misleading. It seems probable that the German sources gave their information to the Swiss General Staff, which in turn passed to Roessler that information which the Swiss wanted to relay to the Soviets.) The key German sources were Werther, Teddy, Anna, and Olga. They have never been identified definitively The Swiss police—almost certainly unaware of the relationship between Swiss intelligence and Roessler—arrested him soon after the arrest of Eduard Hamel in October 1943. The reason was that Hamel had had in his flat information supplied Roessler by the Swiss General Staff. Roessler was arrested on 2 June 1944, along with Duebendorfer, but was released three months later. He was tried again on 23 October 1945 on charges of espionage but was acquitted. He died on 17 December 1958.

ROSENBERG
is the name of a person who supplied false documents to members of the Rote Kapelle in Belgium. In 1938 Malvina Gruber visited Ant-

werp to get false passports from Rosenberg for Rajchmann. Rajchmann, in his statement to the Belgian authorities, indicated that in February 1941 he received on several occasions from a person named Rosenberg in Antwerp, on behalf of Makarov, blank identity cards with seals attached, certificates of good conduct, etc. Rosenberg is possibly identical with Victor Rosenberg, the brother of Lisa Zarubin (alias Helen Zubilin), a known Soviet agent. Victor Rosenberg worked for Ignace Reiss in a photo laboratory used by the Soviets. He has been described as a "photographic expert."

HENRI MARCEL AUGUSTIN DE RYCK or RIJCK
became a shareholder in Simexco in 1941. He was born 7 June 1910 at St. Gilles and by profession was an editor/publisher. In mid-1942 de Ryck worked in Germany for six months. At the end of 1942, on his return to Belgium, he was questioned by the Germans about his part in Simexco and was arrested. De Ryck reportedly died in the Mauthausen concentration camp.

AENNE SAEFKOW
(nee Thiebes), widow of Anton Saefkow, was born 12 October 1902 in Duesseldorf. She was formerly the secretary of Ernst Thaelmann and Heinz Neumann, former German Politburo member. She was in Moscow in 1931 and was a prewar member of the KPD. She became Deputy Mayor of Berlin/Pankow in October 1946 and was elected a representative to the Volkskammer in October 1950. She was reported in *Neues Deutschland* of 11 April 1953 as chairman of the Prenzlauer Berg Council. In July 1954 she attended the World Congress of Mothers held in Lausanne, Switzerland.

In 1946 Aenne Saefkow was associated with Professor Robert Havemann and gave radio talks on the European Union. Professor Havemann in 1947 occupied a comfortable apartment in the Kaiser Wilhelm Institut Building in the U.S. sector of Berlin. Until 1933 he was a research assistant at the Kaiser Wilhelm Institut, but at that time, because the directors under whom he had worked were chiefly Jews who were forced to leave the Institut, he too was required to sever his connections.

ANTON "KURT" SAEFKOW
was born 22 July 1902 in Germany. He had once been a colleague of Ernst Wollweber and engaged in illegal activities after the dissolution of the Communist Party in 1933.

In his book *Out of the Night,* Jan Valtin (alias Richard Krebs) refers to Anton Saefkow as "Tonio." According to Krebs, Saefkow was a member of the Spitzengruppe (leadership) of the underground organization of the party in Fuhlsbuettel. Krebs first met Saefkow in Fuhlsbuettel but knows he had been the illegal Bezirksleiter of the KPD ZX and had been sent to Hamburg to organize the illegal party. When Saefkow was arrested, he pleaded guilty immediately, knowing that under the existing law he could not get more than three years. In 1936 Saefkow started the trend among Communists serving prison terms to write letters to the Gestapo asserting their change of heart; Saefkow himself wrote the first such letter, which was shown to Krebs by Paul Krauss one day during interrogation. It stated that Saefkow had broken with the Communist Party and would have nothing more to do with such work. At about this same time Herta Jentsch mentioned that Saefkow's wife had been sent to Moscow for training at the Lenin School (three-year course). It had been Saefkow's wife who brought in the instructions from the outside to write the letter to Krauss. She passed it to him from her mouth during a kiss, just before she left Germany.

The B.Z. Am Abend, No. 213 issue of 12 September 1959, published the recollections of Anton Saefkow and his comrades, entitled "Unconquered by Death" (Vom Tode unbesiegt) and featuring a photo of Aenne and Anton Saefkow taken in August 1941.

Saefkow was executed by the Gestapo in 1944.

GEORGETTE SAVIN

(nee Dubois, alias Patricia Delage, alias Anne Marie Rendiere) was born 21 November 1918 at La Boule (L.I.). A French national, she was married to Henri Savin, a jeweler at Lyons. She was Mussig's mistress, "Pat," and worked with him in the black market, dealing in gold traffic. She was also involved with Mussig in his collaboration with the Sonderkommando in its infiltration of the Mithridate network. It was Georgette who assisted Moses Gatewood in crossing the frontier into Spain.

RUDOLF VON SCHELIHA,

a German national, was born 31 May 1897 in Tessel bei Oels. A cavalry officer, he received training as a diplomat and had a long career with the German Foreign Office, including posts as vice consul in Kattowitz, Counselor to the German Embassy in Warsaw, and member of the German Foreign Office in Berlin from 1939 to 1942.

As early as 1934 von Scheliha was recruited into a Soviet espionage network. Until his recall to Berlin in September 1939, he provided intelligence obtained through his position in the German Embassy in Warsaw. In Berlin he was posted to the Information Section of the Foreign Office. He continued to furnish intelligence through a cutout to the Soviet Commercial Attache until the withdrawal of Soviet representation in June 1941.

While in the Foreign Office von Scheliha joined up with Ilse Stoebe, who was Rudolf Herrnstadt's mistress, and furnished intelligence in return for money, some of which was deposited in a Swiss bank for safekeeping.

He was arrested on 29 October 1942, shortly after Ilse Stoebe, and executed with her on 22 December 1942.

As early as 1952 extensive investigation of von Scheliha's sister, Renata Johanna von Scheliha, was carried out in connection with her application for a position as librarian in the Office of the Surgeon General, Department of the Army. When interviewed on 26 September 1950 in Cleveland, Ohio, Miss von Scheliha stated that the ten thousand dollars credited to her bank account at the Guaranty Trust Company in New York in 1939 was inherited by Rudolf and his wife from Wilhelm von Medinger, father of Rudolf's wife.

Another source stated, however, that Rudolf's wife, Mary Louise von Scheliha, and her brother, Dr. Wilhelm von Medinger, said during March of 1952 that they knew of no inheritance left by their father to Rudolf or to Rudolf and his wife. Both professed little knowledge of Rudolf's financial affairs, and von Medinger stated that all the family properties and wealth in Czechoslovakia had been lost or confiscated.

Renata von Scheliha, born 16 August 1901 in Germany, was re-interviewed on 16 May 1952 at her place of employment, the Army Medical Library, Cleveland, Ohio. She was asked to furnish specific details of her knowledge concerning the source of the ten thousand dollars acquired by Rudolf and deposited to her bank account. She advised that she had assumed that her brother had inherited this money because it would have been impossible for him to accumulate it from his salary in the German diplomatic service. She denied knowledge of her brother's espionage activities and stated that the ten thousand dollars was credited to her account by her brother.

There is a possible connection between the von Scheliha and Rudolf Roessler cases through the person of Renata von Scheliha, who had family connections among the German generals. She resided in Basle before coming to the United States during the summer of 1948. During the years 1938 to 1940 the account of Rudolf von Scheliha with the bank of Julius Baer and Company, Zurich, showed various transfers of dollar amounts, including some under the name of Renata von Scheliha through the Guaranty Trust Company of New York. At that time Rudolf von Scheliha was a counselor at the German Embassy in Warsaw.

Isidor Koppelmann, a wartime agent of the Polish IS who had a small banking firm in Basle (IKAP, Internationale Kapital-Anlagen Gesellschaft, Rittergasse 12, Basle) rendered great service to the Polish IS by obtaining high class military information from Germany. There seems to be a possibility that Renata von Scheliha, and perhaps Koppelmann, worked through Roessler for the Russian IS.

Rudolf von Scheliha's brother, Ernst Guenther, born 16 December 1909 at Schlawe, a former captain and now lawyer, has been living since March 1950 in East Berlin. Ernst was probably engaged in the agent activity of his brother; and his move from West Berlin to the area of party favorites, Hohenschoenhausen, in which the MGB has numerous support points and hideouts as well as special prisons, was regarded as suspicious by West German intelligence (1955).

CHRISTIAN SCHNEIDER

("Taylor") was born 15 October 1896 in Schierstein, Germany. According to Foote, he was a German Jew by origin. His parents, Christian Schneider and Anna Schmidt, reportedly came from Zurich. His whereabouts during the 1930s are uncertain.

For a number of years Schneider, a Swiss citizen, was employed as a translator for the ILO in Geneva. His address was Rue Carteret, and he also resided on Rue des Alpes, Geneva (1938-1940).

Rudolph Roessler ("Lucy") sought out Taylor because he believed that through Taylor he could find a means to get information to Moscow. Intelligence from Germany went to the Swiss, who passed it to Lucy for transmittal to the RIS.

In a message dated 6 October 1943 from Moscow to the Swiss group, the Director advised Taylor that he could probably be useful after the war, and Moscow would guarantee his future as long as he lived, through any bank in Europe or the USA. According to Foote, Schneider gave up his job with ILO on the promise of a salary for life from Moscow.

Schneider was arrested with Rachel Duebendorfer and imprisoned during the summer of 1944 by the Swiss authorities because of his activities in the Rote Drei case. It is reported that he served only one month in jail for his conviction on security and espionage charges. According to British sources, after his arrest by the Swiss he is said to have talked.

The Rado papers found at Hamel's flat reflected that Taylor was paid a salary by Rado from June 1942 to September 1943.

According to the Sauter papers, Taylor was a Soviet agent before the war and highly valued in Moscow, but after his arrest by the Swiss he fell into disfavor and was probably rejected for any future intelligence assignment.

In 1948 Schneider was employed by UNESCO in Paris, but his whereabouts or activities since then are unknown.

FRANZ SCHNEIDER

(alias Niggi) was in contact with Henri Robinson in 1929 and was probably recruited for Red Army intelligence by Robinson through Konstantin Jeffremov in Brussels in 1936. He was probably less important than his wife, Germaine, nee Clais, who was recruited at the same time. Franz Schneider was probably used solely as a courier, particularly to Switzerland. He is probably identical with "Chimor," Jeffremov's courier to Switzerland.

Franz Schneider was born 19 February 1900 in Basle and was a Swiss citizen. In June 1920 he moved to Belgium from Switzerland. He was probably already a member of the Swiss Communist Party. In 1922 he was employed as a commercial traveler for the Societe Natural, Le Contre et Cie., Antwerp. In January 1925 he married Germaine and with her travelled to Switzerland, returning to Brussels that same year. They undertook to provide services for the Comintern, for which they were recruited by "Leon," probably Leon Nicole. From 1925 to 1929 they were active in the Belgian Communist Party and the Comintern and provided safehouses for travelers. In February 1929 Schneider was expelled from Belgium because of his political activities, but he apparently remained in Belgium illegally. In June 1929 he left for Zurich and returned to Belgium in June 1930. In March 1931 the expulsion order was rescinded, and he was allowed to stay in Belgium.

The Schneiders were recruited for Soviet intelligence in 1936. In 1938 Franz Schneider visited Henri Robinson's mistress, Klara Schabbel, in Berlin. He may also have had contacts with the Schulze-Boysen group before and during the war. In August 1939 Schneider, on an intelligence mission for Henri Robinson, visited the United

Kingdom under cover as a commercial traveler for Lever Brothers. Schneider's contact in London was one "Adolf."

Jeffremov began to organize his network in Belgium in 1939, and the Schneiders agreed to work under his direction. At about this time Herman Wenzel began to live in the Schneider home and probably served as their chief employer under Jeffremov.

In the spring of 1942 Schneider delivered a W/T set from Germaine to Augustin Sesee.

After Wenzel's arrest in July 1942, Schneider received a letter from Germaine admitting infidelity with Wenzel; this was probably a prearranged story designed to establish his innocence and to underplay her responsibilities in the network. Schneider remained in Belgium after Germaine fled to France, and in July 1942 he asked his friend, Ernest Bomerson, to hide Jeffremov in his house at 25 Rue Alfred Orban, Forest. Jeffremov was arrested before he could move to the Bomerson house.

Schneider was interrogated but not arrested after the capture of Jeffremov. He somehow was able to find out that Jeffremov had agreed to work with the Germans, and he sent a warning to Trepper. Nonetheless, Schneider attended a meeting arranged by Jeffremov in November 1942 and was arrested. In April 1943 he was transferred to Germany. He was released from Brandenburg Prison by the Russians in May 1945. He was suffering from lung trouble and was in poor general health. Lever Brothers, his former employer, continued to pay him a salary while he convalesced. Schneider joined his wife in Switzerland in October 1945 and stayed with her until her death in November 1945. He moved back to Belgium, and in the spring of 1947 he lived with Elizabeth Depelsenaire at Anderlecht, Belgium. In June 1947 Schneider left Belgium to join his mistress, Depelsenaire, in Neuchatel, Switzerland. Schneider and Depelsenaire were married 2 August 1947. In October 1948 Schneider was living in Zurich. He was reportedly bitter about his experiences with the Russians, blaming them for Germaine's death. In 1948 Schneider was in contact with Maurice Aenis-Hanslin, a former member of the Rote Kapelle in France and Switzerland.

According to a 1960 report, Schneider and his second wife were separated.

GERMAINE SCHNEIDER

(nee Clais, alias Pauline, alias Odette, alias Papillon, alias Schmetterling) was born in Anderlecht, Brussels, 17 March 1903. In 1925 she married Franz Schneider, and they paid a short honeymoon visit to Switzerland. It was there probably that they were first approached by the Soviet Intelligence Service, for whom they agreed to work.

From 1925 to 1929 Mr. and Mrs. Schneider took part in Belgian Communist Party affairs. They were also concerned in clandestine work for the Comintern, providing a safehouse for travelers.

From 1929 to 1936 they abstained from open political activity, but probably in that year they were approached by an agent of the RIS and were recruited for courier work in the Rote Kapelle network.

From 1936 to 1939 Germaine Schneider was known to have travelled as a courier to France, Holland, Switzerland, the United Kingdom, Germany, and possibly Bulgaria. From 1939 to 1942 she was active for the Rote Kapelle in the Low Countries. She was Henri Robinson's link to the United Kingdom. In 1939 she became associated with Johannes Wenzel, possibly as his mistress, and was trained by him in W/T.

Germaine Schneider was the head of a sub-group in the Jeffremov network which included her sisters, Renee Blumsack, and Josephine Verhimst; Renee's husband, Joseph Blumsack; Josephine's lover, Jean Janssens; and Yvonne Poelmans.

Germaine Schneider was present at a meeting of Trepper and Jeffremov in her house in Brussels in May 1942, at which time Jeffremov was placed in charge of the remainder of Trepper's and Sukolov's networks in the Low Countries. She then became a courier between Jeffremov's organization and Trepper's network in Paris. After Wenzel's arrest, she was able to convince the Germans that she was not involved in intelligence activities. They released her, and she immediately fled to France to give warning to Trepper. She worked for Trepper in Paris during the summer of 1942, making occasional trips back to Belgium. On one of these trips she learned, probably from Rajchmann, that Jeffremov was working with the Germans. In late August 1942 Grossvogel asked Rajchmann to procure false identity papers for her, but Rajchmann was arrested before delivery could be made. In the fall of 1942 Trepper sent Germaine to join the Springer network in Lyons. She was arrested while working for this group in November or December 1942. She was sent to a concentration camp, from which she was liberated by the Russians in May 1945.

In October 1945 Germaine Schneider went to Zurich, where she was joined by her husband. She died of cancer in Zurich 12 November 1945.

KURT SCHULZE

(alias Berg) was born 28 December 1894. He was a member of the KPD at the end of the 1920s. A postal employee, he had a country home in Berlin-Gruenau. He had been a radio operator in the German navy.

Between 1929 and 1931 Schulze worked for the AM Apparat in Brandenburg. Finally he was recruited by the illegal Soviet apparatus "Klara," sent to the USSR, and there attached to the radio network of that apparatus. His liaison man in the Soviet commercial setup was Maschkewitsch, one of the bosses of the Klara-Apparat.

When he started to work for the Soviets, Schulze officially quit the KPD. Later he was put in touch with the Rote Kapelle organization and worked for it as an operator and trainer of future operators, including Hans Coppi.

Schulze's wife, Martha, also belonged to the same circles. She was sentenced at a court martial in January 1943 to five years in prison.

Schulze was executed on 22 December 1942.

HARRO SCHULZE-BOYSEN

was born 2 September 1909 in Kiel, Germany, and was married to Libertas Schulze-Boysen, nee Haas-Heye, born 20 November 1913. She was the granddaughter of Princess Eulenberg, and her parents owned an estate at Giebenburg where important Nazis were frequent visitors. He was the grand-nephew of Admiral von Tirpitz and the nephew of "Grande Dame" von Hassell, who was the wife of Ulrich von Hassell, German Ambassador to Rome, born 12 November 1881, executed February 1945.

By birth and destiny Schulze-Boysen seemed certain to have a grand career in the Air Ministry. He had a wide circle of important contacts who were ideal covers for secret work.

He spoke Swedish, English, French, and German, and in 1939 he learned Russian. He had been a Communist since 1933. As a member of the *Jungdeutsche Orden,* he was arrested in 1933, but his family succeeded in procuring his release. In pre-war days Herman Goering, who was a friend of the family, used to visit the house of Harro's parents-in-law; hence his introduction into the Luftwaffe. At the Air Ministry he was in charge of counterintelligence.

After his recruitment as a Soviet agent, he was told by Alexander Erdberg to form an espionage network. Shortly before Erdberg left Berlin in May or June 1941, he supplied Harnack and Schulze-

Boysen with W/T sets for the groups they were to run. Neither W/T set worked, and Harro continued to send his intelligence to Belgium via courier.

Harro was able to recruit his student, Horst Heilmann, a crypto-grapher in the Luftnachrichtentgruppe in Berlin, who passed Abwehr messages to Schulze-Boysen. Heilmann carried on a love affair with Mrs. Schulze-Boysen and told her of the cracking of the code of the radio messages pertaining to the Rote Kapelle members. Also belonging to the ring were a radio operator, Hans Coppi, and Countess Erika von Brockdorf, who placed her apartment for radio purposes at the disposal of Coppi, with whom she was carrying on a love affair.

In 1938 Schulze-Boysen went to Switzerland, where he visited Wolfgang Langhoff, a prominent Communist in the Freies Deutsch-land movement. In 1941 he was appointed to the liaison staff of the Luftwaffe. He was arrested on 30 August 1942, and he and his wife Libertas, who had participated in his clandestine work, were executed on 22 December 1942 at Berlin-Plotzensee prison.

OTTO SCHUMACHER,
(alias Roger) was born 12 November 1909 in Speyer am Rhein, Ger-many. He fought for the Republicans during the Spanish Civil War. He later went to Belgium where he was a member of the Interna-tional Bureau. He spoke fluent German, French, and Spanish. According to one source Schumacher was a mechanic who had lived in Worms. According to another source he was a book printer.

Schumacher was a member of the Jeffremov group in Belgium in 1942 and had probably performed services for Sukolov as well. Wenzel was living at Schumacher's house in Laeken when he was arrested on 30 June 1942. Schumacher escaped to France and made contact with Hillel Katz, who may have been the original recruiter of Schumacher. Schumacher was sent to Lyons to work under Isidore Springer. He was a W/T technician and was able to construct and repair transmitters for the network.

Following the arrest of Trepper and the latter's denunciation of the Lyons group, Schumacher fled to Paris with his mistress, Helene Humbert-Laroche. They were captured there early in 1943. Schu-macher was subsequently executed.

RENEE SCHWING
was an employee of Simexco and the mistress of Henri Rauch. She

was arrested in the general roundup of Simexco employees in November 1942 and deported to Germany. In May 1945 she was repatriated to Belgium.

HENRI MARIE SIDOINE GHISLAIN SEGHERS
was one of the original shareholders of Simexco when it was officially organized in March 1941. He had been a friend of Sukolov and Margarete Barcza and was approached by them to invest in Sukolov's new firm.

Seghers was born 23 March 1914 in Brussels and was employed by the Belgian Civil Service. He was arrested at the end of 1942 in Antwerp and deported to Germany. In May 1945 he was repatriated to Belgium. Seghers was probably not involved in the intelligence activities of the Sukolov network and may even not have known that they were taking place.

Perrault writes that Seghers occupied the apartment across the hall from Margarete Barcza on the Avenue Emile de Beco in Brussels and was a frequent bridge partner of hers.

AUGUSTIN SESEE,
(alias Jules, alias Ostender, alias Musikant) was a W/T operator for Trepper's Belgian network. He was subordinated to, and probably recruited by, Makarov, with whom he worked at Ostende in 1939 and 1940. Sesee was stationed at Ostende almost certainly for the purpose of establishing a W/T service to London, which may have been put into operation for the receipt and relay to Moscow of information collected by the agents of the Rote Kapelle.

Sesee was a native of Antwerp and served in the Belgian Mercantile Marine as a radio mechanic. According to Perrault, Sesee was employed in Ostende as a police inspector. It is probable that Sesee is identical with Feys, who, according to Piepe, was a radio operator in Ostende for the network.

When Makarov transferred to Brussels in the summer of 1940, Sesee kept a reserve set and was instructed to become active in the event of Makarov's capture. Sesee may eventually have gone to Brussels, where he assisted Makarov and Danilov in the operation of the transmitter at 101, Rue de Attrebates.

After Makarov's arrest in December 1941, Sesee went into hiding. When Jeffremov took charge of the network in May 1942, however, he was instructed to commence transmissions with his own reserve set. It is unlikely that his line ever came into operation. During the period Wenzel sent Sesee a new transmitter by Franz Schneider.

Sesee was arrested in his lodgings at Brussels in August 1942, as a result of Maurice Peper's betrayal. He was imprisoned at St. Gilles, but in April 1943 he was deported to Germany, where he was executed.

PIERRE JEAN DE SOETE

was an agent and courier to France for Henri Rauch on Simexco business, and he may have performed other duties for the Sukolov network. De Soete was an old friend of Hoorickx, by whom he was recruited for Rauch. He was born 30 July 1886 at Molenbeek St. Jean, Belgium. De Soete was the widower of Rosalie, nee Hofmanns, and was divorced from Gabrielle, nee Coenen. In 1941 and 1942 he was living with Marie-Therese Schippers in Brussels. De Soete was a sculptor, and in 1941 or 1942 he visited Vichy to execute a bust of Petain. He subsequently made a bust of General Falkenhausen.

HERSOG SOKOL,

(alias Hersz, alias Russko) was born 25 October 1908 in Bychitok, Poland. He was a medical doctor. He held Polish Passport No. 36399, issued in Berlin in September 1924. He was the husband of Mariam Sokol, with whom he had been active as a Communist in Belgium.

From 1924 to 1931 he travelled in Belgium, France, England, and Switzerland, at one stage on behalf of a South African firm. In 1938 he and his wife Mariam were expelled from Belgium. In 1939 he was interned by the French as a Communist. In 1940 he was recruited by Trepper and trained by Grossvogel as a W/T operator. He later handled the transmissions of the Grossvogel group. In 1942 he was in touch with Claude Spaak, with whom he left money and identity papers. From April to June 1942 he acted as Trepper's only W/T link to Moscow. He was arrested in Paris 9 June 1942 and reportedly died in prison as a result of torture.

JACOB OR JACQUES SOKOL

was born 25 May 1911 in Bialyatok, Poland. He is the brother of Hersog Sokol. He was an architect and an active member of the Belgian Communist Party until his expulsion in 1938. He was arrested by the Germans in about the autumn of 1942. His address was 72 Rue de l'Ermitage, Brussels.

Jacob Sokol was suspected by the Germans of implication in Trepper's espionage activities in France.

In 1960 Sokol and his wife, Kira, nee Soloviegg, alias Kira de Soene, alias Monique, born 26 October 1911 in St. Petersburg, were living at 65, Rue de la Langue Haie, Brussels. They previously lived at 28, Rue de l'Ermitage, Ixelles, which is known to have been a special hideout of the BCP.

The Belgian authorities in 1958 were informed that Madame Sokol was working in the secretariat of the Belgium-China Association as assistant to Madame Deguent, nee Marthe Huysmans.

MARIAM SOKOL,

nee Rachlin (alias Madeleine) was born either 17 March 1908 or 6 October 1909 in Bychitok, Poland. She had a Ph.D. and was the wife of Hersog Sokol. She held Polish Passport No. 950/1557 issued in July 1929 and Polish Passport No. 1049/34 issued in Brussels on 23 July 1934. She arrived in Belgium in 1929, married Sokol in 1934, and was active with him as a Communist in Belgium. She was in touch with Madame Spaak, whom she met in connection with her political activities. She was recruited by Trepper and trained by Grossvogel as a W/T operator. She was arrested in Paris on 9 June 1942 and later executed in Belgium.

In 1939 Andre Labarthe, a suspected Soviet agent in France, made a payment of 10,000 French francs to a woman named Sokol at 27 Rue Chevert, Paris (7), France. This address was the residence of Hersog Sokol and his wife, Mariam Sokol.

JACQUES SOUSTELLE

was born 3 February 1912 in Montpellier, France, son of Jean Soustelle and Germaine, nee Blatiere. He is married to Georgette, nee Fagot, born 2 May 1909. A noted anthropologist of left-wing sympathies, he is a friend and associate of Marcel Prenant.

In the 1920s he accompanied a French mission of scientists to Mexico, and in 1927 he was appointed assistant head of the Paris Anthropological Museum. In May 1942 he arrived in London from Mexico and joined De Gaulle. In 1943 he was appointed head of intelligence on De Gaulle's staff, and in March 1945 he was French Minister of Information.

JEAN CLAUDE SPAAK

was born 22 October 1904 in Bruxelles-St. Gilles, Belgium. A noted author (*La Rose des Vents*), he was a close friend of Trepper and Georgie de Winter and a leading member of a resistance group in France.

In 1943 the Gestapo tried to arrest Jean Claude Spaak, but he escaped capture. His first wife, Suzanne Lorge, was arrested in Belgium and extradited to France. She was imprisoned at Fresnes and later executed.

After Trepper escaped from his Nazi captors, he recontacted Jean Claude Spaak in 1944 and left 150,000 francs with Spaak for Georgie de Winter, who was Trepper's mistress. While Jean Claude was hiding from the Gestapo, he stayed in the Isere Department with his brother Charles' mistress, Alice Perier.

Jean Claude Spaak's second wife is Ruth Peters, born 20 December 1903 in Toronto, Canada. They were married 30 January 1946 in Paris. Ruth Peters was a cousin of Antonia Lyon-Smith, who was also in contact with several members of the Rote Kapelle network.

During the occupation Trepper was anxious to protect his mistress from the Nazis; so in this connection he contacted Antonia Lyon-Smith, who had previously befriended Jean Claude Spaak. Miss Lyon-Smith gave Trepper a letter of recommendation on behalf of Georgie de Winter, and the latter was supposed to go to a safehouse in the Isere Department in St. Pierre de Chartreuse, where a doctor named de Joncher would watch over Georgie. But en route to see Dr. de Joncher, Georgie was picked up by the Gestapo, who searched her and found Miss Lyon-Smith's letter. Georgie was deported and spent the rest of the war in a concentration camp; Miss Lyon-Smith was arrested at Bourg-la-Reine on 21 October 1943.

Charles Spaak, the brother of Jean Claude Spaak, also played a role in the Rote Kapelle, but the significance of his involvement has not been determined.

Paul Henri Spaak, the other brother of Jean Claude Spaak, has long been a member of the Bilderberg Group, an international organization presided over by His Royal Highness, Prince Bernard of the Netherlands. A source believed reliable advised that the KGB had an important contact in Paris with access to files of the NATO Political and Military Committees. This KGB contact produced photographs of NATO documents and reportedly had access to Paul Henri Spaak.

JEAN JACQUES SPIESS
was born 15 September 1916 in Veuhausen. Educated in Paris, he was employed in the Dreyfuss Bank before the war. In September 1939 Spiess went to Switzerland, and in 1943 he became a representative of a firm of Zurich machine brokers.

Spiess, a Foote associate with Communist sympathies, is thought to be "Roger" in the Rote Drei traffic and was to have been trained by Puenter as a W/T operator. The transmitter was to have been concealed in the house of "Roger's" father.

ISIDORE SPRINGER

(alias Romeo, alias Verlaine, alias Walter van Vliet, alias Fred, alias Sabor) was a Belgian national, born 23 July 1912 in Antwerp. His father was Simon Springer, and Irma Kuenlintger was his mother. Rita Arnould, nee Bloch, was his mistress. She was also a Soviet agent. Charlotte or Flora van Vliet, nee Velarts, was known as his wife, but they were not married. She was associated with Springer, working first for Sukolov in Brussels in 1941 and later as a member of Springer's group in Lyons in 1942.

According to one source Springer was by origin a Polish Jew and had been trained in Moscow to carry out Soviet intelligence activities. He was at first sent to Palestine, where he worked with Trepper, Grossvogel, and Joseph Katz. He was later sent to Belgium to work with the Sukolov group.

Springer resided in Paris in 1930-1931, and according to Willy Berg he worked for Trepper in Paris before the outbreak of war, acting as liaison with the Soviet Embassy in Trepper's absence. He probably also spent some time in Germany and belonged to the German Communist Party. By 1940 he had moved to Belgium as an active member of the Sukolov group; here he was probably mainly concerned with recruitment and was a courier between Sukolov in Brussels and Trepper in Paris. Springer was a diamond merchant in Brussels in 1940 and 1941. After Makarov's arrest in December 1941, he fled to Paris with Sukolov and was posted to Lyons, where he established an intelligence group and attempted, but failed, to achieve an independent W/T link with Moscow. His group of agents included his mistress, Flora van Vliet, Germaine Schneider, Otto Schumacher, Joseph Katz, and Jacques Blumsack.

The detection and liquidation of the Lyons group resulted from Trepper's betrayal of certain addresses and a rendezvous which he made with Springer under German orders. Springer was captured 16 December 1942 and reportedly executed 27 December 1942 in Paris.

Another source, probably incorrect, indicates that Springer was able to escape to the United Kingdom with Rita Bloch and was still living there in 1954.

ANNA STARITSKY

was born 27 December 1907 in Poltawa, Russia. She was a Russian national but resided in Belgium after 1932. Anna Staritsky was the mistress of Guillaume Hoorickx and was introduced by him to Makarov in the summer of 1941. She was probably used by Makarov as a courier during the latter part of 1941. She was arrested 1 January 1942 by the Abwehr in Brussels, following the arrest of Makarov, but was subsequently released.

Staritsky was by profession a draftswoman or designer. After the war, probably about 1947, she married Hoorickx, and they are now (1969) living together at 150 Avenue Emile Zola, Paris. In 1960 they also owned a flat at 14 Rue Cafarelli, Nice, where they often went to stay because of Hoorickx' bad health. They reportedly make periodic trips to Brussels, where they have often visited Nikita Koussoff, a known anti-Communist.

ILSE STOEBE

(alias Alte) was born 17 May 1911. Her last residence was Berlin, Saalestrasse 36.

Stoebe was the mistress of Rudolf Herrnstadt. She was a coworker of von Scheliha and was also associated with Schulze-Boysen and Harnack.

Ilse Stoebe was executed on 22 December 1942.

VICTOR SUKOLOV

(alias Vincente Sierra, alias Kent, alias Fritz, alias Arthus Barcza, alias Simon Urwith, alias Manolo, alias Dupuis, alias Lebrun) was probably born in Leningrad 3 November 1911. It is possible, as Pannwitz has reported, that his true name was Gurevitch and that he was a Jew; however, a Uruguayan passport issued in New York 17 April 1936 in the name of Vincente Sierra gave his date of birth as 3 July 1911 and the place as Montevideo.

Heinz Pannwitz has described Sukolov's early years as follows:

> Kent was born some time between 1911 and 1913. He stated that he was a Russian. He was obviously Jewish and obviously a Soviet national. His parents lived in the Leningrad area where he had spent his youth as a factory worker and Komsomol member. He went into hotel service because of his gift for languages and diversified interests. He claimed that he did this to study languages and to broaden his knowledge of people in preparation for intelligence work,

which was his goal. The original idea of becoming an intelligence officer, he said, came to him through his Party work in the Komsomol. He volunteered for fighting in the Spanish Civil War because, according to him, anyone who wished to get ahead at that time had to go to Spain. Allegedly he made the rank of Captain in Spain.

Kent was thoroughly and extensively trained by his military intelligence service, the GRU, in Moscow. He was trained as a Soviet intelligence officer or official both for the internal organization in the Soviet Union and for the special foreign mission. His specialized training for the foreign mission covered more than a year and was carried out with strictest observance of conspiratorial (operational) security methods. The conspiratorial rules were so rigid that he personally knew almost none of the teachers giving the specialized courses. He claimed that he had never really worked in the GRU internal organization in the Soviet Union.

He had been trained in every possible technique needed in intelligence work. There was nothing, quite simply, which he could not do in the field of technical equipment, in photography, in chemistry. He knew all the techniques and had done practical work in all of them.

After the Spanish Civil War, Sukolov was probably posted to France, where he performed some kind of intelligence duties from 1937 to 1939. In 1938 and 1939 he received funds from Mexico, deposited in a Marseilles bank. Sukolov visited Berlin in April 1939 under Moscow's instructions to reactivate the Schulze-Boysen network and to initiate a courier service between Germany and Belgium.

In July 1939 Sukolov entered Belgium and took up residence in Brussels as Vincente Sierra, a Uruguayan student. From 1939 to 1941 he studied commercial subjects at Brussels University. In the summer of 1939 he probably visited Switzerland, and in March 1940 he delivered money to Alexander Rado in Geneva. Sukolov worked as Trepper's assistant in Brussels until Trepper fled to France in July 1940. At that time Sukolov was placed in charge of the Belgian network.

From about June 1940 the Belgian network had been relaying by

W/T to Moscow most of Schulze-Boysen's and Trepper's material, and this was Sukolov's major task as the new head of the network. He had one W/T operator of his own in Brussels, Makarov, and he probably utilized also the link established in Holland by the Winterink group.

In the fall of 1940 Sukolov established the firm Simexco to serve as cover for his intelligence activities. As head of Simexco he was able to travel freely, and in 1940 and 1941 he made trips to France, Germany, Switzerland, and Czechoslovakia on intelligence missions.

In December 1941, when four members of his network were arrested in Brussels, Sukolov escaped to France. There he was joined by his mistress, Margarete Barcza, with whom he had been living since May 1940. In January 1942 Sukolov formed or reactivated a group of Czech agents in Marseilles with cover of a branch of Simex, run by Jules Jaspar and Alfred Corbin. Sukolov was visited occasionally in Marseilles by Trepper. During this period Sukolov frequently discussed with Barcza the possibility of discontinuing intelligence operations and fleeing to Switzerland.

Sukolov and his mistress were arrested in Marseilles 12 November 1942. He was taken first to Paris, then to Brussels, and finally to Gestapo headquarters in Berlin for intensive interrogation. He was returned to Paris 4 January 1943, having agreed to cooperate with the Germans. In March 1943 Sukolov's W/T playback to Moscow ("Mars") was begun; and in July 1943, under Moscow's instructions, he contacted Waldemar Ozols. German control was relaxed at this time to give the appearance that Sukolov was still at liberty.

Sukolov was kept in a villa at 40 Boulevard Victor Hugo, Neuilly; and he was joined there by Margarete Barcza, on 9 September 1943. Also living in this villa were Trepper, Hillel Katz, and Otto Schumacher. About 20 April 1944 Margarete Barcza gave birth to a son named Michel. According to Perrault, Michel Barcza is currently a magician in Brussels.

In January 1944 Sukolov, through Ozols, was put in touch with Legendre and his resistance group. At a meeting with Sukolov on 18 July 1944, Marcel Droubaix and two other members of the resistance group were arrested by the Germans.

Sukolov left Paris with Pannwitz of the Sonderkommando 16 August 1944. They continued the playback from various locations until May 1945. They were captured by a French military force in a mountain hut near Bludenz, Vorarlberg, Austria, 3 May 1945. Sukolov and Pannwitz were taken to Paris and interrogated. They were finally turned over to the Soviet authorities in Paris and left by plane for Moscow 7 June 1945.

According to Perrault, Sukolov was imprisoned at Vorkonta. He was released in 1956 and is now living in Leningrad under the name Gurevitch.

Pannwitz has given the following description of Victor Sukolov:

> Kent was about 5 feet 5½ inches tall and his build was well proportioned for his height, neither too thin nor too stout. His hair was dark but not black, and his head was narrow, not at all a Slavic-type head. His forehead was high and his ears protruded. His lips were full, too full for a man, and the lower lip protruded due to constant pipe smoking. He carried his head forward, especially when standing still, but also when walking. When he was relaxed, his full lips made him look like a pouting child. As with all Russians he loved to eat, so that when he was free he was inclined to gain weight. He could not control his hands and eyes during a tense situation. His hand would begin to tremble slightly. His eyes clearly spoke of whatever he was feeling—anxiety, joy, concentration, or expectant questions. The medical examination revealed that although he was a Jew, he was not circumcised.
>
> He was somewhat vain and could be brought out of his shell by praise and recognition. His vanity also caused him to brag, especially under the influence of alcohol. Because he was a Russian who had been accustomed to a poor standard of living, he liked especially to eat well and much. He patronized expensive restaurants, some even in the luxury class. When the meat course arrived, he would reorder it three times. Before his meal he would drink a phenomenal amount, for the West, of very strong alcohol—for example, a half bottle of vodka. This always attracted the attention of the waiters. Such a client was easy to track in restaurants because the waiters remembered him. He also made himself conspicuous by his naivete in buying mass lots of cigarettes and men's leather shoes, for which his training was to blame. It should never have been

risked during the training in Moscow that an agent being prepared for a foreign mission was not told the difference between the internal Russian propaganda concerning the West and the reality of the West. Kent honestly believed that only by chance had leather shoes appeared in a shoe store, because according to Russian propaganda workers in capitalistic countries wore only paper or straw shoes. He had also never been taught what the proper behavior was in a restaurant.

He was endowed naturally with a lively imagination and the ability to put two and two together for the right answer. He influenced people inconspicuously and without any obvious effort and issued his orders, when necessary, in a positive, commanding manner which allowed no argument. At such times the full force of his personality came into action. General Ozols, Legendre, and others would unconsciously stand at attention in his presence. This trait was not the result of his training in Moscow but was a part of the man's personality. He learned foreign languages very quickly. He also possessed a good understanding of psychology and had a high degree of empathy, which became obvious in our discussion of the tactical problems of the playback operation. I tested him by asking him to analyze some members of my Kommando, and his conclusions were always accurate. He could always see the sensitive spots or weaknesses of his fellow workers and would make some casual observation which disclosed to the latter what an accurate insight he had. His fellow workers were always amazed and surprised that the "Chief" knew such things.

He certainly was not one of the revolutionary types, and made the impression in his appearance and manner of a bourgeois; but he had a definite inclination for adventure, adventure governed by reason. He was not bound by ideological or philosophical concepts, although he knew all the concepts. He could be a well-indoctrinated Communist, but used his Communist education as a chess player who

moves his pieces to carry out his strategy. He was an
independent thinker and capable of making his own
decisions. He felt that his own intelligence was his
only reliable guide.

Kent knew the Soviet system very well and did not
consider anything which happened to himself as especially tragic. His attitude toward life was that every
man in the world had to fight his way and should be
forced to strain his "little head" once in a while. At
the end of the war he believed that the Soviet Union
had finally abandoned its policy of isolation and
would then be capable of entering the political community of the world. Such ideas appealed to him
because he was a very restless and flexible man. He
immediately adapted himself to the new situation
when the interrogations began in Moscow. Every
interrogation would begin with, "After the victorious
Red Army had driven out the Fascists and freed the
homeland . . ." There was actually little opportunity
in his interrogation to use such a militaristic, nation-
alistic style, but he was well acquainted with the
necessary formulas which could be used and he
always used them if the opportunity arose.

He was a strongly sexed man who had no inhibi-
tions about carrying out his sex life with Barcza when
they were sleeping in the hotel room with several
(German) officials. In this regard he was fortunate
that he stayed with one woman . . . Barcza and Kent
lived together as though legally married. She was a
handsome woman, but she was not the beauty subsequent publications have claimed. Most likely she was
Kent's first love affair in Western Europe and he remained faithful to her. His work and the enforced
loneliness made such a relationship very necessary.
His choice of mistress was very wise because she
never caused him any problems. He must have
revealed, at some time, his true identity and the true
nature of his work to her. This must have occurred
before they were forced to flee to Marseilles. She
stayed with him through everything. They were
taken into custody together in Marseilles and they

remained together during the trip to Berlin, Brussels, and finally to Paris. They were separated for very short periods when they were in prison. All of Dallin's descriptions of Barcza in his book, *Soviet Espionage,* are utter nonsense. While the two, Barcza and Kent, were in my Kommando in Paris, they had a two-room apartment with all comforts. There a son was born in March or April 1944 who was baptized in the Catholic Church and named for my oldest son, Michael. Kent selected the name and asked me to be the godfather. Naturally, I agreed to this.

ILONA ROLF SUSS
(also Suess, alias Rolph) was born 27 September 1896 in Lodz, Poland. A Polish Jewess, she was the daughter of George and Rose, nee Schindler. A militant left-wing journalist and author, she served the cause of Chinese Communism.

She was educated in Poland, Silesia, Canada, and the United States. She was employed by the U.S. Consulate in Nuremberg in 1916. From 1917 to 1919 she was in Lodz and from 1919 to 1921 she was part of the Hoover Mission in Lodz and Warsaw. For the next four years Suss was a secretary attached to the U.S. section of the reparations committee in Berlin.

From 1925 to 1928 Suss was a secretary attached to the UFA studios, Berlin, by the U.S. Commercial Attache, Berlin, and by "American Film Trust," Berlin. In 1928 she was assistant to the Anti-Opium Bureau, Geneva. In 1936 Suss went to China for the Keyston Press Agency.

In the summer of 1940 Suss was recruited by Ursula Hamburger, on the recommendation of Marie Ginsberg, as a prospective W/T operator and received preliminary instructions from Foote, who pronounced her inept, nervous, and unsuitable; she was dropped within two months.

In 1941 she came to the United States and lived at 231 E. 54th Street, New York (October 1944).

LOUIS SUSS
(aka Louis de Gaidey de Soos, aka Louis Suss, alias Salter) was born 6 October 1890 in Alsace-Lorraine. He died in Switzerland on 25 April 1955. It was not until after his death that it was determined that he was identical with "Salter."

Suss was employed during World War II in the French Legation in Bern, Switzerland, and was later Press Attache in the French Legation in Prague, Czechoslovakia.

He was a contact of Otto Puenter (Pakbo), a Swiss journalist who was also active for the GRU in Switzerland, both during World War II and in the postwar period.

Rado's financial transactions reflected that Salter was paid two hundred Swiss francs each month from February 1942 to May 1943.

Foote was questioned about Salter on 3 July 1947, after Foote's return from Moscow to Germany in March 1947, when he "came over" to the British in Berlin. He advised that Salter was a sub-agent of Pakbo and was in touch also with the British I.S. He was used by Rado in the approach made in 1943 to the British Legation asking if they would provide asylum for Rado in case of emergency.

His widow, Friedel, nee Kirschbaum, still resides (1968) in Chene-Bourg, Chemin du Saut du Loup, Geneva.

WILLY LOUIS ANDRE ROLLAND THEVENET

was a French national, born 4 January 1903 in Yzeure, France. In December 1941 he was appointed a director of Simexco. He may have provided some assistance to members of the Rote Kapelle in Belgium. In July 1942 Sukolov completed the sale of Simexco to Thevenet. At the time of the general roundup of Simexco employees in November 1942, Thevenet was arrested and imprisoned in St. Gilles.

According to Perrault, Thevenet had been a cigarette manufacturer before the war. Perrault also states that Thevenet died in prison, some time before April 1943.

LEOPOLD TREPPER

was born 23 February 1904—or some other date still unknown—in Neumark, near Zakopane, Poland. Leiba ben Zeharya Trepper was probably his true name. He was known in Warsaw by the name Leiba Domb, but he has used many aliases, among them being Jean Gilbert, Adam Mikler, Vladislav Ivanovich Ivanowski, de Winter, Sommer, Onkel Otto, "Le Grand Chef," Le General, Herbst, Peiper, etc.

A Polish Jew, one of ten children, he came from a family of merchants. Still in his teens, he was obliged to leave school and to work in the mines of Kattowicz. By the time he was twenty-two, he had already been jailed for heading a revolt at Dombrova. After spending eight months in prison, he could find no work in Poland; so he went to Palestine, thanks to Hechalutz, a Zionist organization financed by rich American Jews.

In Palestine Trepper became acquainted with the Grand Mufti of Jerusalem, found his true vocation, and began his apprenticeship as a spy. There he married Sarah Broide, who had previously been married to Joseph Orschitzer. She is probably identical with Luba Alexayevna Brikson, whom Trepper married in 1924. Reportedly he had two sons by Luba, one born in 1931 in Paris; the other, in 1936 in Moscow.

He joined the Zionist movement in the early 1920s and became acquainted in Palestine with his faithful "Old Guard" who later worked with him in Europe.

In 1928 he went to France and joined the Rabcors, a Communist-dominated group providing men and information to Moscow. In February 1932 the famous French commissaire, named Charles Faux-Pas-Bidet, dismantled the Rabcors when he arrested the "Phantomas," Izaia Bir, and his assistant, Alter Strom, both Polish Jews and important Soviet agents. Trepper escaped and proceeded to Moscow, where he was taught that only by supporting Stalin and the Communist cause could the Jewish demands be realized. He learned at the Red Army Academy, where (Alexander) Orlov taught, that war against Fascism and Nazism could be successfully waged only under the guidance of Communism and that support of the Soviet anti-Fascist movement was obligatory for the Jewish masses. Trepper has stated that it was during this period of his studies that his plans for the future crystallized.

New possibilities for the RIS to renew its work in France presented themselves following political developments in that country during the 1930s. These factors were the victory of the Popular Front led by Leon Blum, the setting-up of a left-wing government, and the deterioration of French relations with Hitlerite Germany. Thirty to forty thousand men were purged during the 1936-1937 period; the GRU suffered the most, but Trepper remained loyal to Stalin throughout the difficult purge years.

Five years after the arrest of his Rabcors friends in France, Trepper was back in Paris with a false passport in the name of Sommer. His first successful mission after his arrival in France was the discovery of the traitor responsible for the arrest of the "Phantomas." This traitor had been chief of a Soviet espionage network in the United States and had been reportedly doubled by the FBI, which notified the French police.

In July 1940 Trepper, then in Brussels, realized he was being surveilled by the GIS. Keeping informed on the advance of the German troops, he fled to France and later was joined by his American-born mistress, Georgie de Winter, by whom he had a child, Patrick de Winter, born in Brussels.

France's role in the framework of Soviet intelligence grew considerably during the years of the Soviet-German friendship (1939-1941). In June 1940 German armies moved into Paris, but half the country remained under French rule. The Soviets moved to Vichy, and the chaos of the Vichy regime proved advantageous for a team of experienced underground agents. With the help of the veteran Comintern agent Henri Robinson, of Leon Grossvogel—whom Trepper had known in Palestine—and of his secretary, Hillel Katz, the "Grand Chef" organized his first headquarters in France. From 1940 to 1942 Trepper commanded seven networks of Soviet intelligence, each active in its own field and subordinated to its own chief.

Certainly the "Grand Chef" succeeded in penetrating the enemy at the highest echelons. A decoding by the Germans of the Soviet W/T in Brussels showed that the Soviets had penetrated the OKW. As a result of the information he obtained from Jeip Tours, Trepper was able to figure out the German order of battle. When on 22 June 1941 Hitler attacked Russia, the Rote Kapelle had done its work well. Trepper had notified Moscow through General Susloperof in Vichy of the invasion, but Stalin did not believe "Otto." On 10 October 1941 a radio message from the Center to "Kent" (Sukolov) exposed the Rote Kapelle; and this fact permitted the Germans to identify, to arrest, and partially to control the RIS operations.

On 5 December 1942 Trepper was arrested by Henry Friedrich Piepe of the Abwehr and Karl Giering of the Gestapo. According to Gestapo reports Trepper betrayed his collaborators and was doubled by the Nazis. David Dallin also has written that Trepper betrayed his collaborators: Hillel Katz, Henri Robinson, Anna and Vassili Maximovitch, and others, and that the Nazis "destroyed the Paris network." The Nazis and Dallin were probably mistaken, because it now appears that Trepper was a triple agent while in Nazi hands. Heinrich Reiser of the Sonderkommando has advised: "Don't believe the Gestapo reports if you want to get down to the facts in the Rote Kapelle case." But he was probably also partially wrong because he was unaware of the complicated "Funkspiel," or radio playback, operations.

According to Piepe, if the "Grand Chef" talked it was not because of fear or torture or to save his life. He was not like Johann Wenzel and Abraham Rajchmann. Trepper talked, but he did so upon orders. It was his duty; "he gave us a few morsels and while we were picking them up, he salvaged the rest. He made monkeys of the Germans." Piepe too might be wrong: The French specialists think that Trepper sacrificed his associates to save the CPF underground. Trepper was capable of duping "all the Corbins of the world" and leading them to the execution post rather than compromising his network.

Trepper was glad to see Giering transferred from Paris during the summer of 1943. The "Grand Chef" knew that he could never lower his guard with Giering; so he welcomed his departure and the arrival of Pannwitz, convinced he was the winner in the exchange. Trepper escaped from Willy Berg on 13 September 1943. According to Trepper, Giering had asked him to cooperate in order to bring about peace between Russia and Germany. Berg used to say: "I was a cop under the Kaiser, a cop under the Weimar; I'm a cop under Hitler; I'll be a cop if Thaelmann takes over."

After his escape Trepper wrote to Pannwitz telling him that CI agents accosted him in a drugstore and he had to follow them; he requested that Pannwitz not punish Berg. Trepper advised that he wanted to save the "Grand Jeu" and continue the "Funkspiel," but for a reason different from Pannwitz's.

After his escape Trepper was hidden by Mrs. Queyrie in Suresnes, and Moscow instructed Trepper to hide. Trepper doubted that Moscow believed him; and he wrote to Pannwitz a second time, expressing displeasure over the arrest of so many innocent people. Trepper was the subject of an "identification order" in France, Germany, and Belgium as a "wanted dangerous spy." In November 1943 Pannwitz sent a message to the Center via "Kent," who was under control. In answer the Center advised Pannwitz through "Kent" to stay away from Trepper—"he's a traitor."

In another letter to Pannwitz, Trepper threatened to break off the "Grand Jeu" if arrested persons were not released. Pannwitz was uncertain if Trepper had betrayed the Germans or Moscow; so he was forced to go along with Trepper in order to keep out of trouble himself.

Trepper went to Warsaw after his release from prison. Even there he found no means of livelihood, and he finally decided to emigrate.

His destination was France. After the failure of all efforts to reach France legally, he approached an American emigration enterprise called Haljas, which at that time operated in Warsaw. The Polish government supported emigration, for it hoped to lessen unemployment in this manner and to oppose the Communist danger at the same time. Trepper obtained, with the assistance of the above-named American committee, an emigration pass and arrived in Vienna with a regular emigration train from Warsaw.

Since the age of eighteen Trepper has hidden behind a false identity and worked clandestinely; and Pannwitz, the Gestapo chief, sketched this portrait of the "Grand Chef" twenty-three years after first meeting "his prisoner" in Paris.

> When he knew he wasn't being observed, he looked very tough and distrustful, cold and aloof. The moment someone paid attention to him, his appearance changed and he played the role of an actor. If someone pressed him with questions, he would put his hand on his heart in order to remind his listener he had a heart condition. He was first of all a Jew. The Russians were wrong to put so many Jews in this network—think of it, the Rote Kapelle was 90 percent Jewish—because a Jew is much too malicious to die for a lost cause . . .

Pannwitz claims the Germans succeeded not only in locating and liquidating the clandestine networks in Brussels, Berlin, Amsterdam, and Paris, but also in doubling the Soviet agents, and by virtue of the Funkspiel in intoxicating the Soviets with false information.

What awaited Trepper when he arrived in Moscow in 1945 was a cell in the Lubyanka instead of a hero's welcome. He emerged from jail only after the death of Stalin, was then rehabilitated, and went back to Poland, apparently disillusioned but not disheartened. Trepper explains: "Stalinism was an epidemic. We had to wait for it to pass. The trip from Moscow to Warsaw lasted eleven years . . . trains are often late." Trepper left the Lubyanka as he entered it—a Communist.

Pannwitz has written that Trepper learned to speak Polish, Russian, German, French, and Yiddish. In the beginning Trepper worked in the Comintern field of interest but was also receiving orders from the Military Attache of the Soviet Embassy in Paris. One of his numerous missions was to prevent any scandal or crime resulting from Communist work in France from being brought before a French court. He accomplished this by means of bribes or, if necessary, by force.

Trepper was about 5 feet 7 inches with a broad, squat, stout build. He had dark hair and a full face. His eyes had large dark circles, often very swollen bags under them, which made him appear to be suffering from heart trouble, which was actually true. His hands were always busy. He was capable of great concentration, during which times he had a withdrawn, hard look. His head was round and his lips were normal, perhaps somewhat thin. He generally had a look of alert expectation.

The *New York Times,* 28 March 1968, reported that Leopold Domb, president of the Jewish Cultural Society, "who during World War II ran a Soviet espionage ring in France and Belgium," was among the Poles attacked for the "anti-Polish campaign staged by Zionist centers in the West."

After the Corby case in Canada, the Director of the GRU was fired. The KGB seized this opportunity to settle accounts with the GRU. Three years later there was an anti-Semitic wave in the USSR, and Trepper was queried as to why he had surrounded himself with traitors—Hillel Katz, Grossvogel, Springer, Rajchmann, etc.

Trepper was kept in jail incommunicado (no news from his wife) until March 1953, when Stalin died and Beria was liquidated. Then he was finally exonerated and rehabilitated. He left for Poland. Perrault interviewed him in 1966 and learned that in April 1965 Trepper was at Auschwitz commemorating the liberation of the camp. As Leiba Domb, president of the Jewish community of Poland, he addressed the eighty thousand persons there.

It had been established that Trepper, Alexander Foote, and Alexander Rado left Paris together on a Soviet plane 6 January 1945. Upon his arrival in Moscow Trepper was reportedly arrested and held in prison for several years. But he managed to convince the Soviets that his behaviour when he fell into the hands of the Gestapo was the only way to save himself and at the same time prevent his network from being damaged to an even greater extent. According to Trepper, his "collaboration" with the Nazis was a "big bluff," and his persuading the Germans that he was collaborating with them enabled him to hide numerous important items of information and to stall for time until he was able to escape—as he subsequently did.

Although Trepper was "cleared," it appears he was no longer completely trusted by the RIS, and in 1957 he arrived in Warsaw as a tourist. In Warsaw he has been managing the publication *Yiddish Buch.*

Paris Match, 29 July 1967, carried an account of an interview with "Le Grand Chef" by Gerard Periot. Trepper was then living in Warsaw under the name of Leiba Domb.

With regard to the revolts that broke out in Dombrova in 1927, and Trepper's part in them, an Abwehr report dated 24 March 1943 states that Trepper was arrested by the Polish authorities as one of the leaders and thrown into prison. There he began a hunger strike. He was released after eight months without a sentence and without ever having a regular hearing. The time in prison, as he said himself, "had awakened in him a deep hatred against the Polish feudal economy and changed him from then on into a full believer in the Communist idea."

Trepper said he managed to continue "his resistance work" in France all during the war and to implicate numerous members of the Pfeffer group who wanted to negotiate with the West, with or without the Fuehrer. The Nazis thought that the Rote Kapelle had penetrated the OKW, and many of the Schulze-Boysen group were executed. Trepper made a report to Moscow in Hebrew, Yiddish, and Polish. He sent this message via Jacques Duclos. Trepper claims he also fooled "Kent" in case he was under control. "Kent" was fooled and coded the messages to Moscow, not suspecting that Trepper was playing a triple game.

After the war Novikov arrived in Paris to head the Soviet military mission. The plane that brought Thorez back from Moscow took Trepper to the Soviet Union 6 January 1945. Soviet intelligence must have been delighted to see Trepper arrive in Moscow with Foote and Rado. Then "Kent" and Pannwitz arrived, followed by Ozols and Wenzel. The Director could not afford to have Trepper loose in Moscow telling everyone he had on three occasions vainly warned Stalin of the imminent German attack. Sorge would have suffered the same fate as Trepper if the Japanese had not executed him. The Center could not be persuaded that the Germans had located the Rote Kapelle W/T sets so rapidly; so the Center thought there was a German spy in the Kremlin. Trepper knew too much, and that is why they put him in jail.

MARTHE ANGELE FRANCOISE VANDENHOECK

(nee Baumanns) was born 31 December 1918 in Woluwe St. Pierre, Belgium. She was a courier between Paris and Brussels for the Jeffremov network, working under Elizabeth Depelsenaire. She was arrested by the Germans in July 1942 and was used to stage the arrest of Depelsenaire. She probably assisted in other arrests also, under

German duress. In the spring of 1943 she was deported to Moabit Prison, Berlin, with other members of the Belgian network.

In 1945 Vandenhoeck was liberated from prison and returned to Belgium. In 1946 she was residing at 553/5 Chaussee de Wavre, Etterbeck, Brussels. In November 1946 she attempted to join her husband, a geologist, in Anyama, Ivory Coast, but she was prevented from leaving Belgium by the confiscation of her passport.

ANNE-MARIE VAN DER PUTT
(alias Vera, alias La Noire) was probably recruited by Sukolov in Brussels in 1940 or 1941 and trained by him in coding. In October 1941 she was escorted by Malvina Gruber across the frontier and taken to Trepper in Paris, where she was utilized by the Sokols as an encipherer until their arrest in June 1942. Van der Putt was then transferred to Sukolov in Marseilles. She escaped arrest and probably fled to Switzerland in November 1942.

Anne-Marie van der Putt was probably the assumed name of a Belgian Jewess. She had been the mistress of one Ackermann, who was killed fighting with the Republicans in the Spanish Civil War. She reportedly spoke French, Flemish, and Spanish.

EDOUARD VAN DER ZYPEN or ZIJPEN
(alias Nelly) was a Belgian civilian employee of the Hentschel works in Kassel, Germany, and one of Jeffremov's most important agents. In December 1942 he was arrested by the Germans. In July 1943 he was executed.

FLORA VAN VLIET
(nee Velarts, alias Frau Springer, alias Arlette Rochat) was associated with her lover, Isidore Springer, in work for Sukolov in Brussels in 1941. In 1942 she was a member of Springer's group in Lyons.

Flora van Vliet was born 25 January 1909 in Brussels. Her father was Francois Velarts, and her mother Therese, nee Duffy.

She was arrested 17 December 1942 in Orlienas, Rhone, France. Her ultimate fate is unknown.

JOSEPHINE FRANCOISE VERHIMST
(nee Glais) was the sister of Germaine Schneider and Renee Blumsack. She was used by her sister, Germaine, as a courier for Jeffremov's service in Belgium.

Josephine was born 23 July 1887 in Brussels. She was the wife of

Pierre Verhimst, a Belgian, born 1 March 1880 in Anderiecht. She was the mistress of Jean-Baptiste Janssens, with whom she lived in 1942.

She was arrested with Janssens in January 1943.

JEAN PIERRE VIGIER
(alias Braut) was born in Paris on 16 January 1910. He is the son of Henri Vigier, former League of Nations delegate and representative of the ILO. Jean Pierre obtained his Ph.D. at the University of Lausanne and served in the French Army in World War II as a captain under General Lattre de Tassigny. In 1947 he was attached to the Atomic Energy Commission of France in Paris and served on the staff of Francois Billoux, a known member of the CP of France.

During the late 1930s and early 1940s, Vigier resided in Switzerland, where he was in contact with Alexander Rado. Vigier became a source of the Rote Drei, allegedly having been recruited by Tamara Caspari, whom he later married. Tamara is the daughter of Rachel Duebendorfer by her first marriage. Alexander Foote, in his book *Handbook for Spies,* mentiones Tamara and relates how she acted as a courier for the net. Her mother hid messages under her hair ribbons and Tamara delivered them to other agents.

Vigier provided Duebendorfer with rather unimportant information from Gaullist circles. He and Tamara continued to act as Soviet agents after World War II ended. Tamara considered that the Soviets treated her mother harshly and unfairly after the war ended, and she asked her husband to join her in denouncing them. Still an ardent Communist, he refused, and she obtained a divorce.

About 1 March 1949 Jean Pierre was arrested by the Surete because he had unauthorized possession of French AEC documents. Although he was not convicted, he was transferred to an obscure provincial post.

After the end of World War II President de Gaulle brought back Maurice Thorez, head of the French Communist Party, from Moscow and installed him as Vice President of France. Consequently, numerous Communists were placed in high government positions in France. Francois Billoux, previously mentioned, was one of those seated. He headed the Ministry of Defense. Frederic Joliot-Curie, a Communist, was another individual who was given a government post; he headed the French Atomic Energy Commission, and his chief of personnel was Jean Pierre Vigier.

Vigier is a personal friend of Alexander Abramson, who at one time maintained liaison between French and Swiss Communists in Geneva.

In 1967 Vigier was Secretary General of the Bertrand Russell International War Crimes Tribunal. He went to Hanoi as the leader of an investigation team of the Tribunal to collect documentary proof of U.S. crimes against Vietnamese civilians. Another member of the Tribunal was Guillermo Frank Janes, a Cuban military expert. At a press conference held in Hanoi, Vigier condemned the U.S. bombings of Haiphong as a very important step in genocidal attempts against the population.

L'Humanite on 27 May 1968 announced the expulsion of former Central Committee member Professor Jean Pierre Vigier from the French CP, commenting that during the last few weeks Vigier had taken a very active part in support of the French students, whose demonstrations were condemned by the Communist Party. Vigier had earlier clashed with the Communist Party leadership over the Sino-Soviet conflict.

TAMARA VIGIER

(nee Caspari, alias Vita) is the daughter of Rachel and Curt Caspari. Tamara was born on 8 July 1922. She worked for her mother as a Rote Drei courier.

KATHE VOELKNER

was born 12 April 1906 in Danzig. A German national, she first arrived in France in 1936. She was the mistress of Johann Podsiadlo, who taught her painting. Kathe, an art student and daughter of a Danzig artist, travelled extensively in Europe and Russia before the war.

She was recruited in 1941 by Anna and Basil Maximovitch for Trepper's service in Paris. She was a secretary in the German Kommandantur, with offices in the Chamber of Deputies. One of her assignments for Trepper, in addition to collecting any information available from her office, was to provide blank forms, stamps, and specimen signatures of the heads of departments. A number of blank forms, with genuine stamps and signatures, were later found among Trepper's papers. Voelkner may also have performed services for Robinson's group.

Voelkner handed over her information on sheets of tissue paper which were concealed in her compact, or between two pages of a magazine which had been pasted together, or in a cake, or inside a match box.

Trepper, for some reason, was suspicious that Voelkner might be a "plant" and that the Germans might be using her. He therefore arranged a meeting with her at a metro station. In order to make certain that he was not followed, he chose a station at the end of the line which had only one exit, so that he could see if any of those who got out there were persons whom he had spotted during the journey.

From time to time Trepper would instruct one of his agents to invite Voelkner to dinner. Trepper would select the restaurant, one in which there were plenty of mirrors, and attend the meeting himself, sitting nearby so that he could see whether there were any Germans shadowing them. Most of these meetings took place in the evening.

Voelkner was arrested by the Gestapo on 7 January 1943 and executed. Just before being executed she reportedly exclaimed: "I'm happy that I performed some service for Communism."

Kathe Voelkner and Johann Podsiadlo were the parents of Hans Voelkner, born 21 August 1928 in Danzig. Hans was arrested at Orly Field outside Paris on 19 May 1969. He had disembarked from Germany and was immediately picked up by the DST for espionage.

According to the French, Hans was in a German prison camp during the war, was liberated, and then entered France on 1 June 1945. He was arrested in 1948 at Mayence in the occupied zone of Germany and imprisoned in the Maison d'Arret at Fulda. The French also reported that Hans had come back to France as a student after World War II and had established contact with Trepper to get information about his parents. He was expelled in 1948 "for signing a Communist tract." Hans eventually settled in East Germany and became an officer in the MFS, reportedly a colonel or lieutenant colonel by 1969.

One of Hans Voelkner's contacts in Paris had been a journalist named Jacques Leman, who over the years had made frequent trips to East Berlin on business. A "friend" of Leman's was one Mme. Martha Danilo, employed in the cultural section (also reported in the press as the cipher section) of the Foreign Office, whom he urged to get a job in NATO. When Leman died in January 1969 at the age of sixty-seven, the French finally picked up Danilo in May and learned she had been told to expect a visitor from East Berlin. This turned out to be Hans Voelkner, travelling as West German businessman Hans Martin Richter. The French arrested him.

Another contact Danilo had was a woman known to her as Marise, apparently an EGIS courier or case officer. She may be identical with Marie-Rose Martin, a French national employed in Brussels by a French financial newspaper. Martin was arrested and interrogated by the Belgians at the request of the French. She admitted knowing no one but Leman, and him only nominally. The Belgians said they had planted a story in the Belgian press about Voelkner in the hope that readers knowledgeable of the case would come forward with information.

Jacques Leman was a known "left-wing radical" and a suspected Communist. He was secretary of the France-USSR society in 1952. In February 1960, when he was a *Le Monde* journalist, he tried to contact an eleven-man Chinese Communist technical team then visiting France. Voelkner so far has told the French only what they have shown him they already knew. The press has speculated that the government hopes to hold him for a possible "spy swap" with East Germany.

Voelkner's defense hinged on his claim that he never forgot the memory of his mother, who died under the torture of Nazis who later became members of the West German intelligence service (and thus agents of NATO). He claimed that he did not spy against France but only against NATO. Gilles Perrault appeared for the defense.

In February 1970 Marthe Danilo and Simone Leman, sister of Jacques Leman, received suspended sentences. Voelkner received twelve years.

The *London Times* on 12 February 1970 printed the following account of the case:

> Hans Voelkner, the East German national accused of spying, was today sentenced to twelve years imprisonment by the state security court. Two women charged with him, Marthe Danilo, a former typist in the cipher office of the Quai d'Orsay, and Simone Leman, members of the spy ring Voelkner directed from East Germany, were given short suspended sentences as accessories.
>
> The court followed the summing up of the Prosecutor General, who had yesterday declared himself utterly convinced of the guilt of the three but allowed extenuating circumstances for the two women.
>
> "Voelkner has lost. He must pay," he went on. "In any case, I am not too concerned about his future. He can, as is often the case with spies, benefit from an exchange.

"Certainly, fate was exceptionally cruel to him since youth. But he is, I am convinced, really a senior secret service officer on a special mission and not an occasional agent, as he claims. He constitutes a potential danger."

The main witness for the defense was M. Gilles Perrault, the author of a history of the "red orchestra," the Soviet espionage organization which operated against the Germans during the war. Voelkner's mother was a member of this organization in Paris, and for her part in it she was tortured and executed by the Nazis. Her husband had also been executed.

Herr Voelkner had never got over the execution of his parents, and he never stopped thinking about his mother. M. Perrault told the court, "I do not share his convictions, but as a Frenchman I feel a debt of gratitude towards his parents."

He added that he got much of the information for his book from former members of the Gestapo he rediscovered in Germany. "What are they doing now?" asked Mr. Joe Nordmann, defending counsel. "They are well, and some have been taken on by the secret service of the Federal Republic," was the reply.

Mr. Nordmann said in his plea for Herr Voelkner that he had lived obsessed by the memory of his mother. "He never tried to do anything against France, for NATO is not France. Herr Voelkner was accused of trying to get information from the NATO headquarters. Imagine the grief of this man when he learned that those very men who had arrested and tortured his mother, those former Nazis, had become agents of NATO."

Another article on the Voelkner case appeared in the *London Times* of 13 February 1970:

There is a dramatic quality about the past of Hans Voelkner, an alleged member of the HVA, the East German intelligence organization, who appeared today before the Court for State Security to answer charges of espionage.

The keen eyes and angular features of this small, round-shouldered, rather insignificant man testify to his extraordinary life and suffering. Born in Danzig in 1928 of two acrobats—a German mother whose name he took and a father he presumes to have been Polish—he led all over Europe the hard, wandering life of circus folk until the family came to settle in France in 1937.

They left Nazi Germany because, he explained to the court today, his mother's people were convinced Social Democrats, and an accident suffered by his father at a Leningrad circus opened his mother's eyes to the benefits of social security.

Then came the war and the German occupation. His parents joined the "Red Orchestra," the Communist espionage organization, and because of her nationality his mother also became secretary to the representative in Paris of Sauckel, the head of the Reich organization. The boy was sent to a labor camp in Germany to be indoctrinated and toughened up. There, in 1943, he learned his parents had been arrested by the Gestapo and executed after torture.

He was sent to the Eastern Front in 1944, tried to desert to the Russians, was caught, and sent to Belsen. When the camp was liberated, he returned to France, but he fell afoul of the police.

He was expelled and tried to get into East Germany, but the Russians would not have him. He smuggled himself in and was sentenced by a Russian military court to twenty-five years in a labor camp on charges of spying for France.

Freed by an amnesty in 1955, his health badly damaged by his ordeal, he settled down and eventually obtained a post of responsibility in the official East German travel agency in Berlin, which brought him into contact with French businessmen visiting the Leipzig Fair. The indictment maintains that this was a cover under which he set up an espionage ring in France. Two alleged members of the ring, a woman clerk at the Quai d'Orsay, and another woman, are also on trial.

Herr Voelkner was arrested during a visit to Paris last year. His dramatic tale is having its epilogue in a small dingy court of the Palais de Justice, where the Court for State Security holds its hearings. The president of the court said today that he would be considered "a soldier who has worked for his country and is accused of working against ours."

Herr Voelkner said: "I agreed to do a number of things for my country, but I never did anything against France. I would never have agreed to be the cause of harm to France, to which I owe so much."

GUENTHER WEISENBORN

was born 10 July 1902 in Velbert in the German Rhineland. He studied medicine and philosophy at Cologne and Bonn Universities. He became an author and dramatist and later the dramatic critic of the Schiller Theatre in Berlin during World War II. He married Margaret Weisenborn, nee Schabbel, who was reportedly a Soviet agent. (Her relationship, if any, to Klara Schabbel, who was the mistress of Henri Robinson, is unknown.)

Before World War II Weisenborn had been a member of the "Klara Apparatus," which was a branch of the IVth Section of the Red Army. During World War II he belonged to the closest circle around Schulze-Boysen and Harnack.

Manfred Roeder stated that Weisenborn was sentenced to a prison term for his role in the Rote Kapelle because he did not report the treasonable activity of the Schulze-Boysen group.

Weisenborn has written a book entitled *Memorial,* which concerns the operations of the Rote Kapelle in Germany.

ERNEST DAVID WEISS

was born in Breslau, Germany, in 1902 and attended Breslau University from 1922 to 1927. In May or June 1931 he was contacted by a party named Demetz whom he had met at Breslau University. Demetz asked him if he would be interested in a job travelling abroad, and Weiss advised that he would be. In January 1932, Weiss was introduced to Harry I through Demetz in Paris. On 11 May 1932 Weiss arrived in England, where he commenced doing general research work for Harry I. In 1932 he had various meetings with Harry I, and in June 1932 he was introduced to two seamen couriers with whom he had liaisons thereafter.

In December 1932 Harry I went abroad and may have visited the United States. On 17 September 1933 Weiss was introduced to Robert Gordon Switz from Kensington Gardens, England, by Harry I. It was in December 1933 that Mr. and Mrs. Switz were arrested in France as Soviet espionage agents. Weiss recognized their picture in a newspaper as that of the people he had met in September through Harry I and stated that for the first time he knew he was working for a Russian espionage system. In the fall of 1935 Weiss met Harry II in Enge, Switzerland, and contacted him thereafter when he had any messages to deliver.

In 1936 Weiss obtained confidential information concerning production of airplanes and other war materials from "Vernon" and "Meredith." In December 1936 Harry II asked Weiss to contact Sam Barron and to ask him if he would be interested in employment abroad. From 1936 to August 1941 Weiss continued to have contacts with Harry II and with a party named Andre to whom he gave information obtained from the seamen couriers and from "Vernon" and "Meredith." In 1941 Weiss discontinued his work as a courier for this Russian espionage group.

The British interrogated Weiss and, judging from the report, it appears that the SIS had an operational interest in him after the arrest of Robinson on 21 December 1942.

Weiss told the British that

(1) Andre was one of the aliases of Henri Robinson, a Soviet intelligence officer of long standing. He is thought to have taken over the U.K. network in 1937 and is known to have made many trips to the U.K.

(2) Demetz is probably identical with Hans Demetz; this man's name was given to the British by Krivitsky in 1940. Demetz was born about 1907 and started to work in the Fourth Department in 1925.

(3) Weiss met David Rockefeller through Saul Rae and played squash with Rockefeller at Kensington Palace Mansions. David Rockefeller is now president of Chase Manhattan Bank. He was in OSS during World War II.

(4) Vernon is probably Wilfred Foulston Vernon, born 17 October 1912 in London, who was a "cipher contact" between the RAE and CP headquarters in London. He was associated with scores of persons with Communist sentiments, among them being Meredith, with whom he was on close terms. Frederick William Meredith was born 10 July 1895 in Killiney, Dublin, Ireland. Meredith with about

eight other people from the RAE left for Russia in May 1932, returning in June 1932.

(5) Weiss knew Sam Barron at the London School of Economics, where they first met. Harry II suggested to Weiss that he should approach Barron and ask him whether he was interested in taking a job abroad. Subsequently Barron was in the United States from 1938 to 1941 and working for the War Trade Department of the British Embassy in Washington, D.C. Lauchlin Currie, former White House secretary, was Sam Barron's reference.

The British commented that Weiss probably failed to tell the whole truth or deliberately suffered a lapse of memory. Weiss met Roger King when he was evacuated to Chorley Wood in 1940. Roger King is probably Roger Andrew Ivan King, born 29 March 1922 in Zurich. In 1946 he was working in the SIS. Also, when Vernon was prosecuted, he was defended by D.N. Pritt, to whom, according to Meredith (who was in Vernon's confidence), he told the full story of his dealings with Weiss's organization. Pritt is probably Denis Nowell Pritt, a Socialist member of Parliament who was outspokenly sympathetic to the USSR and Communism.

JOHANNES WENZEL

(alias Hans, alias Herman, alias the Professor, alias Charles, alias Bergmann) was born 9 March 1902 in Niedau, near Danzig. A German national, he was a Communist in his youth and went to Moscow in the 1920s, where he attended a school run by the AM Apparat of the Comintern. In 1930 he was a student at the Political Military School in Moscow.

Wenzel returned to Danzig as a KPD official and was probably a member of the AM Apparat until 1935. During this period he almost certainly was in contact with Henri Robinson.

Wenzel is said to have played a part in the Reichstag fire, and after the Nazis came to power he was probably sought by the German police. In 1935 he was ordered to Moscow, where he was given an intensive course by the GRU preparatory to his appointment as technical advisor in Western Europe.

In January 1936 he arrived in Brussels, where he posed as a student of mechanics and took a course at the technical school. In October 1937 he was denied permission by the Belgian authorities to remain in their country; so he went to Holland, where he contacted Daniel Goulooze, with whom he discussed plans for the construction of a service in Belgium.

In early 1938 he returned to Belgium, probably illegally, and it is probable that he lived with Germaine and Franz Schneider. In 1939 he became technical advisor to Sukolov under Trepper's direction, and he trained a number of W/T operators for the Low Countries and France. Wenzel also acted as technical advisor to Konstantin Jeffremov, whom he probably first met in 1936.

In June 1940 he may have been arrested by the German occupation forces as a German refugee, but he was released shortly afterwards because he was not recognized as a Soviet agent. From December 1940 to 1942 Wenzel transmitted intelligence to Moscow via W/T. In May 1942, following Makarov's capture, Jeffremov took over Sukolov's Low Countries network and invited Wenzel's collaboration in re-establishing a link with Moscow for Sukolov's service. In May 1942, by arrangement with Grossvogel, who visited him from Paris, Wenzel commenced transmissions; and following the capture of the Sokols in France, Trepper also utilized Wenzel's W/T service.

By technical means the Gestapo located Wenzel's transmitter and captured him 30 July 1942. He agreed to collaborate with the Germans, and the playback to Moscow was begun on Wenzel's transmitter ("Weide") 6 August 1942. It was Wenzel's disclosure to the Germans of his W/T codes that enabled them to decipher a large amount of back traffic and to make the first arrests in Germany.

Wenzel escaped from his captors 17 November 1942. According to one report, he went to Holland and joined an underground group. He was able to inform the Soviet Embassy in London, via a British communications line, that Jeffremov had been doubled and that the Germans were conducting playback operations.

According to Gilles Perrault, Wenzel eventually made his way to Moscow, where he was imprisoned at Lubianka with Trepper, Pannwitz, Sukolov, and Ozols. His ultimate fate is unknown.

Perrault interviewed Henry Piepe of the Abwehr in February 1965. Piepe was in charge of the investigations in Brussels in 1941 and 1942, and Perrault quotes him as follows:

"Naturally, it came as a most unpleasant surprise when Berlin informed us that a transmitter was again operating in our area. No agent had ever called to pick up the set concealed in Mathieu's garage; so our trap had been a waste of time, and we had to start from scratch, just as for the Rue des Attrebates.

"The tracking teams came back to Brussels, including my old sergeant technician in charge of the 'suitcase' detector. The Funkabwehr spent the first few days taking the usual bearings from fixed points. It must seem unbelievable, but it's true; the transmitter was operating all night long, which obviously made our task much easier. I must confess I could never understand the Russians' attitude. Were they really so overworked? After all, an underemployed pianist is more use than a pianist locked up in jail. No, I think they simply weren't aware of the advanced techniques we were using. I can't see any other possible explanation. Not unless they were cold-bloodedly sacrificing radio operators.

"Anyway, we very soon discovered that the transmitter was somewhere in the Laeken district. Unluckily, an electric railway ran through the neighborhood. It jumbled the electric fields—or something like that—and much to his annoyance my sergeant had to admit that his 'suitcase' wouldn't work. We had to resort to a Funkabwehr van fitted with equipment powerful enough not to be jammed by the railway. It was camouflaged as a military vehicle, but we hardly had to worry about spotters, because we only operated after curfew. On the other hand, there was a risk that we ourselves might be stopped and questioned, and that was something I wanted to avoid at all costs. I certainly didn't want reports leaking out that a mysterious vehicle was roaming the streets at night, that the police weren't interfering with it, and so on.

"[L]uckily, the transmitter continued to operate five hours a night, and in the end we located the house where it was hidden—a tall building with a lumberyard on one side and a shop on the other. According to my sergeant the set was sure to be on one of the upper floors. It was hard for him to be more specific. Anyway, the rest was up to me.

"My first step, as in the Rue des Attrebates, was to recruit extra manpower. We couldn't allow the bird to escape, and I preferred to take too many precautions rather than too few. I was given twenty-five members of the secret police. In addition, I went back to the Luftwaffe barracks and explained what I was up to. The airmen were very young and enthusiastic; the scheme excited them, and they put themselves at my disposal. I decided to launch the attack at 3 a.m. on June 30.

"It was a marvelously clear, moonlit night, so I instructed the airmen to hide in the lumberyard until zero hour; then they were to emerge from cover and seal off the street. My squad of police and I moved into the ground-floor apartment of the house in question. We woke up the tenant, who proved to be very friendly, offering us coffee and making conversation (Otto Schumacher). At 3 o'clock we went into action. I assigned two men to each floor and told the rest to stand by. We galloped up the stairs. Suddenly I heard a shout from the attic: 'Hurry! Hurry! It's up here!' I raced to the attic. It was divided into small compartments. I hurried to the part where a light showed, and there I found my two men—alone! I ordered them to search the other compartments, while I quickly took stock of the scene. On a small table was the transmitter—still warm. Beside it lay a bundle of documents written in German. Dozens of postcards were strewn about the room, posted from various German towns. It was enough to take one's breath away. On the floor, a jacket and a pair of boots. The pianist must have felt very safe, to put comfort before security. But how could he possibly have escaped? I glanced up and noticed the dormer window was half open. I poked my head out, intending to take a look at the roof. There was a loud shot, and I ducked quickly. Someone down in the street shouted, 'Look out. He's crouching by the chimney!'

"I went downstairs with the documents. My airmen friends had moved out into the street, but they were taking cover in doorways; the fugitive was shooting at them. He was clearly visible as he sprang from roof to roof. He had a revolver in each hand and was blazing away between leaps. I could sense that my boys were dying to get him, but I told them, 'Whatever you do, don't shoot! I want him alive.'

"Our man reached the last building in the block; he was cornered. But he smashed one of the dormer windows and disappeared. We heard a woman calling for help. 'What's going on?' we shouted up at her. She said a man had just raced through her bedroom and down the stairs. We sped to the house and searched every floor. No sign of him! I began to fear the worst. However, some of the airmen went down to the cellar, picked up an overturned bathtub, and found him hiding underneath. They were so angry and worked up that they started beating him with the butts of their rifles. I ordered them to stop and took my prisoner to Gestapo headquarters. He seemed panic-stricken. He was a short, stocky, hard-featured man, about forty years old, terribly working-class. I must say, he didn't make a great impression on me.

"He immediately wanted to know whether I was Abwehr or Gestapo; I set his mind at rest. He spoke French, but none too well and with a heavy accent. Next he asked me to fasten his hands in front of him, instead of keeping them handcuffed behind his back. 'Oh, no,' I said, 'that's an old trick! You're just looking for a chance to jump me and hit me over the head.' He insisted that he had no such intention, but I remained suspicious. As a gesture, however, I laid my gun on the table and said, 'There, you see, I'm unarmed. You have nothing to fear.' He complained of the beating he had received, and I felt obliged to point out that it was his own fault—he ought not to have opened fire; troops never like being shot at when they can't shoot back. He calmed down, and after a while we started chatting in German; he spoke it perfectly.

"Eventually I informed him that I proposed to question him about his identity. He stared uneasily at the two policemen in my office. I ordered them out, removed his handcuffs, and said, 'Go ahead; we're all alone, just the two of us, so you can speak quite openly.' Relaxing visibly, he told me that his name was Johann Wenzel and that he had been born in Danzig in 1902. A German! But he added: 'I warn you here and now, I'm not the kind of man who makes bargains. You needn't expect any disclosures or betrayals from me!' 'Now, now,' I said, 'you aren't being sensible.' But I couldn't get another word out of him. So I packed him off to St. Gilles prison . . .

"Following Wenzel's departure, I went to report to my superiors. They immediately telephoned the news to Berlin. Twenty minutes later, Berlin called back with intense excitement and informed us: 'You've caught one of the most prominent members of the prewar German Communist Party, one of the chiefs of the Comintern's underground apparatus.' The capture was such a major and miraculous event in their eyes that they could hardly believe it could be the same man.

"To finish up with Wenzel, I should add that the Berlin Gestapo sent for him a few days later. He was out of his mind with fear, for obviously the Gestapo had old scores to settle with him. Giering and his men set to work on him. They tortured him for six or eight weeks, then sent him back to Brussels. When I saw him again, I simply didn't recognize him. He was a broken man. He had revealed everything to them, including his code and his cover name, 'the Professor.' He was called that because he was a great specialist in radio communication and had trained many pianists in his time. Giering informed me that the prisoner was now prepared to work for us."

GEORGIE DE WINTER

(alias Elizabeth Thevenet) was born 29 May 1919 in New York City. She was a professional dancer and met Trepper in Brussels in 1938 or 1939. She became his mistress and they had a son, Patrick de Winter, born 29 September 1939 in Brussels. It is possible, as Perrault claims, that Trepper was not the father of Patrick and that Georgie was already pregnant when she met Trepper. Patrick de Winter served in the U.S. Army in 1957. He is now a U.S. citizen and a professor at Columbia University.

Georgie in all probability was not an agent herself, nor did she know the exact nature or extent of Trepper's espionage activities. Trepper fled from Brussels to Paris in July 1940, and in March 1941 Georgie moved to Paris to be with him, using her U.S. passport in the name de Winter. In June 1941 she adopted the name Elizabeth Thevenet and used false papers supplied to her by Trepper. After Trepper escaped from the Germans in September 1943, he visited Georgie at Le Vesinet for two days. She took him to the Queyries' house in Suresnes, where he stayed a week. Trepper then left Georgie and went to Claude Spaak. Georgie left for the unoccupied zone and in about mid-October 1943 she was arrested by the Germans. She had on her person a letter from Antonia Lyon-Smith, which exposed the Maximovitch group. Georgie was transported to Fresnes Prison and subsequently detained in Ravensbrueck Camp until her liberation by the Allies 10 May 1945. She then rejoined her child with the Queyries in Suresnes. From May 1945 until about April 1946 Georgie received periodic payments, to a total of twenty-three thousand francs, from Claude Spaak, this being money left for her provision by Trepper.

After the war Georgie lived with Jules Jaspar at St. Hippolyte du Gard in the south of France, possibly until 1954. According to one report, however, Jaspar died circa 1948-1949. In 1965 she married a Polish aristocrat, Colonel de la Garde. They are now living in Lasalle in the Cevennes mountains in southern France.

Gilles Perrault interviewed Georgie at Lasalle (actually in a nearby hamlet called Les Horts) in the summer of 1965. Her husband was at that time in a Montpellier hospital recovering from a heart attack. Georgie said that after her release from the concentration camp she had gone to see her mother in Belgium. The Belgian security police arrested and interrogated her. She reported that she had also been interrogated in 1962 by the French DST.

ANTON WINTERINK

(alias Tino, alias Tanne) was born 5 November 1914 in Arnhem, Netherlands. He was a Dutch national and an official of the Communist Party of the Netherlands. He resided in Amsterdam.

Winterink was a leading functionary of the Rote Hilfe organization in the Netherlands. In this organization there were factions of the SND. Around 1938 Winterink started to work full-time for the SND. In this capacity he established an agent network which was later used by the Rote Kapelle. Konstantin Jeffremov was, for a time, Winterink's supervisor.

Winterink established a radio technical section and at the beginning of the war he took over the leadership of the group "Hilda" in Holland. On 18 August 1942 he was arrested by the Sonderkommando and since then his whereabouts are unknown. He is presumed dead.

JOSEF KARL WIRTH

was born on 6 September 1879 in Freiburg in Breisgau. He became successively a professor, town councillor, member of the Baden Landtag, member of the Reichstag, federal minister of finance, and federal chancellor—the last from May 1921 to November 1922. During part of this period he also served as the minister of foreign affairs. The major development during his tenure as chancellor was the signing of the Treaty of Rapallo, which established diplomatic relations between the USSR and Germany and which paved the way for the secret agreement by which the two countries gave each other military assistance in violation of the Treaty of Versailles.

For seven years, 1922 to 1929, Wirth ostensibly withdrew from public life. In 1930 he accepted Bruening's offer of the Ministry of the Interior. But in October 1931 President Hindenburg ousted him from office.

When the Nazis seized power in 1933, Wirth went to Austria. A year later he moved to Paris, where he remained until 1939. When the Nazis seized Austria, he fled via Italy to Switzerland.

During the Second World War, Wirth was in contact with Vladimir Alexandrovich Jokolin, who was appointed the Assistant Secretary General of the League of Nations on 18 February 1937. He also had contacts with "Long" and "Salter" of the Rote Drei. He lived in Lucerne. He made rather grandiose plans for a postwar German government strongly oriented toward Communism and supported initially by the USSR. In 1951, in fact, a committee headed by Margarete Buber-Neumann, who had suffered political persecution in both the USSR and Germany, charged, "The Soviet intention to establish a counter-parliament against Bonn with Wirth as federal chancellor . . . endangers security and order . . ."

Wirth appears in the Rote Drei traffic, Moscow to Switzerland, by true name, not by cover name. A message from the Center on 14 January 1943 to Dora begins:

> Request reply about exact substance of talks between Long (George Blun) and Wirth. Especially interested in contents of Wirth's negotiations with the Anglo-Saxons and his intentions regarding negotiations with the USSR. What does he plan to do, as a practical matter, to establish contact?

Six days later Moscow asked about OKW intentions, directed that the requirement be levied on Lucy's sources but added, "if feasible, Long should try to get relevant information from the Wirth group."

On 5 October 1943, Rado informed the Center,

> On 27 September Salter talked with . . .Wirth in Lucerne. Wirth rejects the German Liberation Committee in Moscow . . .According to Wirth the German Embassy in Bern is extremely interested in Sokolin.

Wirth seems to have been dealing, or trying to deal, with the British, the Soviets, the Americans, and even the Germans in an effort to obtain a major governmental position in postwar Germany. It is known that through an SD agent, Richard Grossmann (alias Director) and Ludwig, Wirth supplied information to Walter Schellenberg. The topic, at least ostensibly, was usually peace feelers. But Wirth also entertained strong personal ambitions.